The EU in the Global Investment Regime

The European Union (EU) has emerged as a key actor in the global investment regime since the 1980s. At the same time, international investment policy and agreements, which govern international investment liberalisation, treatment and protection through investor-to-state dispute settlement, have become increasingly contentious in the European public debate.

This book provides an accessible introduction to international investment policy and seeks to explain how the EU became an actor in the global investment regime. It offers a detailed analysis of the EU's participation in all major trade and investment negotiations since the 1980s and EU-internal competence debates to identify the causes behind the EU's growing role in this policy domain. Building on principal-agent and historical institutionalist models of incremental institutional change, the book shows that Commission entrepreneurship was instrumental in the emergence of the EU as a key actor in the global investment regime. It refutes business-centred liberal intergovernmental explanations, which suggest that business lobbying made the Member States accept the EU's growing role and competence in this domain. The book lends support to supranational and challenges intergovernmental thinking on European Integration.

This text will be of key interest to scholars, students and practitioners of European and regional integration, EU foreign relations, EU trade and international investment law, business lobbying, and more broadly to international political economy.

Johann Robert Basedow is a Visiting Fellow at the European University Institute in Florence, Italy, and an Assistant Professor in International Political Economy at the London School of Economics, United Kingdom.

Routledge/UACES Contemporary European Studies
Edited by Chad Damro
University of Edinburgh, United Kingdom

Elaine Fahey
City University London, United Kingdom

David Howarth
University of Luxembourg, Luxembourg, on behalf of the University Association for Contemporary European Studies

Editorial Board: Grainne De Búrca, European University Institute and Columbia University; Andreas Føllesdal, Norwegian Centre for Human Rights, University of Oslo; Peter Holmes, University of Sussex; Liesbet Hooghe, University of North Carolina at Chapel Hill, and Vrije Universiteit Amsterdam; David Phinnemore, Queen's University Belfast; Ben Rosamond, University of Warwick; Vivien Ann Schmidt, University of Boston; Jo Shaw, University of Edinburgh; Mike Smith, University of Loughborough and Loukas Tsoukalis, ELIAMEP, University of Athens and European University Institute.

The primary objective of the new Contemporary European Studies series is to provide a research outlet for scholars of European Studies from all disciplines. The series publishes important scholarly works and aims to forge for itself an international reputation.

For more information about this series, please visit: www.routledge.com/Routledge-UACES-Contemporary-European-Studies/book-series/UACES

33 **Russia's Impact on EU Policy Transfer to the Post-Soviet Space**
   The contested neighbourhood
   Esther Ademmer

34 **Domestic Politics and Norm Diffusion in International Relations**
   Ideas do not float freely
   Thomas Risse

35 **Euroscepticism as a Transnational and Pan-European Phenomenon**
   The emergence of a new sphere of opposition
   Edited by John FitzGibbon, Benjamin Leruth and Nick Startin

36 **Global Power Transition and the Future of the European Union**
   Birol A. Yeşilada, Jacek Kugler, Gaspare Genna and Osman Göktuğ Tanrıkulu

37 **The EU in the Global Investment Regime**
   Commission Entrepreneurship, Incremental Institutional Change and Business Lethargy
   Johann Robert Basedow

The EU in the Global Investment Regime

Commission Entrepreneurship, Incremental Institutional Change and Business Lethargy

Johann Robert Basedow

LONDON AND NEW YORK

First published 2018 by Routledge

2 Park Square, Milton Park, Abingdon, Oxfordshire OX14 4RN
52 Vanderbilt Avenue, New York, NY 10017

Routledge is an imprint of the Taylor & Francis Group, an informa business

First issued in paperback 2019

Copyright © 2018 Johann Robert Basedow

The right of Johann Robert Basedow to be identified as author of this work has been asserted by him in accordance with sections 77 and 78 of the Copyright, Designs and Patents Act 1988.

All rights reserved. No part of this book may be reprinted or reproduced or utilised in any form or by any electronic, mechanical, or other means, now known or hereafter invented, including photocopying and recording, or in any information storage or retrieval system, without permission in writing from the publishers.

Notice:
Product or corporate names may be trademarks or registered trademarks, and are used only for identification and explanation without intent to infringe.

British Library Cataloguing-in-Publication Data
A catalogue record for this book is available from the British Library

Library of Congress Cataloging-in-Publication Data
Names: Basedow, Johann Robert, author.
Title: The EU in the global investment regime commission : entrepreneurship, incremental institutional change and business lethargy / Johann Robert Basedow.
Description: Abingdon, Oxon ; New York, NY : Routledge, 2018. | Series: Routledge/UACES contemporary European studies ; 37 | Includes bibliographical references and index.
Identifiers: LCCN 2017032315 | ISBN 9781138083370 (hardback) | ISBN 9781315112282 (ebook)
Subjects: LCSH: Investments, Foreign—European Union countries. | Investments, Foreign—Law and legislation—European Union countries. | European Union countries—Commercial policy.
Classification: LCC HG5422 .B37 2018 | DDC 332.67/3094—dc23
LC record available at https://lccn.loc.gov/2017032315

ISBN: 978-1-138-08337-0 (hbk)
ISBN: 978-0-367-89057-5 (pbk)

Typeset in Times New Roman
by Apex CoVantage, LLC

To my parents

Contents

List of figures ix
List of tables x
List of boxes xi
Preface xii
List of abbreviations xiii

1 Introduction 1

2 European integration theory and the EU's new international investment policy 13

3 An introduction to international investment and its regime 46

4 An overview of EU international investment policymaking under the Treaty of Lisbon 74

5 The EU in investment-related negotiations during the Uruguay Round 90

6 The EU in investment-related negotiations on the Energy Charter Treaty 114

7 The EU in negotiations on the multilateral agreement on investment and the Singapore Issues 139

8 Investment disciplines in European Preferential Trade Agreements 170

9 The evolution of the EU's legal competences in international investment policy	197
10 Conclusion	230
Index	243

Figures

1.1	A chronology of the emergence of the EU's international investment policy (1980–2017)	5
2.1	A three-stage model of commission entrepreneurship for institutional change	14
2.2	Simplified causal relationship as described in liberal intergovernmentalism	28
2.3	Member states' outward FDI stocks of EU total (2014)	36
2.4	Extra-EU outward FDI stocks by sector (2014)	36
3.1	Number of ratified BITs of leading capital-exporting countries (1958–2012)	65
3.2	World inward FDI stock in trillion US dollars (1980–2012)	67

Tables

2.1	Identifying conceptual overlaps between historical institutionalism and principal-agent research	26
2.2	Share of selected Member States in outward FDI and number of ratified BITs (2017)	38
3.1	Overview of OLI framework	50
7.1	Number of meetings and submissions per year by country (selection)	163
10.1	Summary of empirical observations	231

Boxes

2.1	Economic and policy entrepreneurs	17
2.2	Institutionalism in a nutshell	18
2.3	Who are the stakeholders in the EU's international investment policy?	35

Preface

This book traces and seeks to explain the EU's growing role in international investment policy and the global investment regime from the 1950s until 2017. It has benefited from the support and input of many people and institutions. I am particularly indebted to my PhD supervisor Stephen Woolcock for his guidance. I am grateful for critical and helpful feedback on the various drafts and elements of this book manuscript by Cornelia Woll, Angelos Dimopoulos and Bernard Hoekman. My research and the book manuscript have also benefited from the stimulating intellectual environments at the London School of Economics, the European University Institute, the Directorate General for Trade of the European Commission and the Organisation for Economic Co-operation and Development (OECD). I have discussed my research with many knowledgeable colleagues in these places, which has significantly helped me in developing and refining my thinking. Last but not least, I am deeply thankful for the support of my family and in particular of my parents. I dedicate this book to them.

All errors remain mine.

Abbreviations

ACP	African, Caribbean and Pacific Group of States
BDI	Bundesverband der Deutschen Industrie
BIAC	Business and Industry Advsisory Committee
BIT	Bilateral Investment Treaty
CCP	Common Commercial Policy
CEFIC	European Chemical Industry Council
CEOE	Confederación Española de Organizaciones Empresariales
CETA	Comprehensive Economic and Trade Agreement
CIL	Customary International Law
CIME	Committee on Multinational Enterprise
CIS	Community of Independent States
CJEU	Court of Justice of the European Union
CMIT	Committee on Capital Movements and Invisible Transactions
Confindustria	Confederazione Generale dell'Industria Italiana
DIHK	Deutscher Industrie- und Handelskammertag
DG	Directorate General
ECFIN	Economic and Financial Affairs
ECJ	European Court of Justice (see CJEU)
ECSG	European Communities Services Group
ECT	Energy Charter Treaty
ESF	European Services Forum
EU	European Union
EUSFTA	European Union-Singapore Free Trade Agreement
FCN	Treaties of Friendship, Commerce and Navigation
FDI	Foreign Direct Investment
FET	Fair and Equitable Treatment
FPS	Full Protection and Security
FTA	Free Trade Agreement
GATS	General Agreement on Trade in Services
GATT	General Agreement on Tariffs and Trade
GNS	Group for Negotiations on Services
ICSID	International Centre for Settlement of Investment Disputes

IGC	Intergovernmental Conference
IIA	International Investment Agreement
IMF	International Monetary Fund
IPE	International Political Economy
IR	International Relations
ISDS	Investor-to-State Dispute Settlement
MAI	Multilateral Agreement on Investment
MEDEF	Mouvement des Entreprises de France
Mercosur	Mercado Común del Sur
MFN	Most-Favoured Nation
MNE	Multinational Enterprise
MPoI	Minimal Platform on Investment
NAFTA	North American Free Trade Agreement
NT	National Treatment
OECD	Organisation for Economic Co-operation and Development
OLI	Ownership-, Location-, Internalisation-specific advantages
R&D	Research and Development
Relex	External Relations
REIO	Regional Economic Integration Organisation
SFSRs	Soviet Federal Socialist Republics
SWF	Sovereign Wealth Fund
EC	Treaty establishing the European Communities
TEN-E	Trans-European Energy Networks Initiative
TFEU	Treaty on the Functioning of the European Union
TPA	Third Party Access
TPC	Trade Policy Committee ('113 Committee', '133 Committee')
TPP	Transpacific Partnership
TRIMs	Trade-Related Investment Measures
TRIPs	Trade-Related Intellectual Property
TTIP	Transatlantic Trade and Investment Partnership
TUAC	Trade Union Advisory Committee
UNCITRAL	United Nations Committee on International Trade Law
UNCTAD	United Nations Committee on Trade and Development
UNICE	Union des Industries de la Communauté Européenne
WTO	World Trade Organisation

1 Introduction

In June 2010, the European Commission published a communication and draft regulation dealing with international investment regulation (European Commission, 2010a, 2010b). The communication, entitled *Towards a Comprehensive European International Investment Policy*, underlined that the Treaty of Lisbon (2009) had extended the scope of the Common Commercial Policy (CCP) to the regulation of Foreign Direct Investment (FDI). The EU had thus undeniably become a key actor in the global investment regime. The communication discussed how the Commission envisaged using the European Union's (EU)[1] new exclusive competence in international investment policy to the benefit of Europe. The draft regulation, on the other hand, discussed how to deal with the Member States' regulatory legacy in the form of some 1,300 bilateral investment treaties (BITs). It proposed to review all Member State BITs in view of their legality and conformity to European law and policy objectives.

While the two documents were hardly spectacular in purpose and content, they stirred furore among investment policy officials of the Member States. National investment policy officials, it seemed, had so far lived in denial, or indeed not known about the new legal situation. During the following months, national investment policy officials publically accused the Commission of having surreptitiously usurped the competence to regulate international investment flows. They pointed out that many Member States had clearly opposed the extension of the CCP to FDI regulation during the relevant debates in the Convention on the Future of Europe (2002/2003) and the following Intergovernmental Conferences (IGCs) on the Constitutional and Lisbon Treaties. They, moreover, warned that the Commission lacked the necessary expertise to adequately represent and defend European interests in the international investment regime. They pointed to the Commission's draft regulation on how to deal with existing Member State BITs as an example of the Commission's technical incompetence and disregard for the needs of European investors. They claimed that the proposed review process for Member State BITs would create legal uncertainty for European investors and thereby hinder investment activity. Some Member States such as Germany, France and the United Kingdom, furthermore, continued negotiating and signing BITs with third countries despite being arguably in breach of European law (UNCTAD, 2017). The atmosphere between the Commission and the relevant national ministries was extraordinarily tense at this time. And only in May 2017 – eight years after the entry into force of the Treaty of Lisbon and in the midst of finalising this book manuscript – did the Court of Justice of the European Union (CJEU) finally resolve the simmering competence dispute between the Commission and the Member States. In Opinion 2/15 (European Court of Justice, 2017), the CJEU clarified that the EU indeed largely holds the exclusive competence to enter into international agreements dealing with market access, post-establishment treatment and protection of FDI.

The Member States' opposition to the extension of the CCP to FDI regulation is remarkable in the global scheme of things. It stands in contrast to the Member States' previous behaviour in this policy domain, as they had temporarily empowered the EU on several occasions to participate in international investment negotiations since the 1980s. The Commission represented the Member States, for instance, in investment-related negotiations during the Uruguay Round of the General Agreement on Trade and Tariffs (GATT) and in the Doha Round of the World Trade Organisation (WTO). The Commission was also deeply involved in the most ambitious modern investment negotiations on the Energy Charter Treaty (ECT) and the Multilateral Agreement on Investment (MAI). Since the late 1990s, the Member States even empowered the Commission to seek the inclusion of investment provisions into European Free Trade Agreements (FTAs). Hence, the EU has been playing an increasingly central role and acquiring so-called de facto competences in international investment policy since the 1980s. The term 'de facto competences' refers to the Member States agreeing on informal policymaking rules to jointly govern policy issues predominantly coming under Member State competences. De facto competences are thus tantamount to an informal 'Brusselisation' of policymaking (Woolcock, 2011, pp. 33–34).

The preceding discussion draws a conflicting and intriguing picture of the EU's involvement in international investment regulation. The Member States, on the one hand, cooperated and temporarily empowered the EU to participate in major international investment negotiations. But on the other hand, the Member States – ultimately unsuccessfully – opposed the extension of the EU's legal competences in this key domain of global economic governance. On the whole, these observations seem counterintuitive and inconsistent with mainstream theories of the fields of European Integration and International Relations and trigger several questions. Why did Member States readily cooperate and empower the EU to participate in international investment negotiations since the 1980s? And why did Member States then oppose the extension of the EU's legal competences in this domain? And, finally, why did the Lisbon Treaty extend the EU's exclusive competence to FDI regulation despite the reported opposition from Member States? Existing research on the EU's involvement in international investment policy is scarce (Billiet, 2006; Meunier, 2017; Niemann, 2013; Young, 2001). The few existing studies neither provide exhaustive theoretical nor empirical accounts. This book closes this research gap. The objective is to trace and to explain the emergence of the EU's international investment policy from the EU's first involvement in the global investment regime in the 1980s until the entry into force of the Treaty of Lisbon and the extension of the CCP to FDI regulation in 2009. The overarching research question of the book thus reads as follows: *Why has the EU acquired de facto and legal competences to regulate international investment flows since the 1980s?*

1.1 The argument in a nutshell

The book argues that Commission entrepreneurship was the main driver behind the emergence of the EU's international investment policy. The book builds on principal-agent models and historical institutionalism to develop the argument. Principal-agent models help us understand why and how the Commission could acquire a central role in international investment negotiations since the 1980s despite the EU's limited competences and Member State hesitation (Da Conceição, 2010; da Conceição-Heldt and Meunier, 2014; Kerremans, 2004; Meunier, 2005; Pollack, 2003; Schmidt, 1998; Young, 2001). The Commission used its agency autonomy – for instance through agenda setting, the invoking of fringe and implied competences or international forum shopping – to consolidate its role in international investment negotiations. Historical institutionalism, in turn, offers a promising framework to explain how the EU's growing role in international investment negotiations affected formal integration and led to a comprehensive competence transfer under the Treaty of Lisbon (Büthe, 2016; Mahoney and Thelen, 2010; Stacey and Rittberger, 2003; Streeck and Thelen, 2005). Seen through a historical institutionalist lens, the Commission's short-term strategies to consolidate its role in international investment negotiations amounted to incremental agency-driven institutional change in the form of 'conversion' (re-interpretation of existing institutional rules), 'layering' (adding of new subordinate institutional rules) and 'drift' (change in the policy environment altering the effect of institutions). The Commission promoted for instance 'conversion' by invoking implied and fringe competences from adjacent policy domains to ensure its involvement in investment negotiations. The Commission, moreover, engaged in 'layering' when it had recourse to the CJEU to clarify the EU's legal competences and pushed for – at first sight – unrelated treaty changes to consolidate the EU's role in investment policy. Finally, the Commission fuelled institutional 'drift' when it pushed investment negotiations into policy fora such as the WTO or bilateral trade negotiations, where the EU conventionally speaks through the Commission with a single voice regardless of competence issues. The Commission's efforts gradually consolidated the EU's accepted role, extended relevant legal competences and ultimately reconfigured the preferences of key policymakers in favour of a comprehensive competences transfer. The combination of principal-agent models and historical institutionalism thus offers an illuminating analytical framework to understand how Commission autonomy and entrepreneurship in daily policymaking affect long-term formal integration.

The book, moreover, argues that business preferences and lobbying cannot account for the emergence of the EU's international investment policy. It is widely assumed that European business preferences and lobbying decisively shape international investment policy and may account for the EU's growing role in this domain. The assumption builds on the intuitive reasoning that business is arguably the main stakeholder of international investment policy and should shape policy outcomes to maximise profits. With regard to the emergence of the EU's international investment policy, it is occasionally suggested that growing global competition over lucrative investment opportunities motivated European business to push for a communitarisation of international investment policymaking to maximise bargaining power in international negotiations. This reasoning, which reflects liberal intergovernmental thinking (Moravcsik, 1998), is flawed in two regards. First and foremost, businesses rarely take an interest in international investment policy. International investment policy and agreements – apart from investment liberalisation commitments – have minor, distant and uncertain economic effects on business operations and profits. International investment agreements (IIAs) seek to ensure a minimum level of investor treatment and protection abroad through access to investment arbitration. Businesses investing abroad, however, often discount or internalise the risk of future expropriation, are hesitant to use investment arbitration in case of a dispute with a host country and finally cannot know whether they might win an arbitration case. Investors have won not even a third of known investment arbitration proceedings (UNCTAD, 2014a, p. 10). Businesses thus perceive the benefits of pushing for IIAs as minor, uncertain and distant, while the costs of forming preferences and lobbying policymakers are immediate and substantial. The political economy of international investment policy thus differs significantly from classic trade policy, which redistributes welfare within society through market liberalisation/protection and thereby triggers forceful lobbying (Hiscox, 2002; Krugman et al., 2014; Milner, 1999; Rogowski, 1989; Viner, 1950). More importantly for this study, businesses presumably would only take an interest and lobby for changing the institutional setup of international investment policymaking within the EU, if it affects policy substance and alters the earlier identified economic effects on businesses. The communitarisation of international investment policy, however, is unlikely to have such effects. While it has for instance been argued that the integration of international investment policy increases Europe's bargaining power in international investment policy, it is important to note that IIAs have always been fairly standardised and are becoming even more similar in content (Alschner, 2013; Alvarez, 2009; Dolzer and Schreuer, 2012; Mills, 2011; Salacuse, 2010). Bargaining power is of limited importance in international investment negotiations. It follows that European business should not have held strong preferences or lobbied for the integration of international investment policy.

The book empirically confirms the twofold argument through qualitative in-depth case studies, analysing all concluded international investment negotiations since the 1980s, where the EU participated despite missing legal competences. It focuses on investment-related negotiations during the Uruguay Round (1986–1994); the negotiations on the ECT (1990–1998); the failed negotiations on the MAI at the OECD (1995–1998); the short-lived investment negotiations of the Doha Round; and finally negotiations with Mexico and Chile on the EU's first comprehensive preferential trade agreements (PTAs) to encompass investment provisions (1997–2003) (Figure 1.1). The book assesses for each case study why the EU was allowed

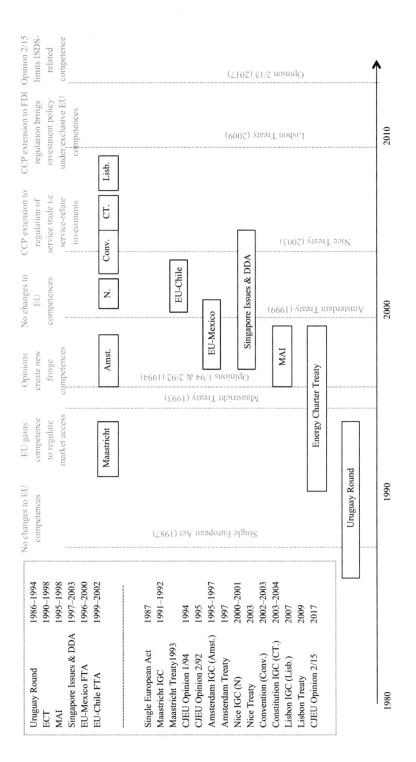

Figure 1.1 A chronology of the emergence of the EU's international investment policy (1980–2017)

to participate in the first place; and what actors and factors shaped the EU's engagement in these fora. Turning to the evolution of the EU's legal competences, the book assesses the long-standing discussions between the Member States and the Commission over the EU's role in international investment regulation as part of IGCs and CJEU proceedings. The assessment covers an extensive time period between the 1950s and 2017. It builds on 42 anonymised interviews with policymakers and business leaders, press and archival research, primary documents and secondary literature.

1.2 Theoretical, empirical and policy contributions

The contributions of this book are of empirical, theoretical and policy nature. First and foremost, it closes an empirical gap in the literature and covers in detail the EU's role in the global investment regime and underlying integration dynamics. Political scientists have only in passing, and for short policymaking instances, assessed the EU's role in international investment policy (Billiet, 2006; Manger, 2009; Meunier, 2017; Niemann, 2013; Young, 2001). These studies do not offer a comprehensive empirical or analytical picture of the EU's role in the global investment regime. Legal scholars, on the other hand, have paid significantly more attention to the EU's role in international investment regulation (Baetens, 2015; Bischoff, 2011; Dimopoulos, 2011; Eilmansberger, 2009; Hoffmeister and Ünüvar, 2012; Kleinheisterkamp, 2014; Poulsen et al., 2015; Reinisch, 2013). They focus, however, on legal questions and do not explain the EU's growing role in this policy domain.

The book, moreover, makes three theoretical contributions. First, it develops an innovative model of Commission entrepreneurship based on principal-agent models and historical institutionalism. It theoretically links the Commission's influence on daily policymaking to long-term, incremental institutional change. In other words, it conceptually connects informal integration in daily policymaking to formal integration through treaty revisions. The book thus breaks with an established research tradition in European studies. Many studies either assess daily policymaking; or analyse intergovernmental negotiations on treaty revisions (Moravcsik, 1998; Pollack, 2003; Rosamond, 2000). The analytical separation of informal and formal integration allows for theoretical parsimony. Informal integration and daily policymaking are subject to different dynamics than formal integration through IGC and treaty revisions. The differences between informal and formal integration create 'noise' hindering the development of theoretically elegant explanations. The drawback of this research approach, however, is that informal and formal integration are often interconnected and mutually condition each other (Bickerton et al., 2015; Büthe, 2016; Pierson, 1994, 2004). In foreign economic policy, informal integration in the form of ad hoc cooperation and delegation typically precede formal integration through treaty revisions (Elsig, 2002; Niemann, 2013). Formal integration indeed is often the outcome of prior informal integration. It is crucial to understand the drivers of informal integration to explain formal integration in this policy domain. This rationale informs the research design and analytical framework developed in Chapter 2.

This book's second theoretical contribution relates to liberal intergovernmental thinking. It challenges liberal intergovernmentalism in two regards (Börzel, 2013; Moravcsik, 1998; Moravcsik and Schimmelfennig, 2009; Rosamond, 2000; Wiener, 2009). First, liberal intergovernmentalism views integration as only occurring if (major) Member States benefit and push for it. The book makes the empirical and theoretical argument that European Integration occurred in international investment policy despite hesitation by (major) Member States. Second, liberal intergovernmentalism assumes that business preferences and lobbying decisively shape Member State preferences and ultimately European Integration outcomes. Business was mostly disengaged from international investment policy and held no strong preferences regarding the institutional setup of international investment policymaking in the complex multilevel governance system of the EU. Indeed, in many cases, the institutional policymaking setup has only limited complex substantive implications and economic effects on businesses. Businesses thus face weak incentives to invest resources in costly preference formation and lobbying. Hence, it may be necessary to reconsider the role of business preferences and lobbying in liberal intergovernmentalism. Business preferences and lobbying may be an important driver with regard to policies related to the development of the Single Market and with direct implications for business operations and profits, but policies which are more removed from markets and daily business operations are unlikely to be subject to strong business preferences and lobbying.

This book's third theoretical contribution relates to societal theories of foreign economic policy. This book scrutinises the burgeoning literature on business preferences and lobbying patterns (Dür, 2008; Eckhardt, 2015; Frieden, 1991; Grossmann and Helpman, 1995; Hiscox, 2002; Krugman et al., 2014; Rogowski, 1989; Woll, 2008; Woll and Artigas, 2007). Studies argue that businesses form preferences as a function of the expected impacts of foreign economic policies on profits. Businesses would consequently lobby policymakers for profit-maximising options. To determine the impacts of foreign economic policies on business profits, most studies build on Vinerian economics. Liberal foreign economic policies should increase the profits of export-competing firms and sectors, whereas protectionist foreign economic policies should benefit import-competing firms and sectors. However, foreign economic policy – and international trade – have evolved significantly during the last decades (Eckhardt, 2015; Young, 2016). In the past, foreign economic policy dealt with classic on-the-border market access barriers such as tariffs and quotas. The imposition or removal of these barriers had direct and well-understood effects on import and export competition and business profits. The formation of business preferences and lobbying patterns were therefore straightforward. Nowadays, foreign economic policy increasingly focuses on complex regulatory issues. It seeks to remove regulatory hurdles and frictions through various instruments of regulatory cooperation and harmonisation (Basedow and Kauffmann, 2016; OECD, 2017). IIAs, for instance, seek to create a minimum level of property protection across borders. The rise of regulatory foreign economic policy has two distinct effects on the formation of business preferences and lobbying patterns. First, regulatory foreign economic policy may have only limited and distant economic effects on business operations and profits. Businesses, therefore, may face weak incentives to form preferences and to lobby for specific policy outcomes. Second, businesses may struggle to understand whether and how complex regulatory foreign economic policy measures affect their operations and profits, and therefore whether they should lobby policymakers. The empirical chapters of this book produce ample evidence of such complexity-induced business lethargy. Preference formation and lobbying have become more complex and difficult to model. This development may increase the causal importance of trade bureaucrats in policy outcomes. They provide businesses with initial information and explanation of policies and thereby shape business perceptions, preferences and lobbying (Woll, 2008; Woll and Artigas, 2007). To conclude, additional research on the formation of business preferences and lobbying patterns in modern regulatory foreign economic policy is needed.

Finally, the book makes a policy contribution. It ties in with debates on reforming IIAs and investor-to-state dispute settlement. Its findings imply that states may strengthen states' right to regulate under IIAs without risking a significant decline in international investment activities and related economic opportunity costs. Many policymakers, media, non-governmental organisations and citizens increasingly worry that IIAs and traditional investor-to-state dispute settlement mechanisms overly constrain states' right to regulate and impose potentially significant financial risks on taxpayers. Demands to reform IIAs and investor-to-state dispute settlement are multiplying (Baetens, 2015; Mestral and Lévesque, 2013; Poulsen et al., 2015). Many proposals foresee more precise language on treatment and protection standards, higher hurdles for the launch of investment arbitration and more transparent arbitration proceedings. Critics have warned that such proposals undermine investment protection and ultimately lead to a decline in international investment activities, foregone growth and development opportunities (Lavranos, 2013; Peterson, 2011; Reinisch, 2013). The findings of the book show that European business rarely takes an interest in international investment policy. Economic research on the impact – or rather non-impact – of IIAs on investment decisions and flows by and large confirms these findings (Blonigen and Piger, 2014; Busse et al., 2010; Colen et al., 2014; Egger and Merlo, 2007; Hallward-Driemeier, 2003; Neumayer and Spess, 2005; UNCTAD, 2014b). Most European businesses seem little aware and knowledgeable of international investment policy. It seems unlikely that European businesses would react to a reform of IIAs by reducing their international investment activities. The costs of reforming IIAs may thus be lower than suggested in the policy debate.

1.3 The structure of the book

The book is structured as follows. Chapter 2 develops in detail the theoretical argument and lays the analytical-theoretical foundations for the empirical chapters. Chapter 3 introduces the non-expert reader to international investment and its regime. It defines international investment, discusses economic and political impacts of international investment activities on home and host economies, and identifies the tools and purposes of international investment policy and its historical roots. Chapter 4 provides an overview of the EU's legal competences in international investment policy and identifies the key actors and their preferences in international investment policy. Chapter 5 turns to the empirical analysis and examines the EU's involvement in investment-related negotiations during the Uruguay Round of the GATT (1986–1994). Chapter 6 shifts the analytical focus to the EU's role in investment-related negotiations on the ECT (1990–1998). Chapter 7 analyses the EU's participation in the MAI negotiations (1995–1998) and the closely related but short-lived investment negotiations as part of the Singapore Issues in the Doha Round (1996–2003). Chapter 8 examines how investment provisions made their way into European FTAs. The focus lies on the EU-Mexico negotiations (1996–1999) and EU-Chile negotiations (1999–2002), which marked the beginning of investment provisions in European PTAs. Chapter 9 examines the EU-internal debates during legal proceedings, IGCs and the Convention on the Future of Europe, which shaped the EU's legal competences. Chapter 10 concludes and discusses the empirical findings and theoretical implications of this study.

Note

1 For the sake of simplicity this book uses the term European Union/EU in order to refer to precursor organisations like the European Economic Communities (EEC) or the European Communities (EC). It does not assume that these organisations had the same political, economic and legal properties as today's EU.

References

Alschner, W., 2013. Americanization of the BIT universe: The influence of Friendship, Commerce and Navigation (FCN) treaties on modern investment treaty law. *Goettingen J. Int. Law* 5, 455–486.

Alvarez, J.E., 2009. *The Public International Law Regime governing international investment, Recueil de cours of the Hague Academy of International Law*. Martinus Nijhoff Publishers, Leiden.

Baetens, F., 2015. *Transatlantic investment treaty protection: A response to Poulsen, Bonnitcha and Yackee*, CEPS Special Report. CEPS, Brussels.

Basedow, R., Kauffmann, C., 2016. International trade and good regulatory practices: Assessing the trade impacts of regulation. *OECD Regul. Policy Work. Pap.* 4.

Bickerton, C., Hodson, D., Puetter, U., 2015. The new intergovernmentalism: European integration in the post-maastricht era. *J. Common Mark. Stud.* 53, 703–722.

Billiet, S., 2006. From GATT to the WTO: The internal struggle for external competences in the EU. *J. Common Mark. Stud.* 44, 899–919.

Bischoff, J.A., 2011. Just a little BIT of 'mixity'? The EU's role in the field of international investment protection law. *Common Mark. Law Rev.* 48, 1527–1570.

Blonigen, B.A., Piger, J., 2014. Determinants of foreign direct investment. *Can. J. Econ.* 47, 775–812. doi:10.1111/caje.12091

Börzel, T., 2013. Comparative regionalism: European integration and beyond, in: Carlsnaes, W., Risse, T., Simmons, B. (Eds.), *Handbook of international relations*. Sage, London, pp. 501–530.

Busse, M., Königer, J., Nunnenkamp, P., 2010. FDI promotion through bilateral investment treaties: More than a bit? *Rev. World Econ.* 146, 147–177. doi:10.1007/s10290-009-0046-x

Büthe, T., 2016. Historical institutionalism and institutional development in the EU: The development of supranational authority over government subsidies (State Aid), in: Rixen, T., Viola, L.A., Zürn, M. (Eds.), *Historical institutionalism and international relations: Explaining institutional development in world politics*. Oxford University Press, Oxford, pp. 37–66.

Colen, L., Persyn, D., Guariso, A., 2014. *What type of FDI is attracted by bilateral investment treaties?* LICOS Discuss. Pap. 346/2014.

Da Conceição, E., 2010. Who controls whom? Dynamics of power delegation and agency losses in EU trade politics. *JCMS J. Common Mark. Stud.* 48, 1107–1126.

Da Conceição-Heldt, E., Meunier, S., 2014. Speaking with a single voice: Internal cohesiveness and external effectiveness of the EU in global governance. *J. Eur. Public Policy* 21, 961–979.

Dimopoulos, A., 2011. *EU foreign investment law*. Oxford University Press, Oxford.

Dolzer, R., Schreuer, C., 2012. *Principles of international investment law*, 2nd ed. Oxford University Press, Oxford.

Dür, A., 2008. Bringing economic interests back into the study of EU trade policy-making. *Br. J. Polit. Int. Relat.* 10, 27–45.

Eckhardt, J., 2015. *Business lobbying and trade governance*. Palgrave Macmillan, Basingstoke.

Egger, P., Merlo, V., 2007. The impact of bilateral investment treaties on FDI dynamics. *World Econ.* 30, 1536–1549.

Eilmansberger, T., 2009. Bilateral investment treaties and EU law. *Common Mark. Law Rev.* 46, 383–429.

Elsig, M., 2002. *The EU's common commercial policy: Institutions, interests and ideas*. Ashgate, London.

European Commission, 2010a. Proposal for a regulation of the European Parliament and the Council establishing transitional arrangements for bilateral investment agreements between Member States and third countries (COM(2010) 344 final). Brussels.

European Commission, 2010b. Towards a comprehensive European international investment policy (COM(2010)343). Brussels.

European Court of Justice, 2017. Opinion 2/15 (ECLI/EU/C/2017/376). Luxemburg.

Frieden, J., 1991. Invested interests: The politics of national economic policies in a world of global finance. *Int. Organ.* 45, 425–451.

Grossmann, G., Helpman, E., 1995. The politics of free trade agreements. *Am. Econ. Rev.* 85, 667–690.

Hallward-Driemeier, M., 2003. Do bilateral investment treaties attract foreign direct investment? Only a bit ? and they could bite, policy research working papers. *The World Bank*. doi:10.1596/1813-9450-3121

Hiscox, M., 2002. *International trade and political conflict: Commerce, coalitions, and mobility*. Princeton University Press, Princeton.

Hoffmeister, F., Ünüvar, G., 2012. From BITS and Pieces towards European investment agreements. Presented at the EU and Investment Agreements, Vienna.

Kerremans, B., 2004. What went wrong in Cancún? A principal-agent view of the EU's rationale towards the Doha Development Round. *Eur. Foreign Aff. Rev.* 9, 363–393.

Kleinheisterkamp, J., 2014. Financial responsibility in European international investment policy. *Int. Comp. Law Q.* 63, 449–476. doi:10.1017/S0020589314000116

Krugman, P., Obstfeld, M., Melitz, M., 2014. *International trade: Theory and policy: Global edition*, 10th ed. Pearson, New York.

Lavranos, N., 2013. The new EU Investment Treaties: Convergence towards the NAFTA model as the new Plurilateral Model BIT text? Vrije Universiteit Brussel. URL https://cris.cumulus.vub.ac.be/portal/files/29952551/SSRN_id2241455.pdf

Mahoney, J., Thelen, K. (Eds.), 2010. *Explaining institutional change: Ambiguity, agency, and power*, 1st ed. Cambridge University Press, Cambridge.

Manger, M., 2009. *Investing in protection: The politics of preferential trade agreements between north and south*. Cambridge University Press, Cambridge.

Mestral, A.L.C.D., Lévesque, C., 2013. *Improving international investment agreements*. Routledge, London.

Meunier, S., 2017. Integration by stealth: How the European Union gained competence over foreign direct investment. *J. Common Mark. Stud.* 1–18.

Meunier, S., 2005. *Trading voices: The European Union in international commercial negotiations*. Princeton University Press, Princeton.

Mills, A., 2011. Antinomies of public and private at the foundations of international investment law and arbitration. *J. Int. Econ. Law* 14, 469–503.

Milner, H., 1999. The political economy of international trade. *Annu. Rev. Polit. Sci.* 2, 91–114.

Moravcsik, A., 1998. *The choice for Europe: Social purpose and state power from Messina to Maastricht*. Cornell Univeristy Press, Ithaca.

Moravcsik, A., Schimmelfennig, F., 2009. *European Integration Theory*. Liberal intergovernmentalism, in: Wiener, A., Diez, T. (Eds.). Oxford University Press, Oxford, pp. 67–87.

Neumayer, E., Spess, L., 2005. Do bilateral investment treaties increase foreign direct investment to developing countries? *World Dev.* 33, 1567–1585.

Niemann, A., 2013. EU external trade and the Treaty of Lisbon: A revised neo-functionalist approach. *J. Contemp. Eur. Res.* 9, 634–658.

OECD, 2017. *International regulatory co-operation and trade: Understanding the trade costs of regulatory divergence and the remedies*. OECD, Paris.

Peterson, L.E., 2011. EU member-states approve negotiating guidelines for India, Singapore and Canada investment protection talks; some European governments fear 'NAFTA-contamination'. Investment Arbitration Reporter. URL https://www.iareporter.com/articles/eu-member-states-approve-negotiating-guidelines-for-india-singapore-and-canada-investment-protection-talks-some-european-governments-fear-nafta-contamination/

Pierson, P., 2004. *Politics in time: History, institutions, and social analysis*. Princeton University Press, Princeton.

Pierson, P., 1994. *The path to European integration: A historical institutionalist perspective*. Harvard University and Russel Sage Foundation, Cambridge, MA.

Pollack, M.A., 2003. *The engines of European integration: Delegation, agency, and agenda setting in the EU*. Oxford University Press, Oxford.

Poulsen, L., Bonnitcha, J., Yackee, J.W., 2015. *Transatlantic investment treaty protection*, CEPS Special Report. CEPS, Brussels.

Reinisch, A., 2013. The future shape of EU investment agreements. *ICSID Rev. – Foreign Invest. Law J.* 28, 179–196. doi:10.1093/icsidreview/sit007

Rogowski, R., 1989. *Commerce and coalitions: How trade affects domestic political alignments*. Princeton University Press, Princeton.

Rosamond, B., 2000. *Theories of European integration*. Palgrave Macmillan, Basingstoke.

Salacuse, J.W., 2010. *The law of investment treaties*, 1st ed. Oxford University Press, Oxford.

Schmidt, S., 1998. Commission activism: Subsuming telecommunications and electricity under European competition law. *J. Eur. Public Policy* 5, 169–184. doi:10.1080/13501768880000081

Stacey, J., Rittberger, B., 2003. Dynamics of formal and informal institutional change in the EU. *J. Eur. Public Policy* 10, 858–883. doi:10.1080/1350176032000148342

Streeck, W., Thelen, K.A. (Eds.), 2005. *Beyond continuity: Institutional change in advanced political economies*. Oxford University Press, Oxford.

UNCTAD, 2017. Investment policy hub [WWW Document]. URL http://investmentpolicyhub.unctad.org/IIA (accessed 7.15.11).

UNCTAD, 2014a. *Recent developments in Investor-State Dispute Settlement (ISDS)*. IIA Issues Note.

UNCTAD, 2014b. *The impact of international investment agreements on foreign direct investment: An overview of empirical studies 1998–2014*. IIA Issues Note.

Viner, J., 1950. *The customs union issue*. Carnegie Endowment for International Peace, New York.

Wiener, A., 2009. *European integration theory*, 2nd ed. Oxford University Press, Oxford.

Woll, C., 2008. *Firm interests: How governments shape business lobbying on global trade, Cornell studies in political economy*. Cornell University Press, Ithaca, NY.

Woll, C., Artigas, A., 2007. When trade liberalization turns into regulatory reform: The impact on business-government relations in international trade politics. *Regul. Gov.* 1, 99–182.

Woolcock, S., 2011. *European Union economic diplomacy: The role of the EU in external economic relations*, Global finance series. Ashgate, Burlington.

Young, A.R., 2016. Not your parent's trade politic: The transatlantic trade and investment partnership negotiations. *Rev. Int. Polit. Econ.* 23, 345–378.

Young, A.R., 2001. *Extending European cooperation: The European Union and the 'new' international trade agenda*, EUI Working Papers. RSC. European University Institute, Economics Department.

2 European integration theory and the EU's new international investment policy

Why and how has the EU acquired *de facto* and legal competences to regulate international investment activities since the 1980s? In other words, what fuelled the emergence of the EU as a key actor in the global investment regime? Two explanations come to mind. Either the European Commission or European business lobbying are typically considered to be the key drivers behind the emergence of the EU's international investment policy. These speculations align with grand theories of European Integration. Supranational thinking suggests that the Member State governments have at least partly lost control over European Integration. Supranational actors such as the Commission, the European Parliament or the CJEU are seen to decisively shape and promote European Integration. Intergovernmental thinking, on the other hand, suggests the Member State governments are in full control of European Integration. Member State preferences on European Integration in turn should reflect the preferences of powerful domestic constituencies, namely national business communities.

This chapter advances a twofold theoretical argument. It first develops the argument that supranational thinking, and in particular Commission entrepreneurship, may explain the emergence of the EU's international investment policy. On the basis of principal-agent models, the chapter explains that the Commission exploited its 'agency autonomy' to consolidate its *de facto* competences in international investment policymaking and negotiations. Drawing on historical institutionalism, it is argued that the Commission's efforts over time amounted to incremental institutional change in the form of institutional 'conversion', 'layering' and 'drift', leading to a gradual increase in the Union's legal competences in international investment policy. The second section of the chapter then theoretically refutes business-centred liberal intergovernmental explanations of the emergence of the EU's international investment policy. Societal theories of international political economy suggest that foreign economic policy affects and redistributes welfare in society between exporters, importers and consumers. Apart from investment liberalisation provisions, international investment policy is of a regulatory rather than redistributive nature. Post-establishment treatment and protection standards have only limited, distant and uncertain effects on business operations and profits. Hence, businesses are unlikely to invest resources to develop and voice preferences regarding international investment policymaking – especially on second-order questions such as its communitarisation. The liberal intergovernmental assumption that businesses may have successfully lobbied Member State governments for a communitarisation of international investment policymaking seems improbable.

2.1 Commission entrepreneurship and historical institutionalism

This book endorses the supranational assumption that the Member States have – at least partly – lost control over European Integration. More specifically, it advances the argument that the Commission acted as a resourceful policy entrepreneur and promoted institutional change by first consolidating its role and influence in daily policymaking and thereby fuelling incremental institutional change in the form of an extension of the scope of the CCP to international investment regulation.

The theoretical argument will be laid out in three steps (Figure 2.1). First, the chapter theoretically evaluates why the Commission may have favoured an extension of Union competences to international investment policy. Neo-functional research often uncritically stipulates that the Commission always favours integration. This assumption seems unrealistic. The section draws on the literature on Commission entrepreneurship to assess the Commission's preferences in more detail. Second, it discusses how the Commission may pursue its preferences and consolidate its role and influence in daily policymaking in policy domains beyond Union competences despite Member State opposition. The section builds on the literature on principal-agent models to explain when and how the Commission enjoys autonomy and may consolidate its role and influence. Finally, the section assesses how the Commission may advance formal integration through its growing role and influence on daily policymaking. It draws on historical institutionalist models of slow incremental change (Mahoney and Thelen, 2010). On the one hand, it argues that the Commission's growing role and influence in daily policymaking must indeed be considered formal integration in the form of 'institutional layering' and 'conversion', as it extended the undisputed scope of Union competences inter alia under the CCP to investment-related issues. On the other hand, the Commission's

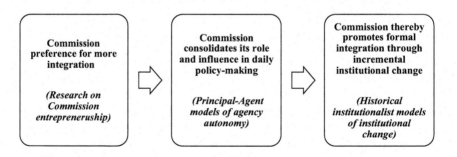

Figure 2.1 A three-stage model of commission entrepreneurship for institutional change

growing role and influence altered the policymaking context, discourse and preferences of relevant actors, thereby promoting relevant treaty revisions.

2.1.1 Supranationalism and the European Commission

David Mitrany's (1943) functionalism is considered the intellectual founding father of modern supranational theories of European Integration (Haas, 1958; Lindberg, 1963; Schmitter, 2009). Mitrany argued that governments should serve human needs and not become ends in themselves like the nation state in realist, liberal or federalist thinking on international relations. In accordance with his technocratic understanding of government, Mitrany suggested that policy issues transcending the boundaries of the nation state should be dealt with at an appropriate supranational or sub-national level of governance. Such effective multilevel governance should shift the expectations and loyalties of domestic interest groups from the nation state to new supranational authorities, thereby promoting international cooperation and integration. Mitrany predicted that a functionalist system of multilevel governance would ultimately bring about a peaceful world order.

Ernst Haas' neo-functionalism (1958) elaborates on Mitrany's reasoning. Neo-functionalism is less normative and more analytical than Mitrany's functionalism. While Mitrany pondered on the questions of why and how states *should* cooperate, Haas sought to theorise on why and how states *actually* cooperate. He observes that an initial integration of a few strategic economic sectors and the creation of a supranational authority which monitors and sponsors further integration trigger functional pressure – i.e. spillovers – to integrate additional economic sectors at the European level. Domestic interest groups slowly shift their expectations and loyalties to the European level and the supranational authority, thus sponsoring further integration. Progressive economic integration requires an ever more intense institutionalisation of European cooperation together with ever more complex and intrusive transnational regulation. Hence, political cooperation and integration are inevitable by-products of initial economic cooperation. Mitrany, Haas and other neo-functionalists argue that cooperation among the Member States of the EU is a self-sustaining process fuelled by functional spillovers, domestic interest groups and supranational institutions (Börzel, 2013; Haas, 1958; Hoffmann, 1966; Lindberg, 1963; Rosamond, 2000; Schmitter, 2009).

Functionalism and neo-functionalism both endorse the assumption that the European Institutions – and more precisely the European Commission – are of causal importance in European Integration and policymaking. A shortcoming of functionalism, neo-functionalism and – not least – liberal intergovernmentalism is their deterministic view of the role of the European Commission and the Member States in European Integration. Supranational and intergovernmental theories typically claim that either the Member States or supranational actors are in full control of European Integration and policymaking. It is manifest, however, that the influence of the Member States and supranational actors varies over time and across policy domains. In certain periods and policy domains, the Member States may be in control of policymaking and European Integration. In other periods and policy domains, supranational actors such as the European Commission may come to shape policymaking and European Integration.

Instead of asking in black-and-white logic whether supranational actors or the Member States control European Integration and policymaking, it is more appropriate to ask *when, why* and *how* supranational actors manage to acquire causal importance. This realisation has fuelled a coming together between scholars of European Integration and comparative politics. Instead of considering European Integration and the EU as a *sui generis* phenomenon, scholars of European Integration are increasingly drawing on theories of comparative politics to understand the workings and evolution of the EU as a political system. This shift in European studies has advanced the discipline and produced important new insights. For the purpose of this study, three strands of research are of particular importance. First, research on policy and Commission entrepreneurship critically scrutinises when and why supranational actors such as the European Commission may seek to shape policy outcomes and European Integration (Hooghe, 2001, 2003, 2005; Kassim et al., 2013; Schafer, 2014). Second, research drawing on principal-agent models provides insights into when and why supranational actors such as the European Commission may successfully pursue their preferences and shape policy outcomes (Copeland and James, 2014; da Conceição-Heldt, 2011; Da Conceiçao-Heldt, 2009; Delreux and Kerremans, 2008; Hooghe and Kassim, 2012; Kaunert, 2011; Laffan, 1997; Meunier and Nicolaidis, 1999, 2006; Schmidt, 1998a, 1998a; Woll, 2006). Third, historical institutionalist research allows for a better understanding of how supranational actors such as the European Commission may – by shaping daily policymaking – promote institutional change in the European political system (Mahoney and Thelen, 2010; Pierson, 2004; Streeck and Thelen, 2005; Thelen, 2004). Taken together, these literatures shed light on how the Commission may have promoted the emergence of the EU's international investment policy.

2.1.2 Understanding Commission preferences on European Integration

Research on Commission entrepreneurship – based on the notion of policy entrepreneurship (see Box 2.1) – critically assesses the preferences of the European Commission on European Integration. Neo-functionalists tend to assume that the Commission categorically seeks to shape policy outcomes and favours greater integration. This assumption is, however, over-simplistic. A growing literature suggests that Commission preferences on European Integration vary significantly across policy domains due to bureaucratic, fiscal federal and ideational considerations (Hooghe, 2001, 2003, 2005; Hooghe and Kassim, 2012; Kassim et al., 2013; Schafer, 2014). It has been suggested that the Commission leadership and staff promote integration if it increases the Commission budget and powers and thereby ultimately improves the career prospects of the civil servants involved. In line with fiscal federalism, other scholars have argued that the Commission leadership and staff favour greater integration if it entails a more efficient and

> **Box 2.1 Economic and policy entrepreneurs**
>
> The concept of 'policy entrepreneurs' derives from Schumpeter's economic theory of entrepreneurship (Schumpeter, 1934). According to Schumpeter, entrepreneurs are the drivers of innovation. Innovation is a disruptive process based on 'creative destruction'. Innovation in products or production processes displaces demand from incumbents to innovating entrepreneurs. Entrepreneurs consequently occupy a dominant position which allows them to extract rents from markets until competitors emulate them. The prospects of temporarily extracting rents motivate entrepreneurs to run risks and to invest resources in innovative projects with uncertain outcomes. Schumpeter concludes that this cycle of innovation, creative destruction and imitation is at the heart of long-term growth and development in capitalist societies.
>
> Dahl (2005) transposed the concept of entrepreneurs from economics to politics. He suggested that like businesses, policy actors might push for policy innovation. Such political entrepreneurs introduce new ideas to shape policy outcomes and institutions. Political entrepreneurs take risks, invest their political capital, use their networks and build coalitions to gain the necessary support for policy innovation. Like economic innovation, policy innovation is a disruptive process. It redistributes resources and power within society and administrations. It weakens the positions of incumbent political leaders and strengthens political entrepreneurs. Political entrepreneurs therefore face resistance from other political actors seeking to protect their power and access to policy resources.

effective provision of public goods (Hooghe, 2003). The Commission leadership and staff are thus unlikely to push for an extension of Union competences if a policy task is better administered at the national or sub-national level. Finally, the Commission leadership and staff also act on ideational considerations – i.e. pro-European ideology. Scholars, however, find that ideational considerations primarily come in to play when the Commission leadership and staff deal with new policy tasks. Ideational considerations serve as a heuristic framework to interpret new challenges and to deal with uncertainty in European policymaking and integration (Schafer, 2014).

Research on Commission preferences suggests that the Commission leadership and staff favour a greater role for the EU and an extension of Union competences in foreign economic policymaking and thereby in international investment policy (Hooghe, 2001, 2012; Hooghe and Kassim, 2012; Kassim et al., 2013; Schafer, 2014). This preference arguably reflects the fact that the functioning of the Single Market requires a common foreign economic policy. As the Commission, the CJEU and academics have suggested in the past, maintaining national foreign economic policies may distort competition within the Single Market and thereby undermine European Integration. However, coordination of national policies is often seen as insufficient, as the Member States may defect from common rules and a free ride to attract more trade, investment and financial activity. The continual integration of foreign economic policy in line with the evolving international economic agenda is, therefore, often seen as the key to the success of the Single Market and European Integration. Indeed, surveys by Hooghe (2012) and Kassim et al. (2013) find that the Commission leadership and staff consider foreign economic policy to be a domain where the Commission should generally play a greater role and seek an extension of Union competences. In the light of these findings, it is coherent to assume that Commission entrepreneurship promoted the emergence of the EU's international investment policy.

2.1.3 Putting Commission preferences into action

Institutionalist research (Box 2.2) provides insights into how the European Commission may act upon its preferences and consolidate its role and influence in non-integrated policy domains. In particular, principal-agent models are widely used to explain when, why and how the Commission shapes policy outcomes. They have produced a wealth of insights into how the Commission may pursue its preferences despite Member State opposition. These models point to five possible Commission strategies to consolidate its role and influence daily policymaking: 1) agenda setting, 2) information asymmetries, 3) international forum shopping, 4) invoking of implied or fringe Union competences and 5) strategic recourse to the CJEU.

Box 2.2 Institutionalism in a nutshell

Institutionalism builds on the assumption that institutions shape policy outcomes. Institutions are often defined as single or complex sets of formal and informal rules and norms. Knowledge of such rules and norms must be widely shared in society for them to be considered an institution. Institutions prescribe and proscribe behaviour. They shape outcomes despite not being actors themselves. They solve social problems through incentives and disincentives (Stacey and Rittberger, 2003). The literature distinguishes between rational choice, sociological and historical institutionalism. Rational choice and historical institutionalism are of interest for this study.

Rational choice institutionalism models institutions as exogenous rules of a game between rational actors. Rational actors know the rules and seek to maximise their welfare within their institutional environment. Principal-agent models are the most prominent variety of rational choice institutionalist research. Principal-agent models assume that principals (Member States) delegate tasks to agents (the Commission) to lower transaction, monitoring and enforcement costs. Delegation, however, is costly. Agents may intentionally or accidentally deviate from the preferences of their principals when fulfilling their tasks. This risk of agents deviating from principals' preferences increases as the agents' autonomy increases. Agency autonomy is a product of 1) the discretion delegated to the agent to act without interference from the principal and 2) the principal's oversight and sanctioning mechanisms. Minimising agency autonomy by circumscribing agents' discretion or by strengthening monitoring and sanctioning may undo the benefits of delegation. Principals must, therefore, find a balance between the benefits and the costs of delegation (Pollack, 2003; Shepsle, 2008). Principal-agent models in essence evaluate when, why and how institutions – such as delegation relationships – shape policy outcomes.

Historical institutionalism shares the assumption of rational choice institutionalism that institutions affect outcomes. However, it focuses on why institutions remain stable or change over time. Institutions are seen as endogenous to politics and not as rules exogenous to politics. Most historical institutionalist research draws on the economic concept of 'positive feedback dynamics' to account for institutional stability. Institutional change, on the other hand, should occur when positive feedback dynamics break down due to exogenous shocks and so-called critical junctures open up. In recent years, scholars have underlined that institutional change may be agency-driven and occur in the absence of exogenous shocks (Pollack, 2003; Shepsle, 2008; Stacey and Rittberger, 2003).

It is crucial to emphasise, however, that the Commission strategies identified in the institutionalist literature primarily come in to play in daily policymaking. This helps to explain how the Commission may informally and on an *ad hoc* and temporary basis *de facto* take on competences in previously non-integrated policy domains. These strategies do not entail formal integration through treaty revisions. Nonetheless, the literature is of great relevance here. Informal integration often precedes and conditions formal integration through IGCs.

Agenda setting

The Commission holds the power to set the policymaking agenda of the EU. Studies suggest that the Commission's first-mover advantage in the form of its right to initiate policy measures and negotiations allows it to shape policymaking outcomes. The Member States must react to a Commission proposal by accepting, amending or rejecting it (Da Conceição, 2010; Delreux and Kerremans, 2008; Kerremans, 2004; Pollack, 2003). To the extent that the Commission proposes measures or negotiations going beyond Union competences, it may consolidate its role in policy domains legally coming under shared or national competence.

The ability of the Commission to exploit its agenda-setting powers partly depends on the content of the initiative. The Member States must accept, amend or reject Commission initiatives on the basis of simple or qualified majority voting or unanimity in the Council of Ministers. Simple or qualified majority requirements leave the Commission some important leeway to shape policy outcomes. It need only convince a majority but not the entirety of the Member States about an initiative. Unanimity requirements constrain the Commission's leeway to shape policy outcomes. It must ensure that all the Member States accept its proposal. Commission initiatives which go beyond Union competence and touch upon shared or national competence require unanimity. Rational choice scholars would, therefore, argue that the Commission's agenda-setting powers are of limited use in consolidating its role and influence in non-integrated policy domains. Such Commission initiatives will only succeed if all the Member States endorse them, which suggests that the Commission is of limited causal importance in integration (da Conceição-Heldt and Meunier, 2014; Meunier, 2005; Pollack, 2003).

A rational choice lens, however, ignores the socialisation and discursive effects of the Commission's first-mover advantage (Hay, 2008; Johnston, 2001; Niemann, 2004). By proposing measures, the Commission can draw attention to and force discussion on salient issues in relevant Council meetings. Over time, the Commission may influence Member State perceptions and preferences on new policy issues beyond undisputed Union competence, such as investment regulation. It may offer heuristic frameworks for Member States to think about certain policy issues. Its agenda-setting powers may thus have a more profound and subtle impact on policymaking and informal integration than rational choice institutionalism suggests.

Information asymmetries

The Commission typically holds an information advantage vis-à-vis the Member States in foreign economic and trade policy, which it may use to consolidate its role and influence in non-integrated policy domains (Da Conceição, 2010; Frennhoff Larsén, 2007; Kerremans, 2004; Pollack, 2003; Tallberg, 2000, 2006). The Commission manages foreign economic and trade policy and acts as the EU's single voice in international negotiations. In comparison to the Member States, it has privileged access to information, with a better overview of third-country preferences, actions and developments in relevant international fora such as the WTO.

The Commission can use these information asymmetries to shape policy outcomes and offer heuristic frameworks to the Member States to interpret the policy context. It may shape the preferences of the Member States, and ultimately Council decisions, by strategically sharing information about international negotiations only in part, or even by misrepresenting the international environment and systemic pressures. The Member States seek to limit information asymmetries through monitoring. For instance, they often send delegates to negotiations between the Commission and third countries to observe. Monitoring is, however, costly. It risks undoing the benefits of delegation. Moreover, many decisive agreements are prepared or struck outside of formal negotiations in informal settings where Member State monitoring is limited. The Commission may use its informational advantage to shape Member State preferences and to make the Council of Ministers endorse initiatives entailing informal cooperation, integration and delegation in non-integrated policy domains.

International forum shopping

The Commission may engage in international forum shopping to consolidate its role and influence and to shape policy outcomes in integrated and non-integrated policy domains (Reiter, 2005; Woolcock, 2011; Young, 2002, 2001). The EU conventionally speaks with a single voice in some international policymaking and negotiating fora such as the WTO or bilateral trade negotiations regardless of the distribution of legal competences under European primary law. The Commission may consolidate its role and shape policy outcomes even in non-integrated policy domains when acting as a single voice, as the Member States are by definition excluded from direct participation in policymaking and negotiating. In other international fora such as the OECD, World Bank, International Monetary Fund (IMF) and UNCTAD, the Member States continue to speak on their own behalf unless an issue indisputably falls under Union competence. The Commission's influence on outcomes should, therefore, be much more limited in these international fora.

The Commission may use its agenda-setting powers and information asymmetries within the EU to build support for managing and negotiating certain issues in Union-friendly fora. In debates with the Member States, it may propose and reiterate the advantages of dealing with a given issue in a Union-friendly forum. It may, moreover, manage the flow of information to the Member States with a view to creating the impression of strong functional and systemic pressures to hold negotiations in Union-friendly fora. On the other hand, the Commission may build coalitions with like-minded third countries to increase systemic pressure to hold negotiations in Union-friendly fora. The choice of international policymaking and negotiating fora is thus endogenous and is likely to affect the Commission's role and influence on policy outcomes.

Invoking implied and fringe competences

The Commission may invoke fringe and implied competences to consolidate its role and influence in issue areas beyond undisputed Union competence (Elsig, 2002; Young, 2002, 2001). The concept of fringe competences refers to competences which have an indirect yet manifest bearing on an issue area. As policies substantively overlap, the EU may unexpectedly start playing a role in new policy domains if it holds competences in adjacent policy domains. On the other hand, the concept of implied competences refers to the so-called *ERTA Doctrine* developed by the CJEU in 1971 in case 22/70 (Kuijper, 2007, p. 1578). It stipulates that if the EU holds internal competences to regulate an issue within the EU it must hold implied external competences to ensure policy coherence and effectiveness.

The Commission may invoke fringe and implied competences to pressure the Member States into accepting its role in a policy domain and to increase its influence on policy outcomes. It may argue to the Member States that it has to participate in an international negotiation either because it holds a crucial fringe competence or because it holds a comprehensive implied and yet disputed competence. From a theoretical point of view, the invoking of fringe and implied competences in many regards resembles the historical institutionalist concept of 'unintended institutional effects' and the neo-functional concept of 'spillovers'. These mean that existing Union competences may over time become relevant in unexpected ways and policy domains entailing European encroachment into national competences and policies without the intent or endorsement of the Member States (Haas, 1958; Lindberg, 1963; Pierson, 2004; Pierson and Skocpol, 2002; Schmitter, 2009).

Strategic recourse to the CJEU

Finally, the Commission may consolidate its role and increase its influence on policy outcomes through strategic recourse to the CJEU (Alter, 2009; Pollack, 2003; Schmidt, 1998b, 1998a; Woll, 2006). Under European primary law, the Commission has the prerogative to bring disputes with Member States to the CJEU. The literature suggests that the Commission uses this prerogative in two ways: 1) to claim disputed competences for the EU outright and 2) to re-shape Member State preferences in line with desired policy outcomes.

The Commission may call on the CJEU to clarify the distribution of competences in disputed policy domains and thereby to claim competence. The CJEU may find that a disputed competence lies with the Union or is of shared rather than national nature. The Commission may thereby consolidate its role in, and ultimately influence on, policymaking and outcomes in these domains. Recourse to the CJEU to clarify the distribution of competences is indeed a frequent phenomenon in the European legal order (see Opinions 1/75, 1/94, 2/92 or 2/15). The Commission typically advances an extensive interpretation of the Union's competences, whereas the Member States typically endorse a restrictive interpretation.

The Commission may call on the CJEU to alter the preferences of the Member States on controversial policy initiatives. It may thereby tilt the balance of power in the Council of Ministers in its favour, push for its desired policy outcomes and consolidate its role in new policy domains (Schmidt, 1998b, 1998a; Woll, 2006). Schmidt (1998a, 1998b) provides an illuminating example of the Commission skilfully using this practice. In line with the European Treaties and Single Market programme, in the 1990s the Commission pushed for the liberalisation of service sectors, which were then dominated by public monopolies. A majority of the Member States were initially opposed to the initiative. The Commission called on the CJEU to clarify Member State obligations under the treaties. The CJEU backed the Commission's reading. A critical mass of Member States consequently endorsed the Commission's initiative to avoid even more far-reaching liberalisation.

2.1.4 From daily policymaking to formal integration – a historical institutionalist perspective

Apart from the last strategy – of strategic recourse to the CJEU – the literature reviewed primarily focuses on how the Commission may consolidate its role and influence in daily policymaking. It thus sheds light on informal integration dynamics through temporary *ad hoc* Member State cooperation and delegation. However, the literature remains mostly silent on the question of how the Commission may use its growing role and influence in daily policymaking to promote formal integration through treaty revisions.

The link between informal and formal integration is, nonetheless, of theoretical salience. In many policy domains, informal integration precedes – and conditions – formal integration. In particular, this is the case of foreign economic policies. The Member States often informally cooperate and delegate to the Commission negotiation on policy issues which are beyond the scope of the CCP. In the long run, such informal integration frequently leads to an extension of the EU's legal competences under the CCP (Niemann, 2013; Young, 2002, 2001).

Historical institutionalist research offers an illuminating framework within which to conceptualise the relationship between informal and formal integration. First, it underlines that formal integration does not necessarily take the form of abrupt and wholesale changes to European law through IGCs and treaty revisions. Formal integration – in other words a redrawing of the Union's legal competences – may also come about incrementally and slowly in daily policymaking ('conversion' or 'layering'). Second, it shows that informal integration may shape the overall policymaking context and extra-institutional environment ('drift'). Changes in these areas may trigger new functional pressures and alter policy discourse and preferences, which should ultimately influence treaty revisions. Both of these theoretical arguments are developed in detail next.

Formal integration through 'conversion' and 'layering'

Political scientists working on European Integration typically assume that formal integration proceeds through IGCs and treaty revisions. Formal integration is seen as consisting of abrupt events and wholesale overhauls of the distribution of legal competences between the EU and the Member States. Recent historical institutionalist research challenges this assumption. It observers that institutional change – inter alia in the form of formal integration within the EU – is often slow and incremental. For instance, Mahoney and Thelen (2010) observe that the British House of Lords evolved over centuries from being a bastion of the aristocracy into a defender of individual civic rights. This fundamental change in the composition, powers and mission of the House of Lords was not the result of abrupt and wholesale institutional amendments. It came about through countless minor adjustments to the statutes and vision of the House of Lords.

Historical institutionalist research explains that such slow incremental institutional change is often the result of actors pushing for institutional change.

24 Theoretical framework

Institutions are seen to redistribute power and resources in society and therefore they are internally contested. Some actors favour institutional stability to maintain their welfare. Others seek to change the existing institutions to increase their welfare. Change-oriented actors may find it difficult to push for abrupt and wholesale change due to opposition from stability-oriented actors. They may, therefore, resort to slow incremental institutional change through so-called institutional 'conversion' and 'layering' (Mahoney and Thelen, 2010; Streeck and Thelen, 2005).

Institutional 'conversion' means that change-oriented actors start advancing new interpretations of existing rules. Rules are typically vague and thus subject to the problem of 'incomplete contracting'. The interpretation of institutional rules is an important factor shaping the functioning and/or effect of an institution on society. Actors may seek to give existing rules new meanings without formally revising them. These new meanings may indeed change the functioning and/or effect of an institution on society (Mahoney and Thelen, 2010; Streeck and Thelen, 2005). 'Layering', on the other hand, refers to the process of adding new rules to existing institutional rules. It leaves the core of institutional rules intact but the new ones may nonetheless profoundly alter the functioning and/or effect of an institution on society (Mahoney and Thelen, 2010; Streeck and Thelen, 2005).

The earlier identified Commission strategies to invoke fringe and implied competences and to take recourse to the CJEU indeed echo the logic of institutional 'conversion' and 'layering' in historical institutionalist research. Invoking implied competences is by and large equivalent to 'layering'. The Commission argues that an existing institutional rule actually encompasses another implicit institutional rule. Invoking fringe competences, on the other hand, resembles 'conversion'. The Commission re-interprets and clarifies that an existing rule also has an – often ignored – bearing on a different policy domain. If the Commission manages to convince the Member States of the validity of its claim to implied or fringe competences, it creates a political and legal precedent. Thenceforth, the EU continues to play a role in the given policy domain or similar policymaking fora in the future. Even though the Commission's manoeuvring may not alter codified law, it redraws the shared understanding of the EU's legal competences in a given policy domain and – at times – decisively extends its role beyond old interpretations. If, however, the Commission fails to convince the Member States it may take recourse to the CJEU to force them to accept a specific interpretation of European law. In the case that the CJEU agrees with the Commission's interpretation of European law, this again may qualify as 'conversion' or 'layering'. It bindingly re-interprets existing elements or even adds new ones to an existing competence, which amounts to incremental formal integration.

Formal integration through 'drift'

Moreover, historical institutionalist research provides an illuminating framework for thinking about the impact of informal integration in daily policymaking on fully-fledged treaty revisions. Informal integration often takes place over many years before discussions about formal integration in the form of treaty revisions start. It thus often fundamentally changes the policymaking context and institutional environment ('drift'). This evolution may shape formal integration through several channels. It may trigger new functional pressures and alter policy discourse and actors' preferences on formal integration. Actors may unwillingly realise that further cooperation and delegation has become necessary. They may thus start favouring formal integration, whereas they previously opposed such steps. In other words, informal integration may gradually prepare and tilt the political balance in favour of integration, which may decisively shape negotiations on treaty revisions and therefore formal integration.

The earlier identified Commission strategies to set the policy agenda using information asymmetries and engaging in international forum shopping again reflect the logic of the historical institutionalist concept of 'drift'. They enable the Commission to shape the actual policymaking context and institutional environment, or at least to shape the Member States' perceptions of them. Agenda setting and information asymmetries enable the Commission to push debates and to shape the perceptions and preferences of the Member States in a given policy context. They are thus heuristic tools for the Commission to influence Member State thinking over time. International forum shopping, on the other hand, actually shapes the policymaking context and institutional environment. If the Commission manages to keep policymaking and negotiating in Union-friendly fora where the Member States traditionally speak with a single voice through the Commission, the Member States will agree to cooperate and to delegate regardless of the distribution of competences. If – over time – a policy issue becomes a standard agenda item in such a Union-friendly forum, the Member States may come to the conclusion that formal integration is necessary and unlikely to alter the political status quo. The Commission's ability to engage in international forum shopping may thus alter the policymaking context to such an extent that formal integration becomes a reasonable and consequential little step rationalising existing policymaking procedures.

2.1.5 *Conclusion*

This section has developed the theoretical argument that the Commission acted as policy entrepreneur and drove the emergence of the EU's international investment policy. The argument has been developed in three theoretical steps. First, with reference to research on Commission entrepreneurship, it was clarified why the Commission may have favoured greater integration in international investment policy. Second, on the basis of principal-agent models it was explained how the Commission might pursue its preferences in daily policymaking and consolidate its role and influence in policy domains beyond Union competence, such as international investment policy. Third, with reference to historical institutionalist research on incremental institutional change it was explained how the Commission may use its growing role and influence in daily policymaking to promote formal integration through treaty revisions. The section has thus theoretically bridged a gap in the literature. Most studies on European Integration either seek to explain informal integration in the form of daily cooperation and delegation or they seek to explain it as consisting of grand intergovernmental bargains on treaty revisions. Few studies connect these spheres. A joint assessment of informal and formal integration creates much 'noise' which complicates the development of parsimonious explanations of integration. However, it is manifest that informal and formal integration are interdependent. If we strive to understand and to explain European Integration as an overarching phenomenon, we need to understand and explain the relationship between informal and formal integration. Table 2.1 tentatively summarises the conceptual overlaps between principal-agent models and historical institutionalist concepts of incremental change.

Table 2.1 Identifying conceptual overlaps between historical institutionalism and principal-agent research

Historical institutionalist concepts of incremental institutional change	*Literature on Commission influence on daily policymaking*
Conversion: Existing rules remain intact and unchanged. However, re-interpretation of these rules alters their application and thereby their functioning and/or effect on society	**Invoking fringe and implied competences:** The Commission may invoke fringe and implied competences to consolidate its role in daily policymaking in issue areas beyond undisputed Union competences. The Commission may thereby reinterpret the scope of the CCP. If the Member States accept a new reading of the Union competences, the new interpretation becomes binding and thus qualifies as formal integration.
	Recourse to the CJEU: The Commission may also have recourse to the CJEU to have its interpretation of Union competences endorsed. Again, the strategy is about re-interpreting the scope of the CCP. If the CJEU agrees with an extensive interpretation of Union competences advanced by the Commission, the interpretation becomes binding and qualifies as formal integration.
Layering: Existing rules remain intact and unchanged. However, actors may gradually add new rules which change the functioning and/or effect of an institution on society.	**Invoking fringe and implied competences:** One may also think of the Commission invoking fringe and implied competences as adding new elements to the CCP. Extending the CCP to entirely new trade issues may count as layering rather than a mere conversion. If the Member States accept the Commission's argument, it becomes binding and qualifies as formal integration.
	Recourse to the CJEU: In a similar vein, the Commission may seek to have the CJEU bindingly acknowledge its interpretation of Union competences, thereby adding new elements to the CCP. This qualifies as formal integration.

Historical institutionalist concepts of incremental institutional change	Literature on Commission influence on daily policymaking
Drift: Existing rules remain intact and unchanged. However, change-oriented actors shape the policymaking context and extra-institutional environment, which may alter the functioning and/or effect of an institution on society. This 'drift' may trigger functional pressures and alter policy discourse and preferences and thus in the long run lead to a formal revision of institutional rules.	**Agenda setting**: The Commission has the right to initiate and to set the agenda in integrated policy domains. It may thereby shape the policy discourse and preferences of Member States on cooperation and delegation beyond undisputed Union competences. In the long run, agenda setting may create the sense of a need for formal integration among the Member States. **Information asymmetries**: Similarly, the Commission may use its information advantage to convince the Member States to take common action and to speak with a single voice in issues beyond undisputed Union competences. In the long run, it may convince the Member States to agree to formal integration. **International forum shopping**: The Commission may shape the policy context and institutional environment to consolidate its role and influence in policymaking. By pushing policymaking into Union-friendly international fora, policymakers may get the impression that formal integration is indeed necessary and overdue.

2.2 The limits of business-centred liberal intergovernmental explanations

Business preferences and lobbying play a central role in theorising on European Integration and European politics. In particular, intergovernmentalism models business preferences and lobbying as constitutive of Member State preferences on European Integration. Domestic interest groups, namely national business communities, are seen to shape Member State preferences. These preferences, in turn, are seen to control European Integration. In line with neo-realism (Waltz, 1979), intergovernmentalism considers the Member States to be the only actors of causal importance in international and European affairs. European Integration and politics are seen as state-driven and state-serving processes (Hoffmann, 1966; Moravcsik, 1993).

2.2.1 Business preferences and European Integration

The causal relationship between business preferences, Member State preferences and European Integration is particularly explicit in Andrew Moravcsik's 'liberal intergovernmentalism' (Moravcsik, 1991, 1993, 1998) (Figure 2.2). Liberal intergovernmentalism enjoys great prominence due to its parsimony and analytical clarity. It stipulates that states should engage in integration in a given policy domain if individual action and non-institutionalised cooperation are expected to deliver suboptimal outcomes. Put differently, integration should occur in policy areas where states want to address collective action problems as described in the prisoner's dilemma.

28 Theoretical framework

Figure 2.2 Simplified causal relationship as described in liberal intergovernmentalism

Liberal intergovernmentalism models integration as a three-stage process. First, the Member States must develop preferences on cooperation and European Integration. It is at this first stage that Moravcsik sees a key role for business preferences and lobbying (Moravcsik and Schimmelfennig, 2009, pp. 69–70). Moravcsik suggests that Member State preferences are primarily formed on the basis of demands from powerful domestic interest groups. Governments are thus modelled as arbitrators between competing domestic demands. As European Integration is to a large extent about economic policy issues, business preferences and lobbying play a central role in the domestic struggle to shape government positions. Domestic interest groups and notably businesses assess the expectable economic effects of integration in a given policy domain and lobby their Member State governments to support profit-maximising options. Member State governments, on the other hand, adjust their positions and preferences to the dominant interest coalition at the domestic level in order to maximise national welfare, to increase political support and ultimately to enhance their chances of re-election.

Second, once the Member States have developed their national positions in discussions with their domestic interest groups, they enter into substantive intergovernmental negotiations on integration. Morvacsik draws on bargaining theory to explain the outcomes of such intergovernmental negotiations. These outcomes reflect the asymmetrical interdependence of the Member States in a given domain. In other words, the Member States incurring high opportunity costs from non-integration will be more willing to compromise than the Member States incurring low opportunity costs. The substantive negotiating outcomes will thus be closer to the ideal point of the less dependent Member States than to that of the more dependent ones. Nevertheless, Moravcsik concedes that the Commission or the CJEU may push for certain substantive agreements prior to or during IGCs by providing or manipulating information on the costs and benefits of the integration proposals under discussion. However, scholars of intergovernmentalism caution that supranational actors only dare to push for specific outcomes if a critical mass of Member States explicitly or tacitly support it. At times, Member States may even publicly oppose certain integration proposals to avoid domestic challenges but secretly encourage the Commission, the European Parliament or the CJEU to push for them (Garrett, 1992; Schmidt, 1998a; Weaver, 1986; Woll, 2006).

Finally, the Member States engage in second-order negotiations to determine the exact setup of cooperation and integration. While the Member States preserve comprehensive discretion in certain integrated policy domains, they delegate all policy-making to the European level in others. Moravcsik draws on rational institutionalism and principal-agent models to explain this variation in delegation and institutional setups. The institutional setup and degree of delegation should depend on needs for credible commitment, neutral monitoring, interpretation and enforcement of incomplete contracts, and demand for policy management and technical expertise. Scholars of intergovernmentalism thus highlight that the – even at times very comprehensive – powers the Commission, European Parliament and CJEU have merely reflect Member State preferences (Caporaso and Keeler, 1995; Garrett, 1992, 1995; Pollack, 2003). Moravcsik, nonetheless, concedes that the degree of delegation and the institutional setup may occasionally also reflect a federalist ideology of Member State governments and thus may sometimes defy rational institutionalist thinking.

2.2.2 Extending the liberal intergovernmental logic to informal integration

Liberal intergovernmentalism seeks to account for formal integration through treaty revisions. It does not seek to explain temporary informal *ad hoc* cooperation and integration in daily policymaking. However, as Alasdair Young (2002, 2001) notes, many studies on informal integration in the form of temporary *ad hoc* cooperation and delegation implicitly endorse a liberal intergovernmental logic. This is particularly true for studies on EU foreign economic policy, which is the subject of this book.

Woolcock and Bayne, for instance, observe, "*The broad EU trade policy position over the past decades can be summarised as the defensive interests of agriculture competing against the market opening interests of manufacturing and services. These interests reflect the competitive positions of the respective sectors*" (Woolcock and Bayne, 2007, p. 26). By shaping the substantive policy preferences of the Member States and the EU, business should equally shape informal integration in this domain. Business demands are unlikely to perfectly mirror the EU's – in many cases unclear – legal competences and so business may – unintentionally – push the Member States into cooperation and integration on issues beyond Union competence. Thus, while most studies drawing on business preferences to explain substantive policy outcomes may not actually intend to uncover integration dynamics, they nevertheless convey information about such dynamics (Baccini and Dür, 2012; M. Baldwin, 2006; R. Baldwin, 2006; De Bièvre and Jappe, 2010; Dür, 2007; Manger, 2009; Meunier and Nicolaidis, 1999; Young, 2002, 2001).

Manger's work (2009) on the global proliferation of PTAs illustrates this train of thought. He reports that in the late 1990s European business successfully lobbied the Commission and Member States to conclude competitive PTAs including services and investment chapters with Mexico and Chile in order to mitigate negative effects arising from US PTAs. The Member States gave in to these business demands and empowered the EU to conclude comprehensive PTAs with ambitious services and investment provisions despite the fact that the EU did not yet hold the relevant legal competences to negotiate and to enter into such commitments. Therefore, while business lobbied for substantive policy commitments and did not lobby for the integration of services and investment regulation at the European level, its lobbying efforts *de facto* drove the extension of the EU's *de facto* competences in these domains.

2.2.3 Explaining business preferences and lobbying

Liberal intergovernmentalism is an illuminating framework. It helps business preferences and lobbying to be located and embedded in the process of formal and informal European Integration in general, and in foreign economic policymaking in particular. However, from the perspective of this study, it suffers from a significant weakness. While it assumes that business preferences may decisively shape Member State preferences and thereby European Integration, it does not explain how business preferences are formed and therefore why and when business preferences may promote European Integration. Business preferences are treated as exogenous building blocks factored into the aforementioned model of treaty revisions. This shortcoming of liberal intergovernmentalism is understandable in view of avoiding theoretical overstretches. Nevertheless, it externalises the challenge of explaining European Integration. To fill this explanatory gap, it is instructive to review research on the formation of business preferences. The literature advances both 'thin' materialist and 'thick' cognitivist models of the formation of these preferences (Woll, 2008).

The bulk of the research on the formation of business preferences is rooted in the literature on comparative political economy (Crouch, 2005; DiMaggio and Powell, 1991; Hall and Soskice, 2001; Wildavsky, 1987). It endorses a materialist perspective. It builds on microeconomics and models businesses as rational economic and political actors. Businesses are seen as having a fundamental interest in ensuring their economic survival. This translates into a need to maximise income and profits. Many studies consequently adopt a reductionist view and consider that businesses lobby for short-term profit maximisation, for instance through the dismantling of costly social regulation. Comparative political economy research thus draws an antagonistic picture, with businesses pushing for neoliberal policies to maximise profits and labour pushing for high wages and job protection.

However, scholars have cautioned that in reality business preferences are more complex. At times, businesses lobby for allegedly labour-friendly policies and stringent regulations, and labour occasionally supports allegedly business-friendly policies. Hall and Soskice (2001) invoke the institutional setting to account for these observations. National institutional settings – understood inter alia as labour markets or education and vocational training regimes – may systemically affect and alter business preferences. In line with rational institutionalism, national institutional settings must be thought of as the 'rules of the game', creating specific incentive structures and governing the interactions between businesses, labour and policymakers. They may therefore account for occasional counterintuitive business preferences.

Woll (2008) generalises this train of thought. She observes that businesses have a fundamental interest in securing their economic survival, which translates into a preference to generate profits. However, the preference to generate profits is too broad and underdetermined. Businesses need to gather and interpret information about their economic, political and institutional environment to understand how exactly they can generate profits and what political strategy they may successfully pursue to reach their desired policy outcomes. This context-focused model of the formation of business preferences allows for a more nuanced view of them.

2.2.4 Foreign economic policy, business preferences and lobbying

There is a burgeoning literature on the formation of business preferences and lobbying in foreign economic policy. As international investment policy falls under foreign economic policy, it is illuminating to review this literature. The literature echoes in many regards debates on business preferences and lobbying in comparative political economy. Early research endorses a materialist and demand-side perspective on the formation of business preferences on foreign economic policy (De Bièvre and Dür, 2005; Dür, 2007, 2008, 2012; Frieden, 1991; Hiscox, 2002; Manger, 2009; Rogowski, 1989; Young, 2016). Governments are seen as responsive arbitrators which adopt national preferences in line with dominant interest coalitions at the domestic level. Businesses, in turn, lobby for foreign economic policies that increase income and profits, and oppose policies that lower them. To understand how foreign economic policies may redistribute income in society and thereby affect business profits, scholars of international political economy draw on theories of trade economics. They predict that political cleavages form around production factors, economic sectors or specific products.

Factor-based models assume that preferences in foreign economic policy are formed on the basis of the relative abundance or scarcity of production factors in a given economy. They build on the Heckscher-Ohlin and Stopler-Samuelson theorems. Economies are seen as being differently endowed with the production factors of land, labour and capital. Relative abundances or scarcities affect the returns for the owners of production factors, with scarce factors yielding greater returns than abundant ones. However, the degree of abundance or scarcity of production factors may be affected by the openness of the economy through trade and investment. Owners of scarce production factors will prefer protectionist foreign economic policies to keep out foreign competition and to maximise returns, and owners of abundant factors will favour liberal policies to increase profits through sales abroad. In essence, therefore, factor-based models suggest that political mobilisation regarding foreign economic policies will run along socio-economic classes. Depending on changing coalitions between the landowning class, capitalist entrepreneurs and mass labour, countries will opt for protectionism or open markets. Rogowski (1989) demonstrates that this neo-Marxist class-based view of foreign economic policy accounts for the preferences and policy outcomes in major Western economies in the 19th and early 20th centuries. Moreover, factor-based models are relevant in accounting for the long-term tendencies in countries' foreign economic policies. Nevertheless, it is clear that the preferences of businesses and other domestic interest groups on foreign economic policy are significantly more nuanced and complex in the short-term and in modern developed economies than predicted by factor-based models.

Sector-based models constitute an insightful alternative approach to understanding the formation of business preferences. These models assume that preferences in foreign economic policy are formed on the basis of the international

32 Theoretical framework

competitiveness of given sectors. They build on the Ricardo-Viner theorem, which models factors as immobile across economic sectors in modern developed economies. In other words, the labour or capital allocated to a specific economic sector cannot easily shift to another sector. A worker trained to produce medical equipment cannot simply change sectors and work as an accountant. A firm which has invested in heavy industry cannot easily change sectors and provide telecommunication services. The assumption that production factors are locked into their respective sectors has far-ranging implications for the formation of preferences in foreign economic policy. Market openness should not have a homogenous impact on the returns on production factors *per se*, as is assumed in factor-based models, but should affect returns as a function of economic sectors and their international competitiveness. If an economic sector is import-competing, economic openness should entail a reduction in returns and profits on the capital and labour in that sector. If it is export-competing, however, market openness should lead to rising returns and profits through better export conditions. It follows that capital and labour should face similar income and profit effects from economic openness/closure as a function of the relevant sector and thus have similar preferences in foreign economic policy. Hiscox (2002) shows that sector-based models account rather well for the formation of business preferences in modern developed economies.

Since the 1980s, 'new' trade theory has emerged as another line of thinking. This suggests that preferences on foreign economic policy should be product-specific due to underlying production processes. 'New' trade theory builds on the observation that much world trade takes place between countries with similar factor endowments and levels of productivity. Classic trade theories such as the earlier cited Heckscher-Ohlin, Stopler-Samuelson and Ricardo-Viner theorems cannot account for these trade flows. According to them, traders and consumers should have little interest in such trade. Instead, scholars of 'new' trade theory suggest that countries with similar economic properties nonetheless engage in trade because they specialise in certain sectors and thereby attain important economies of scale (Krugman, 1980, 1990). Such economies of scale provide countries with a competitive edge and cost advantages and drive trade. Milner and Yoffie (1989) deduce from this reasoning that businesses engaged in the production of goods or services with strong economies of scale will favour liberal foreign economic policies to ensure market access abroad. Businesses engaged in the production of goods and services with weak economies of scale should favour protectionist foreign economic policies to limit import competition. Other scholars extend the argument to Global Value Chains (GVCs) (Young, 2016). Certain goods and services are produced through highly decentralised GVCs to benefit from location-specific advantages such as cheap labour, strategic assets or access to rare commodities. Businesses involved in the production of these goods or services need to take advantage of GVCs to remain competitive and will therefore favour liberal foreign economic policies.

Materialist models of the formation of business preferences enjoy considerable prominence due to their theoretical parsimony. However, scholars of comparative political economy and international political economy have cautioned that such models ignore the cognitive component in the process of preference formation. The social universe is complex. Economic actors, including businesses, cannot simply read off their preferences and lobbying strategies from their environment. Businesses and other economic actors draw on paradigms, beliefs, identities and joint cultures to make sense of their environment, to identify relevant causalities and therefore to take action to maximise their welfare or profits. Paradigms, beliefs, identities and culture function as instruction sheets which determine what businesses perceive to be rational and profit-maximising in a given situation (Wildavsky, 1987). Scholars interested in understanding the formation of business preferences therefore need to evaluate how ideas, paradigms, beliefs, identities and culture come about and how they shape preferences. Hall and Soskice (2001) and DiMaggio and Powell (1991), for instance, suggest that the institutional settings play a central role in shaping paradigms, preferences and lobbying of businesses.

Research on the formation of business preferences on foreign economic policy has mostly ignored cognitive approaches. Woll's work (2008) constitutes a notable exception. She argues that materialist models often fail to account for business preferences and political strategies in foreign economic policy. Foreign economic policy – especially on new trade issues – is a highly complex domain. Businesses face considerable uncertainty as they lack experience and expertise in such issues. They struggle to understand and to identify the costs and benefits of foreign economic policy options. Woll argues that to develop situation-specific preferences and political strategies businesses engage in a dialogue with governments. Businesses and governments share their concerns and knowledge in order to jointly define their respective preferences. Woll's framework thus breaks with the demand-side perspective of the models discussed earlier. Business preferences are modelled as endogenous to the policymaking process with governments shaping businesses preferences, and *vice versa*.

2.2.5 Modelling business preferences on international investment policy

The literature review suggests that business preferences and lobbying patterns reflect the economic effects of foreign economic policies on business operations and profits. In order to understand whether business holds preferences and lobbies in international investment policy – and for its communitarisation – it is thus necessary to theoretically assess its economic effects on business. The economic effects of international investment policy are more complex than in classic foreign economic policy focusing on conventional market access. As will be discussed in detail in Chapter 3, international investment policy as implemented through international investment agreements (IIAs) deals with three issue areas: investment liberalisation, post-establishment treatment and protection standards and dispute resolution mechanisms. The IIA provisions relating to investment liberalisation, post-establishment treatment and protection standards as well as dispute resolution have distinct effects on business operations. Business preferences and lobbying are likely to differ across these issue areas and need to be assessed separately.

Investment liberalisation

Investment liberalisation provisions have an economic impact on businesses operations and profits comparable to conventional market access provisions of classic foreign economic policy. The investment liberalisation provisions of IIAs determine the reciprocal market access for national and third-country investors. Investment liberalisation provisions – much like tariffs or quotas – affect competition, price levels and profit margins in a given economy and sector. They redistribute welfare within the economy and society. In line with Vinerian economics and the aforementioned materialist theories, business preferences and lobbying should reflect the expected economic effects of investment liberalisation provisions on business operations and profits. Domestically oriented import-competing firms should favour and lobby for protectionist investment and foreign economic policies to maintain high profit margins. Internationally oriented firms – embedded in GVCs – should favour and lobby for liberal investment and foreign economic policies to take advantage of business opportunities abroad.

Post-establishment treatment and protection standards

IIA provisions regarding post-establishment treatment and protection standards are primarily of a regulatory nature. They do not affect competition, price levels or profit margins. They establish basic standards for the treatment of international investors in host jurisdictions. These standards arguably lie below the equivalent standards provided under Member State and EU law. Hence, the provisions are unlikely to affect business operations and profitability within the EU. They may, however, economically benefit outward investors (Box 2.3) by providing a safer and more predictable investment environment abroad. Business surveys and research on the impact of IIAs on investment flows, however, cast doubts on this assumption. Yackee (2010) and Cotula et al. (2016) find that most US and Chinese investors for instance are not aware of IIAs when taking an investment decision. Investors seem to consider that post-establishment treatment and protection standards of IIAs have no significant effect on their operations and profits. Econometric research also shows that IIAs have limited effects on the volume and geography of FDI flows (Blonigen and Piger, 2014; Busse et al., 2010; Colen et al., 2014; Egger and Merlo, 2007; Hallward-Driemeier, 2003; Neumayer and Spess, 2005; Sauvant and Sachs, 2009; UNCTAD, 2014b; Yackee, 2009). These findings imply that investors rarely take IIAs into account to assess the investment climate in potential host countries and to decide on an investment destination. UNCTAD (2014b) concludes that not IIAs but inter alia access to strategic markets, labour, commodities, the overall business climate and quality of the rule of law shape investment decisions. The disregard of investors for IIAs and their post-establishment treatment and protection standards when deciding on investment destinations implies that they are unlikely to lobby for such provisions.

Dispute resolution mechanisms

Dispute resolution mechanisms in the form of investor-to-state dispute settlement (ISDS) mechanisms are also primarily of a regulatory nature. ISDS provisions are an

Theoretical framework 35

enforcement mechanism. They allow investors to claim compensation if host countries violate post-establishment treatment and protection standards enshrined in IIAs. They do not affect competition, price levels or profit margins. They have – at best – minor, distant and uncertain economic effects on business operations by eventually limiting future losses. Business interest and lobbying for ISDS should be limited for a number of reasons. First, most businesses invest in countries, which they consider to provide a generally save and reliable investment environment. If investors think that they face a significant risk of mistreatment and expropriation, they are unlikely to invest in a country in the first place. It follows that many investors tend to discount for the future need of access to ISDS when carrying out an investment. Major multinational corporations and investors active in high-risk sectors and world regions – admittedly – may be less prone to this cognitive bias. Second, if investors face mistreatment and expropriation at some point in the future, they seek to avoid using ISDS against host countries. Investors normally favour 'soft' dispute resolution mechanisms such as mediation or dialogues with host country authorities. ISDS erodes the work relationship with host country authorities and risks amplifying problems and losses. ISDS is sometimes described as the 'nuclear option' of dispute resolution. Finally, investors cannot know whether they will win an ISDS proceeding. UNCTAD (2014a) for instance reports that investors won not even a third of known arbitration cases against host countries; and received only fractions of claimed damages as award. To sum up, investors tend to discount for the risk of expropriation; are little inclined to actually use ISDS; and face uncertainty regarding whether they might win an ISDS case and get compensation. The limited, distant and uncertain economic effect of ISDS provisions on business operations should translate into limited business interest and lobbying in this domain.

Box 2.3 Who are the stakeholders in the EU's international investment policy?

The main stakeholders in international investment policy are outward investors. They face the greatest economic effects from international investment policy, and by logical extension from a communitarisation of international investment policy. If business lobbying was a driving force behind the communitarisation of international investment policy, they should have been key actors in the policy debate.

A statistical analysis suggests that European outward investors are concentrated in a small number of Member States and economic sectors. Almost half of EU outward FDI comes from the United Kingdom, France and Germany (Figure 2.3). Eight large and medium-sized old Member States account for more than 80% of the EU's outward FDI stock. In terms of economic sectors (Figure 2.4), European outward investors are primarily active in services (59%), but also manufacturing (29%) and mining and other extractive industries (12%). Financial service providers are the EU's most potent outward

36 *Theoretical framework*

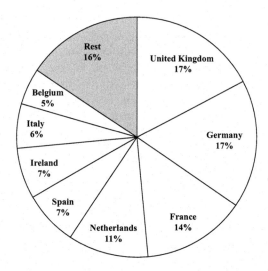

Figure 2.3 Member states' outward FDI stocks of EU total (2014)
Source: Eurostat (2017).

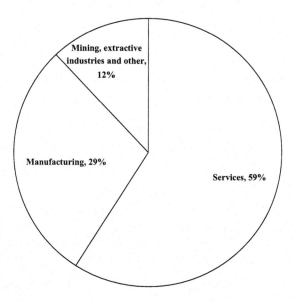

Figure 2.4 Extra-EU outward FDI stocks by sector (2014)
Source: Eurostat (2017).

investors (Eurostat, 2017). While it is in principle possible to further disaggregate data to identify key sectors and sub-sectors, it is little useful. FDI data is notoriously patchy. This holds in particular true for outward stocks and flow statistics.

2.2.6 Modelling business preferences on the communitarisation of international investment policy

For the purpose of this study, it is crucial to assess whether the communitarisation of international investment policymaking may alter the economic effects of international investment policy identified earlier and thereby fuel business lobbying. The communitarisation of international investment policy is thought to yield two important benefits. First, it arguably increases the bargaining power of Europe in international investment negotiations. Second, it may promote the creation of a level playing field for European investors abroad as Member State policies cease to exist. The theoretical assessment suggests that neither of these communitarisation effects is likely to significantly alter the economic effects on business and therefore to have fuelled lobbying efforts.

Assessing the benefits of increased bargaining power

The communitarisation of international investment policy is thought to increase the bargaining power of Europeans in international investment negotiations and thereby to benefit business – arguably the main stakeholder – in the form of better negotiating outcomes (European Commission, 2010, 1995). While at first glance this may seem convincing, a detailed theoretical assessment shows that the communitarisation of international investment policy may have more limited economic effects on businesses than was assumed.

First, in the domain of investment liberalisation bargaining power is indeed important to secure good market access and investment conditions abroad. Negotiations on investment liberalisation resemble traditional trade negotiations on tariff reductions. Countries exchange market access concessions. Market size is considered an important determinant of bargaining power in such negotiations. Major economies can offer access to large markets and thereby extract greater concessions from negotiating partners seeking market access. The communitarisation of international investment policy – and notably dealings with investment liberalisation – may thus, at first sight, benefit European business and the Member States. However, a detailed examination shows that this assumption is flawed. The Member States never negotiated individually but always spoke with a single voice in talks on investment liberalisation. Since the entry into force of the Treaty of Maastricht in 1993, the EU held a shared competence under the chapter on capital movements to negotiate on international investment liberalisation. The Member States were unable to individually negotiate with third countries in this domain. Hence, the Treaty of Lisbon neither *de facto* nor *de jure* changed the bargaining power of the EU in this domain. Communitarisation did not deliver the promised economic gains to European business, which should have translated into a lack of business lobbying.

Second, bargaining power is of limited importance in negotiations on post-establishment treatment standards and protection provisions. These disciplines are predominantly of a regulatory nature. There is fairly little variation in these clauses in the BITs of OECD members. Experts are inclined to see Member State BITs as providing similarly high levels of post-establishment treatment standards and protection, which, for instance, exceed the levels of post-establishment treatment standards and protection provided under US and Canadian BITs (Alschner, 2013; Dolzer and Schreuer, 2012; Gugler and Tomsik, 2006; Reinisch, 2013). Increased bargaining power is unlikely to further enhance the level of post-establishment treatment and protection and so translate into economic gains for business. Moreover, the emerging EU approach to post-establishment treatment and protection in many regards emulates the US and Canadian approach rather than the so-called gold standard of Member State BITs (Alschner, 2013; Lavranos, 2013; Reinisch, 2013). In comparison to Member State BITs, US and Canadian ones strengthen host country rights to the detriment of investors. Some experts have therefore warned that the communitarisation of international investment policy actually harms European business interests by lowering the level of post-establishment treatment and protection for European businesses abroad.

Assessing the benefits of a level international playing field

The communitarisation of international investment policy is thought to benefit European business by creating a level playing field for outward investments. Until the entry into force of the Lisbon Treaty, some Member States had created dense BIT networks to support outward investment activities by their business communities. Other Member States had not negotiated such BIT networks, arguably harming their national business communities in intra-EU and international competition. Disadvantaged business communities may have sought to enhance their economic standing by lobbying for a communitarisation of international investment policy in order to gain access to a network of EU BITs. Again, while this is convincing at first glance, a detailed assessment casts doubts on the assumption.

Almost 80% of outward FDI stocks are held by British, German, French, Dutch, Spanish, Italian and Belgian businesses (Box 2.3). These investors can rely on dense BIT networks[1] (Table 2.2) so they should not have expected significant

Table 2.2 Share of selected Member States in outward FDI and number of ratified BITs (2017)

Country	% in EU outward FDI stock	Number of IIAs
United Kingdom	17%	106
Germany	17%	135
France	14%	104
Netherlands	11%	95
Spain	7%	88
Italy	6%	82
Belgium	5%	94
Total	77%	704

Source: Author's own calculations, UNCTAD (2017).

economic gains from a communitarisation of international investment policy and therefore would not have lobbied for it. The remaining 21 Member States account for about 20% of EU outward FDI stocks (Box 2.3). While business in this group may eventually expect economic gains from a communitarisation of international investment policy, the group seems highly fragmented and relatively small. The heterogeneity of this group in terms of countries, the consequent high coordination costs of lobbying and their limited importance as outward investors at the EU level cast strong doubts on the assumption that they may have successfully pushed for a communitarisation of international investment policy.

2.2.7 Conclusion

It is often assumed in the academic and policy debate that European business was the main driver of the communitarisation of international investment policymaking. By and large, the assumption echoes liberal intergovernmental thinking on European Integration. This holds that business preferences and lobbying decisively shape Member State preferences and European Integration. Political economy research predicts business preferences and lobbying on the basis of the redistributive and economic effects of policies. Business should generally push for profit-maximising policy outcomes. Apart from investment liberalisation provisions, international investment policy is unlikely to have a significant economic effect on businesses and, therefore, trigger business lobbying. Post-establishment treatment standards and investment protection provisions are of a regulatory. They have only minor, distant and uncertain impacts on business operations. Business is therefore likely to hold strong preferences and to lobby for investment liberalisation commitments, but less likely to lobby policymakers over post-establishment treatment and investment protection provisions. More importantly for this study though, the communitarisation of international investment policy is unlikely to fundamentally alter these economic effects of international investment policy. It therefore seems unlikely that business was a decisive driver behind the emergence of the EU's international investment policy.

2.3 The methodological strategy

The preceding sections have developed two theoretical arguments. The validity of these two arguments will be assessed using qualitative methods, namely analytical process tracing. Process tracing is necessary due to the problem of observational equivalence. The book seeks to evaluate whether Commission entrepreneurship or business lobbying accounts for the EU's growing role in international investment policy. It is possible that European business, the Member States and the Commission at times held similar preferences. Only an in-depth assessment of the political processes and causalities underlying the EU's growing role allows evaluating the validity of the advanced arguments. Analytical process tracing is a particular suitable method to uncover causalities in cases of observational equivalence. It goes beyond historiography and a description of a series of events in the past. Instead, it approaches case studies with pre-defined theoretical assumptions about variables and causalities. It recounts in detail the periods examined through an analytical-theoretical lens and summarises the data accordingly (George and Bennett, 2005, p. 211). To gather the necessary data, the study draws on academic literature, policy documents, archival research, extensive press research, 42 semi-structured anonymised research interviews, an internship at the Investment Policy Unit of the Directorate General for Trade at the European Commission and on countless informal discussions with policymakers and academics.

The project examines several in-case studies. In-case studies do not follow the logic of comparative case studies. They seek to shed light on the causalities at work in different fora and points of time within the overarching and long-term process of the EU's new international investment policy emerging (George and Bennett, 2005, pp. 178–179). In line with this approach and the research question, the study examines EU-internal debates on legal competences and international investment negotiations with EU involvement. These policymaking instances shaped the EU's *de facto* and legal competences and allow identifying the causal mechanisms at work. The project examines all the IGCs and relevant CJEU proceedings since 1980. Moreover, it examines all the multilateral negotiations on investment which the EU took part in, namely the GATS and TRIMs talks within the Uruguay Round, the negotiations on the ECT, the MAI in the OECD and the Singapore Issues. Finally, the study analyses how investment disciplines became a standard agenda item in PTAs between the EU and third countries. The analysis focuses particularly on the EU-Mexico and EU-Chile PTA negotiations. While inclusion of comprehensive consolidated investment disciplines in the EU-Mexico PTA unexpectedly failed, the EU-Chile PTA, which quickly followed, does comprise such investment disciplines.

Note

1 As Figure 2.3 shows, Irish firms hold 7% of outward EU stock. They are, nevertheless, ignored here, as Ireland has not concluded IIAs for constitutional reasons.

References

Alschner, W., 2013. Americanization of the BIT universe: The influence of Friendship, Commerce and Navigation (FCN) treaties on modern investment treaty law. *Goettingen J. Int. Law* 5, 455–486.

Alter, K., 2009. *The European court's political power*. Oxford University Press, Oxford.

Baccini, L., Dür, A., 2012. The new regionalism and policy interdependency. *Br. J. Polit. Sci.* 42, 57–79.

Baldwin, M., 2006. EU trade politics: Heaven or hell? *J. Eur. Public Policy* 13, 926–942.

Baldwin, R., 2006. Multilateralizing regionalism: Spaghetti bowls as building blocs on the path to global free trade. *World Econ.* 29, 1451–1518.

Blonigen, B.A., Piger, J., 2014. Determinants of foreign direct investment. *Can. J. Econ.* 47, 775–812. doi:10.1111/caje.12091

Börzel, T., 2013. Comparative regionalism: European integration and beyond, in: Carlsnaes, W., Risse, T., Simmons, B. (Eds.), *Handbook of international relations*. Sage, London, pp. 501–530.

Busse, M., Nunnenkamp, P., Spatareanu, M., 2010. Foreign direct investment and labor rights: A panel analysis of bilateral FDI flows. *Econ. Lett.* 11, 270–272.

Caporaso, J., Keeler, J., 1995. The European Union and regional integration theory, in: Rhodes, C., Mazey, S. (Eds.), *The state of the European Union*. Lynne Rienner Publishers, Boulder, pp. 29–62.

Colen, L., Persyn, D., Guariso, A., 2014. *What type of FDI is attracted by bilateral investment treaties?*, LICOS Discuss. Pap. 346/2014.

Copeland, P., James, S., 2014. Policy windows, ambiguity and commission entrepreneurship: Explaining the relaunch of the European Union's economic reform agenda. *J. Eur. Public Policy* 21, 1–19. doi:10.1080/13501763.2013.800789

Cotula, L., Weng, X., Ma, Q., Ren, P., 2016. *China-Africa investment treaties: Do they work?* IIED, London.

Crouch, C., 2005. Models of capitalism. *New Polit. Econ.* 10, 439–456.

Da Conceição, E., 2010. Who controls whom? Dynamics of power delegation and agency losses in EU trade politics. *JCMS J. Common Mark. Stud.* 48, 1107–1126.

da Conceição-Heldt, E., 2011. *Negotiating trade liberalization at the WTO*. Palgrave Macmillan, London, UK.

da Conceição-Heldt, E., Meunier, S., 2014. Speaking with a single voice: Internal cohesiveness and external effectiveness of the EU in global governance. *J. Eur. Public Policy* 21, 961–979.

Da Conceiçao-Heldt, E.D., 2009. *Delegation of power and agency losses in EU trade politics*, EUI Work. Pap.

Dahl, R.A., 2005. *Who governs? Democracy and power in the American city*, 2nd Rev ed. Yale University Press, New Haven.

De Bièvre, D., Dür, A., 2005. Constituency interests and delegation in European and American trade policy. *Comp. Polit. Stud.* 38, 1271–1296.

De Bièvre, D., Jappe, E., 2010. *The political economy of EU anti-dumping reform*, ECIPE Work. Pap. 03/2010.

Delreux, T., Kerremans, B., 2008. *How agents control principals*, IIEB Work. Pap. 28.

DiMaggio, P., Powell, W., 1991. *The new institutionalism and organizational analysis*. Princeton University Press, Princeton.

Dolzer, R., Schreuer, C., 2012. *Principles of international investment law*, 2nd ed. Oxford University Press, Oxford.

Dür, A., 2012. Key Controversies in European Inegration. Why interest groups dominate the EU's foreign economic policies, in: Zimmerman, H., Dür, A. (Eds.). Palgrave Macmillan, Basingstoke, pp. 177–183.

Dür, A., 2008. Bringing economic interests back into the study of EU trade policy-making. *Br. J. Polit. Int. Relat.* 10, 27–45.

Dür, A., 2007. EU trade policy as protection for exporters: The agreements with Mexico and Chile. *J. Common Mark. Stud.* 45, 833–855.

Egger, P., Merlo, V., 2007. The impact of bilateral investment treaties on FDI dynamics. *World Econ.* 30, 1536–1549.

Elsig, M., 2002. *The EU's common commercial policy: Institutions, interests and ideas*. Ashgate, London.

European Commission, 2010. *Towards a comprehensive European international investment policy* (COM(2010)343). Brussels.

European Commission, 1995. A level playing field for direct investment world-wide (COM(95)42 final). Brussels.

Eurostat, 2017. Foreign direct investments [WWW Document]. URL http://ec.europa.eu/eurostat/web/structural-business-statistics/global-value-chains/fdi.

Frennhoff Larsén, M., 2007. Principal-agent analysis with one agent and two principals: European Union trade negotiations with South Africa. *Polit. Policy* 35, 440–463.

Frieden, J., 1991. Invested interests: The politics of national economic policies in a world of global finance. *Int. Organ.* 45, 425–451.

Garrett, G., 1995. The politics of legal integration in the European Union. *Int. Organ.* 49, 171–181. doi:10.1017/S0020818300001612

Garrett, G., 1992. International cooperation and institutional choice: The European Community's internal market. *Int. Organ.* 46, 533–560.

George, A., Bennett, A., 2005. *Case studies and theory development in the social sciences, BCSIA studies in international security.* MIT Press, Cambridge.

Gugler, P., Tomsik, V., 2006. *The North American and European approach in the international investment agreements*, NCCR Work. Pap. 2006/04.

Haas, E.B., 1958. *The uniting of Europe: Political, social and economic forces, 1950–1957.* Stevens, London.

Hall, P., Soskice, D., 2001. *Varieties of capitalism the institutional foundations of comparative advantage.* Oxford University Press, Oxford.

Hallward-Driemeier, M., 2003. Do bilateral investment treaties attract foreign direct investment? Only a bit ? and they could bite, policy research working papers. *The World Bank.* doi:10.1596/1813-9450-3121

Hay, C., 2008. Constructivist institutionalism, in: Rhodes, R.A.W., Binder, S., Rockman, B. (Eds.), *Oxford handbook of political institutions.* Oxford University Press, Oxford, pp. 56–74.

Hiscox, M., 2002. *International trade and political conflict: Commerce, coalitions, and mobility.* Princeton University Press, Princeton.

Hoffmann, S., 1966. Obstinate or obsolete? The fate of the nation-state and the case of Western Europe. *Daedalus* 95, 862–915.

Hooghe, L., 2012. Images of Europe: How commission officials conceive their institution's role*: Images of Europe. *J. Common Mark. Stud.* 50, 87–111. doi:10.1111/j.1468-5965.2011.02210.x

Hooghe, L., 2005. Many roads lead to international norms, but few via international socialization: A case study of the European commission. *Int. Organ.* 59, 861–898.

Hooghe, L., 2003. Europe divided? Elites vs public opinion on European integration. *Eur. Union Polit.* 4, 281–304.

Hooghe, L., 2001. *The European commission and the integration of Europe: Images of governance.* Cambridge University Press, Cambridge.

Hooghe, L., Kassim, H., 2012. The commission's services, in: Peterson, J., Shackelton, M. (Eds.), *The institutions of the European Union.* Oxford University Press, Oxford, pp. 173–198.

Johnston, A.I., 2001. Treating international institutions as social environment. *Int. Stud. Q.* 45, 487–515.

Kassim, H., Peterson, J., Bauer, M.W., Connolly, S., Dehousse, R., Hooghe, L., Thompson, A., 2013. *The European commission of the twenty-first century.* Oxford University Press, Oxford.

Kaunert, C., 2011. *European internal security: Towards supranational governance in the area of freedom, security and justice.* Manchester University Press, Manchester.

Kerremans, B., 2004. What went wrong in Cancún? A principal-agent view of the EU's rationale towards the Doha Development Round. *Eur. Foreign Aff. Rev.* 9, 363–393.

Krugman, P., 1990. *Increasing returns and economic geography*, Working Paper No. 3275. National Bureau of Economic Research.

Krugman, P., 1980. Scale economies, product differentiation, and the pattern of trade. *Am. Econ. Rev.* 70, 950–959.

Kuijper, P.J., 2007. Fifty years of EC/EU external relations: Continuity and the dialogue between judges and Member States as constitutional legislators. *Fordham Int. Law J.* 31, 1571–1602.

Laffan, B., 1997. From policy entrepreneur to policy manager: The challenge facing the European commission. *J. Eur. Public Policy* 4, 422–438. doi:10.1080/13501769780000081

Lavranos, N., 2013. The new EU Investment Treaties: Convergence towards the NAFTA model as the new Plurilateral Model BIT text? Vrije Universiteit Brussel.

Lindberg, L.N., 1963. *The political dynamics of European economic integration.* Stanford University Press, Stanford.

Mahoney, J., Thelen, K. (Eds.), 2010. *Explaining institutional change: Ambiguity, agency, and power*, 1st ed. Cambridge University Press, Cambridge.

Manger, M., 2009. *Investing in protection: The politics of preferential trade agreements between north and south.* Cambridge University Press, Cambridge.

Meunier, S., 2005. *Trading voices: The European Union in international commercial negotiations.* Princeton University Press, Princeton.

Meunier, S., Nicolaidis, K., 2006. The European Union as a conflicted trade power. *J. Eur. Public Policy* 13, 906–925.

Meunier, S., Nicolaidis, K., 1999. Who speaks for Europe? The delegation of trade authority in the EU. *J. Common Mark. Stud.* 37, 477–507.

Milner, H., Yoffie, D., 1989. Between free trade and protectionism: Strategic trade policy and a theory of corporate trade demands. *Int. Organ.* 43, 239–272.

Mitrany, D., 1943. *A working peace system: An argument for the functional development of international organization, post-war problems.* Royal Institute of International Affairs, London.

Moravcsik, A., 1998. *The choice for Europe: Social purpose and state power from Messina to Maastricht.* Cornell Univeristy Press, Ithaca.

Moravcsik, A., 1993. Preferences and power in the European Community: A liberal intergovernmentalist approach. *J. Common Mark. Stud.* 31, 473–523.

Moravcsik, A., 1991. Negotiating the single European Act: National interests and conventional statecraft in the European Community. *Int. Organ.* 45, 19–56.

Moravcsik, A., Schimmelfennig, F., 2009. *European Integration Theory.* Liberal intergovernmentalism, in: Wiener, A., Diez, T. (Eds.). Oxford University Press, Oxford, pp. 67–87.

Neumayer, E., Spess, L., 2005. Do bilateral investment treaties increase foreign direct investment to developing countries? *World Dev.* 33, 1567–1585.

Niemann, A., 2013. EU external trade and the Treaty of Lisbon: A revised neo-functionalist approach. *J. Contemp. Eur. Res.* 9, 634–658.

Niemann, A., 2004. Between communicative action and strategic action: The Article 113 committee and the negotiations on the WTO basic telecommunications services agreement. *J. Eur. Public Policy* 11, 379–407.

Pierson, P., 2004. *Politics in time: History, institutions, and social analysis.* Princeton University Press, Princeton.

Pierson, P., Skocpol, T., 2002. Historical institutionalism in contemporary political science, in: Katznelson, I., Milner, H. (Eds.), *Political science: State of the discipline.* W.W. Norton, New York, pp. 693–721.

Pollack, M.A., 2003. *The engines of European integration: Delegation, agency, and agenda setting in the EU.* Oxford University Press, Oxford.

Reinisch, A., 2013. The future shape of EU investment agreements. *ICSID Rev. – Foreign Invest. Law J.* 28, 179–196. doi:10.1093/icsidreview/sit007

Reiter, J., 2005. The European Union as actor in international relations: The role of the external environment for EU institutional design, in: Elgström, O., Jönsson, C. (Eds.), *European Union negotiations : Processes, networks and institutions union.* Routledge, London, pp. 148–163.

Rogowski, R., 1989. *Commerce and coalitions: How trade affects domestic political alignments.* Princeton University Press, Princeton.

Rosamond, B., 2000. *Theories of European integration.* Palgrave Macmillan, Basingstoke.

Sauvant, K., Sachs, L. (Eds.), 2009. *The effect of treaties on foreign direct investment: Bilateral investment treaties, double taxation treaties and investment flows.* Oxford University Press, Oxford.

Schafer, J., 2014. European commission officials' policy attitudes. *JCMS J. Common Mark. Stud.* 52, 911–927. doi:10.1111/jcms.12115

Schmidt, S., 1998a. Commission activism: Subsuming telecommunications and electricity under European competition law. *J. Eur. Public Policy* 5, 169–184. doi:10.1080/13501768880000081

Schmidt, S., 1998b. *Liberalisierung in Europa.* Campus, Frankfurt.

Schmitter, P., 2009. Neo-neo-functionalism, in: Wiener, A., Diez, T. (Eds.), *European integration theory.* Stevens, London.

Schumpeter, J.A., 1934. *The theory of economic development: An inquiry into profits, capital, credit, interest, and the business cycle.* Transaction Publishers.

Shepsle, K., 2008. Rational choice institutionalism, in: Rhodes, R.A.W., Binder, S., Rockman, B. (Eds.), *The Oxford handbook of political institutions.* Oxford University Press, Oxford, pp. 23–38.

Stacey, J., Rittberger, B., 2003. Dynamics of formal and informal institutional change in the EU. *J. Eur. Public Policy* 10, 858–883. doi:10.1080/1350176032000148342

Streeck, W., Thelen, K.A. (Eds.), 2005. *Beyond continuity: Institutional change in advanced political economies.* Oxford University Press, Oxford.

Tallberg, J., 2006. *Leadership and negotiation in the European Union, themes in European governance.* Cambridge University Press, Cambridge.

Tallberg, J., 2000. The anatomy of autonomy: An institutional account of variation in supranational influence. *J. Common Mark. Stud.* 38, 843–864.

Thelen, K., 2004. *How institutions evolve: The political economy of skills in Germany, Britain, the United States, and Japan.* Cambridge University Press, Cambridge.

UNCTAD, 2017. Investment policy hub [WWW Document]. URL http://investmentpolicyhub.unctad.org/IIA (accessed 7.15.11).

UNCTAD, 2014a. *Recent developments in Investor-State Dispute Settlement (ISDS).* IIA Issues Note.

UNCTAD, 2014b. *The impact of international investment agreements on foreign direct investment: An overview of empirical studies 1998–2014.* IIA Issues Note.

Waltz, K., 1979. *Theory of international politics.* McGraw-Hill, Boston.

Weaver, R.K., 1986. The politics of blame avoidance. *J. Public Policy* 6, 371–398.

Wildavsky, A., 1987. Choosing preferences by constructing institutions: A cultural theory of preference formation. *Am. Polit. Sci. Rev.* 81, 4–21. doi:10.2307/1960776

Woll, C., 2008. *Firm interests: How governments shape business lobbying on global trade, Cornell studies in political economy*. Cornell University Press, Ithaca, NY.

Woll, C., 2006. The road to external representation: The European commission's activism in international air transport. *J. Eur. Public Policy* 13, 52–69. doi:10.1080/13501760500380734

Woolcock, S., 2011. *European Union economic diplomacy: The role of the EU in external economic relations*, Global finance series. Ashgate, Burlington.

Woolcock, S., Bayne, N. (Eds.), 2007. *The new economic diplomacy*, 2nd ed. Ashgate, London.

Yackee, J.W., 2010. *How much do U.S. corporations know (and care) about bilateral investment treaties? Some hints from new survey evidence*. Columbia FDI Perspect.

Yackee, J.W., 2009. Do BITs really work? Revisiting the empirical link between investment treaties and foreign direct investment, in: Sauvant, K., Sachs, L. (Eds.), *The effect of treaties on foreign direct investment: Bilateral investment treaties, double taxation treaties and investment flows*. Oxford University Press, Oxford.

Young, A.R., 2016. Not your parent's trade politic: The transatlantic trade and investment partnership negotiations. *Rev. Int. Polit. Econ.* 23, 345–378.

Young, A.R., 2002. *Extending European cooperation: The European Union and the 'new' international trade agenda*. Manchester University Press, Manchester.

Young, A.R., 2001. *Extending European cooperation: The European Union and the 'new' international trade agenda*, EUI working papers. RSC. European University Institute, Economics Department.

3 An introduction to international investment and its regime

This chapter introduces international investment and its regime. It seeks to provide background information, which is useful for the comprehension of the following chapters. The chapter does not claim scientific originality and the expert reader may decide to skip it. The chapter first discusses definitions of international investment, its effects on economies, as well as states' policy instruments to deal with the phenomenon. It then traces the legal and economic history of the international investment regime.

3.1 Defining international investment

Many policymakers, academics – and this book – frequently use the layman's term 'international investment'. But what exactly is international investment? International investment is normally used in order to refer to the more technical concept of 'FDI'. The concept of FDI is mainly used in statistics, law and economics and carries similar yet slightly different meanings in these disciplines. The following sections briefly discuss the meanings of the concept in these fields for the sake of completeness. This book builds in the following chapters on a broad economic, rather than purely legalistic reading of the term international investment (see section 3.1.3).

3.1.1 International investment as a statistical concept

Central bankers and statisticians initially created the concept of FDI as a category of balance of payments statistics. These seek to quantify to what degree, and how, an economy is integrated into the world economy. Such statistics list capital stocks and capital flows related to long-term cross-border investments and production processes of multinational enterprises (MNEs) under the category 'FDI'. The category FDI comprises the initial investment[1] to establish, merge or buy an affiliated enterprise[2] abroad as well as consequent bidirectional operational capital flows[3] between the parent and affiliated enterprises. Although FDI has become a widely used term, there is no universally accepted detailed definition. The IMF and the OECD have sought to consolidate existing definitions of FDI in order to facilitate statistical data collection and comparisons, and policymaking debates, and to promote a harmonisation of national legislation on this matter. The official IMF and OECD definitions are by and large identical and state the following.

> *Direct investment is a category of cross-border investment associated with a resident in one economy having control or a significant degree of influence on the management of an enterprise that is resident in another economy.*
> (IMF, 2009, p. 100)

According to the IMF and OECD definitions, the key characteristic of FDI is thus that the investor maintains a lasting economic relationship and exercises influence or control over the affiliated enterprise abroad. The OECD and IMF definitions state that a lasting relationship, influence and control can be assumed if the investor holds 10% of equity share or voting power in the policymaking of the affiliated enterprise (IMF, 2009, p. 100; OECD, 2008, pp. 17–18). In cases where an investor holds less than 10% of equity share or voting power, their investment might still qualify as *indirect* FDI. An investment qualifies as indirect FDI if the investor has an 'effective voice' in the management of the affiliated enterprise through staff or a seat on the board (etc.) (IMF, 2009, p. 100). Cross-border investments which do not fulfil these criteria are considered as portfolio investments. These are typically short-term investments of a speculative nature. The investor does not exercise influence or control over the affiliated enterprise. The investor has a narrow focus on the short-term rate of return (Alvarez, 2009, p. 204; Jones, 2005, p. 5).

3.1.2 *International investment as a legal concept*

The distinction between FDI and portfolio investments might appear at first to be a statistical detail. It is, however, of importance for European policymakers. Since the entry into force of the Lisbon Treaty in 2009, the regulation of FDI comes under the scope of the CCP and exclusive Union competence. The regulation of portfolio investment, on the other hand, comes under shared competence between the EU and the Member States under articles 63–66 TFEU on the free movement of capital (Dimopoulos, 2011, pp. 78, 123; European Court of Justice, 2017; Krajewski, 2005, p. 112). Hence, the applicable European decision-making rules, policymaking objectives, the prerogatives of the Council of Ministers, the individual Member States, the Commission and the European Parliament differ considerably between the two types of investment. It is thus important to define FDI under European law.

The European Treaties refer to the term FDI. They do not, however, define the term in any detail. The scope of the new Union competence under articles 206–207 TFEU is, therefore, a priori unclear. The European Court of Justice (ECJ) has, however, developed a binding definition of the term 'direct investment' and thereby indirectly of the term 'foreign direct investment' in its case law. FDI in the EU context should be understood as cross-border direct investment between EU Member States and third countries instead of cross-border direct investment among EU Member States. The ECJ drew heavily on the aforementioned OECD and IMF definitions as well as the nomenclature of the capital movements directive 88/361/EEC to that effect. The nomenclature states the following:

> *[Direct investments are . . .] investments of all kinds by natural persons or commercial, industrial or financial undertakings, and which serve to establish or to maintain lasting and direct links between the person providing the capital and the entrepreneur to whom or the undertaking to which the capital is made available in order to carry on an economic activity. This concept must therefore be understood in its widest sense.*
>
> (European Communities, 1988, p. 11)

The ECJ clarified in its case law that an investment should be considered a direct investment under European law, if the investor holds a lasting interest and exercises control or influence over the enterprise abroad. Referring to the OECD and IMF definitions, the ECJ stated that a lasting relationship and control could generally be assumed, if the investor held at least 10% of equity shares and voting power in the policymaking of the affiliated firm (Johannsen, 2009, pp. 11–13). The ECJ qualified, however, that this was only a rule of thumb. So-called golden share rules, for instance, decouple ownership and influence on management decisions, which might increase or decrease the relative influence of an investor on the policymaking of an affiliated enterprise. The corporate law of host countries can decisively shape the degree of control of investors and hence affect the legal status of an investment (Johannsen, 2009, pp. 13–14). Furthermore, the ECJ stressed the IMF and OECD concepts of an *effective voice* and *indirect FDI* were valid in EU law. These concepts imply that an investment might still qualify as FDI in cases where the investor holds less than 10% of votes or shares, but dispose of other influence channels. The literature draws on a position paper of the EU and Member States on FDI tabled in 2002 at the WTO in order to concretise possible influence channels. Accordingly, non-vote based influence stems from representation on the board of the affiliated enterprise, participation in the decision-making, exchange of managerial staff, inter-company transactions and provisions of loans at lower than market rates (Johannsen, 2009, p. 14; WTO, 2002, p. 4). The ECJ endorsed this argument in a series of judgements (Johannsen, 2009, pp. 14–15).

3.1.3 International investment as an economic concept

The preceding paragraphs discussed statistical and legal definitions of FDI, which advance a simplistic view of FDI. Economists think of FDI as a much more complex phenomenon than the mere cross-border movement of capital. In economics, FDI designates the international investment and production activities of MNEs. The following paragraphs present the major economic theories of FDI, MNEs and international production.

The understanding of FDI as financial capital – dominant in the aforementioned statistical and legal definitions – has its roots in the convenient measurability of capital as well as neo-classical theories on international trade (Jones, 2005, p. 7). Neo-classical theories like the Heckscher-Ohlin Theorem seek to explain international trade patterns through diverging factor endowments of national economies. From a neo-classical perspective, MNEs represent vehicles of excess capital leaving capital-rich economies for capital-scarce ones in order to increase rates of return for capital. Scholars increasingly questioned this understanding of MNEs and FDI during the 1960s. They found that the bulk of FDI was exchanged between economies with comparable factor endowments. Capital invested abroad could not have yielded superior rates of return than domestically invested capital. Hence, neo-classical theories of trade failed to account for the increasing number of MNEs, international production chains and the rising volume of FDI among industrialised economies since World War II.

In the 1960s, scholars started investigating this theoretical puzzle and sought to explain the diffusion of MNEs and growth of FDI flows. They found that firms turned into MNEs in order to get access to cheap input factors or new consumer markets and to exploit firm-specific technological and managerial expertise as well as intellectual property rights (Jones, 2005, pp. 7–8). In the scholarly debate, FDI turned from mere financial excess capital into a more comprehensive concept encompassing immeasurable and intangible assets like managerial know-how, intellectual property rights, patents, licences or access to transnational distribution, sales and financial networks. It became clear that MNEs and FDI played a central role in the diffusion of economic and technological progress.

John Dunning's so-called *OLI* framework (Table 3.1) outlines this new view of MNEs and FDI. It seeks to explain why and when firms become MNEs and start placing FDI abroad. Dunning identified in his *OLI* framework three categories of factors, which condition the transformation of a firm into a MNE (Dunning, 1981, 2008). First, firms need to hold *ownership-specific* advantages, which give it a competitive edge over other firms in a potential host economy. Ownership-specific advantages can be technological and managerial expertise, economies of scale or intellectual property rights (etc.). Second, firms must identify a *location-specific* advantage in a potential host economy in order to expand abroad and invest there. Location-specific advantages might be the geographical position of a country, good infrastructure, a cheap input like labour, scarce raw materials, high trade barriers or membership in a Regional Economic Integration Organisation (REIO) or trade agreements. Finally, firms must perceive the *internalisation* of business activities abroad as preferable to arm's-length contractual relations via markets. Factors influencing the choice between internalisation and market-based coordination might be the insufficient protection of intellectual property rights, patents, licences or high costs and scarce information for identifying partner firms. If the firm finds ownership-specific, location-specific and internalisation advantages, it is likely to turn into a MNE and to place FDI abroad (Jones, 2005, p. 12).

Dunning's model seeks to explain why firms turn into MNEs and place FDI abroad. But FDI can take different forms. Horizontal FDI seeks to replicate the entire parent company abroad. Vertical FDI replicates or 'offshores' only certain production steps abroad. A second-order question is therefore what determines

Table 3.1 Overview of OLI framework

Advantages	Examples for OLI advantages
Ownership-specific	Economies of scale, intellectual property rights, patents, technological expertise, managerial expertise, transnational sales and production networks, access to cheap capital, etc.
Location-specific	Raw materials, cheap input factors, market size, jumping trade barriers, geographical location, etc.
Internalisation	State of rule of law and enforcement, reputation concerns, lack of adequate local partner firms, etc.

the organisational form of FDI? The question is of importance, because vertical and horizontal FDIs have different side effects on the home and host economies of MNEs (Navaretti and Venables, 2004, p. 39). Scholars have identified three factors, which arguably determine the organisational form of FDI. First, plant-level economies of scale determine whether a firm is likely to concentrate or disperse production processes. If plant-level economies of scale are high, firms should concentrate production processes in few places with low input factor prices. Hence, firms are likely to engage in vertical FDI. If plant-level economies of scale are low, firms should replicate their entire production process in several places. Firms should thus engage in horizontal FDI. Second, trade costs – including transport, customs, licensing, etc. – determine how far firms should engage in intra-firm trade or produce locally. High trade costs should foster horizontal FDI, whereas low trade costs should trigger vertical FDI. Finally, the factor endowment of involved economies should influence the choice between vertical and horizontal FDI. MNE activities between countries with comparable factor endowments should promote horizontal FDI. MNE activities between differently endowed countries should trigger vertical FDI (Navaretti and Venables, 2004, pp. 30–35).

The preceding discussion has implicitly pointed to four motivations underlying FDI flows and MNE activities (Dunning, 2008). First, many firms place FDI abroad in order to access scarce resources, like crude oil, gas or rare earths. Such *resource-seeking* FDI drove most early MNE activities. Second, firms often place FDI abroad in order to access strategic assets like innovative technology, know-how or acquire an advantageous position in a newly emerging sectorial market. Such *strategic asset-seeking* FDI is likely to help firms in maintaining a competitive edge. It normally takes the form of mergers and acquisitions instead of green field investments. Third, many firms establish affiliated enterprises abroad in order to access consumer markets. The literature refers to this as *market-seeking* FDI. Firms engaging in market-seeking FDI often consider a regional presence as important for acquiring new clients or seek to circumvent high trade barriers. Finally, many firms engage in *efficiency-seeking* FDI. They establish affiliated firms abroad in order to have access to cheaper input like labour. Depending on the underlying motivation, FDI is likely to have different effects on home and host countries.

In conclusion, FDI is not mere capital crossing borders. It is a much more complex phenomenon. It encompasses, besides capital, many other – often immeasurable and intangible – business assets. MNEs and FDI thus promote the diffusion of economic and technological innovation. Moreover, FDI complements and substitutes for traditional trade flows. In the following chapters, this book will build on a broad, economic rather than narrow understanding of international investment and FDI.

3.2 The economic and political impact of foreign direct investment on states

FDI flows and MNE activities have always been the subjects of lively policy debates and populist rhetoric. The reason behind the interest of the general public in FDI and MNE activities is that they are not neutral on home and host countries. FDI and MNE activities have manifold positive as well as negative economic and political effects on countries. The following section first briefly discusses the positive and negative effects of outward FDI on the home countries of investing MNEs. The section then examines the negative and positive effects of inward FDI on the host countries, which welcome foreign MNEs.

Outward FDI has several positive effects on home countries (Dunning, 2008; Navaretti and Venables, 2004, pp. 39–48). Outward FDI should increase the competitiveness and productivity of the investing MNEs. MNEs investing abroad face the choice of whether to invest abroad, invest at home or to save capital. Econometric research suggests that FDI normally yields higher returns than forced domestic investment or saving. The more efficient use of MNEs' capital increases their productivity and competitiveness. Furthermore, the productivity and competitiveness gains are likely to spill over to domestic suppliers and competitors and lastly to the entire home economy. Outward FDI has, moreover, two positive effects on factor markets. On the one hand, outward FDI should promote the upgrading of domestic labour toward higher value-adding activities. It normally increases MNEs' demand in headquarter services like management, research and development (R&D), legal affairs or accounting. On the other hand, outward FDI often unlocks new supply markets. It thereby reduces the costs for input factors like labour, capital, land or natural resources. Access to cheaper input factors again increases productivity and competitiveness while lowering consumer prices.

Outward FDI has also several negative effects on home countries (Dunning, 2008; Navaretti and Venables, 2004, pp. 39–48). Most importantly, outward FDI is often equated with the offshoring of production. Re-imports of goods and services substitute for national production, which is seen to lead to higher unemployment. Econometric research draws a nuanced and complex picture of the relationship between outward FDI and unemployment levels. Outward FDI seems to increase demand for skilled worked in home countries, but often limits demand for unskilled workers. In the absence of corrective welfare policies, outward FDI may increase social inequality. Moreover, outward FDI should increase the price of capital in home countries thereby potentially reducing gross domestic product (GDP) growth rates. Finally, outward FDI might in certain cases reduce the competitiveness of a country due to exports of innovative technologies and managerial skills.

Turning now to inward FDI, it has several positive effects on host countries (Dunning, 2008; Lipsey, 2002, pp. 17–40). Inward FDI should increase labour demand and employment rates. As inward FDI is a capital inflow, it should lower capital prices and increase GDP growth rates. Inward FDI should also promote the diffusion of new technologies and skills to affiliated enterprises, suppliers and the rest of the economy. Research furthermore suggests that MNEs pay, on average, higher wages and provide better working conditions than domestic firms. Inward FDI should also enhance the host economies' access to international markets through MNEs' sales and GVCs. Regarding product markets, inward FDI should increase competition, lower consumer prices and generally increase consumer welfare.

Inward FDI also has negative effects on host countries. It can increase prices on factor markets thereby hampering national economic development and growth. MNEs generally dispose of greater capital reserves and purchasing power than domestic competitors. The presence of MNEs – notably in developing countries – might thus push domestic competitors out of the market. The literature labels this undesired effect of inward FDI as a 'crowding out' of factor markets. Inward FDI might also threaten countries' national security. Inward FDI into defence industries, public services[4] or strategic economic sectors[5] often triggers concerns about the underlying objectives and reliability of foreign investors. These concerns have become particularly salient since state-owned enterprises (SOEs) and sovereign wealth funds (SWF) from emerging markets have become potent international investors. Many countries – and most EU Member States – therefore maintain so-called national security screening mechanisms so as to evaluate, condition or prohibit foreign investments in sensitive economic sectors.

In conclusion, FDI flows have a multitude of positive and negative effects on the involved countries. History and research suggest that FDI is neither exclusively good nor exclusively bad for home and host countries. The impact of FDI on home and host countries depends on the volume, purpose and type of FDI (Dunning, 2008; Velde, 2006). Resource- and strategic-asset-seeking FDI often yield limited benefits for host countries, whereas market- and efficiency-seeking FDI can promote their economic growth and development. On the other hand, efficiency-seeking FDI can have negative labour market impacts on home countries, whereas resource-, market- and strategic-asset-seeking FDI should foster growth in the home countries of MNEs. The volume, purpose and type of FDI generated by economies depend on three variables – countries' resource endowment, their factor endowment and, finally, national investment-related policies. Countries cannot influence their resource or factor endowments in the short or medium term. They can, however, pursue international investment policies, which maximise positive effects while minimising negative effects of FDI flows and MNE activities. International investment policy is, therefore, a key instrument of states in mitigating the effects of economic globalisation on society.

3.3 International investment policy – objectives and policy instruments

Countries seek to minimise negative effects while maximising positive effects of FDI flows and MNE activities. This broad objective by and large translates into the following structural preferences nowadays. Developed and capital-abundant developed countries normally seek to promote outward and inward FDI flows. Developing and capital-scarce countries normally want to attract FDI inflows. Which policy tools do states have at their disposal to pursue these objectives? The following paragraphs present the main investment policy tools, which European governments have traditionally been using in order to influence FDI flows and MNE activities: 1) investment guarantees, 2) political and technical support for national investors, 3) investment review mechanisms and 4) IIAs. It is difficult though to clearly delimit investment policy from other policies. The business activities of MNEs typically touch upon a wide range of economic regulations and public policies like environmental, social or health policies. All these policies might potentially affect investment decisions. It is nevertheless evident that governments cannot and must not adjust all their policies to their investment policy objectives.

3.3.1 Investment guarantees

Many investors seek insurance for investment projects abroad. Most commercial and natural risks can be covered by private insurance companies. So-called non-commercial risks, however, are often not insurable through private insurance companies. Non-commercial risks are, for instance, riots, civil war, terrorism, currency risks, expropriation through host state authorities or breaches of contracts and non-honouring of sovereign financial obligations (MIGA, 2011). The limited availability of insurance coverage might prevent promising investment projects abroad despite a low likelihood that a non-commercial risk materialises. The limited availability of insurance coverage for non-commercial risks is seen to diminish economic activity and to slow down economic growth.

Investment guarantees seek to correct this alleged market failure. Investment guarantees are state-backed schemes, which insure investors against non-commercial risks (Gordon, 2008). They thereby seek to support the realisation of generally promising investment projects abroad. Investment guarantees are a policy instrument to promote outward FDI. Most EU Member States have investment guarantee schemes in place so as to support the internationalisation of national business. Most state-backed investment guarantee schemes are self-supporting in order to avoid waste of tax money and unfair competition.

3.3.2 Political support and technical assistance

Political support and technical support constitute soft yet important policy instruments to promote inward and outward investment (Woolcock and Bayne, 2007). Many states have created specialised agencies, which provide information to national investors going abroad as well as foreign investors entering their economy.[6] These agencies inform about important regulations, the general investment climate and possibilities for cooperation with local enterprises. Moreover, most states use their diplomatic representations and ties so as to help national business abroad as well as to attract foreign business. Such political support can be effective in communicating the problems of investors to host country governments. It might also help to mitigate discriminating and protectionist government policies and anti-competitive behaviour of SOEs. Political support is a particularly important investment policy instrument in host countries with an underdeveloped rule of law and strong state intervention in markets.

3.3.3 National security review mechanisms

Many states use national security review mechanisms to screen sensitive inward investments (UNCTAD, 2016, pp. 93–100). Foreign investment plans may under certain conditions and in certain sectors constitute a national security risk. If foreign investors buy or merge with national companies active in defence industries, controlling critical infrastructure or providing vital public services, it may endanger the national public order and security. Concerns also regularly arise in the European and Northern American public debate that foreign investors may buy or merge with national technology leaders in order to get control over strategic technology and knowledge. Such mergers are seen to undermine the long-term competitiveness and development prospects of countries. Such concerns arise, in particular, if the foreign investor is a state-owned enterprise or SWF. Many countries thus require foreign investors to submit their investment plans in sensitive sectors to a governmental screening. Governments may authorise, impose conditions or prohibit investment projects.

3.3.4 International investment agreements

IIAs are the most important and controversial investment policy instrument nowadays. Most IIAs are bilateral and, therefore, also called BITs. Both terms are largely synonymous. Approximately 3,500 IIAs between more than 150 states have been concluded to date (Mills, 2011, p. 742; UNCTAD, 2017a). IIAs are treaties of public international law between two or more states. They contain by and large three types of provisions (Dolzer and Schreuer, 2012; Dolzer and Stevens, 1995). First, they enumerate binding post-establishment treatment and protection standards. They specify how host states must treat foreign investors established within their jurisdiction. Second, they provide for dispute settlement and enforcement mechanisms. Dispute settlement mechanisms come into play if a host country allegedly violated binding treatment and protection standards by expropriating a foreign investor on a discriminatory basis without paying fair compensation for losses. Finally, a small number of IIAs contain binding investment liberalisation commitments. They specify the sectors and activities open to foreign investors. IIAs are thus interstate agreements, which create rights and enforcement mechanisms for private third parties. Capital-exporting developed countries traditionally conclude such agreements with capital-importing developing states. The former seeks to promote outward FDI, while the later hope to attract inward FDI. This traditional pattern is, however, evolving. Developing countries increasingly sign IIAs with each other, while developed countries have also started entering into IIAs or comprehensive PTAs with investment chapters – such as TTIP, CETA, NAFTA or TPP – with other developed countries.

IIAs allegedly address a key problem in the political economy of international investment activities. The literature refers to it as the *mousetrap problem* or *dynamic inconsistency problem* (Elkmans et al., 2006; Guzman, 1997, p. 658). Foreign investors are in a position of force vis-à-vis potential host states before investing, because most states seek to attract inward FDI. Foreign investors become, however, vulnerable to host state pressure once the investment is made, as it is normally impossible to quickly recover invested capital and resources without major losses. Prior to the placement of an investment, host states have a strong incentive to signal to potential foreign investors that they offer a stable and safe economic and regulatory environment and/or are trustworthy business partners.[7] Once an investment is placed, host states have an incentive to renege on prior commitments and to redistribute the risks, burdens and benefits arising from an investment project. Such state behaviour can take the form of direct expropriation or indirect creeping regulatory expropriation[8] of foreign investors. Even if host states have no intention of engaging in expropriation, they cannot credibly commit this to foreign investors. States are sovereign and cannot credibly bind themselves vis-à-vis private actors located in their jurisdiction. Foreign investors, therefore, face considerable legal uncertainty when investing abroad. They have to evaluate the investment environment and prospects of their project merely on the basis of a host country's reputation and past behaviour. So as to enhance legal certainty for foreign investors, states have started committing to their peers – i.e. other sovereign states to adequately treat and protect their investors. IIAs thereby arguably enhance legal certainty for investors and stimulate international investment activity.

The effectiveness of IIAs is controversial. It is uncontroversial that IIAs enhance the legal certainty for foreign investors notably in countries with a weak rule of law. It is, however, open to discussion whether IIAs actually foster international investment activity (for an overview see UNCTAD, 2014a). Research suggests that international agreements with investment liberalisation commitments have an impact on the volume and direction of international investment flows (Blonigen and Piger, 2014; Sauvant and Sachs, 2009). The matter, however, becomes more complicated with the much more numerous traditional BITs, which contain only post-establishment treatment and protection clauses and ISDS provisions

(Blonigen and Piger, 2014; Busse et al., 2010; Colen et al., 2014; Hallward-Driemeier, 2003; Neumayer and Spess, 2005; Sauvant and Sachs, 2009; Stein and Daude, 2007; Yackee, 2010). While some studies stipulate that BITs have only marginal effects on investment activity, others find statistically significant effects. Yet other studies find that the effects of IIAs vary in function in level of development of the contracting states or economic sectors and activities. The challenge of determining the impact of BITs on investment flows arguably derives from poor data as well as from an endogeneity problem. It is difficult to evaluate whether certain states conclude BITs because their investment relationship is intensifying, or whether the conclusion of BITs leads to an increase in investment activity. Finally, many international investment projects do not directly evolve between the home and host country but are routed through intermediary jurisdictions such as the Netherlands, Luxembourg, Singapore or Hong Kong, which further complicates measurement.

The effectiveness of IIAs in enhancing legal certainty as well as in increasing investment activities critically depends on their content. One can broadly distinguish two types of BITs/IIAs in the global investment regime. Traditional BITs – as developed and promoted by European states since the 1950s – cover post-establishment treatment and protection standards and contain dispute settlement provisions. They are very concise and provide arbitrators with significant interpretative leeway in the application of the agreements. Critiques and proponents of traditional BITs alike thus suggest that these agreements offer high levels of investment protection (Alschner, 2013; Lavranos, 2013; Reinisch, 2013). The second so-called NAFTA-type[9] IIAs have emerged in the mid-1990s. NAFTA-type IIAs contain post-establishment and protection standards, dispute settlement provisions and binding investment liberalisation commitments. They are much longer, more specific in language and intentionally limit the interpretative leeway of arbitrators to ring-fence states' right to regulate. They arguably provide for lower levels of investment protection (Alschner, 2013; Lavranos, 2013; Reinisch, 2013). Traditional European BITs are much more numerous than NAFTA-type IIAs and make up the bulk of IIAs currently in force. The main similarities and differences between these two types are discussed next.

Defining investors and investments

All IIAs seek to regulate international investment and investors. European and NAFTA-type IIAs by and large advance similar definitions of investors (Alschner, 2013; Dolzer and Schreuer, 2012, pp. 40–77; Dolzer and Stevens, 1995; Fontanelli and Bianco, 2013; Lavranos, 2013). Investors are natural and legal persons holding the nationality of one of the contracting states according to its national laws. European and NAFTA-type IIAs, however, advance slightly different definitions of the term 'investment', which translates into differences in coverage. European IIAs typically contain an open-ended list of assets qualifying as investments. NAFTA-type IIAs contain a similar list but also enumerate assets (e.g. commercial loans), which do not qualify as investments under these agreements. The coverage of

NAFTA-type IIAs is thus de jure more limited. Both types of IIAs cover not only FDI but also portfolio investments and other investment-like or related business assets such as real estate, intellectual property rights, patents, licences and alike.

Post-establishment treatment and protection standards

Post-establishment treatment and protection standards are the cornerstone of the global investment regime (Dolzer and Schreuer, 2012). As explained earlier, IIAs first and foremost seek to ensure a save and stable investment environment for international investors and to protect foreign investors against arbitrary and discriminatory state conduct and expropriation. IIAs, therefore, enumerate post-establishment treatment and protection provisions, which host states commit to respect and to afford to foreign investors. European and NAFTA-type IIAs alike contain *relative* and *absolute* post-establishment treatment and protection standards. Relative treatment and protection standards are typically the MFN or NT standard. The contracting states thereby commit not to discriminate against investors from the IIA partner country in comparison to third-country or domestic investors. Of greater legal salience are the absolute treatment and protection standards of IIAs. European and NAFTA-type IIAs alike normally provide for 'fair and equitable treatment' (FET) and 'full protection and security' (FPS) (Dolzer and Schreuer, 2012, pp. 130–166; UNCTAD, 2012). European and NAFTA-type IIAs advance different definitions of the FET and FPS standards though. European IIAs hardly define FET and FPS thereby leaving great interpretative leeway to arbitrators. NAFTA-type IIAs normally define in detail the FET and FPS standard and emphasise that these standards do not require any better treatment or protection than necessary under Customary International Law (CIL). The linkage between CIL and the FET and FPS standard has triggered a lively debate among legal experts. Many experts argue that the narrow CIL-based definitions of the FET and FPS standards limit investment protection (Dolzer and Schreuer, 2012, pp. 134–138; Fontanelli and Bianco, 2013; Lavranos, 2013; Reinisch, 2013). While the Member States hardly defined the FET and SPS standard in their BITs/IIAs, the EU seems to be following the NAFTA-type approach to FET and FPS in its first IIAs. The draft texts of CETA, TTIP and the EU-Singapore Free Trade Agreement (EUSFTA) circumscribe the FET and FSP standards in greater detail than traditional European BITs. As most investment arbitrations evolve around an alleged violation of the FET standard, differences in the delimitation of the standard are of potentially great relevance in the application of IIAs and protection of investors in host countries.

Investment arbitration and enforcement

Commitments to treatment and protection standards risk being useless if not enforceable. IIAs, therefore, contain dispute settlement provisions and enforcement mechanisms. Most IIAs provide for state-to-state and ISDS in the case of conflict over substantive norms (Dolzer and Schreuer, 2012, pp. 232–312). While state-to-state dispute settlement plays no significant role in the global investment regime, the number of ISDS proceedings has skyrocketed since the 1990s. Until the early 1990s, only a handful of investment arbitrations had taken place. Since then, investors have launched some 500 arbitration proceedings against host countries (UNCTAD, 2013). The appeal of ISDS lies in the possibility for foreign investors to circumvent potentially biased, corrupted and inefficient courts of host countries through recourse to an international ad hoc arbitration panel.

IIAs typically provide for ISDS proceedings to be held under the arbitration rules of the Convention of the International Centre for Settlement of Investment Disputes (ICSID),[10] of the United Nations Commission on International Trade Law (UNCITRAL),[11] the International Chamber of Commerce, the London Court of International Arbitration or occasionally the Stockholm Chamber of Commerce. The ICSID Convention and UNCITRAL rules are most frequently used (Dolzer and Schreuer, 2012, pp. 241–242; UNCTAD, 2013). They govern the various aspects and stages of the arbitration process. While UNCITRAL rules are really only rules governing arbitration proceedings, the ICSID Convention encompasses procedural rules and creates an institutional framework hosting and overseeing arbitration proceedings. The following paragraphs briefly describe – in non-legal terminology – the main stages of arbitration proceedings held under ICSID and UNCITRAL rules:

- First, a foreign investor must formally launch an investment arbitration proceeding (Dolzer and Schreuer, 2012, pp. 264–270). The launch of an arbitration proceeding tends to be easier under traditional European BITs than NAFTA-type IIAs. While European BITs rarely limit access to arbitration, NAFTA-type IIAs may require investors to exhaust local remedies (i.e. use as far as possible national courts and legal systems) before turning to arbitration; may require investors to opt for either a domestic court proceeding or international arbitration process ('fork in the road clause'), or impose lengthy mediation and cooling-off periods. Once an investor fulfils the requirements for the formal launch of an arbitration proceeding, it must notify the host country and – in the case of ICSID arbitrations – the ICSID Secretariat. The investor and the host state must each nominate one arbitrator. The two arbitrators then nominate a third arbitrator, who chairs the arbitration process. The nomination process is often lengthy and subject to a complex vetting process. The parties often spend significant time and resources on scrutinising the neutrality and qualifications of the nominated arbitrators. Any doubts over the neutrality of arbitrators may lead to the annulment of an award (see the following).
- Once the arbitration panel is constituted, it assesses, in essence, three questions: Is arbitration panel actually competent under the invoked IIA to assess a case? To what extent does a disputed measure of a host state violate post-establishment treatment and protection standards under the relevant IIA? And finally, how high are the incurred economic damages and therefore how high should be a fair compensation for the investor? It is important to

note that arbitration panels cannot order states to repeal laws or regulations. Arbitration panels can only order payment of a financial compensation. States thereby seek to protect their right to regulate and sovereignty. According to UNCTAD (2015, p. 5), ISDS had produced 356 publically known awards by 2014. States had won 37%, while investors had won 25% of publically known ISDS proceedings. The remaining ISDS cases had ended in a settlement or were discontinued.

- Unlike in most national legal systems, revisions or appeals against arbitration awards are impossible under existing investment arbitration rules (Dolzer and Schreuer, 2012, pp. 300–309). The investor and the host state may, however, seek an annulment in case an arbitration proceeding and award grossly violate basic principles of the rule of law. Typical reasons stated for the annulment of an award are a manifest breach of the principles of due process, lacking neutrality of arbitrators, failure to state reasons for an award or a manifest excess of powers (Rajoo, 2016). There are different procedures for the annulment of ICSID and UNCITRAL awards. A special Committee of the ICSID Secretariat assesses requests for the annulment of ICSID awards. There is no special committee for UNCITRAL awards. Investors or host states may, however, ask a domestic court in the jurisdiction hosting an UNCITRAL arbitration process to annul an award. Arbitration panels typically reside in a third country – not involved in an investment dispute – and take place under national arbitration regulations. Local courts thus have jurisdictions to assess whether arbitration awards satisfy minimum standards.
- Finally, the enforcement of an award may pose problems (Dolzer and Schreuer, 2012, pp. 310–312). Host states may refuse to recognise an award and to pay compensation to investors. In this rare case, the 'New York Convention on the Recognition and Enforcement of Foreign Arbitral Awards' (1958) enables investors to call on third countries, which have signed the Convention, to confiscate assets of non-complying host states. If the investor becomes aware that a non-complying host country holds assets abroad – not protected by diplomatic immunity – it may ask local authorities to confiscate the assets.

ICSID and UNCITRAL rules for investment arbitration proceedings are overall fairly similar. A key difference – until recently – was, however, the degree of transparency in arbitration proceedings (Dolzer and Schreuer, 2012, p. 286; Euler et al., 2015). While ICSID rules require at least the publication of arbitration awards, UNCITRAL rules did not require any dissemination of information on arbitration proceedings and awards. The secrecy surrounding many arbitration proceedings triggered critique and opposition against the global investment regime. Investment arbitration normally assesses the legality of state measures and actions and may have significant financial implications for taxpayers. Investment arbitration thus often touches on issues of general public interest. There is a legitimate public interest in arbitration proceedings. The criticism led to the elaboration of the new 'UNCITRAL Rules on Transparency in Investor-to-State

Arbitration' in 2014. The new transparency rules ensure a high degree of transparency in arbitration proceedings and are quickly becoming the new gold standard in the field. A growing number of countries have legally committed under the so-called Mauritius Convention on Transparency to use these new rules for future arbitrations.

Finally, it is important to note that the EU cannot take part in ICSID arbitration proceedings (Reinisch, 2016). The ICSID Convention stipulates that only states can use the ICSID arbitration system. To open up the ICSID system to the EU – from an international public law perspective an international organisation – would require amending the ICSID Convention. Amending the ICSID Convention would require consensus of all 159 signatory states. In the current geopolitical climate, it is unlikely that the EU will probe such an amendment. Future investment arbitration proceedings involving the EU as a defendant are therefore most likely to take place under UNCITRAL rules.

Market access

A handful of NAFTA-type IIAs contain binding investment liberalisation commitments (Dolzer and Schreuer, 2012, pp. 88–90). They mostly adopt a so-called negative list approach. The 'negative list approach' stipulates that in principle all sectors are open to foreign investors with the exception of the listed sectors. The 'negative list' enumerates all protected sectors not open to foreign investors. While binding, investment liberalisation commitments are nonetheless not normally subject to dispute settlement mechanisms. So foreign investors cannot use ISDS to force access or to demand compensation if states do not comply with their liberalisation commitments. So far, European IIAs/BITs do not contain binding market access provisions. They merely include declaratory non-binding 'best endeavour' statements, which encourage the parties to gradually dismantle market access barriers (Dolzer and Schreuer, 2012, p. 89). Prior to the Lisbon Treaty, market access provisions mostly came under shared competence between the EU and the Member States. Hence, neither the Member States, nor the EU could individually regulate in this domain and include such provisions into their IIAs (Dimopoulos, 2011, pp. 78, 86). The EU and the Member States however jointly negotiated and/or concluded several 'mixed' trade agreements with market access provisions for investors since the 1990s. The most notable agreements being: the General Agreement on Trade in Services (GATS) (see Chapter 4), the ECT (see Chapter 5), the MAI (see Chapter VI) and several FTAs (see Chapter 7).

Today's international investment agreement landscape

About 3,500 IIAs have been concluded among ca. 150 states. Almost all of these IIAs are bilateral. And despite this high number, these IIAs/BITs only cover approximately 13% of all possible interstate investment relations (Mills, 2011,

p. 472; UNCTAD, 2011, p. 84). On the other hand, only a few plurilateral and multilateral investment agreements exist. The European Treaties establishing the EU, the North American Free Trade Area, the ECT and the GATS are the only binding multi- and plurilateral agreements which contain noteworthy market access, post-establishment treatment and/or investment protection rules. If the negotiating parties come to an agreement, TTIP and TPP may fall into this category. The OECD Guidelines on Multilateral Enterprises and the OECD Codes of Liberalisation of Capital Movements and Current Invisible Operations are furthermore plurilateral gentlemen's agreements, which encompass rules on pre-establishment treatment, market access commitments and post-establishment treatment. Attempts to negotiate truly global, comprehensive and binding investment agreements have failed on several occasions during the last 60 years (see Chapters IV and VI) (Dattu, 2000; Vandevelde, 1997).

Academics debate whether the network of 3,500 BITs forms an international investment regime. In international law and political science, regimes are conventionally defined as coherent "*sets of implicit or explicit principles, norms, rules, and decision-making procedures around which actors' expectations converge in a given area of international relations*" (Krasner, 1982, p. 186). Scholars are opposing the idea to qualify today's BIT network as an international regime advance two arguments (Alvarez, 2009; Mills, 2011). They stress that the treatment and protection standards enshrined in the 3,500 BITs vary. Today's BIT network arguably does not create a coherent and uniform level of investment protection. States, moreover, arguably conclude BITs to acquire a competitive edge in the world economy. States hope to become more attractive for inward investments and to support national investors competing on foreign and world markets. Other scholars reject this view and qualify today's BIT network as a complex global regime. They observe that almost all countries – even North Korea and Somalia – have entered into BITs. States thus agree on the basic principle enshrined in BITs – to treat foreign investors in line with minimum standards and only to expropriate for public purpose, on a non-arbitrary and non-discriminatory basis and against payment of fair compensation. Small textual differences across BITs in the wording of the FET, FPS or ISDS provisions should not be construed as disagreement over this core principle (Alvarez, 2009; Mills, 2011). BITs, furthermore, normally contain MFN provisions, which allow for the 'import' of substantive and procedural commitments from other BITs. If India, for instance, has concluded a BIT affording for high levels of investment protection with Bangladesh but a BIT affording for low levels of investment protection with Germany, a German investor may invoke in an ISDS proceeding against India the substantive investment protection standards and arguably even procedural arbitration rules afforded under the India-Bangladesh BIT. The MFN provisions in BITs thereby level out differences across BITs. Schill (2009) argues that such MFN provisions fuel a 'multilateralisation' of international investment law. It produces increasingly uniform levels of investment protection across BITs. As its title suggests, this book sides with the latter group of scholars qualifying today's network of BITs as a complex global regime.

3.4 A brief history of international investment

The preceding sections might have created the impression that investment policy is a technocratic, dull and dry matter. This impression is erroneous. International investment flows and their regulation have always been an ideological battleground between left- and right-wing politicians, cosmopolitan and sovereignty-focused thinkers of international relations. The following pages first summarise the development of the modern international investment regime since the 18th century. Afterwards, it briefly discusses geographical and sectorial trends of international investment flows in the recent past.

3.4.1 The emergence of the modern international investment regime

The economic phenomenon of international investment is as old as humanity. As long as 3,000 years ago, Phoenicians merchants invested outside their home territories and established trading posts around the Mediterranean Sea. During the Middle Ages, the merchants of the English Russia Company and of the Hanseatic League established *kontors* in trading hubs all over Northern Europe. During the Renaissance, Florentine and Lombard banking houses founded branches in London and the Low Lands. Since these times, states have pursued – at least implicitly – investment policies and concluded investment-related agreements.

The origin of the modern international investment regime can be traced back to the late 18th century. In 1778, the USA and France concluded a Treaty of Amity and Commerce, which is sometimes considered to be the precursor of the first modern investment agreement. It sought to protect the property of French and US nationals abroad. It referred to the principle of due process, which is similar to the FET standard in modern IIAs (Dattu, 2000, p. 303; The Avalon Project (Yale Law School Lillian Goldman Law Library), 1999).

In 1789, the French National Constituent Assembly adopted the *Declaration of Rights of Man and of the Citizens*. The declaration established the right to property. States should only expropriate property in exceptional circumstances, for public purposes, on a non-discriminatory basis and following due process of law. Other European and American states gradually endorsed the fundamental right to property in the early 19th century, which also affected CIL on the protection of foreign property (Dattu, 2000, pp. 280–281). Since the Middle Ages, it was assumed in Europe that states had the right to protect their nationals abroad against harm from other states. When the right to property became a fundamental right in Europe and Northern America in the early 19th century, the right of diplomatic protection was logically extended to the protection of nationals' property abroad (Vandevelde, 1997, p. 379).

In the first decades of the 19th century, the *opinio juris* formed that foreigners were entitled to non-discriminatory treatment and fair compensation in case of expropriation. In cases where the overall level of protection of property or compensation was deemed inadequate in a host state, home states were entitled to seek redress with legal and military means in the name of their injured nationals (Dolzer and Schreuer, 2012, pp. 1–12). CIL thus established national treatment of foreign investors and set a minimum standard of treatment, protection and compensation for foreign-owned property. This CIL standard later became known as the Hull Doctrine.[12] The Hull Doctrine prevailed as a CIL standard during the entire 19th and first half of the 20th century (Dolzer and Schreuer, 2012, p. 12). CIL standards are non-codified albeit binding obligations of public international law. A legal standard becomes part of CIL if a vast majority of states adhere to it. It needs to be mentioned that this Hull Doctrine and CIL did not de facto play a central role in investment protection in the 19th century (Sornarajah, 2013, pp. 21–24). Large parts of the world were under the colonial rule of Western capital-exporting countries. Western colonial powers ensured through the political and military presence that colonies and dependent territories afforded appropriate treatment and protection to foreign investors.

In 1868, Carlos Calvo published an economic nationalist critique of the Hull Doctrine. The so-called Calvo Doctrine suggests that CIL merely requires states to afford national treatment to foreign investors. CIL arguably does not establish a minimum treatment and protection standard or the right of foreign investors to financial compensation for mistreatment (Dolzer and Schreuer, 2012, pp. 1–12, 378–381; UNCTAD, 1999, p. 13; Vandevelde, 1997, pp. 378–381). Foreign investors should only seek legal redress for controversial treatment through national courts of the host country. Home country governments must not resort to diplomatic protection and physical violence in order to protect the property rights of their nationals abroad. The Calvo Doctrine was a reply to the aggressive 'gunboat diplomacy' of capital-exporting European and Northern American states during the 19th century. Although the Calvo Doctrine stood in the tradition of economic nationalism, which flourished in Europe and Northern America in the 19th and early 20th centuries, it was never endorsed by leading nations. European and Northern American capital-exporting states as well as their dependencies and colonies held on to the Hull Doctrine in order to protect assets abroad. In 1907, European and Northern American countries, nevertheless, partly conceded to critics like Calvo. The second Hague Conference on International Peace adopted the so-called Drago-Porter Convention, which prohibited the use of force in case of commercial, investment or financial interstate disputes (Vandevelde, 1997, pp. 378–381). The prohibition on the use of military intervention reduced the appeal of the Calvo Doctrine among capital-exporting states and their dependencies.

In 1917, a third doctrine regarding the treatment and protection of foreign property emerged. The new Bolshevik government of the Soviet Union nationalised all private property – regardless of the owner's nationality – and refused to pay compensation (Vandevelde, 1997, pp. 380–381). Private property and its protection were seen as incompatible with the socialist *ordre public* of the Soviet Union. From a Marxist-Leninist perspective, the non-compensated nationalisation of foreign-owned investments was just and desirable. It arguably weakened the international class of capital owners, strengthened the proletariat and promoted the world revolution (see Cain, 1978).

The Socialist assault on the Hull Doctrine remained, at first, without consequences. It was only in the late 1940s that three developments gradually eroded the status of the Hull Doctrine as CIL standard. First, the failure to establish the International Trade Organisation (ITO), inter alia due to disagreement on investment disciplines in the USA and its closest allies, indicated the absence of a policy consensus among Western, capital-exporting democracies (Dattu, 2000, pp. 287–288). Second, the gradual expansion of socialism in Eastern Europe, Asia, Latin America and Africa was accompanied by large-scale nationalisations of private property without any form of compensation. This wave of nationalisations decisively weakened the Hull Doctrine (Vandevelde, 1997, pp. 383–384). Third, the decolonisation of large parts of Africa and Asia between 1945 and the mid-1970s was a further blow for the Hull Doctrine (Vandevelde, 1997, pp. 383–384). The newly independent states engaged in large-scale expropriation of foreign-owned property without paying compensation to foreign investors. Foreign investors were mostly from the former colonial motherlands and were active in agriculture, mining and extractive industries. They thereby controlled vast parts of national territories and natural resources. Many newly independent countries felt it necessary to expropriate these foreign investors in order to gain not only de jure independence on paper, but to re-assert their economic, territorial and ultimately political sovereignty.

The demise of the Hull Doctrine as a standard of CIL became undeniable during the 1950s. Several resolutions of the General Assembly of the United Nations (UN) – where developing and socialist countries represented the majority – documented this change in public international and customary law. In 1962, resolution 1803 on *the permanent sovereignty over natural resources* was adopted (Dolzer and Schreuer, 2012, p. 4). The resolution clarified that states had the right to expropriate foreigners' assets, but should pay appropriate compensation. The wording of the resolution neither invalidated the Hull Doctrine nor confirmed the Calvo or Socialist Doctrine as a standard of CIL. An international consensus emerged in 1973/74, when the UN General Assembly adopted by a large majority a declaration and several related resolutions on the establishment of a so-called *New International Economic Order* (NIEO) (Dattu, 2000, pp. 283–285; Dolzer and Schreuer, 2012, p. 5; Vandevelde, 1997, p. 384). The NIEO documents stressed that states have the right to nationalise foreign-owned property and should pay 'appropriate compensation'. In cases where an expropriation or compensation gives rise to disputes, these should be settled using the host country's laws and courts, unless a host country had agreed to other dispute settlement procedures. The NIEO declaration thereby decisively weakened the Hull Doctrine and implicitly confirmed the Calvo Doctrine as a new standard CIL. Rather than having a right to 'fair compensation', foreign investors could only ask for compensation deemed appropriate by a host country government or court as suggested by the Calvo Doctrine.

The demise of the Hull Doctrine entailed the so-called *treatification* of the international investment regime. As CIL did not provide sufficient protection of international investments, governments of capital-exporting states started concluding BITs in order to restore adequate standards of treatment and protection for national businesses abroad (Vandevelde, 1997, p. 386). The Federal Republic of

An introduction to international investment 65

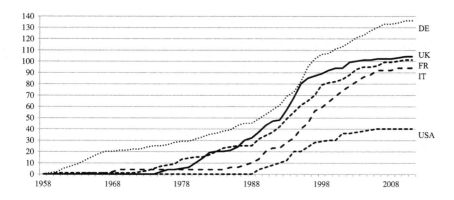

Figure 3.1 Number of ratified BITs of leading capital-exporting countries (1958–2012)
Source: UNCTAD (2017a), author's own calculations.

Germany led the way in the treatification of the international investment regime. It concluded the first modern BIT with Pakistan in 1959. Today, Germany is the state with the highest number of BITs with third countries; it is party to 134 BITs (UNCTAD, 2017a, 2014a). Other European states did not immediately follow the West German example. It was only in the 1970s that other European states like the United Kingdom, France, the Netherlands, Belgium and Italy started negotiating BITs with developing economies (see Figure 3.1).

The number of BITs in force has surged since the 1980s. Between 1959 and 1980, less than 200 BITs had been signed. By the end of the 1980s, states had signed about 400 BITs. Today some 3,500 agreements are in force (UNCTAD, 2006, p. 3, 2017a). Most BITs have been concluded between capital-exporting OECD economies and capital-importing developing economies. BITs between OECD economies remain rare. Three developments fuelled the abrupt diffusion of BITs since the 1980s. First, the economic decline of the Soviet Union and its partners apparently demonstrated the superiority of the Western market economy. In this context, developing countries came to see BITs as 'admission tickets' to the Western international economy (Dolzer and Schreuer, 2008, p. 5). Second, in the 1980s, many developing, and in particular Latin American, countries suffered from severe financial crises. These countries badly needed capital and hard currency inflows in order to recover. As former proponents of the Calvo Doctrine, these countries felt the need to send a signal to Western investors that their capital was welcome and secure. Hence, many Latin American countries altered their stance on BITs and started concluding them (Vandevelde, 1997, pp. 387–390). Third, the USA finally endorsed BITs as an instrument of investment policy in the early 1980s. Until then, the US government did not conclude BITs, because it sought to defend the status of the Hull Doctrine as a standard of CIL. After World War II, the US government initially only signed so-called Treaties on Friendship, Commerce and Navigation (FCN). FCN treaties were agreements developed in the 19th century and reiterated parties' commitments to basic investment policy principles without providing for dispute settlement and enforcement mechanisms. The USA, however, revised its position in the early 1980s and concluded its first BITs. The reorientation of the USA to BITs arguably motivated other countries to follow suit (Weiss, 2007).

The 1990s were a crucial decade in the development of the international investment regime in four regards. First, the speedy diffusion of IIAs practically re-established, and even enhanced, the worldwide level of investment treatment and protection vis-à-vis the previously abandoned Hull Doctrine (Alvarez, 2009; Mills, 2011). States also launched negotiations on a codified multilateral investment regime for the first time since the early post-war years and the failure of the ITO in 1950. NAFTA and the ECT are, for instance, products of the spirit of the 1990s. Negotiations on a multilateral set of investment rules were also conducted in the Uruguay and Doha Rounds of the GATT/WTO (see Chapters 5 and 7) as well as in the OECD (see Chapter 7). These multilateral attempts, however, ultimately failed. Second, investment disciplines gradually became part of the standard agenda of international trade talks. Whereas investment and trade policy were neatly separated policy areas until the late 1980s; in particular, the USA started including IIA-like investment chapters in bilateral and regional trade agreements and pushed for investment negotiations in the GATT. As will become clear in the empirical chapters, the extension of the standard agenda of international trade negotiations to investment disciplines triggered functional pressures on the Member States to cooperate and to delegate negotiating on investment disciplines to the EU/Commission. After all, the EU traditionally speaks with a single voice in trade policy fora such as the GATT/WTO and PTA negotiations regardless of the EU-internal distribution of legal competences. Third, until the 1990s investment arbitration was a sporadic occurrence. It was only in the 1990s that investors started frequently launching arbitration proceedings against host countries thereby giving proper meaning to the ISDS clauses of modern IIAs. By 2012, at least 514 cases had been filed and the number is rising (UNCTAD, 2005, 2013, p. 1; Weiss, 2007). Finally, the late 1990s were characterised by an unprecedented increase in the volume of international investment flows mostly due to major advances in communications and transport technology as well as continued deregulation and privatisation policies (see Figure 3.2).

The last ten years have brought a further increase in FDI flows and stocks, arbitration proceedings and IIAs. One noteworthy development affecting the political economy of the global investment regime is the partial reversal of global investment flows. In the past, international investment activities were heavily concentrated within the OECD. Non-OECD countries only played a minor role in the global investment regime as FDI recipients. In the last two decades, the situation has started changing. Firms from emerging economies have developed into noteworthy investors in both the world economy and OECD countries. The share of developing countries in total global outward FDI stocks more than doubled from 9,9% in 2000 to 21,1% in 2015 (UNCTAD, 2016, p. 200). And while in 2001 firms from the so-called BRICS economies held direct investments worth €9.7 billion

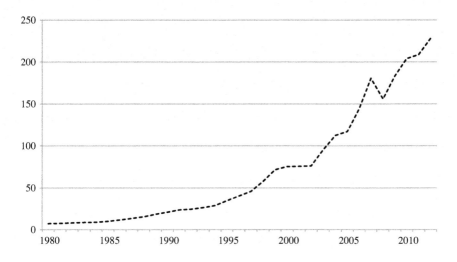

Figure 3.2 World inward FDI stock in trillion US dollars (1980–2012)
Source: UNCTAD (2014b).

in the EU, they held direct investments worth €201 billion in 2012. This amounts to a twentyfold increase in the volume of BRICS-owned assets in the EU within a decade. The partial reversal of investment flows and the emergence of non-OECD investors fundamentally alters the effect of IIAs and ISDS on OECD countries. In the past, IIAs and ISDS de facto only constrained non-OECD countries receiving FDI. As firms from non-OECD countries now invest and start using investment arbitration against OECD countries, IIAs and ISDS also constrain the latter. The emergence of NAFTA-type IIAs is in part a policy response to these developments. As explained earlier, the US government developed NAFTA-type IIAs to ring-fence its regulatory space and to limit its financial exposure in ISDS proceedings (Alvarez, 2009, pp. 301–305). Other states – including the EU – are gradually adopting this new approach in light of the changing global investment landscape.

3.4.2 Geography and sectors of international investment activity in historical perspective

The volume and direction of international investment flows affects the substantive provisions of IIAs, national investment policies and lastly the international investment regime. The following paragraphs briefly trace the evolution of FDI flows in terms of volume, geographical direction and economic sectors for the last century in order to complete the picture.

Prior to World War I (1914–1918), international investment was of comparable economic importance to Western European and Northern American economies as in the late 1980s (Velde, 2006, p. 5). International investment was then, to a large extent, a North-South phenomenon. Firms from Northern America and Europe – and notably the United Kingdom – invested in colonies and developing countries in the south. Two economic sectors attracted the bulk of investment during this time. European and American MNEs invested heavily into the transport sector and in particular in railway networks. Furthermore, investment flowed into mining industries (Velde, 2006, p. 5). International investment was primarily strategic asset- or resource-seeking and unlike the bulk of modern international investment.

The interwar period (1918–1939) brought considerable economic, financial and political turmoil. During World War I, economic nationalism and protectionism had spread in Europe and Northern America and persisted during the interwar period. Furthermore, the war had irrevocably destroyed the former international currency system. Attempts to restore the pre-war gold standard de facto failed. States engaged in 'beggar-thy-neighbour' policies by under-valuing their currencies as well as adopting inflationary monetary policies. These developments led to a disintegration of the international economy and considerable decline in MNE and international investment activities. Nevertheless, Western European and Northern American countries partly saw rising inward FDI stocks in relation to GDP (Jones, 2005, pp. 29–31). Two factors explain this counterintuitive observation. First, many countries prohibited MNCs from disinvesting or repatriating profits in order to stop capital flight. MNCs had to reinvest their profits into their affiliate, which led to growing inward FDI stocks. Second, inward FDI stocks remained stable or grew in absolute terms while in many countries the GDP shrank in response to the war and economic crises. Hence, the ratio of inward FDI stocks to GDP went up.

After World War II, the United Kingdom and the USA intended to prevent the economic mistakes of the interwar period. They sought to establish an open and liberal international economy under the auspices of the Bretton Woods System (Ruggie, 1982). This attempt succeeded in part. States in Western Europe, Northern America and Japan gradually opened up their economies to trade and investment flows during the decades following World War II. Until the mid-1960s, US capital accounted for 85% of worldwide FDI flows (Jones, 2005, p. 33). Then Western European states and Japan started investing abroad and became important creditor regions. FDI flows, however, remained primarily transatlantic. By 1980, two-thirds of worldwide FDI stocks were concentrated in the EU, the USA and Canada (Jones, 2005, p. 33). FDI was mostly market- or strategic-asset-seeking. It was concentrated in the manufacturing and, to a lesser extent, service sectors (Jones, 2005, p. 33; Velde, 2006, p. 7). It was only in the late 1980s that FDI stocks attained comparable levels and economic importance in Western European and Northern American countries to those of the pre-1914 period (Jones, 2005, pp. 33–34). The increasing concentration of FDI flows and stocks in the manufacturing sectors in North America and Western Europe was mirrored by a marginalisation of developing and socialist countries in the international investment landscape at that time (Velde, 2006, pp. 5–7). As previously explained, many developing and socialist countries engaged in large-scale nationalisation of foreign-owned property in the late 1940s and 1960s (Jones, 2005; Vandevelde, 1997). These nationalisation programmes scared off inward FDI. Most developing countries also adhered to economic nationalism and adopted protectionist foreign economic policies. Inward FDI was generally undesired (Jones, 2005, p. 31; Vandevelde, 1997).

Since the 1980s, several developments fundamentally reshaped the international investment landscape. Developed, developing and socialist economies alike gradually adopted more liberal foreign economic and investment policies. Western economies switched from the Keynesian to the neoliberal economic paradigm after Keynesian policies had failed to resolve the stagflation crises of the 1970s. Policymakers sought to limit Keynesian state intervention and to strengthen market mechanism to ensure a more efficient allocation of resources. The adoption of more liberal foreign economic and investment policies formed part of these efforts. Sovereign debt crises in many developing countries and structural crises in socialist economies also made these countries reconsider their macroeconomic paradigms (Vandevelde, 1997). To modernise their economies, to get access to badly needed hard currencies and to attract fresh foreign capital, they gradually adopted liberal macroeconomic, trade and investment policies.

The global shift toward more liberal economic policies coincided with important technological innovations. New transport, logistical and telecommunication technologies facilitated trade, the coordination of GVCs and the operation of MNCs. An unprecedented surge in the global volume of FDI flows was the consequence of these political and technological innovations (Jones, 2005, p. 35; Velde, 2006, p. 5). In the mid-1990s, the volume of FDI flows started exceeding the volume of traditional trade in goods and services. Only the *Dot-com* and *Global Financial* crises temporarily interrupted the growth of FDI stocks and flows (UNCTAD, 2016, 2011, p. 3). The surge in the volume of global FDI flows was not limited to developed countries as in previous decades. Developing and emerging countries also experienced increasing volumes of FDI stocks and inflows. While in the decades following World War II FDI flows into developing countries had been minimal, they received more than half – 52% – of global inward FDI flows in 2010 (UNCTAD, 2011, p. 3). It is important to note though that the diversification of international investment flows remains limited. Since 1980, eight developing and emerging economies[13] have accounted for more than 75% of inward FDI flows into this group of countries. The leading 25 developing and emerging countries account for 95% of inward FDI flows in this group (Velde, 2006, p. 6).

Other important developments concern the origin of investors, sectorial composition and form of international investment activities. As mentioned in the previous section, developing country investors emerged as new actors in the global investment landscape. Firms from developing countries started investing abroad. The last 20 years saw, in particular, the rise of south-south FDI flows and IIAs. Moreover, firms from emerging and developing countries started investing in Northern America, Europe and Japan. International investment activities also evolved in their sectorial composition and organisation form. During the last decades, the share of FDI flowing into the services sector has constantly increased, while the share flowing to the manufacturing and agriculture sectors has decreased. In 2015, 65% of global FDI stocks were in service sectors (UNCTAD, 2017b). This trend is noteworthy as many service sectors – such as telecommunications, healthcare or finance – are politically sensitive (UNCTAD, 2014c, pp. 9–10, 2016). Finally, so-called greenfield investments constituted the bulk of FDI flows in the past. Greenfield investments refer to foreign investors entering a foreign economy and building up new production sites. Nowadays, many investment projects take the form of mergers and acquisitions. In other words, foreign investors do not build up new companies and production sites but buy up or merge with existing foreign companies (UNCTAD, 2014c, p. 7, 2016). The economic effects of greenfield investments, mergers and acquisitions on home and host countries tend to differ. While greenfield investments for instance create new jobs in host economies, mergers and acquisitions typically coincide with restructuring efforts and layoffs due to synergies. The exact impact of different forms of international investment, however, is context and case specific.

Notes

1 This includes, for instance, the acquisition of real estate, licences or machinery and most other expenditures related to setting up or buying an affiliated enterprise abroad.
2 Three types of affiliated enterprises exist. First, *branches* belong 100% to the investor or parent company. Second, *subsidiaries* belong 99–50% to the investor. Finally, *associates* belong 49–10% to the investor.
3 This includes the repatriation of profits, disinvestment, re-investment, intra-firm loans, etc.
4 Under European law the term public services typically comprises telecommunications, postal services, transport services, education, emergency services and hospitals as well as water and energy supply.
5 Countries consider different sectors as strategic or sensitive. Typical sectors, however, are extractive and mining industries, aviation and high-tech industries, as well as financial services.
6 See Ubifrance, Trade and Invest Germany, etc.
7 Foreign investors frequently enter into direct business relationships with host states. In other words, the host state does not only offer a market for the foreign investor to operate in, but the foreign investor and the host state cooperate as business partners inter alia in joint ventures or private public partnerships. Host states thus have a direct stake and interest in the operation of joint business operations and may use their jurisdictional powers to rewrite the terms and conditions of their business relations with foreign investors. Direct business relations between foreign investors and host states typically occur in the mining sector and other extractive industries or if foreign firms provide public services such as transport, waste management, health care or telecommunication.
8 If governments renege on their prior commitments and/or introduce new costly regulations, it may undermine business plans and reduce the investment value and profitability of projects. Lawyers call this phenomenon indirect or creeping expropriation. Creeping expropriation is today more common than direct expropriation through outright and abrupt taking of foreign assets.
9 NAFTA stands for North American Free Trade Area. It is a comprehensive regional trade and investment agreement concluded between the USA, Canada and Mexico (1994). The NAFTA model agreement is generally synonymous with the US model BIT.
10 ICSID is part of the World Bank Group and based in Washington, DC, USA.
11 UNCITRAL is part of the United Nations system and based in Vienna, Austria.
12 The doctrine was named after Cordell Hull, who was US Secretary of State in the 1930s.
13 China, Hong Kong, Mexico, Brazil, Singapore, Russia, Chile and India.

References

Alschner, W., 2013. Americanization of the BIT universe: The influence of Friendship, Commerce and Navigation (FCN) treaties on modern investment treaty law. *Goettingen J. Int. Law* 5, 455–486.

Alvarez, J.E., 2009. *The Public International Law Regime governing international investment, Recueil de cours of the Hague Academy of International Law*. Martinus Nijhoff Publishers, Leiden.

The Avalon Project (Yale Law School Lillian Goldman Law Library), 1999. Treaty of amity and commerce between the United States and France, February 6 1778 [WWW Document]. URL http://avalon.law.yale.edu/18th_century/fr1788-1.asp (accessed 11.24.11).

Blonigen, B.A., Piger, J., 2014. Determinants of foreign direct investment. *Can. J. Econ.* 47, 775–812. doi:10.1111/caje.12091

Busse, M., Nunnenkamp, P., Spatareanu, M., 2010. Foreign direct investment and labor rights: A panel analysis of bilateral FDI flows. *Econ. Lett.* 11, 270–272.

Cain, P.J., 1978. J. A. Hobson, Cobdenism, and the radical theory of economic imperialism, 1898–1914. *Econ. Hist. Rev.*, new series 31, 565–584.

Colen, L., Persyn, D., Guariso, A., 2014. *What type of FDI is attracted by bilateral investment treaties?*, LICOS Discuss. Pap. 346/2014.

Dattu, R., 2000. A journey from Havana to Paris: The fifty-year quest for the elusive multilateral agreement on investment. *Fordham Int. Law J.* 24, 275–316.

Dimopoulos, A., 2011. *EU foreign investment law*. Oxford University Press, Oxford.

Dolzer, R., Schreuer, C., 2012. *Principles of international investment law*, 2nd ed. Oxford University Press, Oxford.

Dolzer, R., Schreuer, C., 2008. *Principles of international investment law*. Oxford University Press, Oxford.

Dolzer, R., Stevens, M., 1995. *Bilateral investment treaties*. M. Nijhoff, The Hague.

Dunning, J., 2008. *Multinational enterprises and the global economy*, 2nd ed. Edward Elgar, Cheltenham.

Dunning, J., 1981. *International production and the multinational enterprise*. Allen & Unwin, Crows Nest.

Elkmans, Z., Guzman, A., Simmons, B., 2006. Competing for capital: The diffusion of bilateral investment treaties, 1960–2000. *Int. Organ.* 60, 811–846.

Euler, D., Gehring, M., Scherer, M. (Eds.), 2015. *Transparency in international investment arbitration*. Cambridge University Press, Cambridge.

European Communities, 1988. Nomenclature of the capital movements referred to in article 1 of the directive. *Off. J. Eur. Communities L-178*, 8–12.

European Court of Justice, 2017. Opinion 2/15 (ECLI/EU/C/2017/376). Luxemburg.

Fontanelli, F., Bianco, G., 2013. The inevitable convergence of the US and the EU on the protection of foreign investments: BITs, PTAs, and incomplete contracts, in: European Society of International Law Conference Paper Series. Presented at the Amsterdam Research Forum, Amsterdam.

Gordon, K., 2008. *Investment guarantees and political risk insurance: Institutions, incentives and development: OECD invest*. Policy Perspect.

Guzman, A., 1997. Why LDCs sign treaties that hurt them: Explaining the popularity of bilateral investment treaties. *Va. J. Int. Law* 38, 639–688.

Hallward-Driemeier, M., 2003. Do bilateral investment treaties attract foreign direct investment? Only a bit? and they could bite, policy research working papers. *The World Bank*. doi:10.1596/1813-9450-3121

IMF, 2009. *Balance of payments and international investment position manual*, 6th ed. Washington, DC.

Johannsen, E.L., 2009. *Die Kompetenz der Europäischen Union für ausländische Direktinvestitionen nach dem Vertrag von Lissabon*. Beiträge zum Transnationalem Wirtschaftsrecht.

Jones, G., 2005. *Multinationals and global capitalism*. Oxford University Press, Oxford.

Krajewski, M., 2005. External trade law and the constitutional treaty: Towards a federal and more democratic common commercial policy? *Common Mark. Law Rev.* 42, 91–127.

Krasner, S., 1982. Structural causes and regime consequences: Regimes as intervening variables. *Int. Organ.* 36, 185–205.

Lavranos, N., 2013. The new EU investment treaties: Convergence towards the NAFTA model as the new Plurilateral Model BIT text? Vrije Universiteit Brussel.

Lipsey, R.E., 2002. Home and host country effects of FDI. Presented at the ISIT Conference on Challenges to Globalization, Lidingö, Sweden.

MIGA, 2011. Types of coverage [WWW Document]. URL www.miga.org/investment-guarantees/index.cfm?stid=1797#toc5.

Mills, A., 2011. Antinomies of public and private at the foundations of international investment law and arbitration. *J. Int. Econ. Law* 14, 469–503.

Navaretti, G.B., Venables, A., 2004. *Multinational firms in the world economy*. Princeton University Press, Princeton.

Neumayer, E., Spess, L., 2005. Do bilateral investment treaties increase foreign direct investment to developing countries? *World Dev.* 33, 1567–1585.

OECD, 2008. *OECD benchmark definition of foreign direct investment*. Paris. OECD Publishing.

Rajoo, S., 2016. Annulment of investment arbitration awards. *Int. Invest. Treaty Arbitr. Rev.* 1, 159–215.

Reinisch, A., 2016. The European Union and investor-state dispute settlement: From investor-state arbitration to a permanent investment court. *CIGI Invest.-State Arbitr. Ser.* 2.

Reinisch, A., 2013. The future shape of EU investment agreements. *ICSID Rev. – Foreign Invest. Law J.* 28, 179–196. doi:10.1093/icsidreview/sit007

Ruggie, J.G., 1982. International regimes, transactions, and change: Embedded liberalism in the postwar economic order. *Int. Organ.* 36, 379–415. doi:10.1017/S0020818300018993

Sauvant, K., Sachs, L. (Eds.), 2009. *The effect of treaties on foreign direct investment: Bilateral investment treaties, double taxation treaties and investment flows*. Oxford University Press, Oxford.

Schill, S., 2009. *The multilatrelaisation of international investment law*. Cambridge University Press, Cambridge.

Sornarajah, M., 2013. *The international law on foreign investment*, 3rd ed. Cambridge University Press, Cambridge.

Stein, E., Daude, C., 2007. Longitude matters: Time zones and the location of foreign direct investment. *J. Int. Econ.* 71, 96–112.

UNCTAD, 2017a. Investment policy hub [WWW Document]. URL http://investmentpolicyhub.unctad.org/IIA (accessed 7.15.11).

UNCTAD, 2017b. *World Investment Report 2017: Investment and the digital economy*. UNCTAD, Geneva.

UNCTAD, 2016. *World Investment Report 2016*. UNCTAD, Geneva.

UNCTAD, 2015. *Investor-State Dispute Settlement review of developments in 2014*. IIA Issues Note 2.

UNCTAD, 2014a. *The impact of international investment agreements on foreign direct investment: An overview of empirical studies 1998–2014*. IIA Issues Note.

UNCTAD, 2014b. UNCTADSTAT [WWW Document]. URL http://unctadstat.unctad.org/ReportFolders/reportFolders.aspx (accessed 3.1.14).
UNCTAD, 2014c. *World Investment Report 2014*. UNCTAD, Geneva.
UNCTAD, 2013. *Recent developments in Investor-State Dispute Settlement (ISDS)*. IIA Issues Note 1.
UNCTAD, 2012. Fair and equitable treatment. UNCTAD Ser. Issues Int. Invest. Agreem. II.
UNCTAD, 2011. *World Investment Report 2012*. UNCTAD, Geneva.
UNCTAD, 2006. The entry into Force of Bilateral Investment Treaties (BITs). IIA Monit. 3.
UNCTAD, 2005. Latest developments in investor-state dispute settlement. IIA Monit. 3.
UNCTAD, 1999. Trends in international investment agreements: An overview (UNCTAD/ITE/IIT/13).
Vandevelde, K., 1997. Sustainable liberalism and the international investment regime. *Mich. J. Int. Law* 19, 373–399.
Velde, D.W. te, 2006. *Foreign direct investment and development: An historical perspective*. Overseas Development Institute, London.
Weiss, M., 2007. *The U.S. Bilateral Investment Treaty Program: An overview*. CRS Rep. Congr. RL33978.
Woolcock, S., Bayne, N. (Eds.), 2007. *The new economic diplomacy*, 2nd ed. Ashgate, London.
WTO, 2002. WG/WGTI/W/115 Communication from the European Community and its Member States.
Yackee, J.W., 2010. *How much do U.S. corporations know (and care) about bilateral investment treaties? Some hints from new survey evidence*. Columbia FDI Perspect.

4 An overview of EU international investment policymaking under the Treaty of Lisbon

This chapter provides readers with a non-technical introduction the EU's international investment policy from a legal and political perspective. It can be read alone but may also facilitate understanding of the following empirical analytical chapters. It discusses the EU's legal competences, identifies the key policy actors, their structural preferences and relevant decision-making procedures in the EU's international investment policy. The EU's international investment policy, however, is legally and politically a moving target. The chapter represents the situation as of May 2017.

4.1 The EU's legal competences

This section – and the entire book – primarily focuses on the EU's legal competence to conclude IIAs. For the sake of completeness, it also briefly evaluates the EU's legal competences regarding investment guarantee schemes, political and technical support and national security reviews for foreign investments. The regulation of international investment activities is highly complex under EU law. It touches inter alia on the CCP, capital movements, establishment and development policy. The discussion in this section offers a basic overview for non-expert readers. For an exhaustive detailed discussion of the EU's competences, the reader may consult the rapidly evolving legal literature (Benyon, 2010; Bischoff, 2011; Bungenberg et al., 2011; Bungenberg and Herrmann, 2013; Cremona, 2015; Dimopoulos, 2011, 2014; Eilmansberger, 2009; Krajewski, 2005).

It needs to be emphasised here that the delimitation of the EU's competences in international investment regulation remains controversial. The publication of Opinion 2/15 – in the midst of finalising this book manuscript – is a case in point. Opinion 2/15 (see Chapter IX) assessed the EU's competence to ratify the EU-Singapore PTA. The EU-Singapore PTA is considered as a blueprint for future EU PTAs. Opinion 2/15 is thus of general importance and found that the provisions relating to ISDS and portfolio investments come under shared competences rather than exclusive Union competence under the CCP or the EU's otherwise implied exclusive competences. It is difficult to predict whether this is the end of competence quarrels; and how it affects future EU international investment policy.

4.1.1 *The EU and international investment guarantees*

The EU mostly plays a supervising role regarding state-backed investment guarantee schemes (Bourgeois, 2003, pp. 738–762; Dimopoulos, 2011, pp. 103–104; Vedder, 2008, p. 28). State-backed investment guarantee schemes insure national investors abroad against non-commercial risks such as expropriation, political violence or non-convertibility of currency (Dolzer and Schreuer, 2008, p. 207). They seek to address a hold-off problem and to enhance the national economic performance. The probability of non-commercial risks materialising might be limited. In many cases though, private insurers do not offer appropriate protection. To enable investors in need of insurance so as to get access for instance to affordable finance, states have created public investment guarantee schemes. These schemes offer protection and enable investors to pursue a priori secure and profitable investment projects abroad (Gordon, 2008).

Article 112 EC provided the EU with a competence to harmonise Member States' export policies including investment guarantee schemes to avoid unfair and wasteful export policy competition among Member States. In 1975, the CJEU confirmed in Opinion 1/75 (see Chapter IX) that the EU was competent under the article 112 EC of the CCP to adopt autonomous measures and to conclude international agreements relating to the harmonisation of export policies (Seidl-Hohenveldern, 1977, pp. 56–57). Since then, the EU transposes OECD rules on the harmonisation of export policies into European secondary law. EU primary law, however, does not provide for a direct EU involvement in export policies including in the provision of investment guarantees. Article 112 EC was deleted during the drafting of the Treaty of Nice. The EU remains, nonetheless, competent to adopt general rules aiming at the harmonisation of Member States' export policies.

4.1.2 *The EU and political support for investors*

The EU and the Member States may both offer practical and political support to European investors. Many Member States and the EU provide European investors with information about the investment environment in third countries. National export and investment promotion agencies, embassies and ministries offer information on the economic, regulatory and political environment in target markets. The Member States and the EU, moreover, often provide crucial political support in relation to third-country authorities. Political support – through diplomatic representations or bilateral cooperation committees – often unlocks doors for investors wishing to enter a third country. It might also help to amicably resolve disputes between investors and host country authorities. The EU and the Member States both maintain a multitude of diplomatic representations and bilateral cooperation committees with third countries, which provide ample opportunity to raise concerns of European investors with host countries. As informal political support does not involve binding international commitments, it is not subject to EU-internal legal controversies over the distribution of competences.

4.1.3 The EU and national security reviews of foreign investments

Many states – including many Member States of the EU – maintain national security reviews for foreign investments in sensitive sectors. Governments screen whether a planned foreign investment – typically in the form of a merge or acquisition – might endanger vital national interests. Foreign investments for instance in defence industries, strategic infrastructures or vital public services often have to undergo a national security review. Governments may authorise, veto or condition foreign investments in these sectors in order to safeguard national security and the *ordre public*. The EU's new competence under the CCP to regulate FDI triggers the question whether the EU and/or the Member States are competent to review foreign investments in view of their compatibility with national security and the *ordre public*. The dominant legal opinion is that the Member States remain competent under the Treaty of Lisbon to screen and authorise foreign investments in order to protect national security and the *ordre public*. Article 65 TFEU allows the Member States to take measures restricting the free movement of capital '*justified on grounds of public policy and public security*'. European law and the jurisprudence of the CJEU have, however, developed over time narrow definitions of public policy, order and security to prevent the abuse of these clauses for hidden discrimination and protectionism. The European legal order thus sets clear limits to Member State action to review and to restrict foreign investment.

4.1.4 The EU and international investment agreements

IIAs – or IIA-like investment chapters in PTAs – are the most prominent, legally complex and controversial tool of international investment policy today. Since the entry into force of the Treaty of Lisbon in 2009, the EU is exclusively competent to regulate extra-EU FDI flows under the CCP and more precisely articles 206 and 207 TFEU. It implies that the Member States have by and large lost their competences to regulate international investment and to enter into IIAs with third countries. From a pragmatic-political perspective, the EU is now in charge of international investment policymaking. From a legal perspective, the situation is more complex – notably after the CJEU released its Opinion 2/15 in May 2017. The following paragraphs summarise the current state of play in the legal debate on the distribution of competences regarding the main components of standard IIAs:

> **FDI versus portfolio investments:** Standard IIAs regulate FDI and portfolio investments (see chapter III). Opinion 2/15 clarifies that the EU holds an exclusive competence to regulate FDI under the CCP as specified in articles 206–207 TFEU. It holds only a shared competence to regulate portfolio investments under article 63 TFEU on capital movements and article 216(1) TFEU on the conclusion of international agreements (Dimopoulos, 2011, pp. 104–105; European Court of Justice, 2017). International agreements regulating not only FDI but also equally portfolio investments

are likely to require mixed ratification through the EU and the individual Member States.

Investment liberalisation: The EU is exclusively competent to regulate market access for FDI and the initial establishment of foreign investors under articles 206–207 TFEU. Only the EU can negotiate international agreements containing FDI-related liberalisation commitments (Dimopoulos, 2011, pp. 94–108, 123). It needs to be emphasised that the Treaty of Lisbon did not fundamentally change the legal situation in this domain. The EU was already exclusively competent under article 133 EC of the Treaty of Nice (2003) to regulate market access and initial establishment for service-related FDI. The Treaty of Nice brought the regulation of services trade – including the 'establishment of a commercial presence' (GATS mode III) largely equivalent to FDI – under the scope of the CCP. The entry into force of the Treaty of Lisbon, in essence, extended the EU's exclusive competence toward the regulation of market access and initial establishment for FDI beyond services.

Post-establishment treatment standards: The Lisbon Treaty, however, established under the CCP a crosscutting competence for post-establishment treatment of FDI. Under articles 206–207 TFEU, the EU is exclusively competent to regulate post-establishment treatment standards such as 'Most-Favoured Nation' (MFN) or 'National Treatment' (NT) for FDI. The EU is furthermore competent to regulate trade- and currency-related performance requirements under articles 207 and 219 TFEU. The EU also holds the exclusive competence to regulate the movement of investment-related key personnel under article 207 TFEU. Article 90 TFEU on the Common Transport Policy provides the EU with an implied exclusive competence for the regulation of transport-related investments. Finally, the EU holds a shared competence regarding the treatment of other established investments under article 54 TFEU (freedom of establishment) and article 56 TFEU (free provision of services) (Dimopoulos, 2011, pp. 94–108, 123). To summarise, the EU is the key regulator in this domain, while the Member States exercise varying influence on European regulatory activity in function of the concerned investment and policy domain. The EU was already competent to regulate many of the discussed issues before the Lisbon Treaty.

Investment protection and ISDS: The EU's competence in the field of investment protection has been the most disputed since the entry into force of the Treaty of Lisbon (Dimopoulos, 2011, pp. 108–116). Prior to Opinion 2/15, some scholars argued that rules on investment protection interfere with the system of ownership of the Member States and thus run counter article 345 TFEU. Article 345 TFEU stipulates that European measures must not affect the system of ownership of the Member States. Investment protection provisions of IIAs, however, seek to circumscribe states' right to expropriate – i.e. to freely regulate the national ownership system. Critics concluded that the EU could not hold an exclusive competence under the CCP in this domain. Other scholars cautioned that article 345 TFEU does not bring Member States' systems of ownership under exclusive Member State competence. The EU has, for instance, adopted many measures concerning intellectual property rights. The ECJ has, moreover, delivered judgements, which contributed to the harmonisation of expropriation procedures and compensatory rules across Member States. Article 17 of the Charter of Fundamental Rights of the European Union, which is an integral part of European primary law, furthermore, jointly obliges the EU and the Member States to protect the right to property. Finally, lawyers have argued that alongside articles 206 and 207 TFEU, article 352 TFEU (extension of Union competence if necessary by unanimity in Council of Minister) as well as Articles 114 and 115 TFEU (approximation of laws) also provide a competence basis for the EU to enter into investment protection commitments (Dimopoulos, 2011, pp. 108–116).

After years of legal and political controversy, Opinion 2/15 finally offers an authoritative delimitation of the EU's competences in the field of investment protection (European Court of Justice, 2017). The CJEU holds the view that the EU is exclusively competent to adopt rules and to enter into agreements with substantive investment protection standards such as 'full protection and security' (FPS) or 'fair and equitable treatment' (FET). The CJEU argues in Opinion 2/15 that such provisions may indeed have an impact on trade and therefore come under the CCP. The CJEU, however, cautions that the EU does not have an exclusive competence to enter into agreements with ISDS provisions. ISDS – as a procedural mechanism to enforce substantive protection provisions – empowers foreign investors to circumvent national legal systems and courts. The CJEU finds that ISDS provisions come under shared competence. The EU cannot enter into agreements on behalf of the Member States, which allow for the bypassing of the national legal system. Agreements with ISDS provisions are likely to require mixed ratification.

An evaluation of the Treaty of Lisbon: The discussion suggests that the EU holds comprehensive legal competences in international investment policy under the Treaty of Lisbon. It shows, however, that the EU held already important competences prior to the entry into force of the Treaty of Lisbon. The Treaty of Lisbon's main implications are that it creates a crosscutting competence for FDI and that it finally brings investment protection under the scope of exclusive Union competence. Opinion 2/15, however, relativitises the practical importance of the latter. Policymakers consider that only access to ISDS turns substantive investment protection provisions into effective norms. Unlike substantive investment protection standards, however, ISDS provisions come under shared competence and may typically require mixed ratification. Unanimous support for IIAs and PTAs with ISDS provisions as necessary for mixed ratification is fairly unlikely in the current political climate. The Treaty of Lisbon may thus have created a 'joint decision trap' (Scharpf, 1988) rather than streamlined the EU's capacity to pursue in international investment policy. Neither the EU nor the Member States can now individually conclude IIAs or PTAs with ISDS provisions.

4.2 The policymaking procedures

4.2.1 The 'ordinary legislative procedure'

Article 207 TFEU specifies that the EU's international investment policy is subject to the 'ordinary legislative procedure'. The 'ordinary legislative procedure' as set out in article 294 TFEU governs the elaboration and adoption of regulations and directives in the EU. Most EU policies come under the EU's 'ordinary legislative procedure'. Hence, it is not specific to international trade and investment policymaking. In the context of trade and investment policymaking, the 'ordinary legislative procedure' has been used for instance to develop and enact the so-called Grandfathering Regulation (No. 1219/2012) dealing with the Member States' regulatory legacy of hundreds of BITs (see Chapter IX) and the 'Financial Responsibility Regulation' (No. 912/2014) dealing with the distribution of costs and representation modalities of the EU and the Member States in joint ISDS proceedings. The following paragraphs provide a brief overview of the main steps in the 'ordinary legislative procedure' (European Union, 2011; Woolcock, 2011):

- **Commission proposal:** Under the 'ordinary legislative procedure', the Commission normally takes the initiative and develops a draft measure. The Treaty of Lisbon, moreover, foresees that a citizens' initiative may call on the Commission to become active. A citizens' initiative requires one million signatures of citizens from at least seven Member States. The Commission needs to carefully assess and reply to successful initiatives. In a similar vein, the Council of Ministers may call on the Commission to take action if at least a quarter of Member States supports it.
- **First reading:** Once the Commission has developed a draft regulation or directive, the European Parliament discusses, adopts or amends the measure in a first reading by simple majority. Afterwards the Council of Ministers discusses the draft measure – and potential amendments of the Parliament – in its first reading. The Council can adopt the draft measure and amendments by qualified majority. In this case, the draft regulation enters into force and becomes binding European legislation. The vast majority of EU legislation enters into force at this stage. The Council of Ministers may, however, disagree with a draft regulation and the amendments of the Parliament. If the Council disagrees with the amendments of the Parliament, it adopts its own position by qualified majority. The draft regulation and Council position are then sent to the European Parliament for a second reading. It needs to be emphasised here that while the European Parliament indeed votes on draft measures, the Council almost never holds formal

80 *The EU and international investment*

votes. The Council Presidency – chairing work in the various Council working groups and committees – normally scopes the distribution of Member State preferences and seeks to forge compromise positions. Voting rules matter in the background. They affect the willingness of the Member States to compromise on critical issues (Kleine, 2013).

- **Second reading:** In the second reading, the Parliament can adopt the Council position by simple majority. In case the Parliament rejects the Council position, the legislative process ends here. As a third option, the Parliament can amend the Council's position by qualified majority. The newly amended draft measure is then sent back to the Council for a second reading. The Commission can table a formal opinion on the Parliament's new amendments. If the Commission gives a positive opinion on the Parliament's new amendments, the Council may adopt the draft regulation by qualified majority. If the Commission delivers a negative opinion on the Parliament's new amendments, the Council has to adopt it by unanimity.

- **Conciliation procedure:** In the exceptional case that the Council disagrees with the Parliament in the second reading, they establish – with the Commission – a joint conciliation committee. The conciliation committee in entrusted to develop a compromise text. If the committee is successful and manages to draft a compromise text, the text is sent to a third reading in the Parliament and the Council. As per usual, the Parliament may endorse the compromise text by simple majority while the Council may endorse a text by qualified majority. If one of the two institutions rejects the text, the legislative initiative has failed.

4.2.2 *Negotiating international investment agreements*

Several important regulations dealing with the operation of the EU's international investment policy have been adopted over the last years. At the heart of international trade and investment policy, nonetheless, lie international agreements. The negotiating and ratification of international trade and investment agreements are subject to distinct rules set out in articles 207 and 218 TFEU. For the sake of this book, it is important to briefly review the EU-internal rules governing international negotiations between the EU and third countries. The discussion that follows summarises the main steps and rules as foreseen in the Treaty of Lisbon. While the detailed decision-making modalities and the role of the European Parliament have evolved over the last decades, the overall procedure governing international negotiations between the EU and third countries has remained stable (Woolcock, 2011, pp. 45–84).

- **Launching negotiations:** As for the 'ordinary legislative procedure', the Commission holds the right to recommend and to initiate international trade and investment negotiations. In line with the 'Better Regulation' agenda (European Commission, 2015), the Commission first conducts an internal impact assessment and stakeholder consultations to assess the costs and benefits of various policy options. The Commission may for instance assess as part of this process whether it should aim for 1) a classic IIA focusing on investment protection, 2) a modern IIA with investment liberalisation commitments or 3) a full-fledged PTA with investment chapter (for an example see European Commission, 2013). On the basis of this assessment, the Commission then develops the so-called negotiating directives and submits them to the Council of Ministers. The Commission is not legally required to submit 'negotiating directives'. Such directives are, however, of great practical significance. The Council normally discusses and authorises by qualified majority the launch of international negotiations. If negotiations, however, deal with 1) trade in cultural, audiovisual, social, health or education services, 2) issues of shared competence and 3) issues requiring unanimity if adopted in an EU-internal context, the Council must authorise the launch of negotiations by unanimity. In light of Opinion 2/15, it is manifest that the launch of negotiations on IIAs or comprehensive PTAs with investment chapters requires unanimity. Once the Council has authorised the opening of international negotiations, the European Parliament is formally informed. The Parliament legally does not play a central role at this stage. The Parliament, nonetheless, must give its consent before the EU can ratify an agreement. The Parliament's veto power ensures that the Commission and the Council informally consult with the Parliament from the earliest stages to avoid a last-minute collapse of international negotiations.

- **Managing negotiations:** The Commission negotiates on trade and investment agreements on behalf of the EU and the Member States. International trade and investment negotiations between the EU and third countries proceed in negotiating rounds. Each negotiating round normally encompasses two or three negotiating days. The Commission would regularly brief the Trade Policy Committee (TPC) of the Council of Ministers and the International Trade Committee (INTA) of the European Parliament on new developments in negotiations. The Commission and the TPC typically meet on a weekly/biweekly basis. While article 218(10) TFEU states that the European Parliament is immediately and fully informed of international negotiations, the Commission and the Parliament tend to meet less frequently. Informal exchanges between the Commission and key Members of the European Parliament (MEPs) are, however, the norm. The meetings between the Commission, the Council and the Parliament shall ensure the dissemination of information and continuous political support for agreements among the Member States and the Parliament in view of ratification.
- **Closing negotiations:** Once the Commission and a third-country government have agreed on a text, they 'initial' the trade and investment agreement. The agreement does not become legally binding through initialling. It merely signals preliminary agreement over substance between the negotiators. In the following weeks, the agreement text undergoes 'legal scrubbing'. Legal experts analyse whether the agreement is coherent and complies with the parties' manifold domestic and international legal commitments. After the 'legal

scrubbing', the agreement is translated into the 24 official languages of the EU. Each Member State government must thereafter verify the authenticity of the translation.
- **Signing and provisional application:** Following the initialling, the Council must adopt – on recommendation of the Commission – a 'decision' authorising the signing of the agreement. The Council adopts this 'decision' by qualified majority unless the concerned agreement contains provisions requiring unanimity (see the aforementioned). The agreement does not become binding at this point. The 'decision' to authorise signing underlines the EU's political commitment to an agreement. The Council may, however, decide at this stage to apply certain parts of an agreement on a provisional basis. While not enshrined in European primary law, the inter-institutional agreement between the Commission, the Council of Ministers and the European Parliament specifies that the European Parliament must give its consent to the signing and provisional application of an agreement.
- **Conclusion and ratification:** Finally, the Council must – again on recommendation of the Commission – adopt a 'decision' on the conclusion of the agreement. In function of the agreement's content, the Council must act by qualified majority or unanimity. Before the Council can take this 'decision', however, it must formally ask the European Parliament for its consent. The Parliament cannot amend but only reject or endorse proposed agreements. Nonetheless, it normally invests considerable time in assessing proposed agreements and does not shy away from rejecting them. In 2012, the Parliament for instance rejected the Anti-Counterfeiting Trade Agreement (ACTA) after many years of negotiations. The ACTA example highlights the importance of the Commission continuously consulting with the Parliament to avoid a last-minute veto. Once the Parliament has given its consent, the Council can adopt its 'decision' making the agreement legally binding on the EU. In many cases and in particular for IIAs and PTAs with investment chapters, mixed ratification is, however, likely to be a legal necessity. Mixed ratification means that each Member State in line with its national Constitution has to ratify the agreement. Mixed ratification multiplies the number of veto players and strongly increases the risk that the EU and the Member States fail to ratify an agreement.

4.3 The policymaking actors

Under European law, the key actors in EU international investment policymaking are the European Commission, the Council of Ministers and the European Parliament. Other actors also manifestly exert influence on EU trade and investment policymaking and outcomes. The heated public debate on TTIP for instance illustrated the importance of non-governmental organisations (NGOs) and businesses representatives in policymaking. To better understand policymaking dynamics and outcomes, the following section discusses these actors in more detail.

4.3.1 The European Commission

A 'political duopoly' consisting of the European Commission and the Council of Ministers has dominated international trade policymaking in the EU from 1958 until 2009 (Bourgeois, 2003; Elsig, 2002; Vedder, 2008; Woolcock, 2011). Within this duopoly, the European Commission has been playing a powerful conceptual role. Under European primary law, the Commission has always held the right to initiate autonomous trade policy measures and international trade negotiations. It has moreover been overseeing the daily operation of EU trade policy. The Commission's legal powers and political influence on policy outcomes in trade policymaking thus always exceeded its standing in most other policy domains.

The Commission is a complex public administration (Hooghe and Kassim, 2012). It comprises a number of specialised directorate generals (DGs). Like ministries in national governments, each DG manages a specific policy area, seeks to advance a distinct policy agenda and objectives. International trade and investment policymaking comes first and foremost under the responsibility of DG Trade. DG Trade has been described as holding on average more liberal economic policy preferences than the average Member State government (Meunier and Nicolaidis, 1999; Young and Peterson, 2014). DG Trade counts some 200 officials and is subdivided into directorates and units with geographical foci (e.g. Far East, Latin America) and substantive foci (e.g. services, intellectual property rights). Geographical units typically coordinate and lead international negotiations with third countries. Substantive units, on the other hand, deal with their specific agenda items within the overall negotiating process. Other DGs such as DG for International Cooperation and Development (DEVCO), DG for Neighbourhood and Enlargement Negotiations (NEAR), DG Internal Market, Industry, Entrepreneurship and Small and Medium-Sized Enterprises (SMEs) (GROW) or the European External Actions Service occasionally also touch in their work on investment policy questions but are expected to coordinate or to follow the lead of DG Trade.

Before the entry into force of the Treaty of Lisbon, the unit for services trade dealt with investment-related questions. The administrative setup reflected that services trade is closely tied to investment activity. Service companies hold a significant share of global FDI. GATS mode III ('establishment of a commercial presence'), moreover, is by and large identical with FDI. After the entry into force of the Treaty of Lisbon in 2009, the unit for services trade split up and a specialised 'investment unit' was created. The investment unit had a twofold work focus during the first years after the competence transfer. First, the investment unit started negotiating on investment provisions inter alia with Singapore, Malaysia, Vietnam, India, Canada and the USA as part of comprehensive PTA talks. It, moreover, initiated a number of stand-alone IIAs for instance with Myanmar and China. Second, it developed in close cooperation with DG Trade's 'legal unit' a number of regulations to operationalise the EU's new international investment policy. The units jointly drew up the 'Grandfathering Regulation' (No. 1219/2012) dealing with the Member States' legacy of hundreds of BITs with third countries. They also developed the 'Financial Responsibility Regulation' (No. 912/2014). Under future EU IIAs, foreign investors may bring claims against the EU, which may challenge the legality of national measures or national transposition measures of EU legislation rather than legal acts of the EU per se. The 'Financial Responsibility Regulation' establishes rules regarding the representation of the Member States and the EU in such complex investment arbitration proceedings and the financial responsibility for potential awards.

4.3.2 The Council of Ministers

The second key player in EU trade and investment policymaking has traditionally been the Council of Ministers. Prior to the entry into force of the Treaty of Lisbon, the Council, as the sole legislator in trade policy, authorised, monitored and decided on the conclusion of international trade negotiations and agreements. Much like the Commission, the Council of Ministers is a complex body. It meets in different formations and working levels. At the top level, the Foreign Affairs Council oversees work on EU trade and investment policy (Consilium, 2017). The Foreign Affairs Council brings together the ministers of foreign affairs of the Member States. This top-level body, however, only rarely discusses trade and investment policy. It typically focuses on issues of 'high politics'. The substantive trade policy work is mostly carried out at the working level in the so-called TPC (previously called '113 Committee' or the '133 Committee'). The 'full members' of the TPC are senior Member State technocrats, who oversee trade and investment policy within their national governments. They discuss the most sensitive issues and take the most important substantive decisions. The 'full members' meet once per month in Brussels. The so-called deputies of the TPC meet once per week and discuss more technical questions in trade and investment policy. Over the years, the TPC has set up three additional issue-specific configurations: 1) steel, textiles and other industrial sectors (STIS); 2) mutual recognition agreements (MRAs); and 3) services and investment. The TPC Services and Investment typically meets biweekly. It comprises the lead officials in charge of investment policy and IIAs in national governments. A Commission official is typically present in most TPC meetings – in its various formations – to brief the Member States on new developments for instance in international negotiations, trade defence proceedings and to discuss further steps.

As discussed earlier, the Council de jure takes decision mostly by qualified majority but on certain issues also by unanimity. In practice, however, the Council rarely holds formal votes (Kleine, 2013; Woolcock, 2011). The rotating Council Presidency, which chairs Council meetings, always seeks to forge a broad compromise acceptable to all Member States. Students of European politics, moreover, often assume that all Member States are equally active in Council meetings. At least in the TPC Services and Investment, the quality and intensity of Member State participation significantly varies. The delegates of Germany, France, the Netherlands, Belgium, Spain and the United Kingdom are often fairly active and engage in technical discussions with present Commission representatives. Other Member States may occasionally voice their views, read out positions prepared beforehand

and take note of discussions for their home ministries. Finally, it is noteworthy that at least in the early years after the entry into force of the Treaty of Lisbon many Member State delegates tended to be generally critical of the Commission in discussions in the TPC Services and Investment. The reasons for this were not only of substantive nature. Many Member State delegates had been in charge of national BIT programmes prior to the competence transfer. They had suddenly lost 'their' competence to the EU and found themselves in the position to observe and comment on the Commission's efforts to develop its own approach to IIAs. As lies in human nature, many delegates struggled with their new role as mere observers. This early scepticism toward the Commission is, however, receding as younger delegates take over representation in the TPC Services and Investment.

4.3.3 The European Parliament

The European Parliament has not been a key actor in EU international trade and investment policy before the entry into force of the Treaty of Lisbon in 2009. It mainly played an informal consultative role (Van den Putte et al., 2015). It had no powers in the adoption of autonomous trade policy measures or in negotiations and the ratification of international trade agreements. Nonetheless, the Commission and the Council started informally consulting with the Parliament prior to the signing and conclusion of association and trade agreements in the 1960s. In the 1980s, these consultations were formalised without, however, giving the Parliament a real say over outcomes (Van den Putte et al., 2015).

The Treaty of Lisbon altered the situation. As discussed earlier, the Parliament has now the legal power to reject international trade and investment agreements and is under the 'ordinary legislative procedure' co-legislator for autonomous trade and investment policy measures. The literature suggests that the Parliament's new powers reflect the need for parliamentary legitimation of ever more intrusive trade policy and echoes the skilful negotiating of the Parliament's representatives during the drafting of the Lisbon Treaty (Niemann, 2013; Young and Peterson, 2006). While some scholars initially qualified the Parliament's new powers as a codification of pre-existing practices (Woolcock, 2010; Young, 2011), others saw them as game changing (Deyvust, 2013; Eeckhout, 2011). The Parliament's bold rejection of ACTA in 2012 indeed lends support to the latter view. The Commission and the Council had to realise that they had to keep the Parliament 'on board' in a post-Lisbon world to ensure ratification of trade and investment agreements. Today, the Parliament is accepted as an actor of significant causal importance shaping trade and investment policy outcomes. Van den Putte et al. (2015); Woolcock (2010); and Gstöhl (2013), however, note that the Parliament is still not on entirely equal footing with the Council. The Council is seen to exert greater influence on policy outcomes than the Parliament, because it is more cohesive as a political actor and holds greater trade policy expertise. Under the Treaties, the Council, moreover, has the right to establish a special committee to 'assist' the Commission in negotiations, whereas the Parliament has only the right to be 'informed' about negotiations.

The Parliament's work on trade and investment policy is concentrated in the International Trade Committee (INTA). The INTA Committee – formerly a committee of secondary importance – has emerged as one of the most prominent and visible parliamentary committees over the last years. The INTA Committee evaluates draft measures, develops reports and amendments, follows international negotiations and its members give voting recommendations to their respective parliamentary groups regarding legislative initiatives and international agreements. Following the entry into force of the Treaty of Lisbon, concerns rose that the Parliament may push for a more protectionist and normative trade and investment policy. Van den Putte et al. (2015) find little evidence to support the claim of surging protectionism. The Parliament tends to support trade-friendly Commission proposals. The major centrist groups – the European Peoples Party, the European Socialists and Democrats and the Alliance for Liberals and Democrats in Europe (ALDE) – cohesively vote in favour of trade-friendly Commission proposals. Only the European Greens and the European United Left (GUEL) regularly oppose trade-friendly Commission proposals. In a similar vein, evidence does not point to a normative turn in EU trade and investment policy under the influence of the Parliament (Van den Putte et al., 2015). Scholars have suggested that the Parliament – as an access point to the policy debate for citizens, NGOs, trade unions and alike – may force the Commission and the Council to put greater emphasis on normative concerns such as Human Rights, sustainable development or environmental protection (Bungenberg and Herrmann, 2013). Van den Putte et al. (2015) find that the Parliament only insists on normative concerns in EU trade and investment policymaking, if agreements and measures are seen to directly and negatively affect EU citizens such as arguably in the case of ACTA. The current debate on ISDS under TTIP and CETA confirms these observations. The looming opposition of the Parliament against these clauses is primarily framed in a normative way and threat to European citizens and democracy.

4.3.4 Non-state actors

Non-state actors also play an important – yet less formalised – role in EU trade and investment policymaking. The most prominent types of non-state actors involved in EU trade and investment policy debates are business representatives and NGOs. In general, business representatives seek to advance policies, which economically benefit their constituency – i.e. firms or sectors. NGOs, on the other hand, seek to advance non-economic objectives such as environmental protection, sustainable development and labour rights. An extensive literature deals with the preference formation, political mobilisation and factors shaping the influence of non-state actors in foreign and trade policymaking (Bernhagen et al., 2015; De Bièvre and Dür, 2005; Dür, 2007, 2008, 2012; Dür and De Bièvre, 2007; Frieden, 1991; Hiscox, 2002; Klüver et al., 2015; Quick, 2007; Rogowski, 1989; Voltolini, 2016; Woll, 2008).

In the EU trade and investment policymaking context, non-state actors typically use three lobbying access points to influence the policy debate and outcomes. First, they seek to shape the Commission's position on policy issues. To that end, business representatives and NGOs may try to bilaterally meet with Commission officials, participate in 'stakeholder consultations', civil society meetings and alike. Second, business representatives and NGOs seek to shape EU trade policymaking and outcomes through lobbying vis-à-vis Member State governments. The exact influence channels vary in function of Member States' political institutions and culture. The underlying rationale is that Member State governments may defend the desired position in the Council of Ministers vis-à-vis other Member States, the Commission and the European Parliament. Finally, the European Parliament's new powers in international trade and investment policy have made it an important access point for business representatives and NGOs. Business representatives and NGOs meet with specific MEPs and observe parliamentary committees. In all three settings, lobbyists may primarily draw on two influence resources. Research shows that lobbyists, who can credibly claim to represent an important constituency and/or can offer technical expertise, are more successful in shaping policy debates and outcomes (Woll, 2008; Woll and Artigas, 2007).

In the EU's international investment policy, non-state actors have so far played an ambivalent role (see empirical chapters). As this book argues, business representatives are surprisingly disengaged from policy debates with the notable exception of the highly mediatised debate on TTIP. In a similar vein, the efforts of NGOs to influence policymaking on international investment provisions flared up and strongly focuses on the TTIP and CETA negotiations. NGOs are little active with regard to other investment negotiations. Particularly visible NGOs in the context of the TTIP and CETA debate have been inter alia the transnational 'Stop TTIP' initiative, Attac, Campact, Greenpeace, certain national trade unions and alike.

References

Benyon, F., 2010. *Direct investment, national champions and EU treaty freedoms: From Maastricht to Lisbon*, Modern studies in European law; 24. Hart, Oxford.

Bernhagen, P., Dür, A., Marschall, D., 2015. Information or context: What accounts for positional proximity between the European Commission and lobbyists? *J. Eur. Public Policy* 22, 570–587.

Bischoff, J.A., 2011. Just a little BIT of 'mixity'? The EU's role in the field of international investment protection law. *Common Mark. Law Rev.* 48, 1527–1570.

Bourgeois, J., 2003. Title IX: Gemeinsame Handelspolitik, in: Groeben, H. von der, Schwarze, J. (Eds.), *Kommentar Zum Vertrag Über Die Europäische Union Und Zur Gründung Der Europäischen Gemeinschaft*. Nomos, Baden-Baden, pp. 638–762.

Bungenberg, M., Griebel, J., Hindelang, S. (Eds.), 2011. *International investment law and EU law*. Springer, Heidelberg.

Bungenberg, M., Herrmann, C. (Eds.), 2013. *Common commercial policy after Lisbon*. Heidelberg, Springer.

Consilium, 2017. *Trade policy committee*. Brussels.

Cremona, M., 2015. Negotiating the Transatlantic Trade and Investment Partnership (TTIP). *Common Mark. Law Rev.* 52, 351–362.

De Bièvre, D., Dür, A., 2005. Constituency interests and delegation in European and American trade policy. *Comp. Polit. Stud.* 38, 1271–1296.

Deyvust, Y., 2013. European Union law and practice in the negotiation and conclusion of international trade agreements. *J. Int. Bus. Law* 12, 259–316.

Dimopoulos, A., 2014. The involvement of the EU in investor-state dispute settlement: A question of responsibilities. *Common Mark. Law Rev.* 51, 1671–1720.

Dimopoulos, A., 2011. *EU foreign investment law*. Oxford University Press, Oxford.

Dolzer, R., Schreuer, C., 2008. *Principles of international investment law*. Oxford University Press, Oxford.

Dür, A., 2012. *Key Controversies in European Integration*. Why interest groups dominate the EU's foreign economic policies, in: Zimmerman, H., Dür, A. (Eds.). Palgrave Macmillan, Basingstoke, pp. 177–183.

Dür, A., 2008. Bringing economic interests back into the study of EU trade policy-making. *Br. J. Polit. Int. Relat.* 10, 27–45.

Dür, A., 2007. EU trade policy as protection for exporters: The agreements with Mexico and Chile. *J. Common Mark. Stud.* 45, 833–855.

Dür, A., De Bièvre, D., 2007. Inclusion without influence? NGOs in European trade policy. *J. Public Policy* 27, 79–101.

Eeckhout, P., 2011. *EU external relations law*, 2nd ed., Oxford EU law library. Oxford University Press, Oxford.

Eilmansberger, T., 2009. Bilateral investment treaties and EU law. *Common Mark. Law Rev.* 46, 383–429.

Elsig, M., 2002. *The EU's common commercial policy: Institutions, interests and ideas*. Ashgate, London.

European Commission, 2015. Better regulation guidelines. Burssels.

European Commission, 2013. Impact assessment report on the EU-China investment relations (SWD(2013) 185 final). Brussels.

European Court of Justice, 2017. Opinion 2/15 (ECLI/EU/C/2017/376). Luxemburg.

European Union, 2011. Guide to the ordinary legislative procedure. Brussels.

Frieden, J., 1991. Invested interests: The politics of national economic policies in a world of global finance. *Int. Organ.* 45, 425–451.

Gordon, K., 2008. *Investment guarantees and political risk insurance: Institutions, incentives and development: OECD invest*. Policy Perspect.

Gstöhl, S., 2013. The European Union's trade policy. *Ritsumeikan Int. Aff.* 11, 1–22.

Hiscox, M., 2002. *International trade and political conflict: Commerce, coalitions, and mobility*. Princeton University Press, Princeton.

Hooghe, L., Kassim, H., 2012. The commission's services, in: Peterson, J., Shackelton, M. (Eds.), *The institutions of the European Union*. Oxford University Press, Oxford, pp. 173–198.

Kleine, M., 2013. *Informal governance in the European Union: How governments make international organizations work*. Cornell University Press, Ithaca, NY.

Klüver, H., Braun, C., Beyers, J., 2015. Legislative lobbying in context: The policy and polity determinants of interest group politics in the European Union. *J. Eur. Public Policy* 22, 447–461.

Krajewski, M., 2005. External trade law and the constitutional treaty: Towards a federal and more democratic common commercial policy? *Common Mark. Law Rev.* 42, 91–127.

Meunier, S., Nicolaidis, K., 1999. Who speaks for Europe? The delegation of trade authority in the EU. *J. Common Mark. Stud.* 37, 477–507.

Niemann, A., 2013. EU external trade and the Treaty of Lisbon: A revised neo-functionalist approach. *J. Contemp. Eur. Res.* 9, 634–658.

Quick, R., 2007. Business in economic diplomacy, in: Woolcock, S., Bayne, N. (Eds.), *The new economic diplomacy*. Ashgate, Aldershot, pp. 105–121.

Rogowski, R., 1989. *Commerce and coalitions: How trade affects domestic political alignments*. Princeton University Press, Princeton.

Scharpf, F., 1988. The joint decision trap: Lessons from German federalism and European integration. *Public Adm.* 66, 239–278.

Seidl-Hohenveldern, I., 1977. *Verischerung nichtkommerzieller Risiken und die Europäische Gemeinschaft, Kölner Studien zur Rechtsvereinheitlichung, Band 1*. Carl Heymanns Verlag KG, Köln.

Van den Putte, L., De VIlle, F., Orbie, J., 2015. The European Parliament as an international actor in trade, in: Stavrids, S., Irrera, D. (Eds.), *The European Parliament and its international relations*. Routledge, London.

Vedder, C., 2008. Title IX: Gemeinsame Handelspolitk, in: Grabitz, E., Hilf, M., Nettesheim, M. (Eds.), *Das Recht Der Europäischen Union*. C.H. Beck, München.

Voltolini, B., 2016. Non-state actors and framing processes in EU foreign policy: The case of EU-Israel relations. *J. Eur. Public Policy* 23, 1502–1519.

Woll, C., 2008. *Firm interests: How governments shape business lobbying on global trade*, Cornell studies in political economy. Cornell University Press, Ithaca, NY.

Woll, C., Artigas, A., 2007. When trade liberalization turns into regulatory reform: The impact on business-government relations in international trade politics. *Regul. Gov.* 1, 99–182.

Woolcock, S., 2011. *European Union economic diplomacy: The role of the EU in external economic relations*, Global finance series. Ashgate, Burlington.

Woolcock, S., 2010. *The Treaty of Lisbon and the European Union as an actor in international trade*, ECIPE Work. Pap. 1/2010.

Young, A., 2011. The rise (and fall?) of the EU's performance in the multilateral trading system. *J. Eur. Integr.* 33, 715–739.

Young, A., Peterson, J., 2014. *Parochial global Europe: 21st century trade policy*. Oxford University Press, Oxford.

Young, A., Peterson, J., 2006. The EU and the new trade politics. *J. Eur. Public Policy, Young* 13, 795–814.

5 The EU in investment-related negotiations during the Uruguay Round

The EU first acquired de facto competences to negotiate on international investment disciplines during pre- and core negotiations of the Uruguay Round of the GATT. The Member States decided to temporarily cooperate and to empower the Commission to speak on their behalf in investment-related negotiations. This chapter analyses and seeks to explain with reference to the analytical framework the initial decision of the Member States to cooperate and to empower the Commission as well as the EU's subsequent use of its new de facto competences in investment-related negotiations. The findings lend support to institutionalist and supranational thinking and challenge societal theories and liberal intergovernmentalism.

The USA pushed in the early 1980s for a new GATT round and the inclusion of investment-related negotiating items. The Commission – after an initial learning phase – became a policy entrepreneur calling on European business and the Member States to endorse the US proposal to negotiate on the so-called *new trade issues* including investment and services. In line with principal-agent research, the Commission used its agenda-setting powers in EU-internal debates, its credibility as technical expert and pointed to the evolving trade agenda requiring an adjustment of Member State cooperation. The Commission acted as policy entrepreneur at this stage mostly for functional considerations. It came to the conclusion that the multilateral liberalisation of investment and services complemented its Single Market programme, that such negotiations allowed for new trade-offs between Member State preferences and that the EU was competitive in these domains and thus stood to significantly benefit from a multilateral framework. European business was, however, little receptive to the Commission's campaigning. Most investors and service suppliers did not yet apprehend the meaning of multilateral investment and services negotiations, their potential effects on their operations and did not have the necessary lobbying structures to develop an informed position and to influence policymaking. Several Member States after initial reluctance started supporting the idea to negotiate and to cooperate on investment and services in the Uruguay Round due to Commission's pedagogical campaigning and despite a manifest lack of business demands. They came to the realisation that their economies would significantly benefit from a multilateral liberalisation of investment and services trade. The Member States consequently agreed to cooperate and to empower the Commission, so as to speak, with a single voice and to wield greater barraging power vis-à-vis more than 100 third countries participating in the Uruguay Round. As stipulated in historical institutionalist models on incremental institutional change, the Member States nonetheless also put on record that their decision to cooperate and delegate was of temporary nature and that they did not cede powers to the EU. The analysis of how the EU actually used its new de facto competences in investment-related negotiations in the TRIMs[1] and GATS[2] negotiating groups draws a similar picture. The Commission sought to proactively advance in particular the GATS negotiations supported by many Member States but hardly by business.

5.1 The way toward Punta del Este

5.1.1 The pre-negotiations on a new multilateral trade round

Discussions on a new multilateral trade round under the GATT started in the early 1980s. In June 1981, the so-called Consultative Group of Eighteen[3] first discussed how to strengthen and to extend the GATT regime to new issue areas beyond the traditional trade in goods. As these questions ultimately required political answers, the GATT Council decided to hold a ministerial meeting in November 1982 (Glick, 1984, pp. 151–152; Paemen and Bensch, 1995, p. 31). In November 1981, the GATT Secretariat circulated a draft ministerial declaration (GATT, 1981) in preparation of the upcoming ministerial meeting. The draft declaration proposed holding a new multilateral trade round, which should tackle leftover issues from the Tokyo Round (1973–1979) and extend the GATT regime to the regulation of international investment and trade in services (Croome, 1995, p. 12; Paemen and Bensch, 1995, pp. 31–32; Schott, 1994, pp. 4–5). Many developing and developed countries were, however, sceptical of these plans. When the ministers met in Geneva in November 1982, they agreed on a more cautious approach. They merely decided to engage in a two-year reflection period on the future of the GATT regime and, notably, its extension to 'new trade issues' like trade in services (European Commission, 1982; Paemen and Bensch, 1995, pp. 32–37; Schott, 1994, p. 5; Stewart, 1993, p. 2062).

Behind the scenes, the USA had been the initiator and driver of these debates. It wanted a new multilateral round in order to advance the liberalisation of agricultural trade, to cut industrial tariffs and to establish full-fledged multilateral frameworks for international investment flows and services trade under the GATT regime. The draft declaration of the GATT Secretariat was thus widely seen as a hidden attempt by the United States to set the GATT agenda (European Commission, 1982, p. 12; Paemen and Bensch, 1995, p. 33; Interview, Brussels, 24 September 2013). The outcome of the ministerial meeting of 1982 caused considerable frustration and disappointment in Washington (Glick, 1984, p. 161; Paemen and Bensch, 1995, p. 32). The USA emphasised its determination to launch a new round by resorting to a twofold strategy. First, it engaged in informative debates with third countries in order to highlight the potential benefits of a new round and an extension of the GATT regime to trade in services and investment regulation. Most governments had never examined the possibility of multilaterally liberalising services trade and investment. They did not know whether, and to what degree, such liberalisation efforts would benefit or harm their economies (Croome, 1995, pp. 20–27; Stewart, 1993, p. 2347). Second, the USA announced that if the GATT parties did not agree to hold a new extensive round, the USA would pursue its foreign economic policy objectives outside of the GATT regime. Non-cooperative countries would, therefore, get locked out of the policymaking process and the US economy in these booming domains of the world economy. To emphasise its threat, the USA presented its first model BIT in 1982 (Wayne, 1984). It also started negotiations on comprehensive FTAs covering, for the first time, services and investment disciplines with Israel and Canada (Auerbach, 1985) and announced the establishment of a comprehensive 'mini GATT' with interested parties if need be (Stewart, 1993, p. 2355; Tyler, 1985).

US pressure for a new comprehensive multilateral trade round succeeded in the end. By September 1985, the USA had built sufficient support among developed and developing countries to launch the formal preparations for a new multilateral trade round. Only a few developing countries like Brazil and India were still strongly opposed, but they could not stop the course of events (Croome, 1995, pp. 20–27; Stewart, 1993, pp. 2357–2358). In the following months, a preparatory committee was commissioned to determine the agenda of the upcoming round. This task proved to be challenging. The USA insisted on including services and investment on the agenda, while the Group of Ten – led by India and Brazil – argued that these issues did not fall within GATT competence. Debates on the guidelines for agriculture were, moreover, complicated due to the clashes between the EU and major agricultural producers (Stewart, 1993, p. 2356). The so-called Swiss-Colombian draft agenda, which foresaw negotiations on trade in services and 'trade-related investment measures', gained the greatest albeit not unanimous support in the preparatory committee. In the end, the preparatory committee failed to define a negotiating agenda (Croome, 1995, pp. 28–29).

The ministers reconvened in the Uruguayan city of Punta del Este in September 1986 in order to formally launch the new multilateral trade round. The first task of the ministers was to finally pin down the negotiating agenda of the new round. The USA continued its efforts to include services and investment on the negotiating agenda. In the weeks before the ministerial meeting, US diplomats spread the rumour that the USA would still walk away from the negotiating table in the event that services and investment were not part of the new round (Croome, 1995, p. 30). US President Ronald Reagan, moreover, sought to personally convince the leaders of several opposing countries in telephone calls and underlined in a radio address on the eve of the ministerial meeting that a new round had to liberalise trade in services and investment so as to take account of the changing realities of the modern economy (Paemen and Bensch, 1995, p. 51; Reagan, 1986). At the end of the ministerial meeting, a hard-fought compromise emerged. The compromise agenda provided for services negotiations, which, however, would take place as parallel, independent negotiations outside the GATT regime in order to prevent issue linkages. The agenda also foresaw negotiations on trade-related investment measures, which – as result of the opposition of developing countries – provided for much more limited negotiations than the USA had hoped. The USA had entered the debate with a maximalist position demanding the establishment of a full-fledged multilateral investment framework within the GATT (Croome, 1995, p. 138; Guisinger, 1987, pp. 222–223; Woolcock, 1990, p. 25). The reference to 'TRIMs' did not preserve much of this US objective. The ministers adopted the agenda in the form of a ministerial declaration on 20 September 1986. The core negotiations of the Uruguay Round started in early 1987.

5.1.2 The EU in the pre-negotiations

What role did the EU play in the pre-negotiations? The Commission was initially hesitant regarding the plan to hold a new multilateral trade round and to extend the GATT regime to services and investment (Interview, Brussels, 24 September 2013). As the Commission's lead negotiator recalled, the Commission at first perceived the proposal primarily as a US attempt to dismantle the Common Agricultural Policy (CAP), which would hardly entail adequate compensation in the form of enhanced industrial market access for European exporters. Many leading Commission officials – even within the DG for Trade – moreover struggled with the idea that the liberalisation of services trade and investment could qualify as trade policy and thus be dealt with within the GATT regime. The question reportedly triggered turf wars within the Commission. Some Commission officials also challenged the assumption that the international liberalisation of services trade and investment would be beneficial to the European economy. The Commission thus stressed on the eve of the ministerial meeting of 1982 that the meeting should not be misinterpreted as the prelude to a new round (Paemen and Bensch, 1995, pp. 32–34).

Toward the mid-1980s and after lengthy internal debates, the Commission nonetheless gradually bought into the US proposal. The Commission consequently started campaigning and using its agenda-setting powers but also invoked the changing economic realities and policy agenda at the domestic level and in international trade to convince the Member States and European business of the opportunities of a new comprehensive GATT round. The Commission's change in mind reflected three realisations and functional considerations. First, the Commission understood that a new trade round extending the GATT regime to investment and services would actually deliver significant economic gains for the EU (Interview, Brussels, 24 September 2013). In late 1982, Christopher Tugendhat, vice-president of the Commission, thus publically endorsed the British proposal for an international standstill clause for services trade, which implied a generally positive view on the liberalisation of international service trade (Agence Europe, 1983). In the following year, Leslie Fielding, Director General in charge of trade policy, lamented that the EU and the Member States did not know yet what they wanted regarding the liberalisation of services trade and investment despite the fact that Europe was the world market leader in these domains (Cheeseright, 1983). The link between the liberalisation of services trade and economic growth, he added, had not yet been universally accepted within Europe. He called upon the Member

States to finally step up their efforts to study these issues and to develop informed positions on these new key issues of national and international economic policy. He regretted that – with the exception of British business – European service providers were not organised and invested in these debates. The Commission therefore demanded European service providers to get involved and asked the Member States to finally prepare studies on the effects of international liberalisation on their service sectors (Cheeseright, 1985a). The Commission even started funding a research centre to further study these issues (Tyler, 1983).

The Commission's change in mind, secondly, reflected the insight that the proposed multilateral liberalisation of services trade and investment within the GATT complemented the Single Market programme put forward by the Commission. The Single Market programme focused on dismantling the remaining barriers to trade in goods, labour mobility, trade in services and investment activities within the EU. The overarching objective was to lift the European economy out of recession. The investiture of the Delors Commission in January 1985 and the publication of the white paper 'Completing the Single Market' in June 1985 illustrated this reorientation of the EU and its Member States from Keynesian policies toward liberal economic ones. The Commission declared in policy debates that the proposed multilateral liberalisation of services trade and investment to be in accordance with its domestic liberalisation agenda (Interview, Brussels, 24 September 2013; Interview, Oxford, 11 October 2013).

Finally, the Commission realised that the proposed comprehensive GATT agenda would facilitate its role as administrator of the CCP. The proposed extensive GATT agenda allowed for new trade-offs among the Member States in the Council of Ministers. It in particular promised to facilitate dealing with France. France had met the US proposal of a new round with considerable hesitation as it expected a new US attack on the CAP. France, however, was also a leading exporter of services and stood to significantly gain from a new comprehensive GATT round. The Commission thus started highlighting the economic opportunities of a new comprehensive round in particular vis-à-vis France and other sceptical Member States in EU-internal debates (Buchan, 1992; Paemen and Bensch, 1995, pp. 34–35; Stewart, 1993, p. 2350).

European business initially remained silent in debates on a new multilateral trade round and an extension of the GATT regime to services and investment (Tyler, 1983; Interview, Brussels, 24 September 2013; Interview, Oxford, 11 October 2013; Interview, telephone, 17 June 2013; Interview Brussels, 25 September 2013b). British service providers marked a notable exception. The Liberalisation of Trade in Services (LOTIS) Committee brought together banks, law firms, and accounting and insurance companies from the City. The LOTIS Committee welcomed the plan to hold a new round and to extend the GATT regime to trade in services and investment regulation. Similar cross-sectorial associations of service providers did not exist in other Member States or at the European level. Architects, lawyers, management consultants or hoteliers did not apprehend themselves as 'service providers' with common interests and thus took little interest in debates on the creation of the GATT framework for the liberalisation of services trade

(Agence Europe, 1983; Tyler, 1983; Interview, Brussels, 25 September 2013b). The LOTIS Committee, in cooperation with its US-American counterpart – the International Committee on Trade in Services – sought to raise awareness and to mobilise service providers from other Member States like Germany; this, however, was of little success (Tyler, 1983). Over the next years, similar attempts of the Commission also failed and caused considerable frustration in Brussels. The LOTIS Committee remained the only proactive business voice during the pre-negotiations on an extension of the GATT agenda to services trade and investment (Dullforce, 1986).

Most Member State governments met the US demand for a new comprehensive multilateral trade round with considerable mistrust at first. Like initially the Commission, they perceived the US proposal as another 'attack' on the EU's CAP (Paemen and Bensch, 1995, p. 32). The plan to extend the GATT regime to trade in services and investment was, at first, a secondary issue for most Member States, and did not receive a lot of attention (Interview, Oxford, 11 October 2013). Many European policymakers initially took the view that the GATT parties should first fully implement their commitments of the Tokyo Round before aiming for a new round (Woolcock, 1990, p. 4). France and Italy were the most vocal exponents of this view, while Germany and the Netherlands adopted more welcoming positions and rhetoric (Farnsworth, 1982; Paemen and Bensch, 1995, p. 34; Interview, Brussels, 24 September 2013). The subsequent nomination of Clayton Yeutter – a renowned expert of agricultural economics – as new US Trade Representative (USTR) amplified hesitation in many Member State capitals. As a high-ranking Commission official recalled, Yeutter made it clear that he saw it as a matter of personal honour to reverse the agricultural concessions made to the EU by the USA in previous rounds (Interview, Brussels, 24 September 2013). A notable exception was the British government in this context. The British government was barely preoccupied with the implications of a new round for British farmers, but primarily focused on the potential gains for its growing service sector. During the ministerial meeting of 1982, Peter Rees, the British Minister for Trade, thus proposed to his colleagues to agree on a standstill clause to prevent the erection of new barriers to services trade and, moreover, supported the idea of holding a new round in order to discuss the creation of a framework for the LOTIS within the GATT regime (Financial Times, 1982).

Toward the mid-1980s, several Member States started tentatively reconsidering their stances on the US plan to launch a new round and to extend the GATT regime to services trade and investment. This change in mind at least partly reflected the Commission's campaigning but not lobbying of European business. Many Member States slowly realised that a reform of the CAP was inevitable regardless of a new multilateral trade round. In 1985, the OECD released a report which qualified the CAP as unsustainable and wasteful. The potential costs of a new round in the form of agricultural concessions were thus limited (Paemen and Bensch, 1995, pp. 34–35). Second, the German, French and other Member State governments underwent a learning process after the ministerial meeting of 1982. On insistence of the Commission – acting as a proactive policy entrepreneur – the Member States studied their services sectors, external trade balances for services and likely effects of a multilateral liberalisation in these domains for the first time. They gradually understood that the liberalisation of services trade and investment indeed promised considerable benefits (Paemen and Bensch, 1995, pp. 34–35). As the Commissioner for Trade, Willy De Clercq emphasised vis-à-vis the Member States, the EU was actually the "*superpower in trade in services, with exports three times higher than those of the US*" (Dullforce, 1986). Finally, many Member States agreed with the Commission that the proposed multilateral liberalisation of services trade and investment was complementary to the EU's new liberal economic orientation enshrined in the Single Market programme.

By late 1985, international support for a new round had grown to such an extent that the GATT Council formally launched preparations and commissioned the preparatory committee to define the negotiating agenda of the upcoming round. In the following months, the Commission vigorously supported the plan for a new round and the extension of the GATT regime. It continued highlighting that a liberalisation of services would be beneficial for Europe and had to go hand in hand with the creation of a multilateral framework for investment (Dullforce, 1986). In June 1986, the Commission submitted to the Council of Ministers the so-called overall approach outlining the EU's position for the upcoming round. The 'overall approach', inter alia, indicated that the EU sought negotiations on services trade and investment disciplines. The Member States generally agreed to this objective and did not raise competence concerns. Only Greece and Italy criticised that the EU should not aim for an across-the-board liberalisation of services trade (Paemen and Bensch, 1995, pp. 43–48; Peel, 1986). The Council endorsed the 'overall approach', which did not, however, represent a legally binding negotiating mandate for the Commission. But despite the EU's documented interest in negotiating on services trade and investment, the EU did not push for these issues during negotiations on the agenda of the upcoming round. During debates in the preparatory committee and at the ministerial meeting of Punta del Este, the EU primarily focused on defending its agricultural interests against developing countries. The EU left it to the USA to battle for the inclusion of services trade and investment, as the EU arguably did not want to fight developing countries in yet another domain (Paemen and Bensch, 1995, p. 49). Even without the active support of the EU, the USA managed to strike a deal with the developing countries at the ministerial meeting in Punta del Este, which paved the way toward negotiations on trade in services and investment in the upcoming round.

5.2.3 The Commission's non-mandate of Punta del Este

The ministers of the GATT parties adopted the negotiating agenda and formally launched the Uruguay Round on 20 September 1986 – the last day of the ministerial meeting of Punta del Este. Until this day, the Commission and the Member State had managed to sidestep formal discussions on competence questions. The Council of Ministers had not yet adopted any legal measures in these domains, which would have triggered debates about the appropriate competence basis and distribution of competences between the EU and the Member States. And as customary in GATT debates, the Member States had tacitly agreed that the Commission should speak on their behalf in the run-up to the Uruguay Round even on issues like services trade and investment. The pending opening of the Uruguay Round put an end to this pragmatic approach. The Council of Ministers, on the one hand, had to formally endorse the draft ministerial declaration of Punta del Este and the therein-enshrined negotiating agenda so as to establish the EU's assent to opening the Uruguay Round. On the other hand, the Council of Ministers had to issue a negotiating mandate in order to legally empower the EU and Commission to participate in the Uruguay Round. In other words, the Member States had to take an explicit decision on whether and how to cooperate on investment disciplines in the context of the Uruguay Round.

The Commission invited the Council of Ministers to convene on the fringes of the ministerial meeting in the early hours of 20 September 1986 in order to establish the EU's assent to the draft ministerial declaration and to adopt the legal negotiating mandate for the Commission. The Commission and the British Presidency of the Council of Ministers energetically pleaded for the endorsement of the draft ministerial declaration and the opening of a comprehensive and ambitious multilateral trade round (Paemen and Bensch, 1995, p. 56). The British minister chairing the meeting was very much inspired by the proactivity and vigour of the US delegation during the weeklong ministerial meeting and sought to emulate this atmosphere within the Council of Ministers (Paemen and Bensch, 1995, p. 56). But while all Member States endorsed the draft ministerial declaration, it became evident that many Member States were not yet fully convinced by the economic opportunities of the new round (Interview, Brussels, 24 September 2013).

The then following discussions among the ministers on the negotiating mandate drew an interesting picture. In essence, it shows that the Commission and the Member States agreed that as customary the Commission should speak on the EU's behalf on all GATT agenda items, including this time services trade and investment. Senior Member State and Commission officials recalled that the representation modalities were never the subject of serious discussions among the minister or in the '113 Committee' (Interview, telephone, 17 June 2013; Interview, Oxford, 11 October 2013; Interview, Brussels, 24 September 2013). This tacit agreement, on the one hand, reflected the long-established division of labour among the Member States and the Commission under the CCP. In the absence of a veritable bilateral trade strategy, the CCP and the DG were practically the EU's mouthpiece for GATT negotiations. Member State and Commission officials met in small circles once or twice per month over years to determine the EU's positions within the GATT and came to trust and respect each other. Nobody, therefore, seriously challenged the Commission's traditional role and claim to be the EU's single voice on all items of the evolving trade agenda in this key policy forum. The expanding trade agenda functioned as an external constraint promoting Member State cooperation and delegation of powers for '*new trade issues*'. On the other hand, the ministers seemed to agree that the Commission should act as their single voice in order to wield greater bargaining power. The Member States perceived cooperation and delegation as capability-maximising strategy (Interview, telephone, 17 June 2013; Interview, Oxford, 11 October 2013; Interview, Brussels, 24 September 2013). Only the French delegation occasionally 'grumbled' about the Commission intruding into domains of Member State competence. A high-ranking Commission official commented in that regard: *"If the Member States believe that it is in their interest to negotiate through the Commission, competence issues never play a role. Competence questions only surface, if somebody wants to block things"*. (Interview, Brussels, 24 September 2013). But while the ministers agreed on cooperating and empowering the Commission to negotiate, inter alia, on services trade and investment disciplines on their behalf, they also feared that this pragmatic decision might compromise their legal competences in the long run. The ministers thus put on record the following formal statement in Punta del Este:

The Council, acting on a recommendation from the Commission, approved the Punta Del Este Declaration annexed to these minutes and authorised the Commission to open the negotiations provided for in that declaration within the framework of the directives which the Council will issue to it. The Representatives of the Governments of the Member States also approved that Declaration to the extent that they are concerned. The decision does not prejudge the question of the competence of the Community or the Member States on particular issues.

(as cited in Paemen and Bensch, 1995, p. 56)

The ministers apparently held the view that the '*new trade issues*' – with the notable exception of TRIMs – came under Member State competence and anticipated a future competence dispute with the Commission. They manifestly worried that the Commission could exploit the mandate in order to later claim legal competences over these issues. These concerns were justified, as Opinion 1/94 (discussed in Chapter 9) demonstrated. At the end of the Uruguay Round in 1994, the Commission endorsed a teleological interpretation of the Treaty articles on the CCP and indeed argued that all so-called *new trade issues* would come under exclusive Union competence. At the end of the meeting in Punta del Este in September 1986, the ministers announced they would be issuing negotiating directive empowering and guiding the Commission in negotiations on all issue areas of the Uruguay Round in due course. While it did not affect the Commission in its function as negotiator, it needs to be mentioned here that the Council of Ministers never issued these negotiating directives. The Council of Ministers only provided the Commission with directives for agricultural negotiations. Regarding all other issues, the Commission represented the EU and the Member States on the basis of the overall approach of 1986 and continuous coordination meetings with the Council of Ministers and the '113 Committee' (Interview, Brussels, 24 September 2013).

To sum up, the pre-negotiations draw an interesting picture of the EU's first steps in the international investment regime. The USA pushed for a new GATT round and for an extensive negotiating agenda comprising investment disciplines. The analysis showed that the Commission – after initial hesitation – became for functional considerations a proponent of the US proposal to hold a new GATT round encompassing negotiations on the multilateral liberalisation of services trade and investment. It consequently started acting as policy entrepreneur, sought to raise awareness and to inform the Member States and European business about the economic opportunities of a new comprehensive GATT round. But whereas a critical mass of Member States showed receptive to the Commission's campaigning, European business remained by and large passive and uninterested in these debates. The Member States and the Commission finally agreed in Punta del Este that the Commission should act as the EU's single voice – including on investment – as customary in the GATT. The Member States generally endorsed the rationale for a new round and far-reaching delegation, but they also remained cautious and underlined that they held the legal competences over these new trade issues.

These observations lend support to supranational thinking on European Integration. In accordance with principal-agent research, the Commission drew on its agenda-setting powers and invoked the evolving international trade agenda to convince the Member States of the need to cooperate and to delegate international investment policymaking to the EU level in this instance. The Commission as an agent thereby gradually reconfigured the preferences and perceptions of its principals. The Member States nonetheless immediately realised in line with historical institutionalism, that their decision to temporarily cooperate and delegate policymaking to the Commission might set legal precedence and trigger institutional change, and, therefore, put on record their continuous claim to competence. The observations go against societal theories of foreign economic policymaking and liberal intergovernmental thinking on European Integration. European business was little interested in discussions on extending the GATT regime inter alia to investment regulation. The growing support among the Member States reflected Commission activism but not business preferences and lobbying. The following sections examine how the EU used its new de facto competences in the TRIMs and GATS negotiations and evaluate how these observations reflect assumptions formulated in the analytical framework.

5.2 The TRIMs negotiations

5.2.1 *A brief negotiating history*

A senior GATT official once commented, "*The TRIMs negotiations were to be among the most frustrating and least productive of the Uruguay Round*" (Croome, 1995, p. 138). Several factors explain this observation. The TRIMs negotiations were a domain of stark confrontation between the USA, Japan and major developing countries. The USA and Japan advanced a maximalist position in the TRIMs negotiations. The USA adopted an extensive definition of TRIMs[4] and sought to establish a multilateral framework agreement prohibiting the use of these measures against foreign investors (GATT, 1987a, 1987b). Most developing countries – and notably India and Brazil – categorically rejected the plan to establish a framework agreement regulating the use of TRIMs in the first place. They were unwilling to accept any limitation of their sovereignty in this domain. They underlined that TRIMs were essential instruments of their development policies. They stressed that the vague negotiating agenda of the Uruguay Round merely provided for an examination of 'the applicability of GATT articles to trade-distorting effects of TRIMs'. The agenda did not allow for negotiations on a new framework agreement limiting, or even prohibiting, the use of TRIMs (Croome, 1995, pp. 138–142; GATT, 1987c, 1987d). The EU held an intermediate position. As explained in more detail in the following subsection, the EU adopted a more limited definition of TRIMs than the USA and pleaded for the creation of a framework agreement, which would circumscribe and only prohibit the use of certain TRIMs (GATT, 1987e, 1988, 1989a). The starkly contrasting positions between developed and developing countries made the negotiations in the TRIMs Negotiating Group a tedious enterprise. The situation was further exacerbated by the unwillingness of the key actors to invest political capital into advancing the TRIMs negotiations. All countries – even the USA which had initially spared no efforts to include investment into the negotiating agenda of the Uruguay Round – considered TRIMs to be a secondary issue within the overall negotiating process of the Uruguay Round (Croome, 1995, p. 138).

The TRIMs negotiations produced no results in the first two years of the Uruguay Round. The USA and major developing countries fought over the interpretation of the negotiating agenda and the definition of TRIMs without any signs of a convergence of minds. When the ministers reconvened for the midterm review in Montreal in December 1988, the ministers did not even discuss TRIMs as no controversial issue had reached the decision-making stage yet (Croome, 1995, pp. 141–142). After the midterm review, the TRIMs Negotiating Group sought to overcome the deadlock. It limited its discussion on studying the trade-distorting effects of certain TRIMs (GATT, 1989b). Progress seemed possible at first; notably, when the USA moved away from its maximalist position and endorsed a narrower definition of the term TRIMs (GATT, 1989c). In the run-up to the ministerial meeting in Brussels in December 1990, which was intended to close the Uruguay Round, it became clear, however, that all countries were sticking to their entrenched positions. The USA, the chairman of the TRIMs group Kobayashi and the lead negotiator of Hong Kong successively tabled draft texts of a TRIMs Agreement, which helped to identify the key controversies but failed to gain broad support (Croome, 1995, pp. 259–261; Stewart, 1993, p. 2123). As a high-ranking GATT official recalled *"no negotiating text went to Brussels in worse shape than the one on TRIMs"* (Croome, 1995, p. 261). The ministers would finally try to resolve the controversies over TRIMs in a Green Room session during the ministerial meeting of Brussels. The ministerial meeting, however, ran into complete stalemate over agriculture one day before the scheduled Green Room session on TRIMs (Croome, 1995, p. 284). The Uruguay Round negotiations only restarted in February 1991. The negotiations on TRIMs slowly struck new paths as the USA and developing countries gradually revised their preferences on TRIMs. US policymakers grew concerned with a hike in Japanese FDI in the USA and started pondering about the benefits of TRIMs, while many developing countries adopted more liberal policies toward FDI (Croome, 1995, p. 308). In autumn 1991, George Maciel, the new chairman overseeing the TRIMs negotiations, started bilaterally and informally consulting with countries over a new draft text for a TRIMs Agreement. In December 1991, Maciel released his non-negotiated draft text and sent it to lead negotiators of the Uruguay Round in the trade negotiating committee (TNC). The TNC did not challenge Maciel's draft text, which ultimately became part of the WTO Agreement in April 1994. The final text of the TRIMs Agreement is of rather humble nature. It prohibits TRIMs which are incompatible with GATT articles III (NT) and XI (prohibition of quantitative restrictions), such as investment incentives or trade performance requirements (Croome, 1995, pp. 284–286, 309).

5.2.2 The EU in the TRIMs negotiations

What role did the EU play in the TRIMs negotiations? The EU did not proactively use its new de facto competences in international investment policy in the TRIMs Negotiating Group. And although the EU spoke through the Commission with a single voice, the EU remained a marginal and reactive party in this negotiating forum. As explained earlier, the key bargains took place between the USA and Japan, on the one hand, and major developing countries on the other. The EU did not belong to these camps and did not attempt to play a moderating role. The EU's submissions to the TRIMs Negotiating Group confirm this view. While the USA tabled a draft working agenda, followed by nine position papers and a draft text for a TRIMs Agreement, the EU tabled merely three position papers in the course of the TRIMs negotiations.[5] The EU's submissions did not develop a new, distinctly European approach to the regulation of TRIMs or add decisive ideas and issues to the discussions. The EU's position papers mostly clarified the EU's position in relation to the language and substance of US position papers. Regarding substance, the EU adopted an intermediate position between the USA, Japan and major developing countries. It stressed that only some of the TRIMs, which the USA sought to outlaw within the GATT regime, had a direct and significant effect on trade flows and could therefore be tackled under a TRIMs Agreement (GATT, 1987e, 1988, 1989a). The EU referred to the so-called 'Foreign Investment Review Act' Case[6] in order to evaluate the relevance of existing GATT rules for the regulation of TRIMs and the potential need for new GATT norms in this domain (GATT, 1987e). Neither the USA and Japan, nor major developing countries, showed support or interest in the EU's position.

The Commission did not attach great importance to the TRIMs negotiations. Senior Commission officials recalled that the TRIMs negotiations were only discussed in passing within the Commission. It was a clearly an issue of secondary importance in Commission-internal deliberations (Interview, Brussels, 5 October 2011). A high-ranking Member State official confirmed this and lamented that the Member States occasionally had to figuratively '*drag the Commission to the negotiating table*' in this field (Interview, telephone, 17 June 2013). The Commission's lack of interest in the TRIMs negotiations reflected two considerations. On the one hand, the Commission took the view that the TRIMs negotiations were mostly about the interpretation, application and elaboration of existing GATT articles in regard to TRIMs. The TRIMs Negotiating Group would not work towards a comprehensive multilateral investment framework. Hence, the TRIMs negotiations did not offer the Commission the opportunity to prove itself as international negotiator or the opportunity to shape the global political economy. As will become clear next, moreover, the Commission did not get pressure from the Member States or European business to push for specific TRIMs disciplines. This combination translated into the Commission dealing with the TRIMs negotiations as a mandatory exercise rather than economic and political opportunity (Interview, Brussels, 24 September 2013).

Business also showed little interest in the TRIMs negotiations. This observation holds true for European as well as national business federations. The European umbrella federation UNICE, the Confederation of British Industries, the German Federation of Industries or the German Chamber of Industry and Commerce and others occasionally encouraged negotiations on TRIMs, but according to all accounts did not engage in meaningful lobbying in order shape the negotiations (Agence Europe, 1992; Montagnon, 1988; Thomson, 1990; Interview, telephone, 17 June 2013). How can one explain that European business representatives by and large disregarded these negotiations while US business reportedly pushed for ambitious TRIMs disciplines? First, many European investors had arguably already put up with TRIMs and the related costs in developing countries, because they had been active in many developing countries since colonial times. US investors, on the other hand, had been less active in most developing countries in the past and perceived TRIMs as significant market entry barrier. This dynamic may explain that – despite the USA being generally a laggard in the conclusion of BITs in the 1980s – it was the first country to include clauses prohibiting the use of performance requirements into BITs (Dolzer and Schreuer, 2012, pp. 91–92; Nikièma, 2014; Salacuse, 2010, pp. 329–333). Second, those European companies which nonetheless showed some interest in the TRIMs negotiations, cautioned that the EU should not push for overly ambitious TRIMs disciplines in the GATT so as not to antagonise developing countries. A TRIMs Agreement would only make sense if developing countries would agree to sign up to such an agreement (Woolcock, 1990, pp. 25–26). Finally, and in line with the aforementioned, many European investors felt that the TRIMs negotiations tackled irrelevant investment barriers. The position of the European Chemical Industries Federation (CEFIC) – a very investment-intensive sector – illustrates this view. CEFIC stressed that European chemical companies were interested in the creation of a multilateral investment framework under the auspices of the GATT. CEFIC and its national members strongly lobbied the Member States and the European Institutions to this end. CEFIC clarified, however, that European chemical companies mainly sought enhanced market access for investments and a better protection of their patents abroad. Both issues were not discussed in the TRIMs Negotiating Group, which therefore received little attention from European chemical producers (Montagnon, 1989).

The Member States, on the one hand considered the TRIMs negotiations as an issue of secondary importance in the big scheme of things. The TRIMs negotiations were unlikely to generate important benefits for the European economy and business. Unlike the USA, several Member States had already started establishing sizeable BIT networks with third countries, which limited the applicability of certain TRIMs to their investors. The Member States concentrated their attention and political capital on the economically more potent negotiations on agriculture, non-agricultural market access and services (Interview, Brussels, 5 October 2011; Interview, telephone, 17 June 2013). On the other hand, the Member States had difficulties agreeing on a clear-cut position and strategy for the TRIMs negotiations. The lead negotiator of the Commission observed that the EU constantly sat on the fence in the TRIMs negotiations (Paemen and Bensch, 1995, pp. 86–87). The divisions among the Member States mirrored in many respects the divisions at the international level in the TRIMs Negotiating Group. All Member States used TRIMs to regulate inward FDI, but certain Member States imposed TRIMs much more frequently on foreign investors than other Member States. The United Kingdom, the Netherlands and Germany for instance used TRIMs only in a few circumstances. France, on the other hand, drew heavily and frequently on TRIMs. France considered TRIMs an indispensable instrument for its industrial policy and its national economic development strategy. So while liberal Member States were ready to limit the use of TRIMs within the GATT regime so as to facilitate the operations of their multinational companies abroad, protectionist Member States were sceptical (Paemen and Bensch, 1995, pp. 86–87; Interview, telephone, 17 June 2013; Interview, Brussels, 24 September 2013). In 1988, this divide between the Member States came forcefully to the fore. France restricted the import of Nissan cars produced in a plant in the United Kingdom. It argued that the cars produced in the British Nissan plant did not attain a local content threshold of 80% so as to qualify as European produce. Hence, they had to be considered as Japanese imports and counted against France's unilaterally imposed import quota for Japanese cars. So far, the French import quota had gone unchallenged within the EU and the GATT, but the Commission and the British government now announced that they would challenge the French measure. Italy expressed its sympathy for the French position (Buchan, 1989; Montagnon, 1988; Montagnon and Dullforce, 1988). The Nissan dispute raised question marks about the legality of TRIMs in the context of the Single Market. As the Member States and the Commission got into internal quarrels about the legality of certain TRIMs, the EU could not play a leading role in international negotiations. The Nissan dispute, moreover, complicated negotiations in the TRIMs Negotiating Group, as it signalled to developing countries that not even the developed countries could agree on a common position.

The EU was generally rather disengaged in the TRIMs negotiations. The European Commission, the Member States and European businesses took little interest in the TRIMs negotiations. The observations thus neither confirm the assumed role of the European Commission as policy entrepreneur nor of European business as powerful advocates of European Integration. They highlight, however, the importance of institutionalist dynamics in European cooperation and policymaking. The Member States cooperated and delegated investment policymaking to the EU level due to the evolving negotiating agenda within the GATT regime.

5.3 The GATS negotiations

In the beginning, the TRIMs negotiations were the focus of investment-related negotiations in the Uruguay Round. As the Round progressed, it became clear that the GATS negotiations would build on an extensive definition of services trade encompassing service-related investments. The GATS negotiations thus evolved into talks on the liberalisation of service-related investments and the creation of post-establishment treatment standards. The GATS negotiations turned into the epicentre of investment-related negotiations in the Uruguay Round and marginalised the TRIMs negotiations.

5.3.1 A brief negotiating history

The negotiations on services trade were highly complex and controversial. As explained earlier, the USA had fought hard with developing countries to set services trade on the negotiating agenda of the Uruguay Round. In the end, the developing countries accepted negotiations on services trade, but their hesitation translated into a vague and contradictory negotiating mandate for the Group on Negotiations on Trade in Services (GNS). The negotiating agenda of the Uruguay Round stipulated that the GNS should, on the one hand, establish a framework for the liberalisation of services trade and, on the other hand, preserve the policy space of governments to regulate – and de facto to protect – their national services sectors (Stewart, 1993, p. 2359). The GNS was, therefore, set for onerous negotiations. In order to facilitate the negotiations, they proceeded in a two-step approach. Until the midterm review, the GNS should examine definitions, volume and geography of services trade and should eventually draft a framework agreement. After the midterm review, the GNS should then start negotiations on liberalisation commitments.

The initial stocktaking phase was meant to ease tensions among the parties by disseminating knowledge about services trade. It evolved, however, into a confrontational exercise. Discussions started out with an argument between the USA, the EU and developing countries over the representativeness of the examined data on the volume and geography of services trade. Several developing countries suspected that behind this data lay a hidden attempt by developed countries to reduce the developing countries' bargaining power in subsequent negotiations on liberalisation commitments (Stewart, 1993, pp. 2362–2363). Moreover, the parties could not agree whether the definition of services trade should encompass service-related investments and the movement of natural persons. The USA had initially proposed a narrow definition, which only encompassed cross-border supply and consumption abroad (GATS mode I & II). The USA had feared that a broad definition including service-related investments would antagonise developing countries too much. Developing countries, however, rejected this narrow definition. They stressed that the definition had to encompass the movement of natural persons (GATS mode IV) in order to allow the competitive advantages of developing countries to play out (Hindley, 1990, p. 14; Stewart, 1993, pp. 2362–2363). Thereupon, the USA and the EU underlined their demand to include the establishment of commercial presences (GATS mode III) – i.e. service-related investments into the definition of services trade (Sidhu, 2004, p. 188). The USA, the EU and other developed countries repeatedly pushed for ending this stocktaking phase and to start with veritable negotiations on a framework agreement and liberalisation commitments. Developing countries, however, resisted these demands (Croome, 1995, pp. 127–128).

The first two years of negotiations produced no results. Only the midterm review during the ministerial meeting in Montreal delivered progress. The ministers decided that the term services trade should encompass cross-border supply, consumption abroad, movement of natural persons and the establishment of commercial presences (Stewart, 1993, p. 2369). The GATS negotiations thereby became multilateral investment negotiations. The adoption of this broad definition of services trade had reportedly become possible, as major developing countries like India and Brazil had slowly warmed to the idea of a comprehensive multilateral services agreement (Croome, 1995, p. 242). In the following two years, the USA and a group of developing countries tabled and discussed several draft texts for a future GATS, while the EU gave detailed comments (GATT, 1989d, 1989e, 1989f, 1989g, 1990). The discussions in the GNS, inter alia, focused on four questions.

- First, how could one apply GATT principles like MFN or NT to trade in services? It was unclear at that point whether and how existing GATT principles could be applied to services trade. The GNS carried out several sectorial tests to determine the likely impact of applying these principles to services trade (Stewart, 1993, pp. 2372–2373, 2376–2378).
- Second, should a framework agreement cover all or only selected service sectors? The EU and many other countries were pleading for a framework agreement applying to all sectors in order to facilitate an equitable liberalisation of services trade. The EU argued that if need be, the parties could add sector-specific protocols to complement general rules. The USA rejected the EU's position and pleaded for a framework agreement applying to a limited number of service sectors. The USA added that sensitive sectors like financial services required sector-specific rules and discussions (Croome, 1995, pp. 250–251; Interview, Oxford, 11 October 2013; Interview, Brussels, 24 September 2013).
- Third, should the MFN principle apply unconditionally or conditionally? The USA stressed the need for a conditional MFN clause in order to promote the liberalisation of services trade. The USA explained that an unconditional MFN clause would provide protectionist countries with full access to liberal services markets like the USA, while US service providers would gain no additional market access to generally closed markets. The EU, and almost all other parties, harshly criticised the US position. They argued that the reasoning of the USA ran counter to the very purpose of the MFN principle and was incompatible with general GATT rules (Croome, 1995, pp. 250, 282; Stewart, 1993, pp. 2378–2379, 2393–2394).

- Finally, should investment liberalisation proceed on the basis of a positive or negative list? And relatedly, should liberalisation commitments take force immediately or be the result of ongoing negotiations? The USA and the EU pleaded for liberalisation on the basis of negative lists. Developing countries opposed this proposal. They argued that negative lists would result in a too speedy and comprehensive liberalisation of service sectors. The USA, moreover, demanded an immediate liberalisation, whereas the EU and developing countries initially favoured a progressive liberalisation. In the end, the parties agreed to undertake some immediate liberalisations as well as to continue negotiations on the basis of positive lists (Croome, 1995, pp. 245–246; Stewart, 1993, pp. 2371–2372, 2397–2399). As the Brussels ministerial meeting approached, the GNS drew up a draft text of the GATS in mid-1990, which consolidated the state of negotiations and was rife with brackets (Stewart, 1993, pp. 2394–2395).

The ministers convened in December 1990 in Brussels with the formal – while unrealistic – objective of concluding the Uruguay Round. The key priority of the ministers regarding the GATS negotiations was to finalise the framework agreement. The objective slowly shifted beyond reach, as the USA voiced ever more radical demands in the days prior to the ministerial meeting. The USA now demanded to exclude entire service sectors from the negotiations and emphasised that it would only accept a conditional MFN clause (Dullforce, 1990). The USA thereby transformed from being the engine driver to being the brakeman of the GATS negotiations. The shift in US attitude de facto put the EU, as second economic heavyweight and major liberal actor, into the driver's seat of the GATS negotiations (Croome, 1995, pp. 250–251). The following ministerial negotiations could not resolve the many disagreements on the GATS, but ran anyway into complete deadlock over agriculture. The GNS reconvened in June 1991 and subsequently focused on three issue areas. The negotiators sought to finalise the framework agreement. The task was difficult taking into consideration that the central questions of the scope of the framework agreement and the MFN controversy could only be resolved in the light of countries' final liberalisation efforts (Croome, 1995, pp. 312–314). The negotiators, moreover, started talks on sector-specific annexes notably for telecommunications, maritime transport and financial services (Croome, 1995, pp. 314–316). The negotiators finally started with discussions on liberalisation commitments. The scheduling exercise was challenging, as the negotiators at first did not know how to identify and measure barriers or how to codify commitments (Croome, 1995, pp. 316–318). As the extended deadline of December 1991 for the conclusion of the Uruguay Round approached, the chair of the GNS drew up a draft framework agreement based on his personal judgement. The draft foresaw universal coverage of the framework agreements, but allowed countries to file temporary MFN exceptions for certain sectors (Croome, 1995, pp. 317–318; Stewart, 1993, pp. 2394–2395). The TNC – the highest negotiating organ of the Uruguay Round under the ministerial level – accepted the draft, which became part of the final WTO Agreement. The as yet incomplete liberalisation schedules for services trade and in particular frictions over agriculture, however, prevented the end of the Uruguay Round. The Uruguay Round continued for another two years. The negotiations on services trade mostly focused on finalising the liberalisation schedules for particularly sensitive sectors like financial services, maritime transport or cultural and audiovisual services. The USA and the EU stood at the very centre of this nerve-wrecking bargaining exercise (Croome, 1995, pp. 332–333, 355–358; Paemen and Bensch, 1995, pp. 233–235). On 15 December 1993, the negotiating parties were finally ready to sign the WTO Agreement. The final text of the GATS covers all services sectors, provides for general MFN treatment and contains several sector-specific annexes. The GATS decisively liberalised service-related investment flows and until today constitutes the most important multilateral investment agreement.

5.3.2 The EU in the GATS negotiations

What role did the EU play in the GATS negotiations? It shone through in the preceding subsection that in comparison to the TRIMs negotiations, the EU proactively used its new de facto competences in international investment policy in the GNS. The EU spoke through the Commission with a single voice and became a central negotiating party in the GNS. The EU's important role in the GNS manifested itself in several ways. First, the EU acted as driver and broker in the GNS negotiations. While the EU was clearly part of the liberal camp, it successfully managed to maintain the dialogue with the opposing camp of developing countries (Paemen and Bensch, 1995, p. 132). As discussed earlier, the EU supported the developing countries, for instance, in rejecting the US demand for a conditional MFN clause. The EU also pushed for a framework agreement covering all service sectors in order to enable the adoption of an equitable package of liberalisation commitments. Second, the EU gradually became nonetheless the leader of the liberal camp in the GNS talks. The EU pushed for a comprehensive liberalisation of service trade including service-related investments on the basis of a negative list. The EU – together with the USA – thereby spearheaded the liberal camp in the GNS negotiations. When the USA gradually adopted a more protectionist position in the GNS negotiations after 1990, the role of leader of the liberal camp quite naturally fell to the EU (Croome, 1995, p. 163). Finally, the EU played a decisive role in the GNS negotiations, because it possessed badly needed expertise for the highly technical negotiations in the GNS. Due to the EU's ongoing internal liberalisation of services and capital flows in the context of the Single Market programme, the Commission and the Member States had acquired expertise which most other countries lacked. In summary, it seems fair to say that the EU proved itself for the first time in its history as a serious actor in investment regulation in the context of the GNS talks.

Commission preferences and behaviour had a decisive influence on the EU's proactive use of its de facto competences and central role in the GNS talks. As explained in the section on the pre-negotiations, the Commission had turned into an outspoken supporter of multilateral negotiations on services trade within the EU in the mid-1980s. From the Commission's point of view, the negotiations promised to deliver significant welfare gains for the European economy and offered the rare opportunity to design a new central building block of the future global political economy. The Commission thus attached great importance to the GNS negotiations and promoted them in EU-internal debates (Interview, Brussels, 24 September 2013; Interview, Brussels, 5 October 2011). The Commission's policy entrepreneurship for a proactive and ambitious use of the EU's de facto competences came to the fore in several ways.

The Commission drew on its agenda-setting powers and expertise to mobilise and maintain support for the GNS talks and to consolidate the EU's role in services and investment regulation. The Commission, for instance, conducted inter-service consultations so as to elaborate an informed position and strategy papers and to guide the initial debates in the Council of Ministers (Interview, Oxford, 11 October 2013). The Commission also strongly propelled the Member States to conduct similar inter-service consultations and to share their results in Council meetings. These inter-service consultations brought together officials from diverse ministries with different outlooks and preferences, which made them a challenging, while very productive, exercise. The Member States developed increasingly informed positions (Interview, Oxford, 11 October 2013). The Commission also called upon the Council of Ministers to establish a new '113 Subcommittee' on trade in services so as to finally create a permanent forum for expert discussion and build up an institutional memory. The debates in the new sub-committee were complex and the Commission had the influential yet challenging task of reconciling the many Member State demands with those from third countries in the GNS. The Commission's lead negotiator on services commented that his work sometimes felt like '*herding cats*' (Interview, Oxford, 11 October 2013). At the same time, the Commission continued calling on European business to get more engaged in these debates. As discussed in detail next, European business showed little responsiveness to these invitations (Interview, Oxford, 11 October 2013).

The Commission, moreover, used the progressing EU-internal liberalisation of services trade in order to consolidate the EU's role in international services and investment regulation. The finalisation of the Single Market – inter alia for intra-EU service trade and related investments – clearly shaped and facilitated the EU's central role in the GNS talks. While many GNS parties struggled, for instance, with a broad definition of the services trade encompassing service-related investments and movements of persons, the Commission could easily convince the Member States of this broad approach by pointing to EU-internal legislation and the Single Market programme, which built on a similarly broad definition of cross-border service provision. Hence, the broad definition of services – encompassing cross-border investment – showed uncontroversial within the EU, which enabled the Commission to push in the name of the EU for a multilateral service framework encompassing service-related investments (Interview, Oxford, 11 October 2013). What is more, the Single Market programme supported the formation of fairly homogenous Member State preferences and thereby a strong European position on service-related investment liberalisation commitments. The EU-internal liberalisation facilitated international liberalisation, as it incidentally also eliminated barriers to international services trade and service-related investment. It fostered the competitiveness of European service providers and prepared them for global markets (Messerlin, 1990, pp. 132–134, 137). In consequence, the Member States and thus the EU generally held firm offensive positions in EU-internally liberalised service sectors, while they continued holding rather defensive preferences on yet protected service sectors such as postal, telecommunications, audiovisual or cultural services. Homogenous Member State preferences generally facilitate the Commission's role as single voice, which allows the Commission and the EU to build up a reputation as serious negotiating parties and skilful negotiators thereby consolidating their role in new policy areas such as investment regulation.

Sectorial preferences, on the other hand, cannot account for the EU's central role and proactive use of its de facto competences in the GNS negotiations. All business representatives, Member State and Commission officials interviewed for this book agreed that – with the exception of very few sectors and associations – European business did not take a genuine interest and shape debates within the EU on the GNS negotiations. National and European federations and business leaders occasionally and publically supported ambitious negotiations on services trade, but did not get wholeheartedly involved in policymaking debates or provide technical expertise to the Member States and Commission (Agence Europe, 1991; Cheeseright, 1985b). The Member States and the Commission repeatedly called on service companies to provide technical expertise. The Commission, moreover, demanded European service providers to finally get organised and learn a lesson from the International Committee on Trade in Services in the USA, which played a decisive role in shaping the US position and strategy in the GNS negotiations. The Commission's calls showed, however, only limited success. Some time after the launch of the Uruguay Round, the European Communities Services Group (ECSG) formed in order to provide European service providers with a common voice across sectors and Member States in the GNS negotiations (Dullforce, 1987). But the ECSG reportedly did not exert great influence on European policymaking, as service providers from different Member States and sectors found it difficult to identify common objectives and to agree on common positions (Interview, Brussels, 25 September 2013b). Among the few proactive and interested business representatives in this domain were reportedly the LOTIS Committee, audiovisual service companies, maritime transport companies, the Dutch business federation and the German Chamber of Industry and Commerce (DIHK) (Interview, telephone, 17 June 2013; Interview, Brussels, 25 September 2013b). This heterogeneous group could not, however, make up for the general lack of business interest and input.

Despite the lack of business lobbying, many Member State governments took a sincere interest in the GNS negotiations. In comparison to other negotiating formations of the Uruguay Round, the Member States held rather homogenous and overall offensive preferences regarding the liberalisation of services trade. All in all, Member State governments considered the liberalisation of services trade to be in their national economic interest and therefore readily cooperated and delegated negotiating powers to the Commission in order to attain a good deal. As discussed earlier, the Member States' support for ambitious negotiations and readiness to cooperate to a large extent reflected the Commission's pedagogical campaigning prior and during the Uruguay Round. The United Kingdom, the Netherlands and, to a lesser extent, Spain, Belgium and Germany were eager to see a comprehensive liberalisation of services trade (Interview, Brussels, 24 September 2013; Interview, Oxford, 11 October 2013, Interview, telephone, 17 June 2013). Italy, Portugal and Greece, on the other hand, were initially sceptical and then neutral regarding the plan to liberalise services trade within the GATT regime (Interview, Brussels, 24 September 2013; Peel, 1986). France, finally, held a peculiar position in these debates. France had manifestly offensive interests in services trade. The French economy comprised a large and competitive services sector, which stood to significantly gain from a multilateral liberalisation of services. France was nevertheless ready to sacrifice gains for its services sector to protect its agriculture (Buchan, 1992; Interview, Oxford, 11 October 2013). It repeatedly applied the brakes to the GNS negotiations if, for instance, the USA voiced unacceptable agricultural demands. These observations suggest that the size and competitiveness of their respective service sectors strongly shaped government preferences and willingness to cooperate – not however business lobbying.

The EU played a proactive role in the GNS talks and fully exploited its new de facto competences in international investment regulation. The EU's central role and proactive use of its new de facto competences primarily reflected Commission entrepreneurship. The Commission's proactive attitude, its recourse to agenda-setting powers and referral to the emerging Single Market managed to mobilise and to convince the Member States to closely cooperate in this forum of international investment policymaking. The Member States bought into the Commission's argument that participation and cooperation in the GNS promised to deliver considerable economic benefits. European business, on the other, remained passive and lethargic. Apart from some few national sectorial associations, European business did not lobby policymakers and promote cooperation and delegation.

5.4 Conclusion

The EU made its first steps in international investment regulation during the pre- and core negotiations of the Uruguay Round of the GATT (1982–1994). The analysis of these negotiations draws a rather homogenous picture of the cooperation, delegation and integration dynamics at work. The observations lend support to institutionalist and supranational thinking and challenge societal theories and liberal intergovernmentalism. The USA pushed in the early 1980s for a new GATT round and the inclusion of investment-related negotiating items. The Commission – at first hesitant – gradually endorsed US calls for a new GATT round and broad negotiating agenda. The Commission realised that the EU would economically benefit from a comprehensive new GATT round. During the pre- and core negotiations, the Commission used its agenda-setting powers and referred to the evolving trade agenda so as to convince European business and the Member States of the benefits to endorse the launch of investment negotiations within the GATT. It encouraged and funded research on services trade and investment, promoted the establishment of a dedicated Council committee for services trade, called on business to establish lobbying structures and pointed to the complementarity between the EU-internal liberalisation enshrined in the Single Market programme and the upcoming GATT round. While European business hardly responded to the Commission's proactive stance, the Member States gradually came around and bought into the Commission's argument and agreed to cooperate and to delegate on investment regulation in the GATT. The Member States, nevertheless, underlined that this decision was of temporary and not permanent nature. These observations confirm principal-agent research, which suggests that agents may shape policy outcomes by shaping principals' preferences. They equally support historical institutionalist research, as the Member States indeed worried about the long-term institutional and legal consequences of their decision to temporarily cooperate and to delegate negotiating to the Commission.

Notes

1 Trade-related investment measures form a subcategory of post-establishment treatment measures applied to foreign investors and their produce. TRIMs are, for instance, local content requirements or export performance requirements. Local content requirements force investors to use a certain quantity of local input products so as to stimulate domestic demand and growth. Export performance requirements oblige foreign investors to export a certain amount of their produce abroad in order to strengthen the external trade balance of their host country. TRIMs artificially inflate or reduce the volume of countries' trade flows. What is more, they come with often substantial costs for the investors concerned, who are limited in their managerial decision-making.
2 The General Agreement on Trade in Services enumerates four modes of services trade: 1) cross-border supply, 2) consumption abroad, 3) commercial presence and 4) presence of natural persons. Mode 3 is by and large equivalent to foreign direct investment. The GATS thus regulates not only services trade but de facto also contains provisions relating to market access and post-establishment treatment of foreign investors.
3 The 'Consultative Group of Eighteen' reassembled the Geneva-based representatives of the USA, the EU Member States, Canada, Japan and major developing countries. While it was an informal grouping, it had considerable influence on the work of the GATT.
4 See endnote 1 for a definition and explanation of TRIMs.
5 See GATT Digital Library of Stanford University for a comprehensive archive of negotiating documents http://gatt.stanford.edu.
6 The acronym FIRA stands for Foreign Investment Review Act. The USA brought a claim against Canada, because it took the view that local content and export performance requirements imposed on US investors under FIRA were illegal under the GATT. The FIRA case thus had a direct bearing on the TRIMs negotiations and may generally be considered as the upbeat to US efforts to establish a multilateral investment framework.

References

Agence Europe, 1992. Statement on U.S. policy on foreign investment (19 February 1992).
Agence Europe, 1991. European and US industrialists call for conclusion to Uruguay round (20 June 1991).

Agence Europe, 1983. Vice-President of the European Commission, Mr Tugendhat, has announced the commission's intention of proposing a stand-still on new restrictions on services business to be followed by a gradual unfreezing of the international services trade (4 November 1983).

Auerbach, S., 1985. U.S. – Israel sign trade agreement (23 April 1985). *Wash. Post.*

Buchan, D., 1992. World Trade News: French ready to fight Gatt concessions (9 October 1992). *Financ. Times* 4.

Buchan, D., 1989. World Trade News: Andriessen takes liberal line on investment in EC (21 July 1989). *Financ. Times* 3.

Cheeseright, P., 1985a. World Trade News: EEC badly placed for trade-in-services talks (21 November 1985). *Financ. Times.*

Cheeseright, P., 1985b. Plea for free trade in Europe (9 January 1985). *Financ. Times* 2.

Cheeseright, P., 1983. World Trade News: Gatt consensus may soon emerge on code for trade in services (24 October 1983). *Financ. Times* 4.

Croome, J., 1995. *Reshaping the world trading system: A history of the Uruguay round.* World Trade Organization, Geneva.

Dolzer, R., Schreuer, C., 2012. *Principles of international investment law*, 2nd ed. Oxford University Press, Oxford.

Dullforce, W., 1990. World Trade News: Splits remain on end to investment flow curbs (6 November 1990). *Financ. Times* 8.

Dullforce, W., 1987. World Trade News: EEC service industries call for freer markets (14 April 1987). *Financ. Times* 7.

Dullforce, W., 1986. World Trade News: EEC shifts stance to back trade in services pact (28 May 1986). *Financ. Times* 12.

European Commission, 1982. GATT ministerial meeting, information note submitted by the commission to the Council of Ministers COM(82)678. Brussels.

Farnsworth, C., 1982. Trade conferees reach consensus despite disputes (29 November 1982). *N. Y. Times.*

Financial Times, 1982. The UK government is seeking a standstill agreement in order to stop the introduction of further barriers to trade in services (24 September 1982). *Financ. Times.*

GATT, 1990. MTN.GNS/W/95.
GATT, 1989a. MTN.GNG/NG12/W/22.
GATT, 1989b. MTN.GNG/NG12/W/14.
GATT, 1989c. MTN.GNG/NG12/W/15.
GATT, 1989d. MTN.GNS/W/50.
GATT, 1989e. MTN.GNS/W/75.
GATT, 1989f. MTN.GNS/W/76.
GATT, 1989g. MTN.GNS/W/77.
GATT, 1988. MTN.GNG/NG12/W/10.
GATT, 1987a. MTN.GNG/NG12/W/2.
GATT, 1987b. MTN.GNG/NG12/W/4.
GATT, 1987c. MTN.GNG/NG12/2.
GATT, 1987d. MTN.GNG/NG12/7.
GATT, 1987e. MTN.GNG/NG12/W/8.
GATT, 1981. GATT/1303.

Glick, L.A., 1984. *Multilateral trade negotiations: World trade after the Tokyo round.* Rowman and Allanheld, Totowa.

Guisinger, S., 1987. Investment related to trade, in: Finger, J.M., Olechowski, A. (Eds.), *The Uruguay round: A handbook for the multilateral trade negotiations*. IBRD, Washington, DC, pp. 217–225.

Hindley, B., 1990. Principles in factor-related trade in services, in: Messerlin, P., Sauvant, K. (Eds.), *The Uruguay round*. World Bank, Washington, DC, pp. 12–18.

Messerlin, P., 1990. The European Community, in: Messerlin, P., Sauvant, K. (Eds.), *The Uruguay round*. World Bank, Washington, DC, pp. 132–149.

Montagnon, P., 1989. World Trade News: Keeping gatt talks on the front burner: Why the Uruguay round is seen as crucial for EC chemicals (14 March 1989). *Financ. Times* 8.

Montagnon, P., 1988. World Trade News: Nissan row touches a raw nerve: A dispute over local content requirements (30 September 1988). *Financ. Times* 8.

Montagnon, P., Dullforce, W., 1988. Montreal trade talks: Signs of progress on yardsticks for liberalising services (1 December 1988). *Financ. Times* 4.

Nikièma, S., 2014. *Performance requirements in investment treaties*. IISD Best Pract. Ser.

Paemen, H., Bensch, A., 1995. *From the GATT to the WTO: The European Community in the Uruguay round, studies in social and economic history*. Leuven University Press, Leuven, Belgium.

Peel, Q., 1986. World Trade News: EEC bid to defend farm policy/call for all subsidy policies to be included in Gatt talks (18 June 1986). *Financ. Times* 6.

Reagan, R., 1986. Presidential radio address [WWW Document]. URL http://en.wikisource.org/wiki/Presidential_Radio_Address_-_13_September_1986 (accessed 3.9.14).

Salacuse, J.W., 2010. *The law of investment treaties*, 1st ed. Oxford University Press, Oxford.

Schott, J.J., 1994. *The Uruguay round: An assessment*. Institute for International Economics, Washington, DC.

Sidhu, K., 2004. *Die Regelung von Direktinvestitionen in der WTO: Das TRIMs-Abkommen und das GATS*. V&R Unipress GmbH, Osnabrück.

Stewart, T., 1993. *The GATT Uruguay round: A negotiating history*. Kluwer Law and Taxation Publishers, Deventer; Boston.

Thomson, R., 1990. World Trade News (GATT): Quietly, Japan moves to lift rice import ban: Politicians work behind scenes on area of once-loud disagreement (20 November 1990). *Financ. Times*.

Tyler, C., 1985. World Trade News: Washington 'will go ahead with trade talks in 1986'/ US proposes alternative to Gatt (20 June 1985). *Financ. Times* 6.

Tyler, C., 1983. World Trade News: New move to boost trade in services (18 April 1983). *Financ. Times* 3.

Wayne, S., 1984. The new U.S. bilateral investment treaties. *Berkeley J. Int. Law* 2, 192–224.

Woolcock, S., 1990. *The Uruguay round: Issues for the European Community and the United States, RIIA discussion paper*. Royal Institute of International Affairs, London.

6 The EU in investment-related negotiations on the Energy Charter Treaty

This chapter shifts the focus of enquiry to the EU's involvement in the negotiations on the ECT. The ECT is little known to the general public. Its content and geographical scope make it a milestone agreement of global economic governance. The much discussed arbitration award of some $50bn in the case of *Yukos Universal Limited (Isle of Man) vs Russia* (ITA Law, 2014) and the pending proceeding *Vattenfall vs Germany (II)* (Bernasconi-Osterwalder and Hoffmann, 2012) concerning Germany's nuclear phase-out were both filed under the ECT and underline the political salience of the agreement. The ECT was negotiated between 1990 and 1998 and governs energy trade and investment among the contracting parties. It contains, inter alia, soft law provisions on market access for investors in the energy sector, and binding post-establishment treatment and protection standards as well as ISDS provisions. The content of the ECT is thus in many regards identical to BITs. Fifty-two parties from Europe, Asia and Oceania have signed the ECT and some 20 parties from the Americas, Middle East and Africa have observer status under the agreement (Energy Charter Secretariat, 2003). Hence, the ECT is the only existing truly multilateral investment agreement. The ECT is, moreover, of special importance to this study. The EU was closely involved in the negotiations on the ECT and acceded – next to its Member States – as full-fledged party to the agreement. The ECT is the only veritable investment agreement, which has been concluded by the EU so far. What is more, the ECT is the only agreement in force which entitles investors to file investment arbitration claims against the EU.

Why and how did the EU become a key player in the ECT negotiations? The analysis produces a nuanced picture of cooperation and delegation dynamics. From the outset of the ECT project, the Member States were keen to cooperate and to speak with a single voice in negotiations with the collapsing Soviet superpower. They sought to maximise their bargaining power to gain access to Soviet energy resources and to wield greater geopolitical influence over their neighbour. From the beginning, the Commission was allowed to play a central role in the conceptualisation and negotiation of the ECT. The Commission, nonetheless, skilfully consolidated its role over time and took over the role as EU lead negotiator from the Council Presidency. It used its agenda-setting powers, invoked fringe, implied and domestic de facto competences to impose itself as the central policy actor within the EU dealing with the ECT. It underlined in EU-internal debates that it held relevant competences under the CCP, that the ECT was in essence the external relations element of its milestone project of a Single Market for energy and that it sought to prove itself as a proactive capable broker in international affairs. While these findings confirm principal-agent research, they also blend with historical institutionalist thinking on incremental institutional change through 'conversion' and 'layering'. The Commission managed to reinterpret and to add new meanings to existing competences in trade, transport and energy policy ('conversion' and 'layering') and thereby consolidated its de facto competences in external relations. European businesses, finally, were mostly uninterested. And European utilities – the only businesses closely following the negotiations – vehemently opposed the ECT project as a Commission-led attack on their downstream monopolies. The chapter thus lends primarily support to institutionalist and supranational thinking rather than societal and liberal intergovernmental explanations for European cooperation, delegation and integration. The chapter first provides a detailed overview of the lengthy and complex ECT negotiations. It then evaluates from a theoretical point of view why and how the EU could acquire such a central role in the ECT negotiations despite lacking legal competences.

6.1 A negotiating history of the Energy Charter Treaty

The negotiations on the ECT evolved in four stages. First, the EU conceived the ECT project as 'Lubbers Plan' and conducted pre-negotiations with the Soviet Union (June 1990 – July 1991). Second, the parties negotiated the European Energy Charter, which was a political agreement (July 1991 – December 1991). It documented the overarching objectives of the ECT project and the intention of the contracting parties to subsequently enter into a binding 'basic agreement'. The 'basic agreement' is better known today as the ECT and is referred to here as such henceforth. Third, the parties then engaged in negotiations on the binding ECT (February 1992 – December 1994). Finally, the parties conducted negotiations on the so-called supplementary protocol of the ECT (January 1995 – autumn 1998). The parties had initially agreed to include binding investment liberalisation commitments into the ECT but failed to reach a compromise on this issue. Hence, they decided to exclude the issue from the ECT negotiations and to deal with it in a 'supplementary protocol'. The negotiations on the 'supplementary protocol' produced an elaborate draft text, but ultimately collapsed. The chapter examines each stage in turn. The analytical focus of this section primarily lies on international negotiating activities between the EU and third countries. EU-internal dynamics shaping the EU's negotiating behaviour and de facto competences in international investment policy are analysed in the second section of this chapter.

6.1.1 The Lubbers Plan

Discussions on a 'European Energy Community' started in June 1990. The Dutch Prime Minister Ruud Lubbers proposed the creation of such a community to his fellow heads of state during a session of the European Council. Under his proposal, the 'European Energy Community' should establish a trade and investment regime for the energy sector encompassing the Single Market of the EU, the Soviet Union and the countries of Central and Eastern Europe. The 'European Energy Community' should allow the parties to capitalise on their complementary relationship. While the Member States of the EU were in need of secure and affordable access to energy, the Soviet Union and the Central and Eastern European countries urgently needed Western capital, technology and know-how to modernise their ailing energy sectors and to revive their economies. Lubbers underlined that such a 'European Energy Community' would support a peaceful transition of the Soviet Union and the Central and Eastern European countries from autocratic command economies toward democratic capitalism (Buchan, 1990; Doré, 1996, p. 138; European Commission, 1991). The so-called Lubbers Plan clearly echoed classic liberalism and the paradigm of Western European Integration to overcome entrenched hostility and to foster peace through economic cooperation and the integration of strategic economic sectors. One may recall here that in the early 1950s the EU had started out as an energy community known as the European Coal and Steel Community (ECSC) (Konoplyanik, 1996, pp. 156–157).

The Lubbers Plan reflected the preoccupations of its time. On the one hand, it echoed the mounting geopolitical challenges in Europe due to the upheavals in the Soviet Union and its satellite states since the late 1980s. The Soviet Union had fallen into a state of economic, political and social paralysis during the 1970s and early 1980s. In 1985, Mikhail Gorbachev became general secretary of the Communist Party. Between 1987 and 1989, Gorbachev launched hitherto unseen reforms in order to lead the country out of its paralysis. He introduced private ownership of business to boost the Soviet economy. He loosened control over media, adopted a liberal stance on civic rights and tentatively democratised the electoral system of the country (Hosking, 2012; Thompson, 1998, pp. 268–283). Gorbachev's reforms had, however, unintended dramatic consequences. Instead of reviving the Soviet Union, they spurred destabilising dynamics. The social and political reforms deeply divided the political elite of the country. The economic reforms, on the other hand, did not ease the country's economic problems but exposed its dysfunctional allocation mechanisms, severe shortage of capital and lack of modern technologies and know-how. In the late 1980s, the Soviet economy slipped into an ever-deeper recession. Material scarcity grew, public finances rapidly degraded and the Soviet government had to ask for emergency loans from Western countries in order to ward off sovereign default. The Soviet Union's economic and financial difficulties kindled old ethnic, religious and national tensions within the country. These tensions increasingly undermined the control of the federal government in Moscow over the Soviet territory and the satellite states in Central and Eastern Europe (Evtuhov et al., 2004, pp. 779–799; Hosking, 2012; Lovell, 2009; Thompson, 1998, pp. 283–289). The creeping collapse of the Soviet Union slowly reconfigured the political and security landscape of Europe. Western and Soviet policymakers faced the question of how to ensure a peaceful and orderly disintegration and transition of the Soviet Union. The Lubbers Plan – and the therein-enshrined idea of economic integration for the sake of peacebuilding and friendship – constituted a Western answer to this geopolitical challenge.

The Lubbers Plan, on the other hand, sought to complement the beginning creation of a Single Market for energy. In response to the failure of Keynesian macroeconomic policies in the 1970s and early 1980s, the Member States and the Commission launched the Single Market programme in the mid-1980s. This was a manifestation of the emerging neoliberal economic paradigm at that time. The Single Market programme foresaw the finalisation of the Single Market by 1993 through the strengthening of market mechanisms and the dismantling of persisting barriers to trade in goods, services, capital and labour movements within the EU. The creation of the Single Market should allow for economies of scale, foster efficiency and European competitiveness and ultimately lead the European economy out of crisis (Moravcsik, 1991). The Commission took the view that the Single Market programme also had to encompass Member States' energy sectors (European Commission, 1985, p. 24). The transition from fragmented, monopolistic national markets toward a competitive European energy market should lower energy prices equivalent to 0.5% of the EU's GDP, increase energy security and create vital background conditions for economic prosperity (Eikeland, 2004, pp. 4–5; Padget, 1992, p. 57). As the energy sector had always been a *domaine reservé*, most Member States initially met the Commission's proposal with hesitation (Padget, 1992, pp. 58–59). However, they could not deny the benefits of a Single Market for energy, as they had endorsed the general economic rationale underlying the Single Market programme. In 1988, the Council of Ministers formally endorsed the proposal and asked the Commission to elaborate adequate measures so as to create a Single Market for energy. In the following years, the Commission tabled a number of measures in order to advance this objective. The Commission notably proposed measures providing for 'third party access' (TPA) to energy networks as well as measures providing for greater transparency in energy pricing. TPA proved to be particularly sensitive in Council debates and among national utilities. Progress on the implementation of TPA thus took until the late-1990s. The Commission argued that TPA was a prerequisite for competition in the energy sector, as it enables consumers to buy gas and electricity from any supplier within the market regardless of ownership of interjacent transmission networks (Padget, 1992, p. 59). National utilities questioned the technical feasibility and the Commission's expertise in this domain (Padget, 1992, pp. 69–72). In many regards, the Lubbers Plan can be considered as an initiative to extend the emerging Single Market for energy to the main transmission and supplier countries of the EU. The underlying reasoning was that the Single Market for energy needed to be embedded into an appropriate regional energy regime to properly function (European Commission, 1991, pp. 2, 4).

The European Council welcomed Lubbers's proposal for a 'European Energy Community' in its session in June 1990. The heads of state decided to further study the proposal. They entrusted the Commission to examine it on behalf of the Member States. The central role of the Commission reflected the intention of the heads of state to sell the ECT as a 'European project' and to appear as a unitary actor in order to exert greater geopolitical influence and ensure a better economic deal with the Soviet Union. In the following year, the Commission – and more specifically the DG for Energy (XVII) and for Trade (I) – fathomed the interest of Soviet Union (Buchan, 1990). The Soviet government embraced the proposal for a 'European Energy Community'. The proposal promised to accelerate the modernisation of the antiquated and highly inefficient Soviet energy sector, to boost exports, to deliver technology spillovers into further economic sectors and to generate badly needed hard currency inflows. It thereby bore the opportunity for the Soviet government to lead the country out of its economic crisis and to get away from short-term economic aid from Western countries. Soviet and Western policymakers drew parallels between the Lubbers Plan and the Marshall Plan, which had financed the reconstruction of Western Europe after World War II (Konoplyanik, 1996, pp. 156–158; Laurance, 1991). The Commission, moreover, continued consultations with the Member States in order to pin down the general objectives and institutional layout of a European Energy Community. The Dutch and British governments strongly supported the Commission in these efforts (Buchan, 1991). In November and December 1990, Commission President Delors sketched the Commission's ideas for a European Energy Community in different international fora (Agence Europe, 1990a). The European Council reacted positively to these ideas and expressed its hope of starting negotiations in 1991 (Agence Europe, 1990b).

Following the preliminary green light from the European Council, the Commission published a communication and draft text for a European Energy Charter in February 1991 (Agence Europe, 1990b, 1990c). The draft charter, inter alia, provided for free trade in energy resources, access to transmission networks and provisions on technical and environmental cooperation. More importantly for this study, the draft charter stipulated the liberalisation of the exploration and exploitation of energy resources and the enhancement of the level of post-establishment treatment and protection afforded to foreign investors in the energy sectors of host countries. The Commission's draft charter thereby foresaw the establishment of a full-fledged international investment agreement governing market access, post-establishment treatment and investment protection under the participation of the individual Member States and the EU (European Commission, 1991).

The Council of Ministers of the EU examined and formally endorsed the draft text of the European Energy Charter in April 1991 (Agence Europe, 1991a). The Soviet government also expressed its support. In the following months, the Commission – again in close cooperation with the Dutch government – started the preparations for the launch of the negotiations on the European Energy Charter scheduled for July 1991. Two problems overshadowed this preparation period. The Commission and the Member States initially did not agree on which countries to invite to the negotiations. In the end, the Council of Ministers took the decision to invite all European and OECD countries to the ECT negotiations (Agence Europe, 1991b, 1991c). The second problem concerned the growing political instability in the Soviet Union and the countries of Central and Eastern Europe. In early 1991, the Red Army intervened in Lithuania and Latvia to oppress demonstrations for the independence of the Baltic Soviet Federal Socialist Republics (SFSRs). Several people died during these interventions, which triggered demands in the EU for an end to consultations with the Soviet government (Buchan, 1991; Palmer, 1991). Several SFSRs, moreover, raised first question marks over the competence of the central Soviet government to negotiate with Western Europe on a European Energy Charter. In particular, the Russian SFSR sought to assert exclusive competence over all energy resources within its territory in spring 1991. As the bulk of the Soviet Union's gas and oil deposits were located in the Russian SFSR, these quarrels threatened the ECT project. In the light of this situation, the Member States and the Commission stressed that they would exclusively negotiate with the central Soviet government and not engage in consultations with the SFSRs. The unclear distribution of competences, nevertheless, caused a headache in Brussels (Buchan, 1991).

6.1.2 The European Energy Charter

Despite these obstacles, the negotiations on the European Energy Charter started on time. On 15 July 1991, the delegates of about 50 European and OECD countries gathered in Brussels for the first day of negotiations. During the first session, the delegates elected Charles Rutten, a senior Dutch diplomat, as chairman of the conference. They agreed to structure the negotiations in five working groups,[1] which would jointly elaborate the text of the European Energy Charter and prepare the text of the 'basic agreement'. All negotiating parties sent representatives to all working groups. The Council Presidency and the Commission jointly represented the EU and the Member States in the negotiations. The individual Member States only rarely intervened in the negotiations in order to clarify their national positions in relation to the EU position previously presented by the Council Presidency or the Commission. Such interventions mostly concerned highly technical issues or issues coming predominantly under Member State competence (Interview, London, 16 January 2014). The working groups and their chairmen could draw on the support of a small conference secretariat. The secretariat was formally independent, but staffed with officials and hosted in the offices of the European Commission (Interview, London, 16 January 2014). During the first session, the delegates agreed to meet at first in their respective working groups and to reconvene for a second plenary session in late October in order to adopt the final text of the Charter. The energy ministers of the participating countries should then meet in The Hague on 17 December 1991 in order to sign the Charter (Agence Europe, 1991d).

The tight timetable of the conference reflected the pre-existing, high degree of support for the Commission's draft text for a European Energy Charter as well as the non-binding, political nature of the Charter. The Commission's Director General for Energy, Clive Jones, commented to that effect that the only unclear issue was *"the degree to which the Soviet Union will be willing to accept an attempt to reform its energy policy along market lines to give confidence to western companies and bankers to invest in the industry"* (Hill and Hargreaves, 1991). The timetable also echoed the concerns of the delegates with the increasingly unstable political situation in the Soviet Union (Agence Europe, 1991d). The seriousness of these concerns forcefully manifested itself in mid-August 1991, when conservative forces in the Communist Party, the KGB and the Red Army staged a coup d'état against Gorbachev. The coup was unsuccessful. It nevertheless raised doubts about the prospects of the ECT project and the sustainability of East-West cooperation (Hill and Gardner, 1991). After the coup, a sense of urgency spread among Western policymakers. Jacques Delors voiced the criticism that Gorbachev had managed to destroy the old Soviet system, but had failed in establishing a new order. Delors reasoned that the EU and the G7[2] had to step up their assistance to the Soviet government in managing the transition of the country, and underlined that the European Energy Charter constituted a core element of Western assistance to the Soviet Union (Agence Europe, 1991e).

The delegates reconvened in the working groups in mid-September 1991. Despite the political turmoil in the Soviet Union, the delegates made excellent progress on the substance of the European Energy Charter in the following weeks. In early October the working group overseeing the drafting of the European Energy Charter announced that they had already reached general agreement on content. They added that the Charter could be adopted as planned in the plenary session of the conference in late October (Agence Europe, 1991f). The delegates of the Soviet Union, Eastern and Central European countries merely cautioned that their countries would need a transition period to undertake the economic reforms necessary so as to conform to the objectives of the Charter (Hill, 1991a). Judging from press coverage and secondary literature, one must assume that the swift agreement was possible due to the pre-existing consensus on the general content of the non-binding charter. What is more, it was reported in later stages of the negotiations that the delegates of the Soviet Union, Eastern and Central European countries often did not understand the meaning and implications of the discussed clauses. The Charter project, its concepts and terminology were rooted in Western international economic law, which was yet unchartered territory for the formerly socialist countries. Hence, the delegates from East and West did not, de facto, discuss as equals. Soviet, Eastern and Central European delegates acted as eager students of Western experts, listening to the elaborations of their Western counterparts (Doré, 1996, p. 146).

While the substantive work on the European Energy Charter could be concluded by early October, the overall negotiating process nevertheless stalled in autumn 1991. The failed coup d'état of August 1991 had kicked off the territorial disintegration of the Soviet Union. The Baltic SFSRs gained their formal independence from the Soviet Union and consequently participated in the conference on the European Energy Charter as sovereign states. Other SFSRs followed the example and sent 'observers' to the negotiations in Brussels (Agence Europe, 1991g). The delegation of the central Soviet government tried to reassure Western delegates that it remained fully competent to negotiate on the Charter. This position was, however, soon overtaken by events. On 22 October 1991, several SFSRs signed the Treaty on an Economic Community. The treaty was intended to create an economic community – similar to the EU – among sovereign SFSRs (Brzezinski and Sullivan, 1997, pp. 32–37). The treaty, inter alia, implied that the

SFSRs were in control of energy resources and energy policy. In the following days and weeks, nascent energy companies, local authorities and newly created energy ministries of the SFSRs sought to assume control over the energy sector in the Soviet Union. The transfer of control remained, however, incomplete, and the resultant power vacuum made the planned adoption of the final text of the European Energy Charter in the plenary session of late October impossible. The delegates agreed that the text was ripe for adoption, but nobody knew whether the central Soviet government or the individual SFSRs should adopt the final text (Hill, 1991b; Hill and Lloyd, 1991). The delegates finally agreed on 21 November 1991 that the interstate economic committee of the central Soviet government as well as the governments of the SFSRs should jointly sign the European Energy Charter. The compromise was not intended to prejudge the sensitive competence question of who was in control over energy resources and policy within the Soviet Union (Hill, 1991b).

On 16 and 17 December 1991, the energy ministers of the negotiating parties met in The Hague to sign the European Energy Charter (Agence Europe, 1991h). The group encompassed representatives of 46 parties, namely of the Soviet Union and the SFSRs, Eastern and Central European countries, the Commission, the Member States of the EU, the USA, Canada and Japan.[3] The final text of the European Energy Charter still clearly bore the signature of the Commission. While the wording of the final text (Energy Charter Secretariat, 2004, pp. 209–226) diverged from the Commission's draft text (European Commission, 1991) of February 1991, the general content and objectives of the final document had remained unchanged. The Charter documented the intention of the parties to establish a binding regulatory framework to promote, liberalise and protect investments in the energy sector (Energy Charter Secretariat, 2004, p. 216). At the occasion of the closing ceremony, the Dutch Prime Minister Ruud Lubbers called upon the parties to conclude the subsequent negotiations on the ECT by the end of 1992 in order to quickly harvest the economic and political benefits of the European Energy Charter (Agence Europe, 1991h; Hill, 1991c). Lubbers's optimism was, nevertheless, premature. One week after the signing of the European Energy Charter in Brussels, the SFSRs concluded the so-called Alma Ata Protocols. The signing of these protocols led to the resignation of the Soviet government, the formal dissolution of the Soviet Union and marked the beginning of a decade of considerable political and economic instability within the successor states of the Soviet Union (Hosking, 2012; Lovell, 2009).

6.1.3 The Energy Charter Treaty

The negotiations on the binding ECT started in late February 1992 (Agence Europe, 1992a). Working group II was commissioned to elaborate the draft text of the ECT. As its task overlapped with the work of all other working groups, it rapidly absorbed the entire negotiating process (Interview, London, 16 January 2014). The negotiations on the ECT advanced at a good pace at first. The negotiating sessions of March and April 1992 produced progress; notably on disciplines for investment protection, energy trade, energy transit and environmental protection. The progress reflected, on the one hand, the increased interest of Russia and Eastern and Central European countries in the negotiations. They faced an increasing number of energy-related disputes among themselves and came to see the ECT as a framework to amicably settle these disputes (Hill, 1992). On the other hand, the Commission had come forward with a first draft text of the ECT in order to speed up the negotiations and to ensure the compatibility of ECT provisions and the Single Market for energy. The Council of Ministers endorsed the draft text, sent it to the other negotiating parties and underlined that the ECT negotiations should first forge agreement on trade, post-establishment treatment and investment protection provisions and only then discuss investment liberalisation commitments (Agence Europe, 1992b). But despite this fresh impetus, the negotiations soon ran into stalemate. It became clear that the legal systems of Russia and the Central and Eastern European countries were not sufficiently developed to honour obligations under Western international economic agreements. In April, the delegates therefore agreed to postpone further negotiating sessions. The negotiating pause was intended to allow the delegates of the former socialist countries to enhance their knowledge of Western international economic law (Agence Europe, 1992c, 1992d). The substantive negotiations only started again in September 1992. The hope of concluding the negotiations on the ECT by the end of 1992 rapidly vanished. By spring 1993, a glut of disagreements had piled up, which delayed the negotiations on the ECT for almost two years. The following paragraphs summarise the most important disagreements.

Investment disciplines stood very much at the centre of the deadlock. A key controversy concerned the question of whether investment liberalisation should proceed on the basis of NT or MFN treatment. The EU and the USA favoured the application of NT to the pre-establishment stage including the distribution of exploration and exploitation licences. They thereby sought to unlock the energy reserves of Russia and Central Asia for their national energy companies (Doré, 1996, p. 139; Wälde, 1996, pp. 277–284). Norway – silently supported by other countries – nevertheless rejected these demands. Norway proposed to provide market access for foreign investors on the basis of MFN treatment – i.e. the obligation to treat all foreign investors alike. Norway also sought to keep the possibility of privileged treatment of national energy companies vis-à-vis foreign companies. The EU and the United States strongly opposed the Norwegian proposal. European policymakers reportedly even publicly pondered importing the dispute into the accession negotiations between the EU and Norway in order to increase pressure on Oslo (Agence Europe, 1993a, 1993b).

Another key controversy concerned the scope of acceptable reservations to the envisaged general investment liberalisation commitment under the ECT. Once the delegates had agreed to liberalise market access for foreign investors on the basis of negative lists, several countries – including some Member States – tabled lengthy lists with reservations. The Commission criticised such lengthy lists, saying they would unbalance the benefits of the ECT among the parties and might ultimately obstruct agreement. Russia and most Eastern and Central European countries, moreover, cautioned that they were unable to table conclusive lists of reservations or to commit to a planned standstill clause (Doré, 1996, p. 146). Under a standstill clause, a country must not introduce new restrictive measures, but may dismantle existing ones. As Russia wanted to attract foreign capital and gain access to downstream markets in Western Europe, it was generally in favour of liberalising market access for investors on the basis of NT (Konoplyanik, 1996, p. 173). Russia stressed, however, that its investment and economic law was still in a formative stage (Konoplyanik, 1996, p. 173). It proposed, at first, an open-ended and then a 10-year transition period for the applicability of a standstill clause and most other key provisions of the ECT. The Russian proposal foresaw that transition countries could enact and dismantle restrictive investment measures and reservations under the ECT as deemed necessary by them. The United States and the EU rejected the Russian proposal. Russia was, de facto, asking for a blank cheque to unilaterally determine and alter its liberalisation commitments. It took a considerable time before the EU and the USA came around and accepted a transition period in principle (Agence Europe, 1993c, 1993d; Doré, 1996, pp. 146–147).

Negotiations on post-establishment treatment, protection clauses and dispute resolution mechanisms were less controversial while no less complicated. The specific regulatory challenges of energy investments[4] and the diverging Northern American and European approaches to investment regulation triggered lengthy expert discussions on the design and wording of concepts like expropriation. These expert discussions mostly evolved between the delegates of the EU and other OECD countries. The delegates of Russia, and Eastern and Central European countries, were bystanders in these debates, as they did not possess the necessary expertise (Agence Europe, 1993e; Doré, 1996, p. 146; Interview, Brussels, 19 October 2011).

The USA and the EU, moreover, clashed over the so-called REIO clause and the applicability of the ECT to sub-federal entities. The Commission and the Member States insisted that the ECT had to contain a REIO clause. They wanted to prevent a multilateralisation of all benefits of EU-membership under the MFN clause of the ECT to non-EU members. The USA rejected the European demand as hidden protectionism (Agence Europe, 1994a; Doré, 1996, pp. 149–150). The USA, on the other hand, reiterated that it could not conclude the ECT for constitutional reasons unless the ECT would not apply to its sub-federal entities – i.e. the federal states of the USA. The EU stressed that it was unable to accept such a broad carve-out under the ECT (Agence Europe, 1994a; Doré, 1996, pp. 150–151).

By late summer 1993, the ECT negotiations had ground to a halt. Policymakers started pondering the possibility that the ECT negotiations might collapse without agreement (Agence Europe, 1993f). The chairman of the ECT negotiations called upon the Commission to resume its 'driving seat' and to inject new dynamism into the negotiating process (Agence Europe, 1993g). In order to avert failure, the EU, Russia and the United States met for trilateral talks in Moscow in mid-September to hammer out compromises for the key controversies (Agence Europe, 1993h). The outcome of the trilateral summit was, however, disappointing. The EU, Russia and the United States were unable to bridge their differences; notably on Russia's demand for a transition period (Agence Europe, 1993d).

Following the unsuccessful trilateral meeting, the Commission grew determined to finally achieve a breakthrough. In October 1993, the Commission presented a proposal to resolve the crucial transition period issue. The Commission proposal consisted of a sequenced entry into force of the ECT. The negotiating parties should conclude the ECT as quickly as possible. The provisions on energy trade and transit, as well as on post-establishment treatment, protection standards and dispute settlement, should take effect directly after signing. Regarding investment liberalisation, a transition period of three years should apply. Countries with mature legal systems should table conclusive reservation lists and grant NT at the pre-establishment stage to foreign investors directly after the signing. Countries with as yet maturing legal system should grant MFN treatment to foreign investors during the transition period. They should be allowed to enact new restrictive measures during this period. Toward the end of the transition phase, these countries should compile conclusive reservation lists. The delegates should then reconvene to examine and to jointly approve these lists. The Commission thereby sought to accommodate Eastern demands for a transition phase as well as Western concerns over providing these countries with a blank cheque for investment liberalisation (Agence Europe, 1993c). What is more, the Commission once more assumed international responsibility for the successful conclusion of the ECT negotiations and sought to demonstrate that it was an important actor in international politics capable of taking the lead (Doré, 1996, p. 148).

The Commission's proposal gained broad support among the delegates. In particular Russia praised the new approach as a breakthrough (Agence Europe, 1993c; Doré, 1996, p. 147). In the following weeks, the delegates slightly altered the Commission's proposal. Instead of concluding one international agreement with comprehensive provisions on a transition period, they agreed to conclude two separate agreements in an interval of three years. The ECT should be concluded first and encompass trade, transit, environmental, competition, post-establishment, protection and dispute settlement provisions. The later concluded 'supplementary protocol' should then contain binding provisions on investment liberalisation commitments (Agence Europe, 1993i; European Commission, 1993).

On 4 November 1993, the Commission formally informed the Council of Ministers and the European Parliament about the new two-stages approach in its communication *The European Energy Charter: Fresh Impetus from the European Community*.[5] In this communication, the Commission requested the Council of Ministers to adjust the negotiating mandate to this new approach. The ministers changed the mandate accordingly on 10 November 1993 (Agence Europe, 1993j) and underlined that the ECT had to provide, in any case, for NT at the post-establishment stage and for investment protection provisions (Agence Europe, 1993k).

The Commission had hoped to conclude the ECT negotiations on the basis of the new approach before the end of the year 1993. These hopes were frustrated in

December, when the Commission openly clashed with France. The Commission held on to its plan to include in the ECT a preliminary, albeit binding, MFN treatment obligation for the pre-establishment stage. The NT obligation, enshrined in the supplementary treaty, should later supersede this MFN obligation (Doré, 1996, p. 148). France, on the other hand, opposed to a binding MFN treatment obligation in the ECT. It stressed that some negotiating parties had largely opened their energy sectors and, de facto, granted NT to foreign investors, while other negotiating parties had isolated their energy sectors. A MFN obligation would thus cement vastly different levels of openness and distort the bargaining positions of the parties in the negotiations on the 'supplementary protocol' (Doré, 1996, pp. 148–149). The United States introduced yet a third opinion into this debate. It underlined that it still sought an agreement providing for NT at the pre-establishment stage. It insisted that it preferred no agreement to a shallow agreement (Doré, 1996, pp. 148–149). In search for an ambitious compromise, it proposed allowing parties at least to annexe positive lists containing unilateral commitments to grant NT (European Commission, 1993, p. 5). In the end, the interest to swiftly conclude the negotiations prevailed. The delegates agreed to the French demand that the ECT should merely provide for voluntary MFN treatment. The delegates discarded US concerns that the pre-establishment provisions were not ambitious enough. The European Energy Charter secretariat tellingly commented, "*You need Russia and the EC [to have a treaty], and you hope to have the US as well*" (as cited in Doré, 1996, p. 149).

The final rounds of negotiations took place in early 1994. The delegates mostly focused on the rules for trade in nuclear goods; the cast of an envisaged REIO clause; the applicability of the treaty to sub-federal entities, notably in the United States; technical aspects relating to dispute settlement; and Norway's general concerns about joining the treaty. These remaining disagreements were controversial but manageable details within the overall negotiating process (Agence Europe, 1994a). In late April 1994, the chairman, Charles Rutten, therefore tabled a draft text for the ECT. The Rutten text sought to balance the different positions on these matters and indeed earned considerable support among the delegates. The EU's Council of Ministers expressed its support for the Rutten text in May. The delegates, nonetheless, continued haggling over details until mid-September, when the final text was sent out to the negotiating parties for approval (Agence Europe, 1994b, 1994c).

The signing of the agreement was set to take place on 17 December 1994 (Agence Europe, 1994c). In October, the United States, however, demanded the reopening of the negotiations. The United States expressed the criticism that it was unwilling to conclude an agreement without ambitious pre-establishment commitments, and could not accept the REIO clause or the provisions relating to the application of the treaty to sub-federal entities (Agence Europe, 1994d). Most other parties and the chairman of the negotiations rejected the US demand and held on to the planned signing of the agreement on 17 December 1994. In consequence, the United States announced that it would not sign the ECT. On 17 December 1994, 42 negotiating parties, including the EU and its Member States, signed the ECT.

It immediately entered into force on a preliminary basis and thereby established a new international organisation and multilateral framework for energy investment and trade (Doré, 1996, p. 151). The EU acceded to the ECT as a full-fledged party alongside the individual Member States.

6.1.4 The 'supplementary protocol'

The negotiations on the 'supplementary protocol' started in early 1995, soon after the conclusion of the ECT. The 'supplementary protocol' should enshrine NT for foreign investors in energy sectors of host countries and promote the privatisation and demonopolisation of energy markets (Agence Europe, 1997a). In comparison to the preceding negotiations on the European Energy Charter and the ECT, the negotiations on the 'supplementary protocol' attracted only a little attention. European policymakers primarily focused on speeding up the ratification process and extending the ECT membership to interested third countries. The ratification process of the ECT, moreover, became increasingly complicated. The Russian Duma voiced concerns about the limitation of Russia's sovereignty over its energy resources under the ECT and its 'supplementary protocol'. By 1997, it became clear that Russia was unlikely to ratify the ECT and would abide to the ECT merely on a preliminary basis (Agence Europe, 1997b). Taking into consideration that the ECT project had been conceived in order to subject Russian energy policy and its energy sector to international economic law and market mechanisms, this development was a serious blow. European policymakers spent most of their time trying to convince Russia to ratify the ECT.

The negotiations on the 'supplementary protocol' rapidly progressed in the slipstream of these events (Agence Europe, 1997a). In January 1997, media reported that the negotiations on the 'supplementary protocol' could be wrapped up within hours, if the parties showed the political will to do so (Agence Europe, 1997b). Mostly Russia, Norway, Australia and Iceland remained critical of the 'supplementary protocol' due to the potential limitation of their sovereignty over their energy resources. France, on the other hand, disliked the idea of opening up its energy market to foreign investors. The French position not only slowed down the negotiations on 'supplementary protocol' of the ECT but also undermined the finalisation of the Single Market for energy. France generally rejected measures which would challenge the monopolies of its utilities Electricité de France or Gas de France or allow foreign investors to buy shares in these companies. In particular, the United Kingdom expressed criticism that French utilities were benefiting from the gradual liberalisation of energy trade and investment within the EU, while the French government went to great lengths to keep the French energy sector closed to foreign investors (Johnstone, 1998). In December 1997, the chairman of the ECT, Charles Rutten, nevertheless, informed the public that most sensitive issues in the negotiations on the 'supplementary protocol' had been resolved. He stressed that the conclusion of the talks in early 1998 was realistic (Agence Europe, 1997a). Rutten's optimism was premature. During spring 1998, France re-emphasised its opposition to investment liberalisation in the energy sector. France, moreover, linked the conclusion of the 'supplementary protocol' to the conclusion of the stalled negotiations on the MAI in the OECD. It stressed that the concerns of civil society against the liberalisation of international investment flows, which came forcefully to the fore in the context of the MAI negotiations, could not be discarded in the negotiations on the 'supplementary protocol' of the ECT. France consequently vetoed the assent of the Council of Ministers to the draft text of the 'supplementary protocol' (Interview, telephone, 4 February 2014a). As the EU was unable to formally endorse the draft text of the 'supplementary protocol', the conclusion of the negotiations was repeatedly postponed (Agence Europe, 1998). In December 1998, and under the shadow of the collapse of the MAI negotiations, the negotiations on the 'supplementary protocol' broke down without furore. The ECT thus only contains soft law provisions on investment liberalisation.

6.2 The EU in the negotiations on the Energy Charter Treaty

The preceding section traced the negotiations on the ECT from their earliest stages to the collapse of the negotiations on the 'supplementary protocol'. It constitutes one of the most detailed accounts of the ECT negotiations so far available in the literature. It has already shed some light on the question of why the EU acquired sufficiently comprehensive de facto competences to even enter into investment protection commitments in this forum. The following section complements this account. It first evaluates the EU's role in the ECT negotiations. It then examines whether institutionalist and supranational thinking or societal theories and liberal intergovernmentalism better account for the remarkable role of the EU in this international investment policy forum.

6.2.1 *Assessing the EU's de facto competences*

The EU played a pivotal role and possessed extensive de facto competences in investment negotiations under the ECT. The ECT was from the outset a '*European project*' rather than an '*intergovernmental project*'. When Ruud Lubbers presented his plan to establish a European Energy Community during the session of the European Council of June 1990, his fellow heads of governments immediately decided to cooperate and to empower the Commission to manage the preparations of the ECT negotiations on their behalf across all issue areas (Buchan, 1990). The Member States and the Commission underlined in their discourse during this period that the EU as a cohesive actor of international affairs – rather than a group of states – sought to negotiate the ECT with the Soviet Union. What is more, not the individual Member States but the Commission conducted EU-internal and international consultations with the Soviet Union, drew up a draft text for a European Energy Charter and managed the logistics of the upcoming negotiations on the European Energy Charter and ECT. As the Lubbers Plan only vaguely foresaw the establishment of an energy trade and investment agreement with the Soviet

Union, the Commission necessarily enjoyed some leeway in further defining the project including its investment disciplines.

The EU acquired an even more important role during the core negotiations on the European Energy Charter, the ECT and its 'supplementary protocol' between July 1991 and December 1998. The Member States closely cooperated on all agenda items – including investment liberalisation, post-establishment treatment and protection standards – and sought to speak with a single voice in the ECT negotiations. At the beginning of the ECT negotiations, the Council Presidency was the main representative of the Member States and the EU. The Council Presidency typically outlined the EU position vis-à-vis third countries and then invited the Commission to elaborate on technical aspects of the position. The Member States were generally present in the negotiations and would – if necessary – intervene in order to provide technical expertise or to clarify their national position in relation to the EU position. The working method within the EU delegation was, nevertheless, to keep the number of Member State interventions limited and to confine such interventions to areas of Member State competence (Interview, London, 16 January 2014; Interview, Brussels, 18 January 2012; Interview, telephone, 4 February 2014a). The coordination between the Member States, the Council Presidency and the Commission was generally harmonious and trustful across all issue areas (Interview, telephone, 4 February 2014a).

As the ECT negotiations advanced, the representation modalities evolved. The Commission gradually took over the role as the EU's main representative from the Council Presidency (Interview, telephone, 4 February 2014a). The Commission's increasingly central role was not limited to areas of exclusive or shared Union competence like trade or transport provisions. The Commission became the main representative of the EU in negotiations on investment disciplines, too. Third-country negotiators recalled that the Commission official obviously spoke on behalf of the EU and its Member States in investment negotiations (Interview, Brussels, 19 October 2011). The Commission increasingly stood at the very centre of negotiations on investment liberalisation, post-establishment treatment and protection standards. Negotiators explained that the Commission gradually acquired this central role within the EU delegation, because the negotiations required considerable preparation and technical expertise, which the rotating Council Presidency and the Council secretariat could not provide. What is more, they underlined that the Commission official in charge of the investment negotiations was highly capable, motivated and naturally became a key figure in the negotiations (Interview, Brussels, 19 October 2011; Interview, telephone, 4 February 2014a). Third countries, moreover, strongly felt the cohesiveness and importance of the EU in the ECT negotiations in the form of lengthy negotiating breaks, which the EU delegation frequently demanded in order to coordinate its position. One third-country negotiator recalled that about a third of the negotiating time elapsed while waiting for the EU to pin down its position in internal coordination meetings behind closed doors in a special room located next to the negotiating venue (Interview, telephone, 4 February 2014a). Finally, the preceding analysis of the negotiating history of the ECT demonstrated that the EU was also the main driver of the negotiations. The

EU – and more specifically the Commission – conceived the ECT project, repeatedly tabled draft texts for the Charter and the ECT, developed decisive compromise proposals to successfully conclude the negotiations and ratified the Charter and ECT as a full-fledged negotiating party. In conclusion, the EU was cohesive, proactive and acquired de facto competence in all areas of international investment policy in this forum.

6.2.2 Commission entrepreneurship

In line with principal-agent research on Commission entrepreneurship, the Commission eagerly promoted the consolidation of the EU's de facto competences in international investment policy during the negotiations on the ECT. While the EU was seen as the driver of the ECT project at the international level, the Commission was the main architect of the ECT project within the EU also with regard to its ambitious investment provisions. When, in 1993, the ECT negotiations had for instance ground to a halt, the chairman of the negotiations Charles Rutten called upon the Commission to resume its '*driver's seat*' and to lead the negotiations out of deadlock (Agence Europe, 1993g).

The Commission's policy entrepreneurship reflected power and functionalist considerations. On the one hand, the Commission reportedly sought to prove itself as a capable actor of international affairs beyond the narrow technical field of trade policy. It wanted to play a proper role in global affairs next to the Member States. As this objective comprised in the given context to play a proactive role in investment talks, the Commission also pushed into this domain. On the other hand, the Commission saw the ECT project as a crucial building block of its EU-internal energy policy. It argued that the Single Market would only function smoothly if embedded in an appropriate regional energy regime. From its point of view, it was thus crucial to have the EU and itself play a decisive role in the ECT project so as to ensure policy coherence.

The Commission drew on three strategies to consolidate the EU's role in the ECT negotiations and in particular in investment talks. First, it used its agenda-setting powers in order to ensure its central role in the negotiations. The Commission decisively elaborated on Lubber's first vague proposal of a 'European Energy Community'. It, moreover, tabled decisive drafts of the European Energy Charter, the ECT and critical compromise proposals, which paved the way to the successful conclusion of the negotiations and decisively shaped the investment provisions of today's treaty. The Commission's proactive and skilful negotiating behaviour and technical, administrative knowledge of its officials led to the concentration of all negotiating activity in the Commission's hand with the Council Presidency and the individual Member States gradually withdrawing from the negotiating process (Interview, Brussels, 19 October 2011; Interview, telephone 4 February 2014a).

Second, the Commission invoked fringe competences of the EU to ensure the EU's central role in the novel policy context of the ECT and thereby engaged in 'conversion' and 'layering'. While the ECT is primarily known as an investment agreement, the Commission framed the ECT negotiations in EU-internal debates also as a project touching on various policy fields coming under explicit or implied Union competence. It underlined that many ECT provisions for instance touched on trade in goods (i.e. energy commodities), trade in services (i.e. exploration, exploitation, distribution, sales, etc.) and transport (i.e. gas and oil transmission). The Commission thereby left no doubt that while the ECT project had a strong investment component coming under national competence, it was also a trade and transport policy project coming under Union competence and requiring 'mixed ratification'. The EU's unchallenged legal competences in trade and transport policy thus de facto ensured its involvement in investment policy in the policy context of the ECT. The Member States indeed accepted the Commission's central role in the ECT project and allowed the Commission for effectiveness and efficiency purposes to assist in the elaboration of the project in policy domains beyond legal Union competence (Interview, Brussels, 18 January 2012; Interview, London, 16 January 2014).

Third, the Commission also framed the ECT negotiations as the logical extension of the ongoing creation of the Single Market for energy. The Commission invoked its de facto and legal competences in EU-internal energy policy to consolidate its role in the ECT project. It thereby engaged again in institutional 'conversion' and 'layering'. From the beginning, the Commission stressed that the ECT was indeed conceived as the international relations component of the emerging Single Market for energy. The ECT should extend the Single Market for energy beyond the EU's borders. The underlying reasoning was that the Single Market for energy would only function efficiently and securely, if the supply and transmission countries also embraced a market-based approach to the regulation of their energy sectors. The Commission clearly formulated this view in its communication accompanying the draft text for the European Energy Charter of spring 1992.

> *[The European Energy Charter] . . . finds itself fully integrated within the energy policy which the Commission wishes to promote . . . with a view to completing the internal energy market and providing an external relations policy to back it up.*
> (European Commission, 1991, pp. 3, 4)

And as the Member States had agreed to cooperate on energy policy and had accepted the Commission's decisive role in liberalising and deregulating the Single Market for energy, it was only coherent for the Member States to engage in close cooperation and to extend the EU-internal role of the Commission to the international sphere and thus to the ECT negotiations (Interview, telephone, 4 February 2014a).

The Commission's consolidation strategies – agenda setting, invoking of fringe and domestic de facto and legal competences – confirm principal-agent research on cooperation and delegation in EU foreign economic policy (Pollack, 2003; Young, 2002, 2001). But they also blend with historical institutionalist concepts of agency-driven incremental institutional change of institutional 'conversion' and 'layering' (Mahoney and Thelen, 2010; Streeck and Thelen, 2005). The

Commission managed through its agenda-setting and proactive-negotiating style to consolidate its role in ECT negotiations by giving new meaning to existing competences ('conversion' and 'layering'). While the Commission did not seek to change the formal distribution of competences in the ECT negotiations, it nonetheless acted under the impression that it might thereby prepare a revision of its role in external relations.

6.2.3 European business preferences

European business took little interest in the project during the first two years. It only got involved in the project in early 1992, when the talks advanced from political deliberations on the Lubbers Plan and European Energy Charter to technical negotiations on the binding ECT and its 'supplementary protocol'. It was around that time, moreover, that European policymakers started regular consultations with European business (Interview, telephone, 4 February 2014a).

European utilities were the most active business actors in this process, and their attitude toward the ECT project was outright hostile. They perceived the ECT as a regulatory component of the creation of the Single Market for energy and thus as a threat to their monopolies. European utilities focused their lobbying activity on national ministries, which were often sympathetic to their concerns (Doré, 1996, p. 142; Wälde, 1996, p. 255). European utilities sought to prevent the inclusion of too liberal clauses into the ECT and the supplementary protocol, such as provisions on 'TPA' to gas and electricity grids (Doré, 1996, p. 142; Wälde, 1996, p. 255). Representatives of trade unions from the energy sector backed the concerns of European utilities and warned that the ECT might contribute to increasing energy prices, a degradation of energy infrastructure and compromise the EU's energy security (Agence Europe, 1992e). Representatives of European utilities, moreover, challenged the assumption of policymakers that investment projects in the energy sectors of the Soviet Union and Central and Eastern European countries could even be profitable in the first place (Riley, 1991). Other representatives of European utilities stressed that the key challenge in the Eastern countries was the modernisation of the antiquated energy infrastructure. They warned that a competitive market order and, notably, provisions on 'TPA' would hinder a modernisation of the energy infrastructure in these countries (Müller, 1991). As the ECT negotiations advanced, European utilities did not drop their opposition to the ECT project. They nevertheless understood that it was too late to nip the project in the bud and consequently adopted more nuanced and arguably constructive 'token' positions (Interview, telephone, 4 February 2014a). European upstream energy companies, on the other hand, were more open-minded vis-à-vis the ECT project. Most European energy companies active in upstream markets, like British Petroleum or Royal Dutch Shell, did not own distribution networks or engage in sizeable downstream business activities. Hence, they did not perceive the creation of the Single Market for energy or the ECT project as a major threat. The E&P Forum[6] – a global federation of upstream energy companies – participated in regular consultations with European policymakers and welcomed the plan to agree on binding investment liberalisation commitments, post-establishment treatment and protection standards. It even supported the inclusion of weak provisions on 'TPA' in the form of energy transit provisions. But the E&P Forum, nonetheless, made no secret of its general scepticism regarding the ECT project. It questioned the assumption of policymakers that the ECT would effectively enhance the trade and investment climate in the former socialist countries (Jenkins, 1996). Other business sectors, finally, did not take an interest or get involved in policymaking debates on the ECT project. Secondary literature and interviews with negotiators confirm this finding. Press research produced merely one generic statement of support for the ECT from the Belgian Federation of Large Industrial Energy Consumers (Agence Europe, 1992f). In conclusion, business preferences cannot be considered as a driver of the ECT project or the EU's pivotal role in it.

6.2.4 Member State preferences

Despite the opposition of substantial parts of European business against the ECT project, the Member States generally favoured close cooperation and delegation in the ECT negotiations including for international investment disciplines. The Member States' readiness to cooperate and to delegate reflected several considerations.

Member State support for the Lubbers Plan was very high during the conception and pre-negotiation period of the ECT project. The Member States immediately agreed to closely cooperate on the project due to economic and geopolitical considerations. The Member States felt that potentially cheaper and more reliable access to energy resources was desirable. They also welcomed the prospect of unlocking investment opportunities in up- and midstream energy markets for their national energy companies. All Member States, albeit to varying degrees, came to the conclusion that the Lubbers Plan would benefit their economies (Interview, 17 June 2013; Interview, Brussels, 18 January 2012). The Member States, moreover, supported the Lubbers Plan as a geopolitical instrument to shape the transition in the Soviet Union and its satellite states. As the Soviet Union was still a hostile global superpower with huge armed forces and nuclear arsenal, the Member States considered it to be in their vital interest to stabilise the Soviet Union. They took the view that the Lubbers Plan – much like the ECSC after World War II – would promote cooperation and increase their influence on the country through international economic integration. By the same token, the Member States felt the need to empower the Council Presidency and the Commission to act as their single voice across all issue areas in order to wield more bargaining power vis-à-vis Moscow (Interview, Brussels, 19 October 2011; Interview, telephone, 17 June 2013). Concerns over the distribution of competences between the Member States and the EU therefore never surfaced (Interview, Brussels, 18 January 2012). Commission and Member State officials commented to the effect that European and Member State policymakers were aware that the ECT project was of a unique nature and constituted a '*one-off*' decision. What is more, the ECT negotiations, despite their complexities, were no '*ideological battlefield*' over competing regulatory approaches. Unlike GATT/WTO or the MAI negotiations in the OECD, European policymakers knew and agreed that the ECT negotiations would not set a precedence for the division of labour, legal competences or global regulatory approaches in future trade and investment negotiations, which the Commission could later invoke to demand for greater de facto or legal competences in other fora (Interview, telephone, 17 June 2013; Interview, Brussels, 18 January 2012). Close Member State cooperation and delegation was thus inherently unproblematic. And as the Commission invested considerable resources in proving itself as a serious broker of international affairs, the Member States were willing to allow the Commission to play an increasingly central role in the negotiating process.

During the core negotiations, Member State preferences nevertheless became more nuanced. The Member States started focusing on the economic rather than geopolitical aspects of the ECT. They increasingly evaluated the provisions of the ECT against the background of ongoing policymaking debates on the Single Market for energy (Interview, telephone, 4 February 2014a). While all Member States continued to support the ECT project and were ready to closely cooperate and to speak with a single voice, EU-internal coordination grew slightly more complicated. The surfacing divisions among the Member States also affected the EU's behaviour and position in the investment negotiations. All Member States could agree on the objective of working toward high post-establishment treatment and protection standards for energy investment. Hence, the EU firmly pushed for such provisions in the negotiations on the ECT (Agence Europe, 1992b, 1993k). The Member States nevertheless disagreed on the scope and desirability of investment liberalisation commitments under the ECT. Negotiations on investment liberalisation commitments under the ECT were intimately linked to debates on the liberalisation of energy investments within the emerging Single Market for energy, the privatisation of national utilities and the demonopolisation of national energy sectors through mandatory 'TPA' to gas and electricity networks. The privatisation, demonopolisation and 'TPA' were highly sensitive issues within the Council of Ministers as well as in Member State administrations. The Commission, the United Kingdom, the Netherlands and Belgium were generally in favour of these measures. France, backed by Southern European Member States, sought to contain liberalisation efforts within the EU and under the ECT. Germany held an intermediate position in these debates (Padget, 1992; Interview, telephone, 4 February 2014a). These divisions made it difficult for the EU to develop and to defend a common position vis-à-vis third countries in negotiations on investment liberalisation under the ECT. The divisions repeatedly surfaced in the negotiations on the ECT as well as on the 'supplementary protocol' when, notably, France sought to prevent too extensive investment liberalisation commitments. To conclude, Member State preferences clearly promoted the EU's initial involvement as well as the subsequent use of its de facto competences at different stages of investment-related negotiations on the ECT. While these observations are in line with liberal intergovernmentalism and the assumption that the Member States seek to maximise their capabilities, they show that European business did not shape Member State preferences and promote cooperation and delegation.

6.3 Conclusion

The chapter traced the EU's involvement in the ECT negotiations. It finds that the EU's outstanding role in these negotiations primarily confirms institutionalist supranational thinking. The Commission engaged in policy entrepreneurship and decisively contributed to the EU's central role and extensive de facto competences in this forum. To that end, it drew on its agenda-setting powers, invoked its fringe and implied competences under the CCP and transport policy as well as domestic de facto competences stemming from its central role in the creation of the Single Market for energy. The ECT and this milestone project of the EU, it argued, were linked. While the described dynamics are easily accommodated in principal-agent models, they also echo historical institutionalist concepts. In hindsight, the Commission's activism may be considered as agency-driven institutional 'conversion' and 'layering' fuelling long-term incremental institutional change.

The findings of the chapter challenge societal theories and liberal intergovernmental thinking on cooperation, delegation and integration. The Member States were indeed eager to cooperate and to delegate negotiating to the Commission. They felt that it was in their best economic and geopolitical interest to appear as a unitary actor vis-à-vis the Soviet Union. The Commission's campaigning, its proactive attitude and the perceived *'one-off nature'* of the ECT negotiations further propelled cooperation and delegation. Business preferences and lobbying, nonetheless, did not decisively shape Member State preferences and cooperation. European business was mostly indifferent of the ECT project. European utilities – the most active members of the European business community – opposed the ECT project as a Commission-led attack on their downstream monopolies. The bulk of European business was disengaged. Member State cooperation and delegation in this international investment policymaking instance cannot be considered as the product of underlying business preferences lobbying.

Notes

1 Working group I in charge of drafting the European Energy Charter (chaired by Director General for energy Maniatopoulos); working group II in charge of drafting the ECT (chaired by British diplomat Duncan Slater); working group III in charge of energy efficiency and environmental protection (chaired by Hungarian official); working group IV in charge of questions relating to oil and gas (chaired by Norwegian official); working group V in charge of nuclear energy and safety (chaired by Canadian official).
2 The 'Group of Seven' encompasses Canada, France, Germany, Italy, Japan, the United Kingdom and the United States of America.
3 Albania, Armenia, Australia, Austria, Azerbaijan, Belgium, Belarus, Bulgaria, Canada, Cyprus, Czechoslovakia, Denmark, Estonia, European Communities, Finland, France, Georgia, Germany, Greece, Hungary, Iceland, Interstate Economic Committee of the Soviet Union, Ireland, Italy, Japan, Kazakhstan, Kyrgyzstan, Latvia, Liechtenstein, Lithuania, Luxembourg, Malta, Moldova, The Netherlands, Norway, Poland, Portugal, Romania, Russian Federation, Spain, Sweden, Switzerland, Tajikistan, Turkey, Turkmenistan, Ukraine, United Kingdom, United States of America, Uzbekistan, Yugoslavia.
4 The regulatory challenges of investments in the energy sector differ in two important regards from investments in most other economic sectors. First, investments in the

energy sector are normally of considerable volume, complexity and duration. Energy exploration, exploitation, transport and distribution are highly capital-intensive activities. Investment projects often run over a period of 20 years or more before amortisation. And they are structured in a sequence of sub-projects and investments (construction of base camps, exploration and initial drilling, building of pipelines, roads, harbours, etc.), which blurs the distinction between the pre- and post-establishment stage under international investment law. Second, host country governments normally assume a dual role in the energy sector. Governments act as supposedly neutral regulators of the national energy sector as well as proper economic actors. Many governments, for instance, act as business partners of foreign investors in joint ventures with state-owned energy companies. See Wälde (1996) for more information on this matter.

5 The communication is of considerable relevance for today's policy debate on future EU investment agreements. It addresses the question of how to ensure the supremacy of EU law in intra-EU investment relations as well as how to ensure the judicial monopoly of the European Court of Justice to authoritatively interpret European law. In particular, the latter question is of considerable relevance today.

6 The E&P Forum is the predecessor of today's International Oil and Gas Producer Association.

References

Agence Europe, 1998. Energy Charter: Adoption of Supplementary Charter postponed to end-June (5 May 1998).

Agence Europe, 1997a. Energy Charter (22 January 1997).

Agence Europe, 1997b. EU/Energy Charter: First Charter implementing treaty will enter into force in March 1998 (4 December 1997).

Agence Europe, 1994a. Energy plenary session: Will Russia confirm its hopes for early endorsement? (26 February 1994).

Agence Europe, 1994b. General Affairs Council supports energy charter compromise (19 May 1994).

Agence Europe, 1994c. Energy Charter: First implementation treaty to be signed without knowing if the US can accept it (20 September 1994).

Agence Europe, 1994d. United States calls for negotiations to be reopened on energy charter treaty (14 October 1994).

Agence Europe, 1993a. Chairman of the conference on European Energy Charter hopes that an agreement can be reached by summer (31 March 1993).

Agence Europe, 1993b. European conference makes 'considerable progress' towards signature of energy charter (21 December 1993).

Agence Europe, 1993c. Energy Charter could become legal treaty by early 1994 (12 October 1993).

Agence Europe, 1993d. Energy Charter: Results of trilateral meeting between the EC, Russia and the US (15 September 1993).

Agence Europe, 1993e. Significant political questions and technical problems complicate negotiations on European Energy Charter (24 March 1993).

Agence Europe, 1993f. Russian reticence puts European Energy Charter negotiations in deadlock (1 July 1993).

Agence Europe, 1993g. Progress on Energy Charter (6 July 1993).

Agence Europe, 1993h. Energy: Controversial points on Energy Charter to be discussed at the trilateral meeting (4 September 1993).

Agence Europe, 1993i. Commission wants to provoke debate on member countries' approach to energy charter (5 November 1993).
Agence Europe, 1993j. Results of General Affairs Council (10 November 1993).
Agence Europe, 1993k. Council approves two-phase approach in implementing energy charter (11 November 1993).
Agence Europe, 1992a. Work reopened on implementation of European Energy Charter (7 March 1992).
Agence Europe, 1992b. Preparation of the draft basic agreement giving effect to the European Energy Charter (3 April 1992).
Agence Europe, 1992c. Negotiations on the basic agreement of the European Energy Charter are making headway (11 April 1992).
Agence Europe, 1992d. European energy charter implementation to be speeded up from May (15 May 1992).
Agence Europe, 1992e. Major European energy distributors and trade unions in the sector condemn the commission's energy policy (31 January 1992).
Agence Europe, 1992f. Belgian industry support for proposals on liberalisation of energy markets (3 March 1992).
Agence Europe, 1991a. Community to draw up draft energy charter, organise international conference (17 April 1991).
Agence Europe, 1991b. Energy Council agrees on gas transit directive but not on policy in case of oil supply problems (1 June 1991).
Agence Europe, 1991c. US, Japan and Canada invited to conference on European Energy Charter (19 June 1991).
Agence Europe, 1991d. Participants in energy charter conference stress the need for urgent action (18 July 1991).
Agence Europe, 1991e. Events in USSR lead MEPs to call for an acceleration towards political union (12 September 1991).
Agence Europe, 1991f. The main points of the European Energy Charter have been defined (2 October 1991).
Agence Europe, 1991g. Work resumes on the 'European Energy Charter' (21 September 1991).
Agence Europe, 1991h. Speech by Mr. Lubbers prior to signing of the Energy Charter (17 December 1991).
Agence Europe, 1990a. CSCE Summit; Delors proposal for European Energy Charter Treaty (20 November 1990).
Agence Europe, 1990b. Special edition: European Council Presidency conclusions (16 December 1990).
Agence Europe, 1990c. Rome Summit expected to adopt decisions on cooperation agreement with USSR (24 November 1990).
Bernasconi-Osterwalder, N., Hoffmann, R.T., 2012. *The German Nuclear Phase-out put to the test in international investment arbitration? Background to the new dispute Vatenfall v. Germany (II)*, Briefing Note. IISD.
Brzezinski, Z., Sullivan, P. (Eds.), 1997. *Russia and the commonwealth of independent states: Documents, data, and analysis.* Center for Strategic and International Studies, Washington, DC.
Buchan, D., 1991. European energy charter finalised (14 February 1991) 4.
Buchan, D., 1990. EC seeks Soviet energy charter (19 October 1990). *Financ. Times* 2.
Doré, J., 1996. Negotiating the Energy Charter Treaty, in: Wälde, T. (Ed.), *The Energy Charter Treaty: An East-West gateway for investment and trade.* Kluwer Law International, London, pp. 137–155.

Eikeland, P.O., 2004. The long and winding road to the internal energy market: Consistencies and inconsistencies in EU policy. *FNI Rep.* 8.
Energy Charter Secretariat, 2004. The Energy Charter Treaty and related documents. Brussels.
Energy Charter Secretariat, 2003. The Energy Charter Treaty: A reader's guide. Brussels.
European Commission, 1993. The European Energy Charter: Fresh impetus from the European Community (COM(93)542). Brussels.
European Commission, 1991. European Energy Charter (COM(91)36). Brussels.
European Commission, 1985. Completing the Internal Market (COM(85) 310). Brussels.
Evtuhov, C., Goldfrank, D., Hughes, L., Stites, R., 2004. *A history of Russia: Peoples legends, events, forces*. Houghton Mifflin Company, New York.
Hill, A., 1992. CIS hopes for energy charter (20 June 1992). *Financ. Times*.
Hill, A., 1991a. Commission sets sights on electricity and gas monopolies (21 October 1991). *Financ. Times*.
Hill, A., 1991b. Soviets to sign energy charter (22 November 1991). *Financ. Times* 2.
Hill, A., 1991c. Lubbers in hurry over energy plan (17 December 1991). *Financ. Times* 2.
Hill, A., Gardner, D., 1991. Coup against Gorbachev: EC could halt up to Ecu 1.15bn of aid (20 August 1991). *Financ. Times* 4.
Hill, A., Hargreaves, D., 1991. Mosocow's stance key to European energy charter (15 July 1991). *Financ. Times*.
Hill, A., Lloyd, J., 1991. The European market: Dutch fear their star guest could spoil Europe's energy party: The Soviet situation has changed so radically the whole charter project risks being bogged down (4 November 1991). *Financ. Times* 4.
Hosking, G., 2012. *Russian history: A very short introduction*. Oxford University Press, Oxford.
ITA Law, 2014. Yukos Universal Limited (Isle of Man) v. The Russian Federation, UNCITRAL, PCA Case No. 227 [WWW Document]. URL www.italaw.com/cases/1175 (accessed 10.2.14).
Jenkins, D., 1996. An oil and gas industry perspective, in: Wälde, T. (Ed.), *The Energy Charter Treaty: An East-West gateway for investment and trade*. Kluwer Law International, London, pp. 187–193.
Johnstone, C., 1998. Power battle over UK-France trade (10 December 1998). *Eur. Voice*.
Konoplyanik, A., 1996. The Energy Charter Treaty: A Russian perspective, in: Wälde, T. (Ed.), *The Energy Charter Treaty: An East-West gateway for investment and trade*. Kluwer Law International, London, pp. 156–178.
Laurance, B., 1991. Gas exports still vital to many European economies (21 August 1991). *The Guardian*.
Lovell, S., 2009. *The Soviet Union*. Oxford University Press, Oxford.
Mahoney, J., Thelen, K. (Eds.), 2010. *Explaining institutional change: Ambiguity, agency, and power*, 1st ed. Cambridge University Press, Cambridge.
Moravcsik, A., 1991. Negotiating the single European Act: National interests and conventional statecraft in the European Community. *Int. Organ.* 45, 19–56.
Müller, W., 1991. Managing the enlarged European market: A view from VEBA as a multiproduct energy company, in: Hoffmann, L., Siefen, H. (Eds.), *Energy in Europe: The East-West dimension*. Verlag TÜF Rheinland, Frankfurt, pp. 118–125.
Padget, S., 1992. The single European energy market: The politics of realization. *J. Common Mark. Stud.* 30, 53–76.
Palmer, J., 1991. Reform assurance restores aid from EC (20 February 1991). *The Guardian*.

Pollack, M.A., 2003. *The engines of European integration: Delegation, agency, and agenda setting in the EU*. Oxford University Press, Oxford.

Riley, D., 1991. Risks and opportunities for oil and gas companies, in: Hoffmann, L., Siefen, H. (Eds.), *Energy in Europe: The East-West dimension*. Verlag TÜF Rheinland, Frankfurt, pp. 109–117.

Streeck, W., Thelen, K.A. (Eds.), 2005. *Beyond continuity: Institutional change in advanced political economies*. Oxford University Press, Oxford.

Thompson, J., 1998. *Russia & the Soviet Union: An historical introduction form the Kievan State to the present*. Westview Press, Oxford.

Wälde, T., 1996. International investment under the 1994 Energy Charter Treaty, in: Wälde, T. (Ed.), *The Energy Charter Treaty: An East-West gateway for investment and trade*. Kluwer Law International, London, pp. 251–320.

Young, A.R., 2002. *Extending European cooperation: The European Union and the 'new' international trade agenda*. Manchester University Press, Manchester.

Young, A.R., 2001. *Extending European cooperation: The European Union and the 'new' international trade agenda*, EUI working papers. RSC. European University Institute, Economics Department.

7 The EU in negotiations on the multilateral agreement on investment and the Singapore Issues

The Chapter examines the EU's involvement in the investment negotiations on the MAI in the OECD (1995–1998) as well as in the consequent negotiations on investment as part of the so-called Singapore Issues in the WTO (1996–2003). The negotiations on the MAI and the Singapore Issues are examined in one chapter, as they were intimately linked. The chapter draws an intriguing picture of European Integration. It lends support to institutionalist and supranational thinking, but challenges societal and intergovernmental thinking on cooperation, delegation and integration.

In the early 1990s, the USA proposed negotiations on the MAI in the OECD to increase pressure on developing countries, which were blocking equivalent efforts in the WTO (see Chapter 5). The Member States supported the US proposal, but sought to contain the EU and the Commission's role in the MAI negotiations. The Member States' reluctance to give the Commission a central role in this policymaking forum had two reasons. First, the Member States typically speak on their own behalf in the OECD – unlike in the WTO – on matters coming under national competence. Second, the Member States were under the impression of the recent legal dispute regarding the EU's competences in foreign economic relations, which had surfaced in Opinions 1/94 and 2/92 (see Chapter 9). They were thus determined to keep the Commission's involvement to a minimum to avoid any political or legal precedent. The Commission showed resourceful to nonetheless consolidate its role in these investment negotiations. It invoked fringe competences to impose its involvement in the negotiations. At the same time, it successfully pushed within and beyond the EU for keeping investment on the agenda of the WTO as part of the Singapore Issues. The underlying rationale was that – unlike in OECD-based talks – the Commission was the EU's accepted single voice in the WTO and could thereby keep a 'foot in the door' of investment regulation. When the MAI negotiations broke down due to substantive disagreements and institutional rivalries, the Commission seized the opportunity and managed to upgrade investment discussions in the WTO to proper multilateral negotiations. The Commission consequently served as the EU's single voice in WTO-based investment negotiations. European business, finally, showed moderate support for the negotiations on the MAI and Singapore Issues, but was little interested in the EU's representation modalities. The observations confirm institutionalist and supranational thinking. In line with principal-agent and historical institutionalist research, the Commission invoked fringe competences ('conversion') and shaped the policy environment through international forum shopping ('drift') to consolidate its role in international investment policy.

7.1 The way towards the multilateral agreement on investment negotiations

Plans to negotiate a binding MAI under the auspices of the OECD reach back to the 1960s (Muchlinski, 2000, pp. 1035–1036). In 1962, the OECD produced the Draft Convention on the Protection of Foreign Property, which, however, was never adopted due to disagreements among its members. Instead the Draft Convention served afterwards as a model text for BITs for the coming decades. At the same time, the OECD elaborated the Codes of Liberalisation of Capital Movements and Invisible Operations. The Codes remain until today a key policy instrument in the liberalisation and treatment of capital and investment flows. The Codes are, however, mere gentlemen's agreements, which are enforced through peer review in OECD meetings (Muchlinski, 2000, pp. 1035–1036). In 1988, the OECD countries explored the possibility of upgrading the Codes to a comprehensive multilateral investment agreement. The talks nevertheless quickly ended in stalemate. The United States was unwilling to grant Canada a NT exemption for its cultural sector and started pushing for talks on ambitious investment liberalisation commitments. Negotiations on comprehensive investment liberalisation commitments, however, were not acceptable for most other OECD countries (Corporate Europe Observatory, 1998; Tieleman, 2000, p. 8).

7.1.1 US pressure for multilateral investment negotiations in the OECD

The US government soon revived plans to negotiate a multilateral investment agreement in the OECD (Lawrence et al., 2006, pp. 149–153; Smythe, 1998, pp. 242–245). US pressure led to the decision of the OECD Council of Ministers[1] to commission a feasibility study on the prospects of establishing a MAI. Observers interpreted the US efforts to re-launch negotiations in the OECD as a reaction to the onerous talks on investment disciplines in the Uruguay Round of the GATT. As described in Chapter IV, the US government had pushed investment disciplines onto the agenda of the Uruguay Round and remained throughout the entire negotiating process the *demandeur* of the creation of ambitious investment disciplines under the GATT. Developing countries, however, persistently opposed US plans to establish a full-fledged investment framework. The US government thus started pushing for negotiations on a multilateral investment agreement in the OECD in order to create an outside option to the Uruguay Round. The underlying reasoning of the US government was that developing countries could either cooperate by contributing to the Uruguay Round negotiations on an ambitious multilateral investment framework or else get sidelined in the form of an OECD investment agreement. The US government assumed that negotiations on investment disciplines in the OECD would be an easy and swift enterprise, which would produce a state-of-the-art multilateral investment agreement. The agreement should be open for accession of non-OECD states and thereby, de facto, set global investment policy standards, which would practically also bind the opposing developing countries. The US government – and in particular the US State Department – thereby sought to increase pressure on developing countries to adopt a more collaborative attitude toward investment negotiations in the GATT. This strategy reportedly guided the US government throughout the MAI negotiations (Corporate Europe Observatory, 1998; Lawrence et al., 2006, pp. 149–143; Smythe, 1998, pp. 242–245; Tieleman, 2000, p. 8).

Due to US pressure, the OECD's Committee on International Investment and Multinational Enterprise (CIME) and the Committee on Capital Movements and Invisible Transactions (CMIT) officially re-examined the possibility of establishing a multilateral investment agreement under the auspices of the OECD after 1991 (Henderson, 1999, p. 19). In early 1994, the committees set up five issue-specific working groups[2] so as to examine various technical matters in more detail. The OECD Council of Ministers received a joint draft report of the CIME, CMIT and working groups in June 1994 and requested the OECD Secretariat to prepare a formal negotiating mandate (OECD, 1995a).

7.1.2 Lukewarm business support

Business was involved in the preparations of the MAI negotiations and generally welcomed the project. The US Council on International Business (USCIB) was reportedly the most supportive national business federation and provided significant input. USCIB pointed out that investment had become even more important than traditional trade in goods and thus required multilateral rules (Lawrence et al., 2006, pp. 152–153). The Business and Industry Advisory Committee to the OECD (BIAC) – the official representative of the business community in OECD policymaking – was closely involved in the discussions on the draft mandate and accompanying final report on the MAI. BIAC promoted the MAI negotiations and reportedly markedly influence the negotiating mandate and the accompanying final report. European business federations like UNICE – today BusinessEurope – also welcomed the MAI initiative and participated in discussions on the negotiation agenda of the MAI. UNICE commented at the end of preparatory discussions that it was satisfied with the mandate and final report (Tieleman, 2000, pp. 9–10). Several Member State business federations voiced similar general statements of support without voicing specific requests (Interview, by telephone, 3 July 2013; Interview, by telephone, 17 June 2013). Unlike American business, which primarily focused on investment liberalisation, European business reportedly was mostly interested in enhancing post-establishment treatment and protection standards in developing countries (Woolcock, 1990, p. 25; Interview, Brussels, 13 June 2012). The support of European business thus hinged on the assumption that the MAI would be multilateralised either through subsequent WTO negotiations or the accession of non-OECD countries. Some business representatives however were more hesitant regarding the project. They feared that European policymakers were unfamiliar with the NAFTA approach of investment regulation, which clearly informed the MAI project. They cautioned that European policymakers might therefore lose out in negotiations on investment liberalisation to the detriment of European business (Interview, telephone, 3 July 2013). Finally, the Trade Union Advisory Committee to the OECD (TUAC) was also regularly consulted on the MAI initiative, but got less involved in the preparations (Tieleman, 2000, pp. 10–11).

Many experts though questioned the authenticity of business support for the MAI project. Many business federations, which came out in favour of the MAI initiative, had very close ties with governments. Former diplomats of the US State Department – the main promoter of the MAI negotiations – for instance were heading USCIB. Many experts came to the conclusion that governments artificially triggered business demands for the MAI. Pierre Sauvé, then official at the OECD's Trade Directorate, commented, *"Bureaucracies were proposing an agreement that the private sector in most countries was not necessarily calling for"* (as cited in Lawrence et al., 2006, p. 153).

The OECD Council of Ministers reconvened and examined the proposed negotiating mandate and an attached final report in May 1995 (Lawrence et al., 2006, pp. 153–156). The final report on the MAI initiative stated that the preceding years had brought a surge in international investment activities. It was now the right time to establish a multilateral framework for international investment. The report lay out as negotiating objectives that the MAI should provide for ambitious investment liberalisation, investment protection and investment dispute settlement provisions (Lawrence et al., 2006, pp. 153–156).

On 5 May 1995 and largely in response to US instigation, the OECD Council of Ministers endorsed the final report, the negotiating objectives and the formal mandate without controversy (Graham, 2000, p. 2). It underlined in the formal mandate that the MAI should be a self-standing international treaty and open to accession by OECD countries, the European Communities and non-OECD countries. The Council, moreover, indicated that the OECD ministerial meeting of 1997 should conclude the MAI negotiations. The literature reports that all OECD countries seemed to generally agree on the objectives and content of the MAI and were optimistic about bringing the negotiations to a successful and swift conclusion. Experts observed that the launch of the MAI negotiations took place in the favourable environment created by the recent wave of BIT conclusions, the successful ratification of NAFTA and the ECT. In comparison to these complex negotiations, the MAI negotiations looked like a 'walk in the park' – an easy stocktaking of best practices among like-minded capital-exporting Western democracies (OECD, 1995a).

7.1.3 Commission entrepreneurship for WTO-based investment negotiations

Not all participating parties shared the enthusiasm of the US government for the MAI project (Dymond, 1999, p. 26; Smythe, 1998, pp. 239, 244–245). In particular the European Commission – which participated in all OECD meetings as the representative of the EU – did not hide its half-hearted support for the initiative (Graham, 2000, pp. 23–25; Henderson, 1999, p. 15; Muchlinski, 2000, p. 1039). Functionalist and power considerations explain the Commission's scepticism regarding the MAI negotiations. First, the Commission argued that negotiations on multilateral investment disciplines in the OECD could only deliver second-best solutions in comparison to negotiations in the WTO. About a month before the endorsement of the mandate for the MAI negotiations in the OECD, the Commission published its communication *A Level Playing Field for Direct Investment World-Wide* in which it described its overall approach to international investment policy (European Commission, 1995). The communication underlined that the WTO should be the primary forum for multilateral negotiations on investment disciplines so as to get developing and emerging countries aboard. Most investment barriers resided in developing and emerging countries, whereas OECD countries were already relatively open and granted high levels of investment protection. In the eyes of the Commission, and arguably European investors, the MAI initiative would marginally enhance the investment climate in the least critical countries, while excluding from the outset those countries where European investors suffered most from high market access barriers and insufficient protection. The MAI negotiations could deliver only marginal benefits for business and the contracting states. The Commissioner for Trade, Sir Leon Brittan, did not get tired of reiterating this position in public statements throughout the MAI negotiations.[3] And a former top official of DG Trade, who oversaw the Commission's participation from Brussels, recalled that he continuously qualified the MAI as a '*bad and pointless project*' in Commission-internal debates (Interview, Brussels, 24 September 2013).

The second reason for the Commission's scepticism regarding the MAI negotiations was arguably its de facto representation monopoly in the WTO. The Commission reportedly favoured the WTO over the OECD, because it would act as sole representative of the EU and its Member States in WTO negotiations. It was nevertheless evident that the Commission would have to negotiate together with Member State delegations in the OECD, as the Member States were competent regarding many aspects of international investment policy and traditionally participated and spoke in the OECD on their own behalf. The Commission did not underline this motivation in public statements, but involved experts and the literature on the MAI almost unanimously point to this concern behind the Commission's position. The view is also indirectly supported by the observation that most EU Member States were more supportive of holding multilateral negotiations on investment disciplines in the OECD, as it enabled them to negotiate for themselves (Dymond, 1999, p. 28; Lawrence et al., 2006, p. 151; Muchlinski, 2000, p. 1039).

Even though the Council of Ministers of the OECD formally launched the MAI negotiations on 5 May 1995, the Commission did not drop its reservations or plan to hold negotiations on international investment disciplines under the auspices of the WTO. The Commission continuously expounded the problem that the MAI negotiations could only deliver second-best solutions. In EU-internal debates, the Commission persistently demanded the Council of Ministers of the EU for a mandate to push investment disciplines back onto the working agenda of the

WTO. The Commission, moreover, continued international debates with Canada, developing countries and the United States so as to gather support for also negotiating on investment disciplines under the auspices of the WTO (Smythe, 1998, pp. 244–245; Woolcock, 1993, p. 251). Many developing countries and the United States were very critical regarding the Commission's proposals, while Canada, Japan and South Korea were supportive (Smythe, 1998, pp. 244–245; Woolcock, 1993, p. 251). In 1996, the Commission's two-level game and advocacy for WTO work on investment played out. The Council of Ministers of the EU followed the Commission's recommendations and provided it with a mandate to seek the inclusion of investment into the working agenda of the WTO on the occasion of the first ministerial meeting of the WTO in Singapore at the end of the year (Graham, 2000, pp. 24–25).

The US government criticised the decision of the Council of Ministers of the EU (Graham, 2000, pp. 24–25). The US government felt that the EU – and more specifically the Commission – sought to sideline the MAI negotiations. Frustrated with these developments and the Commission's activism, the US government directly addressed the EU Member States and demanded them to confirm their full commitment to the MAI negotiations in the OECD. In the course of these debates, the US government, the Commission and the EU Member States ultimately reached a shaky compromise. The US government agreed that it would support the EU's initiative to set international investment disciplines back onto the working agenda of the WTO. The EU Member States and the Commission, on the other hand, would publically acknowledge and accept that the MAI negotiations would remain the primary forum for negotiations on multilateral investment disciplines (Graham, 2000, pp. 24–25).

In December 1996, the ministers of the newly created WTO gathered in Singapore so as to discuss the working agenda for the coming years. The discussions took place already under the impression that a new round of multilateral trade negotiations was in preparation. The EU, Canada, Japan and South Korea strongly pushed for establishing working groups on investment, competition, trade facilitation and government procurement (Graham, 2000, pp. 24–25; Kumar, 2003; Woolcock, 1993, p. 251). These working groups should examine the prospects of holding full-fledged negotiations on these issues in the coming round. The four issues became known as *Singapore Issues*. The United States provided half-hearted support to the EU-led initiative during the deliberations in Singapore. Many developing countries strongly criticised the initiative. In the end, the EU and its supporters, however, prevailed and working groups on the four issues were established. The working group on investment started meeting in May 1997 and consulted on the general elements, benefits and risks of a multilateral investment framework under the WTO. The EU and the United States had informally agreed that in-depth discussions and veritable negotiations should only start once the MAI negotiations had ended (Graham, 2000, pp. 24–25; Kumar, 2003; Woolcock, 1993, p. 251). The creation of the WTO investment working group, which should later become the nucleus for investment negotiations during the Doha Round, is the product of the Commission using its agenda-setting powers in EU-internal debates while at the same time mobilising like-minded third countries for its project. The creation of the WTO working group, on the other hand, consolidated the EU's role in international investment policy by making the Commission the EU's single voice in this key forum.

7.1.4 The Commission mandate for the MAI negotiations

Despite only moderate interest of European business, the EU Member States had generally endorsed the MAI project during the preparatory debates on the MAI project. In particular, Germany, Austria, the United Kingdom and the Netherlands had warmed to the project and showed sincere interest. France, on the other hand, formally supported the project, but worried about the implications of the MAI for its often discriminatory and *dirigiste* industrial policy (Interview, telephone, 17 June 2013; Interview, Brussels, 18 January 2012; Interview, Brussels, 24 September 2013). In late 1994, EU-internal discussions on the EU's representation modalities and a potential negotiating mandate for the Commission started.

The Commission reportedly soon tried to convince the Member States to assign it as their sole representative and single voice in the MAI negotiations even though its reservations vis-à-vis the MAI project were well known (Interview, telephone, 3 July 2013). The Commission sought to further consolidate the EU's role in the MAI negotiations by referring to alleged relevant fringe and implied competences. It claimed that the EU was anyway likely to be competent to regulate international investment under the CCP. It added that the upcoming Opinion 1/94 (see Chapter IX) on the scope of the CCP of the ECJ was very likely to confirm its teleological interpretation of the CCP. Disgruntled with the Commission's continuous attempts to expand the EU's competences as inter alia illustrated in Opinion 1/94, the Member States discarded the Commission's proposal and argument. They saw no need to pool negotiating efforts in the hands of the Commission in this forum. National investment policy officials had been successfully representing their governments in the OECD for decades. From their point of view, the pooling of negotiating in the hands of the Commission would merely undermine their competences and was unlikely to deliver a better deal. They, moreover, stressed that the upcoming Opinion 1/94 was likely to prove that most agenda items of the MAI negotiations still came under national competence (Interview, telephone, 3 July 2013). In Council debates prior to the start of the MAI negotiations, some Member States even underlined that they saw no need to coordinate their positions with their counterparts from other EU Member States (Council of Ministers, 1995). In November 1994, the ECJ indeed ruled in favour of the Member States by advancing a remarkably narrow interpretation of the CCP (see Chapter IX). The Commission's attempt to even further extend the EU's de facto competences in international investment policy thus failed as the Member States were fed up with the Commission's competence usurping behaviour.

In May 1995, the Council of Ministers of the EU adopted, without much further debate, a mandate empowering the Commission to participate in the MAI negotiations alongside the Member States (Agence Europe, 1995). The consensus in the

Council of Ministers regarding the joint participation of the Member States and the Commission in the MAI negotiations primarily reflected the EU's undeniable fringe and implied competences in MAI-relevant domains (European Court of Justice, 1994, 1995; Koutrakos, 2006, pp. 40–48) as well as the EU's customary participation – i.e. de facto competences in all OECD meetings as observer. Policymakers from the Member States and the Commission shared the assumption that the MAI would be a 'mixed' agreement. The recent entry into force of the Treaty of Maastricht, and Opinions 1/94 and 2/92, left no doubt that the EU held fringe competences necessary for negotiations (see Chapter IX, Section 3) (European Court of Justice, 1994, 1995; Koutrakos, 2006, pp. 40–48). In particular, the proposed disciplines on investment liberalisation, transfers of funds, trade-related investment measures and certain post-establishment treatment standards indisputably fell into shared or exclusive Union competences according to the Treaty chapter on capital movements and the CCP. The 'mixity' of the MAI obliged the Member States to empower the Commission to participate in the negotiations. As it was impossible to disentangle agenda items in OECD negotiations according to the competence distribution within the EU, European policymakers agreed that the Commission had to participate in all negotiating formations of the MAI talks. In addition to this EU-internal institutional constraint, the OECD functioned as an external institutional constraint promoting the EU/Commission's involvement in the MAI negotiations. The regulatory activity of the EU regarding the Single Market and the work programme of the OECD strongly overlapped, which made close cooperation between the EU and OECD a regulatory necessity. Hence, the EU had been a formal observer in the OECD for many decades. The Commission represented and spoke on behalf of the EU in the OECD meetings. As the EU and the Commission had well-established roles in the OECD, it was coherent for the Member States and other OECD countries to also accept their participation in the MAI negotiations (Dymond, 1999, p. 28; Interview, telephone, 3 July 2013; Interview, Brussels, 18 January 2012).

After the adoption of the mandate, the Council of Ministers further underlined the Member States' claim to competence over international investment regulation vis-à-vis the Commission in the choice of the EU-internal coordination setup for the negotiations. The Council discarded the possibilities of either holding formal coordination meetings on the MAI negotiations in the '113 Committee' or of establishing a specialised Commission working group (Interview, telephone, 3 July 2013). Instead, the Council decided to create an ad hoc Council committee. The committee directly reported to the General Affairs Council and was not linked to a specific treaty chapter such as the CCP or Capital Movements. The Member States thereby underlined that the MAI negotiations primarily came under national competence. They also sought to prevent the creation of a precedent which the Commission could invoke so as to challenge the delimitation of the CCP in Opinion 1/94 (Interview, telephone, 3 July 2013). According to all accounts, European business did not take an interest in these debates, but occasionally repeated its statements of general support for the MAI project. In summary, neither the Member States nor European business were truly interested in speaking with a single voice in the MAI negotiations. Despite the tense relationship with the Member States in the light of Opinion 1/94, the Commission tried to become the EU's single voice but without success. The EU's undeniable fringe and implied competences, nevertheless, ensured a minimum level of EU involvement in the MAI negotiations.

7.2 The MAI negotiations

In September 1995, the delegations of 29 OECD member countries and the Commission started meeting for the first negotiating sessions. The Dutch diplomat Frans Engering was appointed as chairman of the negotiations. The OECD Secretariat hosted and provided technical expertise to the negotiating parties and thereby acquired an important role in the negotiating process. BIAC and TUAC were regularly briefed and invited to submit comments to the MAI negotiations so as to integrate business and labour concerns (Tieleman, 2000, pp. 9–11). Furthermore, representatives of the WTO, the World Bank and the IMF observed the MAI negotiations whenever agenda items concerned their work. In autumn 1997, finally, several non-OECD delegations – Argentina, Brazil, Chile, Hong Kong, China, Estonia, Latvia, Lithuania and Slovakia – gradually joined the negotiations as observers (Henderson, 1999, p. 20).

The negotiating process was structured in several negotiating formations. The so-called Negotiating Group assembled the national lead negotiators and oversaw the entire negotiating process. Deliberations in the Negotiating Group focused on six substantive areas: scope and application of the agreement, investment liberalisation, investment protection, dispute settlement, implementation, accession of non-OECD countries, and the relationship to other investment agreements (OECD, 1995b). The Negotiating Group would determine the general direction of the negotiations as well as resolve disagreements on controversial issues. Negotiations on technical details were delegated to five expert groups and three drafting groups.[4] The similar and narrow foci of the drafting and expert groups underlined the considerable technicality of the MAI negotiations (OECD, n.d.).

7.2.1 The EU in the MAI negotiations

The Member States and the Commission jointly participated and spoke in all negotiating formations of the MAI talks. The Commission typically spoke first in negotiations followed by the individual Member States. The EU was thus much less cohesive in the MAI negotiations than in the Uruguay Round or the ECT negotiations. All interviewees suggested that the Commission was a central negotiating party despite the Member States' initial reservations about involving the EU/Commission in the negotiations. Several interviewees argued that the Commission managed to acquire a central role because of the proactive and constructive negotiating style of the lead negotiators (Interview, Paris, 1 October 2012a; Interview, Paris, 1 October 2012b). The Commission reportedly frequently sought to forge broad coalitions with third countries and came up with compromise proposals so as to advance the negotiations. Despite this general perception, the Commission's powers, and hence role, remained sometimes unclear and became the object of controversy. It was occasionally unclear within the EU delegation – i.e. among the delegations of the EU Member States and the Commission – as well as to third countries, whether the Commission could speak, whether only the Commission could speak and to what extent the Commission's positions in deliberations were authoritative. A former US negotiator commented that the ambivalent powers and role of the Commission sometimes became a problem and slowed down discussions (Interview, Paris, 1 October 2012a; Interview, Paris, 1 October 2012b). In addition to the Commission's role as a proper negotiating party alongside the Member States, it sought to play an important role in coordinating the positions of the then 15 Member States of the EU. The Commission would typically organise coordination meetings in Paris with the delegations of the EU Member States on the morning of each negotiating day as well as before and after important negotiating sessions so as to forge and maintain a common EU position as far as possible.

The readiness of the EU Member States to coordinate their positions nevertheless varied considerably across issue areas (Interview, Paris, 1 October 2012a). Most EU Member State delegations accepted the Commission's coordination attempts on issues like the Regional Economic Integration Clause (REIO) or capital movements, where the EU/Commission was undoubtedly competent to act. In these domains the EU Member States indeed jointly defended a common position, allowed the Commission to speak on their behalf and acted as a 'collective actor' (Interview, Paris, 1 October 2012a). Most EU Member State delegations refused, however, to coordinate on issues falling into national competence like investment protection or questions related to intellectual property rights. What is more, the so-called *big four* – France, Germany, the Netherlands and the United Kingdom – continuously coordinated their positions in these domains among themselves and even with the US government, but deliberately excluded the Commission from these meetings. The Member States – and in particular France, the United Kingdom and Germany – were determined to protect their competences in international investment policy from any attempts by the Commission to interfere and to become active in this domain (Interview, Brussels, 18 February 2012). The Member States' remarkable preoccupation with competences, on the one hand, reflected the great number of investment policy officials involved. Many governments sent – as customary in OECD Committee debates on investment – technical experts in charge of national BIT programmes as negotiators. These expert officials were arguably more concerned with protecting their competences than national trade policy officials and diplomats were, who were already used to close cooperation and did not risk losing any competences from cooperation in this domain. On the other hand, cooperation and coordination between the Commission and the Member States were also clearly influenced by the recent heated debates over the scope of exclusive Union competence under the CCP during the proceedings of Opinions 1/94 and 2/92 (Smythe, 1998, p. 248; Interview, Brussels, 18 January 2012). A former negotiator of the Commission commented to the effect that cooperation with the Member States was very difficult and frustrating in comparison to the preceding ECT negotiations due to the latent struggle over competences (see Chapter VIII) (Interview, Brussels, 18 February 2012).

7.2.2 Substantive disagreements among the negotiating parties

The MAI negotiations quickly gained momentum due to a very intense meeting rhythm. From September 1996 onwards, the Negotiating Group met 23 times – i.e. every six weeks – for three days each time in order to determine the overall direction of the talks. The three-day sessions of the Negotiating Group were followed by three days of technical discussions in the expert and drafting groups so as to examine and hammer out details (Dymond, 1999, p. 29; Interview, Paris, 1 October 2012b). It became soon clear that the MAI negotiations would be a more challenging enterprise than initially thought. The negotiating parties broadly agreed on the key elements of the MAI, as most of them could be found in the more than 1,000 investment agreements which OECD countries had already concluded. Deliberations in the Negotiating Group, expert and drafting groups showed, however, that no common approach to these elements and provisions had emerged among OECD countries. Moreover, the negotiating parties showed unwilling and/or unable to bridge these differences in their national approaches. The following paragraphs briefly summarise technical and political controversies in the Negotiating Group and the degree of European unity on these questions for the period between September 1995 and early 1997 (Dymond, 1999, p. 29).

Disagreements on technical questions were surprisingly frequent (Dymond, 1999, pp. 34–41; Graham, 2000, p. 27; Muchlinski, 2000, pp. 1040–1046; UNCTAD, 1999). Often these technical disagreements reflected the different regulatory approaches under NAFTA-type and European BITs. Many disagreements were thus transatlantic and promoted European unity despite latent competence struggles. The following list contains the most important controversies and is not exhaustive. First of all, the negotiating parties could not agree on a definition of investment. While many European countries favoured a broad, open-ended, asset-based definition, Canada and the USA insisted on a narrow definition of investment, as under NAFTA. Second, the negotiating parties could not agree on disciplines regarding performance requirements and investment incentives. Some delegations considered certain performance requirements as valuable economic policy instruments, while others considered performance requirements as inherently wasteful and discriminatory. Third, the question of whether the MAI should require states to pay financial compensation only for direct or also indirect, creeping expropriation became another point of controversy. Negotiating parties with strong regulatory traditions feared that the obligation to financially compensate for indirect expropriation could become extremely costly and would undermine their right to regulate, while other parties considered such an obligation to be a quintessential element of an IIA. Fourth, the negotiating parties initially also attempted to establish rules preventing discriminatory tax treatment. The Commission, in particular, pushed for negotiations on this issue, as European investors reportedly faced discrimination in many US states. Discussions in a special working group showed to be so complicated that after one year of negotiations all parties agreed to drop the agenda item. Fifth, the inclusion of a non-lowering of standards clause regarding environmental and labour standards became a controversial issue toward the end of the negotiations, when NGOs started criticising the MAI negotiations. While, for instance, the Canadian and US delegations were sympathetic to the idea, many EU Member States rejected such plans. Sixth, although most negotiating parties had ISDS provisions in their BITs, some delegations disliked the plan to provide for ISDS under the MAI and insisted on state-to-state dispute settlement. When, in late 1998, the MAI negotiations collapsed, no compromises had been found for most of these issues (Dymond, 1999, pp. 34–41; Graham, 2000, p. 27; Muchlinski, 2000, pp. 1040–1046; UNCTAD, 1999).

The high number of disagreements on rather technical questions was undoubtedly a burden for the MAI negotiations. Eyewitnesses, nonetheless, agree that it was instead a set of questions relating to investment liberalisation, which seriously endangered and contributed to the collapse of the MAI negotiations. The most significant controversy concerned the question of whether the MAI negotiations should seek commitments on up-front investment liberalisation. The negotiating mandate stipulated,

> *[The MAI] . . . should go beyond existing commitments to achieve a high standard of liberalisation covering both the establishment and post-establishment phase with broad obligations on national treatment, standstill, roll-back, non-discrimination/MFN, and transparency, and apply disciplines to areas of liberalisation not satisfactorily covered by the present OECD instruments;. . . [and] be legally binding and contain provisions regarding its enforcement.*
> (OECD, 1995a)

The negotiating parties interpreted this clause differently. The US delegation argued that the mandate foresaw negotiations on up-front liberalisation commitments. Hence, the United States pushed for bargaining in this area. Canada supported the US delegation. The US demand was widely perceived as an attempt to multilateralise NAFTA. European BITs normally did not bind governments regarding the regulation of inward investment. The chairman of the MAI negotiations, the EU Member States, the Commission and other negotiating parties, on the other hand, were surprised and taken aback by this US demand. The EU Member States and the Commission rejected the US reading of the mandate. They argued that the MAI mandate only foresaw the codification of existing levels of investment liberalisation. The EU Member States and the Commission pointed out that they were not ready to accept any liberalisation commitments in services which went beyond existing GATS and OECD commitments. The Europeans argued that any new liberalisation commitments under the MAI would be multilateralised through the MFN clause of the GATS and thus enable third countries to free ride (Graham, 2000, p. 34). The EU Member States and the Commission instead proposed that the MAI should contain a standstill clause as well as a roll-back obligation like the OECD codes on Capital Movements and Invisible Operations. The US and Canadian delegation in turn disliked the idea of unconditional standstill and rollback clauses. The EU Member States and the Commission moreover stressed that any new liberalisation commitments should be non-reciprocal and arise from the long-established peer review process in the CIME and CMTE after the conclusion of the MAI negotiations (Dymond, 1999, p. 34; Lawrence et al., 2006, p. 157; UNCTAD, 1999, pp. 11–13; Interview, Paris, 1 October 2012b).

Discussions on the question of up-front liberalisation commitments stood increasingly at the centre of the negotiating process. They continued for more than a year without any significant convergence of minds. While the United States strongly insisted on launching negotiations on up-front investment liberalisation, most other countries felt that such negotiations could only start – if at all – once the core text of the MAI was finalised. Unless the core text was agreed, the negotiating parties could not be certain about the actual implications of eliminating reservations. In late 1996, the chairman, nevertheless, proposed that the negotiating parties should table negative lists indicating existing market access reservations for foreign investors. He hoped that the lists would enable the Negotiating Group to find common ground and finally advance on the issue of up-front liberalisation. These hopes were frustrated when the OECD Secretariat received the lists in February 1997. The United States, Canada, many EU Member States and the EU tabled very extensive lists. The US list counted more than 400 pages of highly detailed reservations enumerating non-conforming investment measures as well as a general disclaimer that sub-federal entities would not be bound by the MAI (Marchand, 1998). The lists of the EU Member States and the EU, on the other hand, were often long and very vague in their reservations. Only the Benelux countries tabled few to no reservations (Thomas, 1997). The United States and Canada strongly criticised many EU Member States, as they felt the vague wording of the reservations left many sectors outside the scope of the MAI. Disputes on liberalisation commitments even emerged among EU Member States, which made it impossible to develop and follow a unified EU position in this domain of the negotiations. Spain, for instance, strongly criticised the United Kingdom, which planned to keep access to its fishery sector closed to foreign as well as European investors (Thomas, 1997). A former negotiator recalled that at the end of the negotiations the "*lists of reservations on market access filled three books of the size of telephone directories*" (Interview, Brussels, 24 July 2012a) which clearly showed that the space for agreement among the negotiating parties was extremely limited in this key issue of the negotiations. The extensive lists of reservations made it difficult to strike an acceptable balance of liberalisation commitments among the negotiating parties. Attempts to find solutions to these problems were numerous, but all failed. At the latest, in late 1997, it was clear that the liberalisation commitments under the MAI would not exceed the existing commitments under the OECD codes and GATS. In consequence, US business in particular lost interest in the MAI negotiations (Graham, 2000, pp. 34–35; UNCTAD, 1999, p. 13).

A closely related transatlantic controversy concerned the so-called REIO clause and the applicability of the MAI to sub-national entities (Graham, 2000, pp. 30–31). The EU – and notably the Commission – pushed for the inclusion of a REIO clause into the MAI text. The REIO clause stipulates that liberalisation commitments within regional economic integration organisations like the EU do not have to be granted to third countries under MFN clauses. The EU Member States and the Commission acted very cohesively and sought to prevent the MAI from fully multilateralising access to the Single Market. The US and Canadian delegation criticised the European demand for a REIO clause. They argued that such a clause contradicted the very spirit of the MAI negotiations, as it constituted a huge, open-ended and vague carve-out and would allow for the continued discrimination against foreign investors in the Single Market. The US delegation particularly feared that the REIO clause would enable the EU to circumvent article 54 EC, which stipulates that foreign enterprises incorporated in one Member State had to be treated as European nationals. In other words, the US delegation assumed that a REIO clause could entail a significant de-liberalisation of access to the Single Market. The US delegation, on the other hand, vehemently demanded a clause providing for the non-applicability of the MAI to sub-national entities – i.e. US federal states. The US delegation insisted that it could not conclude the agreement otherwise for constitutional reasons. The Member States, and notably the Commission, stressed that such a clause would constitute a huge carve-out to the MAI and therefore rejected the US demand. The controversy over the REIO and sub-national entities clause could not be resolved before the collapse of the MAI negotiations and increasingly slowed them down (Graham, 2000, pp. 30–31).

The French demand for a general carve-out for cultural industries became a further problem related to the liberalisation of investment flows field (Dymond, 1999, p. 35; Graham, 2000, pp. 31–32; Interview, Brussels, 18 January 2012). The French delegation refused to accept any liberalisation commitments or other obligations in the domain of cultural industries. It argued that cultural industries were central to national identity and culture. The special role of culture for society thus required special treatment under international agreements. Canada, Italy, Belgium, Greece and Australia supported the French demand. The US delegation, on the other hand, strongly opposed it and rejected the alleged special nature of cultural industries for society. The United States argued that the demand for a general exception of cultural industries served to shelter non-competitive national cultural industries. Japan, New Zealand, the Nordic Countries, the United Kingdom, Germany and the Netherlands supported the US position, as they feared that a too broad carve-out would harm their cultural industries abroad (Agence Europe, 1997a). The EU was thus divided on the cultural exception clause. As the matter closely tied into debates on the treatment of intellectual property rights under the MAI – a jealously guarded domain of Member State competence at this time – it was impossible for the Commission to coordinate Member States and define a common strategy in this field (Dymond, 1999, p. 35; Graham, 2000, pp. 31–32; Interview, Brussels, 18 January 2012).

Finally, in summer 1996, the so-called extraterritoriality issue became a major dispute among the negotiating parties and overshadowed the entire MAI negotiations (Dymond, 1999, pp. 37–38; Graham, 2000, pp. 28–31; Muchlinski, 2000,

p. 1047). The Commission and the EU Member States showed great unity in their rejection of the US demand to accommodate the Helms-Burton Act (July 1996) and the Iran-Libya Sanctions Act (June 1996) under the MAI. Most third countries supported the EU position. The Helms-Burton Act, inter alia, enabled US nationals to bring claims before US courts against foreign companies allegedly trafficking in assets expropriated by the Cuban government. The act was particularly controversial as it even enabled persons who had not been US nationals at the time of expropriation to bring claims. The Iran-Libya Sanctions Act, on the other hand, foresaw the imposition of sanctions on foreign firms which invested or traded in oil and gas with Iran or Libya. Most legal experts and negotiating parties agreed that both acts were not in conformity and even contradicted core principles of public international law, international investment law and the key principles of the MAI. The US assertion of, de facto, exporting its legislation to third countries thus caused a severe row between the EU Member States, the Commission and the US delegation. The Commission – in the name of the Member States and the EU – even warned the US delegation that it would file a claim against the Helms-Burton Act at the WTO Dispute Settlement Body as the measure violated the US obligations under the WTO Agreement. The Commission ultimately desisted from this step, when the US government showed its willingness to limit the applicability of both acts against investors and firms from the MAI negotiating parties (Dymond, 1999, pp. 37–38; Graham, 2000, pp. 28–31; Muchlinski, 2000, p. 1047).

In early 1997, technical and political disagreements had become very numerous. Observers agreed that the MAI negotiations had run into serious problems despite the alleged like-mindedness of the negotiating parties. The chairman of the Negotiating Group declared in March 1997 that it was impossible to bring the negotiations to a successful end by May 1997 as stipulated by the negotiating mandate. He advised the negotiating parties to extend the deadline of the MAI negotiations for another year so as to settle the many disagreements (Dymond, 1999, p. 30). The OECD Council of Ministers of May 1997 followed the chairman's advice. The hope that the extension of the negotiating deadline would help to overcome disagreement was soon frustrated. The Negotiating Group showed unable to broker compromises in the following months. During summer and autumn 1997, the question of up-front liberalisation crystallised as the main stumbling block of the MAI negotiations with no agreement between the United States and the EU in sight (Dymond, 1999, p. 30).

The inability of the Negotiating Group to advance the negotiations at this stage was arguably due to the very nature of the MAI negotiations. The MAI negotiations had been conceived and carried out at the bureaucratic level without significant involvement of heads of governments or ministers. With regard to the United States, it is known that Congress never discussed the MAI project before the actual collapse of the negotiations. Also, President Bill Clinton reportedly never looked into the MAI project despite it being a US-led initiative. Politicians from the EU Member States were not involved or interested in the project. The only notable exception was the Commissioner for Trade, Leon Brittan. Commissioner Brittan however was publically in favour of holding multilateral negotiations on investment disciplines in the WTO rather than in the OECD. The absence of political decision-makers from the negotiating process was probably fatal to the MAI negotiations at this stage. Many of the substantive disagreements were too sensitive for bureaucrats to decide. Hence, the MAI negotiations came to halt in the second half of 1997 (Lawrence et al., 2006, pp. 172–173).

7.2.3 Non-governmental organisations and the anti-MAI campaign

NGOs are not of direct relevance to the topic of the study. The NGO community nevertheless claims – rightly or wrongly – to have played a decisive role in the collapse of the MAI negotiations. Hence, the involvement of NGOs in the MAI negotiations should be mentioned at least briefly here so as to provide a comprehensive picture of the negotiating process.

In May 1997 – shortly after the decision of the Council of Ministers of the OECD to extend the deadline of the negotiations – a draft text of the MAI was leaked and widely circulated among NGOs in OECD countries (Tieleman, 2000, p. 11). Most NGOs reacted with outrage. They criticised the fact that the MAI negotiations had been conducted in complete secrecy without democratic scrutiny and that the agreement would significantly circumscribe the regulatory space of the parties. The MAI was depicted as a treaty dictated by multilateral corporations to the detriment of the contracting states and their citizens (Tieleman, 2000, p. 11). The NGO community started an internationally coordinated campaign against the MAI in spring 1997. The campaign sought to explain the content and potential implications to politicians and citizens. In consequence, several trade unions became aware of the issue and pressed their governments to include clauses to ensure the non-lowering of social, labour, health and environmental standards (Dymond, 1999, p. 30). The USA, France and the United Kingdom showed themselves to be sympathetic to these demands, while more orthodox countries like Germany or the Netherlands were only ready to accept preambular language on this point (De Jonquières, 1998a). Due to the NGO campaign, the general public – in particular in France – developed a strong interest in the negotiations. Demonstrations were held outside the premises of the OECD in Paris. And the MAI negotiations even became a hotly debated topic among cineastes at the Cannes Film Festival of 1998 (Interview, Paris, 1 October 2012a). The OECD Secretariat was caught off guard by these developments. In an apparent reaction of panic, it published the draft text of the MAI in spring 1997 and invited the NGO community to consultation meetings (Tieleman, 2000, pp. 12, 15–16). The NGO community saw these measures as hypocritical and laconically reiterated its demand to abandon the MAI project (Graham, 2000, pp. 47–48).

As the opposition from NGOs grew ever stronger during 1997, a well-known structural problem of the MAI negotiations came to bear down on them even more strongly. Business stood to be the beneficiary of the MAI project, but hardly spoke up for the MAI project (Graham, 2000, p. 49; Lawrence et al., 2006, pp. 171–172; Woolcock, 2003, p. 251). American business had lost interest in the project when it had become clear that the MAI would not deliver liberalisation commitments beyond existing GATS and OECD commitments. European business, on the other hand, had always shown rather lukewarm support. And its interest in the project further diminished when it became apparent that the MAI would include special clauses regarding social, health and environmental standards. European business felt that the MAI would set a lower level of investment protection and post-establishment treatment than normally afforded under Member State BITs. It again became evident that the MAI negotiations were mostly a government-driven rather than a business-driven initiative. The lack of business support for the MAI weakened the argumentative position of policymakers in public debates (Graham, 2000, p. 49; Lawrence et al., 2006, pp. 171–172; Woolcock, 2003, p. 251).

7.2.4 The collapse of the MAI negotiations – a tale of competence struggles and institutional rivalries

In May 1997, the OECD Council of Ministers had extended the deadline for the conclusion of the MAI negotiations for another year in the hope of finally resolving the many substantive disagreements, which had surfaced during the first two years (Dymond, 1999, pp. 30–32). Instead, the disagreements further crystallised and the NGO campaign further complicated the negotiations. As the year 1997 elapsed, it became evident that the Negotiating Group would not conclude the technical work on the MAI within the extended deadline. The Negotiating Group announced it would be seeking a political settlement over the remaining controversies until April 1998. The political settlement should comprise the broad structures and key components of the MAI. The details and technical drafting of the agreement should then be completed after April/May 1998 (Dymond, 1999, pp. 30–32).

In January 1998, the USA, however, explained that the remaining time was insufficient for reaching a political settlement on the many outstanding issues (Dymond, 1999, p. 31; Lawrence et al., 2006, pp. 172–173). The Member States and the Commission rejected the US view. It was clear to most delegations that the US government adopted this new position because it had not been able to renew its fast-track authority from Congress for the MAI negotiations. Due to the mounting anti-MAI campaign in the United States and upcoming midterm elections, the US government was not keen on making a fresh attempt in the near future. The US government did not want domestic debates on its trade policy strategy at this point in time and hence had no intention to either conclude or discontinue the MAI negotiations. The main *demandeur* thus de facto withdrew from the MAI negotiations for the foreseeable future (Dymond, 1999, p. 31; Lawrence et al., 2006, pp. 172–173).

The Europeans collectively underlined their continuing commitment to a quick conclusion of the MAI negotiations in March 1998. The Commission tabled a communication demanding the Council of Ministers to adopt a unified position and cohesive negotiating strategy so as to bring the MAI talks to a swift and successful end against all odds (Agence Europe, 1997b). The Commission called in particular for a common approach regarding the applicability of the agreement to sub-national entities, a general limitation of the number of reservations, the controversy over extraterritorial enforcement of national legislation, and related the definition of national security. The EU and the Member States disagreed on all of these points with the United States, which implicitly suggests that the Commission called for a cohesive stance of the EU vis-à-vis the United States (Agence Europe, 1997b). The Council of Ministers acknowledged the Commission's communication and enumerated its proper objectives for the remaining month of negotiations. The Council reply indicated that the MAI should be applicable to sub-national entities, should contain a REIO clause, conform with WTO law, contain the exterritorial applicability of national law and should not contain liberalisation obligations exceeding GATS commitments. The Council reply, moreover, indicated that France insisted on a cultural exception clause, while other Member States were hesitant (Agence Europe, 1997a). European business also called one last time for a swift conclusion of the talks. UNICE stressed that the failure to conclude the MAI negotiations in May 1998 would be particularly detrimental for European SMEs, which relied much more on transparent and predictable investment conditions than big multinational companies. It stressed, moreover, that OECD and WTO negotiations on investment disciplines should not exclude each other (Agence Europe, 1998a).

The Negotiating Group continued its frequent meetings until April 1998 without, however, engaging in serious negotiations. With the USA de facto withdrawn from the process, it was impossible to resolve any outstanding issues. In April 1998, the French government demanded a formal suspension of the MAI negotiations. The underlying assumption was that any negotiating efforts would be in vain until the midterm elections in the United States were over and the US government could seek fast-track authority (De Jonquières and Kuper, 1998). The United States and Canada were sympathetic to the French proposal. Most other negotiating parties rejected it, as they feared that a formal suspension would practically kill off the MAI negotiations. The OECD Council of Ministers thus extended the mandate of the MAI negotiations without setting a new deadline and arranged for the next meeting of the Negotiating Group on 20 October 1998. The negotiating parties should use the pause in the talks to better communicate the advantages of the MAI to their constituencies. Most observers and media interpreted this outcome of the meeting of the OECD Council of Ministers, nevertheless, as the de facto break down of the MAI negotiations (Denny, 1998; Financial Times, 1998; Turner, 1998). And indeed when the 20 October 1998 came, it had become impossible to continue with the MAI negotiations. France had declared its withdrawal from the MAI negotiation on 14 October 1998 (Marchand, 1998). As France was one of the biggest OECD economies and a major hub for foreign investment, the decision seriously undermined the MAI project. Moreover, the French withdrawal cast doubts on the EU's legal ability, and the validity of the Commission's mandate, to further pursue the MAI negotiations (Chatignoux, 1998; Lawrence et al., 2006, pp. 174–175).

What caused these developments of autumn 1998? It is often assumed that the NGO campaign was the straw that broke the camel's back and triggered the collapse of the MAI negotiations. All interviewed negotiators nevertheless rejected this

Multilateral agreement on investment 157

view. They explained that the substantive disagreement among the parties were the underlying reason for the breakdown of the MAI negotiations. They elaborated that rather competence struggles and institutional rivalries between the office of the USTR and the US State Department and, to a lesser degree, between the Commission and the Member States were the catalyst triggering the breakdown of the MAI negotiations. Some interviewees even suggested that the USTR and the Commission deliberately obstructed the MAI negotiations during the third year in order to end the negotiations in the OECD and push investment negotiations into other negotiating fora, like FTAs or the WTO.

The US delegation comprised officials from the State Department, the Treasury and the USTR. The State Department was traditionally in the lead in OECD negotiations and the main driver of the MAI project. The Treasury took part in the talks due to their potential bearing on the American financial sector and primarily sought to prevent any liberalisation of market access for financial services. The USTR participated as it was normally in charge of international investment negotiations and trade policy. Institutional rivalries and competence struggles developed early between the State Department and the USTR (Interview, Paris, 1 October 2012a). The USTR did not hide that it considered the MAI project to be an inappropriate interference of the State Department in its policy domain. Moreover, the USTR made known that it considered the MAI negotiations a futile project. After the failure to establish ambitious investment disciplines in the Uruguay Round, the USTR was convinced that the time was not ripe for multilateral negotiations. When the first disagreements started slowing down the MAI negotiations in the first year, the USTR took it as a confirmation of its view. The USTR decided to scale down its involvement in the daily negotiating process. Its officials no longer regularly participated in the meetings of the Negotiating Group, or of the expert and drafting group. Instead of focusing on the MAI negotiations, the USTR henceforth stepped up its efforts to conclude bilateral trade and investment agreements with third countries. While the behaviour of the USTR illustrated already its tense relations with the State Department, it did not directly threaten the continuation of the MAI project (De Jonquières, 1998b; Interview, Paris, 1 October 2012a; Interview, Paris, 1 October 2012b).

The institutional rivalries became critical in autumn 1998. The State Department still held on to its plan to conclude the MAI negotiations once the US midterm elections were over. The USTR, on the other hand, considered the MAI project as, de facto, failed (De Jonquières, 1998b). At the same time, debates in France took a critical turn. Trade unions, cultural industries, artists and NGOs drew a lot of attention to the MAI project. Anti-MAI demonstrations were held in the streets of Paris and media coverage was intense. The MAI was depicted in the public debate as the surrender of the state and its citizens to the dictate of multinational corporations and their profit-making interests. What is more, some parts of French business, like the film industry and audiovisual companies, demanded the French government to withdraw from the MAI negotiations. Other parts of the French business community were not interested in the negotiating process and public debates as the MAI did not promise significant benefits. Moreover, the Communists and the

Greens – both part of the coalition government with the Socialists – gradually saw the MAI as an election topic. During 1998, politicians from both parties started criticising the MAI project and demanded – together with NGOs, trade unions, certain business groups and artists – the withdrawal of the country from the negotiations (Agence Europe, 1998b; Chatignoux, 1998).

In 1998, Prime Minister Lionel Jospin and the Socialist Party realised that they stood to lose a lot while winning almost nothing from further participating in the MAI negotiations (Interview, Paris, 1 October 2012a; Interview, Paris, 1 October 2012b). In the eyes of Jospin, the only serious risk of withdrawing from the MAI negotiations was a potential deterioration of French-American relations. In autumn 1998, Jospin therefore commissioned his Minister of Economics, Dominique Strauss-Kahn, to discuss with USTR Charlene Barshefsky the possibility of France dropping out of the negotiations. Barshefsky, who was known to describe the draft MAI as a 'lousy agreement', reportedly signalled to Strauss-Kahn that a French withdrawal would not entail a deterioration of French-American relations and thereby clearly encouraged the French government to leave the negotiating table. A former MAI negotiator and official of the State Department commented that Barshefsky's position had not been cleared with the State Department, which officially led the US delegation. The State Department perceived this as an act of betrayal, which contradicted the formal US position (Interview, Paris, 1 October 2012a; Interview, Paris, 1 October 2012b).

On 14 October 1998 – one week before the resumption of the MAI talks – Jospin informed the Assemblée Nationale that France would withdraw from the MAI negotiations (Chatignoux, 1998). Jospin stressed that French key demands were not met and that the current MAI draft was unacceptable. He added that the draft was no longer a suitable basis for the continuation of the talks. Jospin declared that instead his government would seek the opening of multilateral investment negotiations under the auspices of the WTO. In his view this was a more suitable forum for negotiations. Negotiations in the WTO would enable developing countries to participate delivering more balanced and equitable results (Chatignoux, 1998). France thereby became overnight the Commission's strongest ally in the Council of Ministers in demanding the continuation of multilateral investment negations in the WTO. Jospin's decision to withdraw from the MAI negotiations had not been coordinated with his coalition partners – the Communists and the Greens – or with other Member States and the Commission (Interview, telephone, 13 June 2013). Although all negotiating parties knew about the views and concerns of the French government, Jospin's abrupt decision came as a surprise. Observers speculated that Jospin's abrupt decision was intended to signal to the French public that he did not leave the negotiating table due to pressure from civil society. Rather it should look like a deliberate decision of a statesman, which nonetheless remained a political concession to his coalition partners (Lawrence et al., 2006, p. 175; Interview, Paris, 1 October 2012a).

The negotiators interviewed for this book differed over the question of to what extent similar institutional rivalries within the European delegation contributed to these developments. Several interviewees underlined that the Commission had always remained loyal to the Member States and tried to play a constructive role in the MAI negotiations. They nevertheless cautioned that the Commission's public insistence on shifting investment negotiations to the WTO was not helpful for advancing the stalling MAI negotiations (Interview, Paris, 1 October 2012a; Interview, Paris, 1 October 2012b; Interview, email, 13 January 2014). Other interviewees argued that toward the end of the negotiations the Commission and the USTR formed a peculiar alliance with the shared objective of obstructing the MAI negotiations and pushing investment negotiations back into the WTO, where they both held representation monopolies. To that end, the Commission and the USTR arguably reiterated demands which were very difficult for the other side to accommodate for constitutional reasons. While the Commission emphasised its demand that the USA accept the applicability of the MAI to sub-national entities, the USTR vehemently rejected the proposed REIO clause. A Member State negotiator commented that the permanent confrontation between the Commission and the USTR on these issues was unnecessary from a substantive point of view and harmful to the overall negotiating dynamics. It amplified the atmosphere of stalemate, which ultimately became the pretext for the French withdrawal (Interview, telephone, 3 July 2013). While it is difficult to prove which evaluation of the Commission's role is correct, it is certain that the Commission never undertook any actions to bring France back to the negotiating table and to re-establish European unity. Instead, the Commission made no secret of its relief and satisfaction that investment negotiations would now continue in the WTO. On 21 October 1998, only one week after the French withdrawal, Commissioner Brittan explained his position on that matter to the European Parliament in Strasbourg.

> *Let me ... give you my own views on the issue. It seems to me that we have made strong efforts to achieve the kind of transparent framework within the OECD which would benefit both the EU economies and those of other MAI participants. The MAI negotiations have already done much to clear the ground on investment and to highlight those issues which are of key importance to the EU, including civil society. Nonetheless, I have always taken the view that the WTO is the best long-term home for this work for which the MAI has already provided valuable signposts. In present circumstances the chances of bringing the current MAI negotiations to a successful conclusion frankly do not look at all promising.*
>
> (Brittan, 1998)

The Negotiating Group met several times after the French withdrawal. It did not, however, formally continue negotiations on the MAI. It merely consulted on the prospects of successfully concluding the negotiations despite the withdrawal of France. Even though many delegates publically downplayed the impact of France's decision, most were aware that it was too late to save the MAI negotiations. Without France, the EU was unable to negotiate. Without the EU, the MAI project had become useless. On 30 October 1998, the British government informed the public that it was following the French example and would leave the negotiating table (Denny and Atkinson, 1998). On 3 December 1998, the Negotiating

Group announced that negotiations on the MAI were no longer taking place. The MAI negotiations had collapsed (Lawrence et al., 2006, pp. 174–175).

7.2.5 *A theoretical assessment*

The analysis of the MAI negotiations challenges societal and liberal intergovernmental accounts of European cooperation, delegation and integration. US bureaucrats conceived and proposed the MAI project. American and European business showed – at best – lukewarm support for this US initiative. From the business perspective, the MAI arguably sought to address marginal investment problems in open and secure host economies. The Member States, on the other hand, were more interested in the MAI project. They appreciated the fact that they could negotiate on their own behalf in the OECD. Unlike in the WTO, the Commission does not conventionally act as the EU's single voice in this policy forum. In the OECD, the Commission only speaks on policy issues coming under shared or exclusive Union competence. Under the impression of the recent clash over competences in foreign economic relations between the Commission and the Member States in Opinion 1/94 and 2/92 (see Chapter 9), the Member States were determined to keep the involvement of the EU and the Commission to a legal minimum in order to avoid any precedent for the EU's role in investment regulation. Member State and business preferences thus cannot account for the EU's relatively central role in the MAI talks.

The EU's involvement and relatively unified negotiating approach in the MAI negotiations instead echoes Commission entrepreneurship and confirms institutionalist supranational thinking on European cooperation, delegation and integration. In line with principal-agent models, the Commission invoked the EU's fringe and implied competences vis-à-vis reluctant Member States to ensure the EU's involvement in these important investment negotiations. The Commission consequently managed to prove itself through agenda setting as a capable negotiator and sought to promote European unity in talks with third countries. Cooperation with the Member States, however, remained difficult. The Commission thus engaged in international forum shopping to consolidate its role in international investment policy. It started pushing internally and internationally for shifting multilateral investment negotiations back to the WTO, where it conventionally acts as the EU's single voice regardless of competence questions. When the MAI negotiations ran into stalemate in late 1997, the Commission did not seek to prevent a collapse but adopted a welcoming attitude. Some sources even suggested that the Commission 'engineered' the collapse so as to shift multilateral investment negotiations back to the WTO and to consolidate its role in international investment policy. The observations show how the Commission skilfully used its agency autonomy to pursue its policy agenda. Through a historical institutionalist lens, the Commission's efforts can be read as institutional 'conversion' and 'drift'. It invoked implied and fringe competences in policy domains adjacent to investment regulation to ensure its involvement in the MAI and proactively shaped the policy environment by re-launching investment talks in the WTO to consolidate the EU's role in external relations.

7.3 The negotiations on the Singapore Issues

Despite the collapse of the MAI negotiations, the project to establish multilateral investment disciplines was not off the table. The immediate reaction of NGOs reflected this fact. In the days following the breakdown of the MAI negotiations, more than 300 NGOs published a joint letter "*A call to reject any proposal for moving MAI or an investment agreement to the WTO*" (Lawrence et al., 2006, p. 175). The reaction of the NGOs was understandable. As mentioned earlier, France and the Commission called for negotiations on investment disciplines in the WTO. And the EU and the USA had agreed in a gentlemen's agreement in 1996 that work in the WTO on a binding multilateral investment framework should be pending as long as the MAI negotiations were running. From a European – and notably from the Commission's – perspective, the collapse of the MAI negotiations finally opened the door for the launching of veritable investment negotiations in the WTO.

The WTO was already in the starting blocks for taking over from the OECD. On the initiative of the EU – or rather of the Commission – and Canada, South Korea and Japan, the Singapore ministerial meeting of December 1996 had established a working group to examine the relationship between trade and investment. The working group started meeting in May 1997. Most delegations stressed that the mandate of the working group was primarily of an educational nature. In other words, the working group should analyse ties between investment and trade, but not engage in preliminary informal negotiations on multilateral investment disciplines. During the year 1997, discussions and countries' submissions to the working group evolved around the economic impact of investment on home and host economies as well as on trade flows. In spring 1998, the working group started discussing the similarities and differences in countries' international investment policy approaches. Throughout the years 1998 and 1999, discussions in the working group became more lively, and technical as well as political. Delegates discussed, inter alia, the actual need for a multilateral investment framework, and the potential scope and definitions of such a framework as well as the cast of a dispute settlement mechanism (See document series 'WT/WGTI/W/' at https://docs.wto.org/; WTO, 2002; Interview, Brussels, 24 July 2012a; Interview, telephone, 13 June 2013). The consultations were evolving into pre-negotiations on a multilateral investment framework and the collapse of the MAI reinforced this trend.

The EU's representation modalities in the working group on investment in the WTO were never the subject of serious debate in the Council of Ministers. All Member States tacitly agreed that the Commission – and more specifically the DG for Trade – were in charge of representing European interests in the WTO in-line with the ever-evolving international trade agenda (Interview, Brussels, 24 July 2012a). As one interviewed official put it, DG Trade was then still a machinery with the sole purpose of dealing with all WTO agenda items (Interview, Brussels, 24 July 2012a). The EU-internal distribution of competences was of little importance in the WTO context. The Commission was, from the outset of the debates on investment in the WTO, the unchallenged sole representative of the EU and its Member States and possessed significant authority and influence, notably in comparison to the OECD-based MAI negotiations. The interesting twist to this observation is obviously that the Commission was central to setting investment disciplines back onto the WTO agenda in 1996. As discussed earlier, the Commission first sought to contain the MAI negotiations and then pushed investment disciplines back onto the WTO agenda and arguably played a more or less active role in the breakdown of the MAI negotiations. The Commission shaped the international trade agenda, which then shaped the EU's de facto competences. From this angle, the launch of investment negotiations in the WTO constitutes an impressive instance of Commission entrepreneurship to the end of, inter alia, consolidating the EU's de facto competences in international investment policy.

Cooperation between the Commission and the Member States in the '113 Committee' and on-site in Geneva took place in a productive and friendly atmosphere, unlike in the MAI negotiations (Interview, telephone, 13 June 2013). The 'usual suspects' of national and European trade policy officials dealing with WTO affairs – not investment policy officials as during the MAI talks – coordinated and determined the EU's approach in investment negotiations. Most Member States adopted a welcoming attitude toward investment talks in the WTO. France, the United Kingdom and Germany were particularly interested. As expounded earlier, the French government assumed that its interests were better served in the WTO, where negotiations necessarily aimed for lower standards and liberalisation commitments. The British government was particularly interested in unlocking the financial service sectors of other WTO members. Germany, finally, hoped for enhanced investment protection throughout the WTO. Cooperation between the Commission and the Member States, and thus European unity, was moreover relatively easy to sustain as many potentially controversial issues were off the table in the WTO due to the more modest objectives and scope of investment talks in the WTO in comparison to the MAI negotiations (Interview, telephone, 13 June 2013).

The general convergence of minds enabled the Commission to play a proactive and central role in the working group meetings. The Commission reportedly acted as the main driver of discussions in the working group. Several observations support this conclusion. On the one hand, the Commission was the first party to table a comprehensive working paper and proposal for a working agenda (WTO, 1997). The Commission thereby influenced the initial discussions and broad direction of deliberations in the working group. On the other hand, the EU tabled a high number of working papers. While the Commission submitted 18 papers to the working group between 1996 and 2003 on behalf of the EU and its Member States, the US delegation merely tabled six working papers (see Table 7.1). So whereas the US delegation had often taken the lead and decisively shaped negotiations on investment disciplines during the Uruguay Round and MAI talks, the US delegation was relatively passive in the working group in comparison to the EU (Woolcock, 2003, p. 251).

European business was supportive, albeit not enthusiastic, of holding investment negotiations in the WTO. UNICE, as well as most national business and industry federations, expressed their support for the creation of investment rules in the WTO. The newly founded European Services Forum (ESF) encouraged European

Table 7.1 Number of meetings and submissions per year by country (selection)

	Number of meetings	EU submissions	Canada submissions	Japan submissions	South Korea submissions	USA submissions
1996	0	0	0	0	0	0
1997	2	2	1	2	1	0
1998	4	3	1	4	3	5
1999	5	1	0	1	3	0
2000	2	2	0	2	2	0
2001	4	1	2	1	1	0
2002	4	7	5	6	3	1
2003	4	2	3	2	1	0
Total	**25**	**18**	**12**	**18**	**14**	**6**

Source: Author's own calculations; www.wto.org/english/tratop_e/invest_e/invest_e.htm.

policymakers to work toward a multilateral investment framework under the WTO (European Services Forum, 2003a, 2003b). International Financial Services, the association of English financial service providers, supported investment negotiations in the WTO. While being sympathetic to the idea of negotiating a comprehensive investment agreement with market access commitments, the main concerns of European business were post-establishment treatment and protection standards. It was unlikely that developing countries would sign up to ambitious liberalisation commitments going beyond the GATS. So as to create added value, investment negotiations should therefore focus in particular on post-establishment treatment and protection standards, which were not yet comprehensively covered by WTO law (British Parliament, 2004).

In 1999, the developed countries sought to upgrade the consultations on various issues in the WTO to a veritable new trade round. The ministers of the WTO countries convened in Seattle. The Commission, together with Japan and South Korea, pushed hard for having the Singapore Issues, and thus investment, included in the agenda of the new round. The USA lent only lukewarm support, while developing countries were hesitant or rejected the Commission's initiative on investment negotiations. The ministers could only agree on the formula that Singapore Issues and, notably, investment were important and that all countries should show flexibility in their positions on investment and the other Singapore Issues (WTO, 1999). The ministerial meeting failed to launch a new trade round due to opposition from major developing countries as well as hitherto unseen protests, and even riots, by radical social groups, NGOs and other parts of civil society. The failure to launch the new round was a serious blow to the WTO and developed countries. Observers questioned whether the WTO – a relatively young organisation – could ever recover from the Seattle disaster (Schott, 2000).

The ministers gathered again at Doha in 2001. The ministers this time succeeded in launching the so-called Doha Development Round. The inclusion of the Singapore Issues and, notably, investment negotiations on the agenda of the new round was one of the most controversial issues during the ministerial meeting (Kumar, 2003, p. 3178). As before, the EU, Japan and South Korea were the key proponents of the Singapore Issues and investment negotiations, while developing countries, under the leadership of India, sought to prevent the inclusion of the Singapore Issues on the agenda of the new round. They argued that the working group on trade and investment had been commissioned to study the interrelationship between trade and investment, which arguably had not yet been finished. Moreover, they questioned the ability of developing countries to negotiate and domestically implement complex competition, trade facilitation, public procurement and investment disciplines. The proponents of the Singapore Issues, on the other hand, pointed to the central importance of these issues for the world economy (Kumar, 2003, p. 3178). At the end of the Doha meeting, a hard-fought compromise emerged on the Singapore Issues and notably investment. For a start, the Singapore Issues should remain on the negotiating agenda of the new round. Hence, the working group on trade and investment continued to exist. Its main objective should be to elaborate the modalities of investment negotiations – i.e. to delimit in detail the main elements and objectives of investment negotiations. The WTO ministers should then explicitly endorse the modalities for investment negotiations at the occasion of the next ministerial meeting in Cancún, Mexico, in September 2003 (WTO, 2001).

In September 2003, the ministers reconvened in Cancún to discuss the results of two years of negotiating and to eventually endorse the modalities for negotiations on investment disciplines. The EU remained the major proponent of negotiations on investment disciplines and the Singapore Issues, whereas many developing and least developed countries became increasingly assertive in their rejection of negotiations on investment and the other Singapore Issues (Lamy, 2003). What is more, the Member States of the EU supported investment negotiations, but attached only low priority to them in comparison to other issues. In EU-internal discussions, many Member States increasingly criticised the Commission's insistence on the Singapore Issues and investment. The Commission's insistence arguably alienated and antagonised many developing countries, which made compromises on more important issues like agriculture or non-agricultural market access more difficult (De Jonquières, 2003a). After the collapse of investment negotiations in Cancún, a Member State official stated:

> *The Commission should have backed off much earlier . . . Instead of trying pig-headedly to impose the Singapore issues on other WTO members, it should have been asking what concessions the EU was ready to make to get its demands accepted.*
>
> (as cited in De Jonquières, 2003a)

Opposition to the Commission's arguably inflexible negotiating strategy also grew within the Member States. The development committee of the British House of Commons, for instance, criticised the EU/Commission for their insistence on investment negotiations. It demanded the British government to stop strongly supporting the Commission in its efforts and to take development objectives more into account. The parliamentarians argued that investment disciplines harmed the ability of developing countries to develop and catch up (De Jonquières, 2003b). And as it became increasingly unlikely that investment negotiations would deliver market access, high post-establishment or protection standards, support from European business also shrank (De Jonquières, 2003a). The Doha negotiating mandate for the investment working group made it clear that the Doha Development Round could only deliver humble investment disciplines if at all, which hampered business interest in the Commission-led initiative. At the end of the ministerial meeting, the Commission took internal and external pressures into account. It suddenly gave in and proposed dropping the most controversial Singapore Issues – investment and competition – from the round. The Commission instead proposed pursuing negotiations on investment and competition disciplines on a plurilateral basis outside the round's single undertaking (European Voice, 2003). South Korea and Japan, which so far had been the Commission's allies in this domain, had not been consulted on this decision. Taken aback, they refused to follow suit and forged a compromise with the developing countries. In consequence, the developing countries refused to re-confirm the negotiating mandate for the Singapore Issues, which entailed the discontinuation of talks on investment disciplines in the WTO. When the Cancún meeting drew to an end, many observers asked whether the Doha Round had, de facto, collapsed due to the many controversies and deadlocks on the Singapore Issues, agriculture, textiles and non-agricultural market access (De Jonquières, 2003a).

The EU held markedly increased de facto competences in investment negotiations in the WTO in comparison to the MAI negotiations. The Member States happily cooperated and delegated negotiating on investment to the Commission as per usual in WTO-based negotiations. The sudden readiness of the Member States to entrust the Commission with negotiations on inter alia investment provisions did not reflect business demands. European business showed only moderate interest in negotiations on investment provisions in the WTO. The Member States' readiness to cooperate reflected the altered negotiating environment in the WTO. As shown earlier, the Commission had gone to great lengths to put investment on the work agenda of the WTO in 1996 and played a central role in upgrading the WTO work on investment to proper negotiations after the collapse of the MAI negotiations. The section thus points to an intriguing instance of the Commission shaping the policy environment ('drift') to consolidate its role in international investment policy.

7.4 Conclusion

The chapter traced the EU's involvement in investment negotiations on the MAI in the OECD (1995–1998) and in the WTO as part of the so-called Singapore Issues (1996–2003). The observations confirm institutionalist and supranational thinking – rather than societal and liberal intergovernmental thinking – on European

166 *Multilateral agreement on investment*

cooperation, delegation and integration. European business took generally little interest in the MAI project or the EU's representation modalities. All OECD countries were already secure and investor-friendly economies. From a business perspective, the MAI would thus not significantly improve the investment climate. The Member States, on the other hand, were more interested in the MAI project but sought to contain the EU's role in these negotiations. In light of the competence struggle underlying Opinions 1/94 and 2/92 (see Chapter 9), the Member States were determined to keep the Commission at bay and to avoid any legal or political precedence, which might strengthen the EU's role in international investment policy. The MAI negotiations in the OECD – where the Member States speak on their behalf on matters coming under national competence – were ideal to emphasise the Member States' continued claim to competence over international investment policy. The Commission, nonetheless, managed to ensure the EU's participation in the MAI project. In accordance with principal-agent models, the Commission invoked fringe competences and used agenda setting to nonetheless acquire a fairly central role in the negotiations. Cooperation between the Commission and the Member States however remained difficult. The Commission thus started pushing for multilateral investment negotiations in the WTO, where it normally acts as the EU's single voice regardless of competence questions. When the MAI negotiations ran into stalemate and collapsed the Commission adopted a welcoming attitude and seized the opportunity to upgrade WTO-based negotiations thereby also consolidating its role in international investment policy. The Commission consequently became the main driver of investment negotiations in the Doha Round. These observations confirm historical institutionalist thinking. The Commission reinterpreted existing competences ('conversion') and shaped the policymaking environment ('drift') to consolidate the EU's role in international investment policy. As becomes clear in the following chapters, the EU's involvement in international investment regulation in the WTO was decisive for the inclusion of investment provisions into European PTAs with third countries and ultimately for the extension of the CCP to FDI regulation under the Treaty of Lisbon.

Notes

1 OECD membership comprised the following 29 countries at this point in time. Australia, Austria, Belgium, Canada, the Czech Republic, Denmark, Finland, France, Germany, Greece, Hungary, Iceland, Ireland, Italy, Japan, South Korea, Luxembourg, Mexico, the Netherlands, New Zealand, Norway, Poland, Portugal, Spain, Sweden, Switzerland, Turkey, the United Kingdom and the United States. The European Communities, represented by the European Commission, took part in the Council of Ministers as observer and was allowed to speak but not to vote.
2 The working groups examined existing liberalisation commitments under OECD instruments, liberalisation commitments in new areas, institutional matters, investment protection and dispute settlement arrangements as well as the involvement of non-OECD countries.
3 See for instance Commissioner Brittan's speech on the MAI at the European Parliament on 10 October 1998 (EP reference: Speech/98/212).

4 Expert group No. 1 focused on selected issues of dispute settlement and geographical scope. Expert group No. 2 examined the treatment of tax measures under the MAI. Expert group No. 3 focused on the so-called special topics like investment incentives, state monopolies, corporate practices and the movement of key personnel. Expert group No. 4 discussed institutional matters. Finally, expert group No. 5 finally addressed matters related to financial services. Discussions on more typical components of IIAs were held in three drafting groups. Drafting group No. 1 examined selected topics of investment protection. Drafting group No. 2 discussed selected topics concerning definition and treatment of investors and investments at the pre- and post-establishment stage. Drafting group No. 3, finally, examined selected topics of definition, treatment and protection of investors and investments.

References

Agence Europe, 1998a. EU/OECD/INVESTMENT: UNICE concerned about delays in negotiation of the multilateral agreement on investment (28 March 1998).

Agence Europe, 1998b. EU/United States (17 October 1998).

Agence Europe, 1997a. UE/OCDE/Investissement (28 March 1997).

Agence Europe, 1997b. UE/OCDE: Investissements directs (20 March 1997).

Agence Europe, 1995. Ecofin Council discusses anti-fraud and compensation for investors (23 May 1995).

British Parliament, 2004. Memorandum by International Financial Services, London [WWW Document]. URL www.publications.parliament.uk/pa/ld200304/ldselect/ldeucom/104/4020302.htm (accessed 8.10.14).

Brittan, L., 1998. The Rt Hon Sir Leon Brittan QC Vice-President of the European Commission Declaration: MAI European Parliament Plenary Session Strasbourg, 20 October 1998 (SPEECH/98/212). Strassburg.

Chatignoux, C., 1998. A quelques jours de la reprise des negociations sur l'Accord multilateral sur l'investissement (AMI), le Premier ministre, Lionel Jospin, a fait savoir hier que la France n'y participerait pas. Echos 6.

Corporate Europe Observatory, 1998. MAIGALOMANIA! Citizens and the environment sacrificed to corporate investment agenda: A briefing by Corporate Europe Observatory [WWW Document]. URL http://archive.corporateeurope.org/mai/index.html (accessed 5.3.13).

Council of Ministers, 1995. 7118/95 Limite GATT 97 Ecofin 68.

De Jonquières, G., 2003a. Crushed at Cancun (15 September 2003).

De Jonquières, G., 2003b. Call for UK to stop supporting line on 'Singapore issues' (14 July 2003). *Financ. Times.*

De Jonquières, G., 1998a. Ambitions slimmed for foreign investment pact (8 January 1998). *Financ. Times.*

De Jonquières, G., 1998b. World trade: US cool about investment pact (14 July 2003). *Financ. Times.*

De Jonquières, G., Kuper, S., 1998. Push to keep alive effort to draft global investment rules (29 April 1998). *Financ. Times.*

Denny, C., 1998. Globalisers run into the buffers (24 March 1998). *The Guardian.*

Denny, C., Atkinson, M., 1998. Britain drops support for MAI (30 October 1998). *The Guardian.*

Dymond, W., 1999. The MAI: A sad and melancholy tale, in: Hampson, F.O., Hart, M., Kudner, M. (Eds.), *A big league player? Canada among nations.* Oxford University Press, Oxford, pp. 25–53.

European Commission, 1995. A level playing field for direct investment world-wide (COM(95)42 final). Brussels.
European Court of Justice, 1995. Opinion 2/92 (competence of the community or one of its institutions to participate in the Third Revised Decisions of the OECD on national treatment), in: European Court of Justice Reports. European Court of Justice, Luxemburg, pp. I-00521–I-00578.
European Court of Justice, 1994. Opinion 1/94 (competence of the community to conclude international agreements concerning services and the protection of intellectual property – Article 228(6) of the EC Treaty), in: European Court of Justice Reports. European Court of Justice, Luxemburg, pp. I-5267–I-5422.
European Services Forum, 2003a. ESF call for an effective launch of negotiations of a multilateral agreement on trade and investment.
European Services Forum, 2003b. Press release: European services business call upon WTO Members to ensure success in Cancun.
European Voice, 2003. Commission relaxes stance in 'Singapore issues' (27 November 2003).
Financial Times, 1998. Bye-bye, MAI? (19 February 1998) 17.
Graham, E., 2000. *Fighting the wrong enemy: Antiglobal activities and multinational enterprises*. Institute for International Economics, Washington, DC.
Henderson, D., 1999. *The MAI affair: A story and its lessons*. Royal Institute of International Affairs, International Economics Programme, London.
Koutrakos, P., 2006. *EU international relations law: Modern studies in European law*. Hart, Oxford.
Kumar, N., 2003. Investment on WTO agenda: A developing country perspective and way forward for Cancun Ministerial Conference. *Econ. Polit. Wkly.* 38, 3177–3188.
Lamy, P., 2003. Cancun's delegates must aim high (8 September 2003). *Financ. Times*.
Lawrence, R.Z. et al., 2006. The Multilateral Agreement on Investment. in: Lawrence, R.Z., Devereaux, C., Watkins, M.. *Case Studies in US Trade Negotiations, Volume 1: Making the rules*. Institute for International Economics, Washington D.C., 135–186.
Marchand, S., 1998. La France claque la porte de l'AMI (15 October 1998). *Le Figaro*.
Muchlinski, P., 2000. The rise and fall of the Multilateral Agreement on Investment: Where now? *Int. Lawyer* 34, 1033–1053.
OECD, 1995a. DAFFE/CMIT/CIME(95)13/FINAL.
OECD, 1995b. Multilateral Agreement on Investment: Check list on substantive issues (DAFFE/MAI(95)1.
OECD, n.d. Multilateral Agreeement on Investment: Documentation from the negotiations [WWW Document]. URL www.oecd.org/daf/mai/.
Schott, J., 2000. *The WTO after Seattle*. Institute for International Economics, Washington, DC.
Smythe, E., 1998. The multilateral agreement on investment: A charter of rights for global investors or just another agreement? in: Hampson, F.O., Appel Molot, M. (Eds.), *Leadership and dialogue: Canada among nations*. Oxford University Press, Oxford, pp. 239–266.
Thomas, R., 1997. Fish clog up OECD deal (24 May 1997). *The Guardian*.
Tieleman, K., 2000. The failure of the multilateral agreement on investment (MAI) and the absence for a global public policy network [WWW Document]. URL www.gppi.net/fileadmin/gppi/Tieleman_MAI_GPP_Network.pdf (accessed 5.1.13).
Turner, M., 1998. Delegates determined to fight on to save belingered MAI deal (2 April 1998). *Eur. Voice*.

UNCTAD, 1999. Lessons from the MAI. UNCTAD Ser. Issues Int. Invest. Agreem. UNCTADITEIITMISC 22.

Woolcock, S., 2003. The Singapore issues in Cancun: A failed negotiation ploy or a litmus test for global governance? *Intereconomics* 38, 249–255.

Woolcock, S., 1993. The European acquis and multilateral trade rules: Are they compatible? *J. Common Mark. Stud.* 31, 539–558. doi:10.1111/j.1468–5965.1993.tb00479.x

Woolcock, S., 1990. *The Uruguay round: Issues for the European Community and the United States, RIIA discussion paper*. Royal Institute of International Affairs, London.

WTO, 2002. WT/WGTI/INF/3.

WTO, 2001. WT/MIN(01)/DEC/1.

WTO, 1999. WTO Briefing note: Ministers start negotiating Seattle Declaration.

WTO, 1997. WT/WGTI/W/1.

8 Investment disciplines in European Preferential Trade Agreements

This chapter shifts the analytical focus away from multilateral to bilateral negotiations between the EU and third countries on PTAs. The chapter examines the question of why the Member States started cooperating and empowered the Commission to negotiate on investment disciplines in PTA talks since the late 1990s. It analyses for this purpose the first PTA negotiations between the EU and third countries to cover noteworthy investment liberalisation commitments and post-establishment provisions[1] – the negotiations on the EU-Mexico PTA (1996–1999) and EU-Chile PTA (2000–2002) (Ceyssens, 2005, p. 266). The comparison between these two negotiations is, moreover, particularly interesting due to their differential outcomes. Both PTAs would initially encompass ambitious investment provisions, but while the Member States vetoed such provisions in the EU-Mexico negotiations in a last-minute revolt, they accepted their inclusion in the EU-Chile negotiations. All following PTA negotiations encompassed similar investment disciplines.

The chapter finds that business lobbying and global competitive pressures led to the decision to conclude ambitious PTAs with Mexico and Chile. Both PTAs were meant to mitigate adverse effects of US PTAs. While the Member States at first agreed to ambitious investment provisions in the EU-Mexico negotiations, they ultimately vetoed them in a sovereignist backlash. In the following EU-Chile negotiations, the Commission engaged in policy entrepreneurship to avoid another diplomatic debacle. The Commission stressed in EU-internal debates that the EU could not credibly push on behest of the Member States for an ambitious new WTO round, but conclude out-dated humble PTAs excluding new trade issues such as investment provisions. PTAs were in essence a trade policy instrument to go beyond WTO commitments. The evolving policy environment and agenda of WTO talks thus required the EU to conclude ambitious PTAs. The Commission omitted in these discussions that it had put considerable energy in keeping investment on the WTO agenda (see Chapter 7). The Commission's framing indeed convinced critical Member States, which finally accepted the inclusion of a proper investment chapter into the EU-Chile PTA. From a theoretical point of view, the chapter documents an intriguing instance of Commission entrepreneurship. The observations confirm both principal-agent and historical institutionalist thinking. The Commission used its agenda-setting powers to highlight the evolving policy environment and to politically link WTO and PTA negotiations in view of consolidating the EU's role in international investment policy. The evolving policy environment arguably required an extension of the EU's de facto competences.

8.1 A theoretical note on agenda setting in bilateral and multilateral negotiations

Multilateral and bilateral negotiations differ in important regards. Multilateral negotiations involve a high number of states. Hence, agenda setting is a complex exercise, which requires finely tuned compromises among all involved states (Odell, 2000; Tallberg, 2003). No single country can impose its ideal agenda and objectives. The previously discussed breakdown of negotiations on the so-called Singapore Issues – and more generally the recent collapse of the Doha Round – illustrate the significance of agenda setting. Disagreement over the agenda and overarching negotiating objectives decisively contributed to the collapse of these talks (Cottier and Elsig, 2011).

Bilateral negotiations comprise only two parties. The two involved countries often differ in their political and economic power. Hence, bilateral negotiations are often characterised by a significant degree of asymmetry, which shapes the negotiating agenda (Odell, 2000). Powerful countries insist on negotiating on certain issues, whereas weak countries find it difficult to resist such pressure. Weak or small countries often act as *demandeur* in international economic negotiations, and seek access to a larger market. Hence, agenda setting is often manifestly biased in bilateral negotiations and reflects the preferences of the more powerful country.

The EU is no international power in the classic sense. It wields little influence in geopolitics. The EU is nevertheless a major power in the international political economy (Baldwin, 2013; Woolcock, 2011; Zimmerman, 2007). The size and potency of the Single Market provide the EU with considerable bargaining power and influence in international economic affairs. The EU is normally the bigger and more powerful negotiating party in bilateral negotiations. The involved third country, on the other hand, typically acts as *demandeur* for enhanced market access to the EU's Single Market. It follows that the EU should hold considerable sway over the agenda of bilateral negotiations. So if PTA negotiations between the EU and third countries encompass investment disciplines, it is reasonable to assume that it reflects to a large extent EU-internal considerations rather than the demands of third countries.

This train of thought is important for this book. It clarifies that the examination of the negotiations on the EU-Mexico and EU-Chile PTA should shed additional light on EU-internal factors promoting the EU's growing role in international investment policy. In methodological terms, the chapter puts the spotlight on the EU-internal factors driving the emergence of the EU's international investment policy.

8.2 Investment disciplines in the negotiations on the EU-Mexico PTA

Debates on a PTA between the EU and Mexico can be traced back to the early 1990s. In 1991, the EU and Mexico institutionalised their relationship through a first cooperation agreement. The agreement should support the democratic and economic reform processes in Mexico. It was, however, of symbolic nature. It established general structures for political and economic relations between the EU and Mexico, but did not contain noteworthy provisions on bilateral trade and investment liberalisation. The shallowness of the agreement, notably in regard to bilateral trade and investment relations, reflected a lack of European interest. The Mexican government had proposed negotiating a veritable PTA in parallel with the political cooperation agreement, but European policymakers were preoccupied with finalising the Single Market, the Uruguay Round and had to cope with the geopolitical turmoil in Eastern Europe (Manger, 2009, p. 106).

8.2.1 The pre-negotiations on the EU-Mexico PTA

The entry into force of NAFTA between the USA, Canada and Mexico in 1994 fundamentally changed the situation. Three effects of NAFTA are particularly noteworthy. First and foremost, NAFTA cut or completely abolished tariffs for US and Canadian imports to Mexico, making equivalent European imports less attractive to consumers. Mexican consumers started switching away from European imports, entailing falling market shares for European firms in Mexico. Mexico reinforced this trend by increasing tariffs for non-NAFTA members in 1995 and 1999 (Dür, 2007, p. 838). Second, under NAFTA Mexico transformed into an ideal entry point, investment and low-cost production hub for the US market. Products and services from Mexico benefited from preferential access to the US market (Manger, 2009, p. 97). Third, NAFTA was the first PTA to cover ambitious investment liberalisation commitments. These made it particularly easy for Canadian and US investors to establish and operate subsidiaries in Mexico. In turn, this implies that the relative ease and costs of investing in Mexico deteriorated for European firms. European firms incurred through NAFTA a competitive disadvantage vis-à-vis US and Canadian investors, further eroding their position in the Mexican and Northern American economy.

NAFTA spurred international regulatory and economic competition. This effect was not limited to the narrow scope of traditional PTAs. The highly comprehensive scope of NAFTA carried international regulatory and economic competition into new policy domains. NAFTA extended the standard agenda of PTAs, inter alia, to investment regulation. It encouraged third countries to emulate the NAFTA approach and to conclude similarly comprehensive PTAs. This effect was indeed observable within the EU following the entry into force of NAFTA. European business started lobbying Member State policymakers for the conclusion of a competitive PTA with Mexico comprising ambitious services and investment disciplines so as to re-establish a level playing field (Heydon and Woolcock, 2009, pp. 109–113;

Manger, 2009, pp. 106–118). Many Member State policymakers were receptive to such business demands, as they grew increasingly worried about the falling European market share in Mexico. At the same time, they understood the new interest in the Mexican economy as an entry point into the potent NAFTA market. The Commission welcomed and sought to cultivate the interest of European business and the Member States in a competitive PTA with Mexico.

Mexico welcomed the new attitude of European business and policymakers. Mexico hoped that a PTA with the EU might help rebalance its current account, stabilise its currency, promote its liberal economic reforms and reduce its dependence on the US economy. The Mexican government campaigned for an EU-Mexico PTA and sent several delegations to Brussels to advance discussions (Manger, 2009, pp. 96–97). In late 1994, the Commission and the Mexican government started preliminary consultations on a PTA.

In the following months, the Commission constantly underlined that the PTA should be ambitious and indeed reach for NAFTA-parity and create a free trade area. European business active in Mexico expressed its support for such plans (Agence Europe, 1995a; Manger, 2009, pp. 106–107). The Member States welcomed the plan to negotiate a PTA. Several Member States, however, signalled that the establishment of a free trade area – i.e. the dismantling of all tariffs – would go too far. In February 1995, the Commission released a communiqué to the Council of Ministers and the European Parliament, which laid out its vision of the potential cast of a future EU-Mexico PTA. The Commission avoided using the term 'free trade area' in its communiqué. It nonetheless underlined its intention to reach for an ambitious PTA, which would provide for NAFTA-parity in trade in goods, trade in services, investments and capital movements. The Commission warned that a failure to conclude an agreement of NAFTA-parity would result in the erosion of EU-Mexico economic relations in the long run. While the proposed agenda of the PTA by far exceeded the normal scope of European PTAs and the Union's competences under European law, the Council of Ministers nevertheless endorsed the communiqué on 11 April 1995 (Agence Europe, 1995a; Manger, 2009, pp. 106–107). The Council, moreover, called for a swift start of the negotiations with Mexico (Agence Europe, 1995b). In May 1995, the Commission and Mexico signed a solemn declaration, which formally documented their intention to start negotiations on a new political and economic framework agreement (Manger, 2009, p. 106; Sanahuja, 2000, p. 48).

8.2.2 The Commission mandate

The evolving international trade agenda and consequent systemic pressures shaped the EU-internal debates on the Commission mandate for the upcoming EU-Mexico PTA. The Commission drew up a draft mandate for the so-called EU-Mexico Political Coordination and Cooperation Agreement during summer 1995. The agreement should encompass one chapter on political cooperation and another on economic cooperation. The economic chapter should, de facto, become the EU-Mexico PTA. The Commission used its first-mover advantage to put post-establishment treatment and investment liberalisation on the agenda of the PTA negotiations. The Commission even briefly toyed with the idea of aiming for the inclusion of investment protection provisions into the EU-Mexico PTA, but Germany, the Netherlands and, in particular, France signalled their opposition. Such provisions arguably interfered too much with their BIT programmes and encroached upon national competences (Interview, Brussels, 24 July 2012b). On 25 October 1995, the Commission released a press communication which underlined the ambitious and unseen agenda for the economic chapter – i.e. PTA with Mexico.

Economic chapter: The Commission and Mexico will gradually establish a favourable framework for the development of trade in goods, services and investments, including through gradual and reciprocal liberalization, taking account of the sensitive nature of certain products and in accordance to the relevant WTO rules. The conclusion of the agreement will mark the beginning of a process which in the long-run will lead to the establishment of a favourable framework for the development of trade in goods, services and investments.

(as cited in Agence Europe, 1995c)

The Council of Ministers discussed the draft mandate in February 1996. The substantive provisions regarding 'new trade issues' like investment, services and capital movements proved to be rather uncontroversial according to press coverage, secondary literature and interviews. Given the new regulatory context in Mexico, most Member State governments considered it to be in their interest to reach for ambitious commitments in these domains. In the end, the mandate provided, nevertheless, for negotiations on the liberalisation of service-related investment, services trade and capital movements. It thus clearly exceeded the scope of Union competence and previous European PTAs or association agreements. The Member State governments, moreover, agreed with the implicit assumption of the draft mandate that the Commission would act as their single voice in the PTA negotiations across all agenda items regardless of the EU-internal distribution of competences. The Member State governments thought that the Commission was in charge of negotiating PTAs (Interview, telephone, 14 November 2013).

But while the remarkably broad substantive agenda of the Commission's draft mandate did not cause veritable frictions within the EU, the Member States were divided over the procedural provisions it contained. The Commission and Mexico had agreed that the political and economic chapters should be negotiated in parallel in one single phase. This so-called single phase approach diverged from the EU's standard 'two-phase' approach. The EU normally first concludes a political cooperation agreement. Depending on the satisfactory implementation of this agreement, the EU then eventually concludes a PTA. In the case of Mexico, the Commission wanted to speed up the negotiations so as to mitigate the negative effects of NAFTA on European business and thus proposed a 'single phase' approach. Mexico, on the other hand, had insisted on a 'single phase' approach in order to make sure that any political concessions by Mexico would be balanced by economic and trade concessions by the EU (Manger, 2009, p. 107; Sanahuja, 2000, p. 48).

Spain and the United Kingdom – and to a lesser extent Luxemburg, Sweden and Germany – supported the Commission's plan to engage in swift 'single phase' negotiations. Of the EU's Member States, their national business communities had arguably the closest ties with the Mexican economy and thereby incurred the highest opportunity costs from NAFTA (Sanahuja, 2000, p. 48). In March 1996, Spain published a forceful memorandum in favour of the Commission's proposal. It, inter alia, stressed the need for swift negotiations, the reduction of Mexican tariffs, investment liberalisation and better investment protection. The memorandum, inter alia, raised the problem that the rules of origins of NAFTA had reduced the profitability and value of European investments in Mexico.

France – supported by Austria, Denmark, Portugal, the Netherlands and others – rejected the proposed 'single phase' approach (Agence Europe, 1996a, 1996b; Manger, 2009, p. 107; Sunahuja, 2000, p. 48; Interview, Brussels, 25 September 2013a). They lamented that the effects of bilateral trade liberalisation had not been sufficiently studied yet. They demanded to slow down talks with Mexico and to return to the 'two phases' approach. France voiced the widely shared concern that Mexican agricultural produce could displace imports from African, Caribbean and Pacific Group of States (ACP States) and European overseas territories. It warned that an EU-Mexico agreement might set a negative precedent and deteriorate the EU's future bargaining position in particular in the upcoming trade negotiations with the Mercosur.[2] In addition, France underlined that it worried about the cumulative effects of the growing number of PTAs with third countries. France's scepticism reportedly reflected its general aversion to free trade.

The Italian Council Presidency, nonetheless, managed to strike a compromise between the two camps on 13 May 1996 (Agence Europe, 1996c). The ministers accepted in principle the Commission's 'single stage' approach. They amended, however, the negotiating mandate so that the negotiating process would, de facto, resemble the traditional 'two phases' approach. The EU and Mexico should first agree on a so-called global agreement. This should enumerate the objectives, issues areas and define the institutional framework of cooperation. The global agreement should moreover contain a clause comparable to a 'fast-track authority' for the Commission and Mexican government to engage in subsequent PTA negotiations without further domestic authorisation. The ministers cautiously underlined, however, that any provisions of the PTA coming under shared competence – like investment, services and capital movements – would still require unanimous consent in the Council of Ministers and that the PTA and the global agreement would only jointly enter into force in the form of a new EU-Mexico Cooperation Agreement (Agence Europe, 1996c). The compromise was satisfactory to for the Commission and both camps in the Council of Ministers. The Commission procured a broad mandate, which empowered it to act as the EU's single voice regarding all agenda items including investment, services and capital movements. The Member States in favour of swift and ambitious PTA negotiations secured a firm mandate to open talks with Mexico, while hesitant Member States secured the explicit right to veto the conclusion of the PTA (Agence Europe, 1996c, 1996d).

8.2.3 The core negotiations of the EU-Mexico PTA

The EU and Mexico met for the first negotiating session on 14 October 1996. The Directorate General for External Relations (DG Relex) supported by the Directorate General for Trade (DG Trade) and the Directorate General for Economic and Financial Affairs (DG Ecfin) represented the EU and its Member States on all agenda items. Trade policy officials of the Member State governments typically sat at the back of the negotiating room to observe, take notes and, if necessary, to pass written comments to the Commission negotiators (Interview, Brussels, 25 September 2013a). The Commission embarked on the first negotiating sessions with the objective of swiftly agreeing on the cast of the global agreement so as to subsequently launch the PTA negotiations. The Commission presented a first draft of the global agreement in October 1996, which in principle received a positive echo from Mexico. Mexico, nevertheless, criticised the 'democracy clause'[3] and the de facto 'two phases' approach proposed in the Commission's draft. Mexico complained that the de facto 'two phases' approach ran counter to the spirit of the solemn declaration of May 1995 and stressed that the standardised 'democracy clause' was a manifestation of European arrogance (Agence Europe, 1996e, 1997a; Sanahuja, 2000, pp. 50–51). In June 1997, the Commission and Mexico, nonetheless, managed to resolve their differences and agreed on a draft text for the global agreement,[4] an Interim Agreement Concerning Trade and Trade-Related Issues[5] as well as a Joint Declaration on Services and Intellectual Property Matters.[6] Support for the draft texts seemed high. The ratification of the global agreement by late 1997 and the subsequent start of the PTA negotiations in early 1998 seemed possible (Agence Europe, 1997b; Sanahuja, 2000, pp. 51–52).

Several disagreements nevertheless surfaced within a week. France was critical of the fact that the draft texts contained more commitments on the future liberalisation of trade in goods than on services and was therefore biased in favour of Mexico (Agence Europe, 1997c). France, moreover, forged a coalition of 12 Member States, which criticised the Commission for agreeing to a slightly altered 'democracy clause' in the draft text of the global agreement. They lamented that the Commission had overstepped its mandate and warned that they would veto the global agreement unless Mexico endorsed the standard clause. Only Spain, the United Kingdom and Denmark reportedly thought that that the altered clause of the draft text was in line with the mandate of the Commission (Sunahuja, 2000, p. 52). The controversies increasingly delayed the negotiations. The Commission harshly criticised the double standards of certain Member State governments, and notably France. It pointed out that earlier that year France had decided to not take a position in a similar discussion in the Council on the 'democracy clause' of the EU-China cooperation agreement (Agence Europe, 1997d; Sanahuja, 2000, p. 52). In early July 1997, Mexico decided to end this 'charade'. It accepted the standard 'democracy clause' while releasing a unilateral declaration on the non-intervention of third countries in Mexico's domestic affairs (Manger, 2009, p. 107; Sanahuja, 2000, p. 51). This first clash between the Commission, on the one side, and France and sympathising Member States, on the other, would set a precedent and the atmosphere for the following two years of negotiations. France repeatedly applied the breaks to the negotiations and exhibited its hesitant and occasionally destructive attitude during the talks.

The Council of Ministers consequently endorsed the text in late July 1997 and the Commission signed the agreement on behalf of the EU in December 1997 (Agence Europe, 1997e; Financial Times, 1997). The European Parliament and the Mexican Senate ratified the global agreement in spring 1998. The responsible rapporteur of the European Parliament, Miranda de Lage, cautioned that the assent of the European Parliament was not a blank cheque for the Commission negotiators. While the future PTA did not have to undergo separate ratification again, she underlined that the European Parliament expected the future PTA to reach for NAFTA-parity notably in the fields of investment, public procurement as well as telecommunications, financial, transport, cultural and audiovisual services (Agence Europe, 1998a).

The ratification of the global agreement paved the way for the launch of the actual PTA negotiations. These started with a first symbolic meeting of the joint EU-Mexico committee in mid-July 1998 (Agence Europe, 1998b). The substantive negotiations began in November 1998. The joint EU-Mexico committee, which was handling the PTA negotiations, established three working groups focusing on 1) market access for goods, 2) services and capital movements and 3) regulatory issues like rules of origins, competition policy, public procurement and intellectual property rights (Agence Europe, 1998c, 1998d). The first negotiating rounds, until early summer 1999, focused primarily on the reduction of industrial tariffs, rules of origin and agricultural tariffs. The negotiating focus reflected the main preoccupation of European business, which worried that the tariff differentials for European and NAFTA products eroded its market share in Mexico. The Commission thus demanded an equal and simultaneous reduction of Mexico's industrial tariffs as foreseen under NAFTA. What is more, the Commission wanted to make sure, through new rules of origin, that European exports could easily enter the Mexican market, while US and Canadian exporters should find it difficult to free ride on the EU-Mexico agreement. The negotiations on the rules of origins were among the toughest of the entire PTA talks, as Mexico had already adjusted its policy to the complex rules under NAFTA. Finally, Mexico wanted also a bite off the EU's huge agricultural market, which caused frustration for many Southern European Member States (Agence Europe, 1999a, p. 199, 1999b, 1998e).

Investment-related negotiations in the working group on services and capital movements were initially only an issue of secondary importance within the overall negotiating process. Several reasons explain this observation. First, services, capital movements and investment were less important to European business and the Member State governments than tariffs for industrial goods and rules of origin (Interview, telephone, 14 November 2013). The Mexican government, on the other hand, held rather defensive interests in these areas and did not push for swift negotiations (Interview, Brussels, 24 July 2012b). Second, the Europeans, in principle, held an offensive interest – in particular in unlocking the Mexican financial and insurance markets – but held no common position regarding other sectors (Agence Europe, 1999c; Manger, 2009, pp. 101–103). The lack of a common European position slowed down talks and reduced the EU's ability to press for ambitious negotiations. Third, the EU and Mexico wanted to take bilateral negotiations on investment, services and capital movements slowly in order to see the outcome of the negotiations on the MAI in the OECD as well as the next steps in the WTO toward the Millennium Round (Interview, Brussels, 25 September 2013a). Last but not least, discussions on investment, services and capital movement were tedious and slow because they fell under shared or national competence. Decisions required unanimous support from all Member States (Agence Europe, 1999d).

The Commission started seriously preparing for negotiations on investment, services and capital movement early in autumn 1998. The Commission asked the Member States to draft lists indicating the sectors and activities which should be excluded from negotiations on the LOTIS and capital movements. All Member States – except for France – transmitted their reservations to the Commission by the end of the year (Interview, Brussels, 25 September 2013a). Mexico and the Commission agreed to exchange their first offer for services in spring 1999. Mexico reportedly even proposed to negotiate on investment liberalisation beyond service sectors as well as post-establishment treatment and protection standards (Interview, Brussels, 24 July 2012b; Interview, Brussels, 25 September 2013a; Interview, telephone, 14 November 2013). The Commission, however, insisted on limiting talks to investment liberalisation for services so as not to displease the Member States. The negotiating guidelines for the Commission reportedly only provided for negotiations on market access. As mentioned earlier, the Member States considered post-establishment treatment and investment protection as core elements of their BIT programmes and thus as *domaine reservé*. In parallel, Mexico and the Commission also discussed the liberalisation of capital movements, which had an indirect bearing on investment regulation. The Commission initially proposed that Mexico transpose the European directive 88/361/EEC on the free movement of capital into its domestic legislation so as to free bilateral capital movements – including direct investments – between the EU and Mexico. The Mexican government rejected the proposal, mostly on symbolic grounds and not due to its content. Mexico disliked the European demand to transpose the EU's *acquis communautaires* into national legislation (Interview, Brussels, 24 July 2012b; Interview, Brussels, 25 September 2013a; Interview, telephone, 14 November 2013).

The Commission and the Mexican government exchanged their first offers on services and service-related investments in the fourth round of negotiations in May 1999. Initial discussions on the European and Mexican offers showed that there was still considerable disagreement between the two sides, notably on financial, insurance and maritime services. The negotiations made, however, considerable headway during the following rounds in summer 1999. Common ground notably emerged regarding capital movements (Agence Europe, 1999a). At the seventh round in July, the Commission agreed to the Mexican proposal to liberalise services and investments on the basis of a negative list like under NAFTA. The Commission supported the Mexican proposal, as it facilitated attaining its main goal – to procure NAFTA-parity. Some Member States, on the other hand, criticised the Commission's assent to the Mexican proposal as an unnecessary concession to Mexico and the NAFTA approach to services and investment liberalisation. The Member States had become used to the GATS-like positive list approach and felt that a positive list allowed for a more cautious liberalisation of services and investment. In early October, the Commission expressed confidence that the new approach of negative lists would pave the way toward a compromise on the liberalisation of services and service-related investments between the EU and Mexico, but also within the still-divided Council of Ministers (Agence Europe, 1999d; Harding, 1999). The eighth round of negotiations in October 1999 should ultimately conclude the PTA negotiations. And progress was indeed manifest. The Commission and Mexico agreed on liberalisation offers for services and service-related investments in the form of a negative list and a rendezvous clause, which stipulated that the EU and Mexico would re-examine their bilateral commitments in this domain after three years so as to adjust them to developments in upcoming WTO negotiations. The Commission and Mexico, moreover, agreed on provisions indicating an almost complete liberalisation of bilateral capital movements including FDI (Interview, Brussels, 25 September 2013a). The Mexican Minister for Trade, Herminio Blanco, commented that the issue of services and investment "*that seemed to have dragged the negotiations out for a long time, have been resolved in this eighth round*" (as cited in Agence Europe, 1999e). Older disagreements like rules of origin, agricultural trade and public procurement, however, unexpectedly resurfaced and made the planned conclusion of the negotiations impossible. The negotiators thus decided to reconvene for a ninth round to close the negotiations in November 1999 (Agence Europe, 1999e).

8.2.4 Clashing over competences on investment regulation

The weeks between the eighth and ninth round brought considerable turmoil regarding the agreed provisions on investment, services and capital movements. Media reports hardly covered these developments. They merely indicated that the comprehensive provisions on investment, services and capital movements had mostly vanished from the draft agreement when the ninth round started. Research interviews shed light on this episode.

The reasons behind the sudden changes to the draft agreement were not the result of a clash between the EU and Mexico, but instead one between the Commission and the French government in the '113 Committee'. The French government suddenly objected to the use of negative lists for the liberalisation of services and service-related investments (Agence Europe, 1999f). France reportedly thought that their use was an unnecessary concession to Mexico. France feared that the use of negative lists might entail a much more comprehensive liberalisation of services and investments than initially intended. France wanted to keep its bargaining chips for the upcoming Millennium Round in the WTO. It demanded the deletion of the negative lists. France nevertheless wanted to maintain the rendezvous clause and endorsed the Commission's spontaneous proposal to integrate a standstill clause on services and related investment into the agreement (Agence Europe, 1999g; Interview, telephone, 14 November 2013; Interview, Brussels, 25 September 2013a).

France, moreover, claimed that the Commission had overstepped its mandate by agreeing with Mexico on a comprehensive 'capital movements' clause. It expressed criticism that the agreed clause would, inter alia, liberalise FDI and portfolio investment flows. France took the view that the term 'capital movements' in the negotiating guidelines only referred to 'transfers of payments' (Interview, telephone, 14 November 2013; Interview, Brussels, 25 September 2013a). France's claim was, however, implausible. The term 'capital movements' was clearly defined under community law,[7] OECD codes and IMF guidelines. According to these widely accepted definitions, the term comprised FDI, portfolio investments and many other forms of cross-border transactions. It needs mention, though, that these clauses merely liberalise the cross-border transfer of FDI but do not liberalise the subsequent act of establishment, mergers or acquisitions of subsidiaries in the host country.[8]

France threatened to veto the entire draft agreement unless the Commission deleted the negative lists for services and service-related investments as well as the comprehensive capital movements clause (Interview, Brussels, 25 September 2013a; Interview, telephone, 14 November 2013; Manger, 2009, p. 119). The French threat was credible, as all the clauses negotiated within the working group on services and capital movements were subject to unanimous endorsement in the Council of Ministers. France was, initially, on its own with these demands. But what had started out as an isolated French veto soon grew into a broad majority of Member States. France skilfully convinced, but also pressured, other Member State governments into supporting its position. In the end, only the Commission and Spain still sought to save the controversial provisions. They had to give into the demands of the French-led coalition so as to save the rest of the draft agreement.

France's opposition reflected competence concerns as well as the government's general protectionist attitude in international economic affairs. Interviewed negotiators recalled that France was clearly worried about the implications of comprehensive service, investment and capital movement provisions for its national competences and sovereignty (Interview, Brussels, 25 September 2013a; Interview, 14 November 2013). It feared that such provisions might set a precedent, which could entail a limitation of its legal competences in the long run. France is traditionally more preoccupied with its national competences and sovereignty than many other Member States. Interviewees moreover stressed that the French government, under the socialist Prime Minister Lionel Jospin, was sceptical of globalisation, free markets and trade. The French government repeatedly voiced concerns over a too comprehensive liberalisation of bilateral trade and consequently applied the brakes to the PTA negotiations. The year before – in September 1998 – the Jospin government had, moreover, withdrawn from the MAI negotiations in the

OECD without prior coordination with its European partners and triggered the collapse of the negotiation (see Chapter 7). These observations are important for this study. They suggest that while the Commission promoted the extension of the EU's de facto competences, government preferences on the whole still sought to contain an extension of the EU's de facto competences in this policymaking sphere.

The negotiators reconvened for a ninth and last round in November 1999. The round had a twofold focus. On the one hand, the Mexican and Commission negotiators sought to resolve the outstanding disagreements on rules of origin, public procurement and the like. On the other hand, they had to deal with the considerable damage to the investment, services and capital movement sections of the draft agreement. It seems that the debates between the EU and Mexico on the latter issues were relatively uncomplicated. Investment, services and capital movements were no priority for Mexican negotiators. Rather, certain Member States, like Spain and the United Kingdom, had pushed for these issues during the negotiations. The absence of media coverage regarding these issues therefore suggests that the crucial discussions on the consolidation of the investment, service and capital movement provisions evolved behind the scenes among the Member States rather than between the Commission and Mexico. The PTA was finally initialled in December 1999, signed in March 2000 and gradually entered into force between October 2000 and February 2001 (Agence Europe, 2000a, p. 200; European Commission, 2014a).

8.2.5 An assessment of the investment commitments in the EU-Mexico PTA

So which investment-related provisions does the final EU-Mexico PTA[9] actually contain? As discussed earlier, the PTA could have delivered highly ambitious investment, services and capital movement disciplines. Or as a Commission official phrased it, the EU-Mexico PTA could have contained a *"sexy investment chapter better than NAFTA"* (as cited in Manger, 2009, p. 119). The Council of Ministers, on the initiative of France, nevertheless put a stop to these provisions. But despite this unseen EU-internal clash, the PTA still comprises – arguably by accident – several noteworthy investment-related commitments.

The PTA provides for NAFTA-plus investment market access to Mexican service sectors. The PTA liberalises bilateral trade in services across all modes of supply on the basis of MFN and NT. European service providers entering the Mexican market must thus receive equal treatment to Canadian and US service providers under NAFTA. And while the PTA does not contain a negative or positive list for the liberalisation of services trade, it comprises a standstill clause. The standstill clause prohibits the introduction of new trade barriers across all modes of supply. Taking into consideration that in 1999, Mexico's unilateral market access commitments clearly exceeded its commitments under NAFTA or the GATS, the standstill clause locked in a considerable level of openness. Some caveats nevertheless apply to this reading of investment commitments in the EU-Mexico PTA. The PTA entirely excludes trade in cabotage, maritime, air transport and audiovisual services. On the other hand, the Commission and Mexico never drew up a schedule of the commitments under the MFN and standstill clause. The exact scope of market access commitments remains opaque. European service providers and investors thus find the PTA difficult to use and to enforce (Heydon and Woolcock, 2009, pp. 95–96; Interview, telephone 14 November 2013).[10]

The PTA, moreover, contains a noteworthy special chapter for trade and investment in financial and insurance services, which explicitly provides for NAFTA-parity across all modes of supply. European, Canadian and US banks thus enjoy the same market access and treatment in Mexico. The special deal on financial and insurance services reflects the greater lobbying activity of, notably, British and Spanish banks during the negotiations (Manger, 2009, pp. 115–117). While European business lobbying could not prevent the last-minute deletion of the bulk of investment provisions from the draft PTA, the preservation of the financial services chapter underlines that business preferences and lobbying had some effect on outcomes.

Finally, the PTA contains basic provisions on the 'free transfer of payments' recalling the parties' commitments to relevant OECD instruments and a rendezvous clause providing for new negotiations on capital movements and services within three years.[11] It moreover encourages the parties to conclude BITs in order to complement the PTA with regard to post-establishment treatment and investment protection. The rendezvous clause was never used. Only recently have the EU and Mexico started discussing the possibility to launch negotiations to update the PTA (European Commission, 2017, 2001).

8.2.6 Conclusion

This section comprises the book's first case study, which points to noteworthy business interest and lobbying for investment provisions in international negotiations. European business sought to maintain a level playing field in the Mexican economy after the entry into force of NAFTA. In line with assumptions formulated in the analytical framework, European business was mostly interested in investment liberalisation commitments rather than post-establishment treatment and protection provisions. The Member States – while at first receptive to business demands and the Commission proposal to aim for NAFTA-parity including for investment provisions – reconsidered their stance and ultimately blocked investment provisions in order to protect their competences against EU encroachment. The Commission had to ultimately give in, but managed to safeguard some noteworthy yet often ignored investment provisions. What theoretical conclusions may one draw on the basis of this account of the EU-Mexico negotiations? The main observation of theoretical relevance is that the Commission used agenda setting to push for ambitious investment provisions and sought to protect these provisions against a sudden sovereignist backlash among the Member States. The case study thus suggests that Member States cooperation, delegation and the informal integration of international investment policymaking resulted from intsitutionalist and supranational dynamics rather than intergovernmental dynamics.

8.3 Investment disciplines in the negotiations on the EU-Chile PTA

The negotiations between the EU and Mexico are an interesting episode in the emergence of the EU's international investment policy. The negotiations become, however, even more intriguing if analysed in comparison to the negotiations on the EU-Chile PTA. The latter started around the time of the conclusion of the EU-Mexico PTA in late 1999 and came to an end in early 2002. The EU-Chile PTA is the first European PTA to contain comprehensive investment commitments in service and non-service sectors. Taking into consideration the proximity in time between the two negotiations and the marginal importance of the Chilean economy in comparison to the Mexican economy, one must wonder why the EU-Chile PTA finally encompasses ambitious investment commitments. This section traces the negotiations on the EU-Chile PTA. It finds that Commission entrepreneurship through agenda setting and reference to ongoing investment negotiations in the WTO was instrumental to ensuring the enduring support among Member States for the final inclusion of ambitious investment provisions. The section thus again uncovers institutional and supranational dynamics behind Member State cooperation, delegation and informal integration.

8.3.1 The pre-negotiations on the EU-Chile PTA

The plan to negotiate a EU-Chile PTA was born out of similar considerations as the EU-Mexico PTA. Following Chile's democratisation in the late 1980s, the country pursued a liberal economic and trade policy strategy. It reduced trade and investment barriers and sought to attract foreign investors. In 1995, Chile intended to join NAFTA but failed due to opposition within the USA. In consequence, Canada signed a PTA with Chile in 1996 and Mexico updated its PTA with Chile in 1998. In 1997, Chile and the USA announced their plan to negotiate on a Free Trade Area of the Americas (PTAA) (Manger, 2009, pp. 169–170). The EU was no bystander in this process. The EU concluded a first shallow and rather symbolic cooperation agreement with Chile in 1990. In 1996, the EU and Chile concluded a more comprehensive 'Framework Agreement for Cooperation'. The framework agreement documented the intention of the EU and Chile to conclude a PTA in the near future and constituted the first step in the EU's traditional 'two phases' approach to PTA negotiations. The framework agreement came into force in 1999 (Dür, 2007, p. 844; Manger, 2009, pp. 169–172).

In the early 1990s, the Chilean government had invited foreign companies to invest in Chile so as to diversify and modernise its economy. US firms had mostly ignored Chile's campaign to attract foreign investment and know-how. European, and in particular Spanish, service providers – due to their linguistic and cultural proximity – had followed Chile's courting and had invested in the banking, telecommunications and energy sectors (Manger, 2009, pp. 159–161). By the mid-1990s, several Spanish banks, telecommunication and energy companies had acquired commanding market shares and considerable stakes in Chilean service companies due to their first-mover advantage in service sectors with strong network effects and oligopolistic market structures. Their investments showed to be highly profitable. Many Spanish companies realised higher margins in Chile than through their core activities in Europe (Manger, 2009, p. 165).

In the mid-1990s, US plans to negotiate a comprehensive PTA with Chile – called the Preferential Trade Agreements of the Americas (PTAA) – were taking form (Dür, 2007; Manger, 2009). European business and notably Spanish service providers grew worried over the likely adverse effects of such PTAA on their operations in Chile. They feared that the liberalisation of bilateral economic relations between the United States and Chile might attract US competitors and endanger their dominant positions and profits in Chile. Spanish service providers therefore started lobbying for a comprehensive EU-Chile PTA. As these companies already held dominant positions in the Chilean economy, they were hardly interested in enhancing market access. They voiced demands, which sought to cement their dominant market positions. First, the PTA should codify and lock in Chile's current level of openness (Dür, 2007, pp. 845–846; Manger, 2009, pp. 174–177). Chile's openness was based on unilateral decisions and not bound by international commitments. Spanish service providers apparently feared that Chile might re-introduce protectionist measures against European firms after the conclusion of a highly comprehensive NAFTA-like US-Chile PTA. Second, most companies stressed that an EU-Chile PTA should contain MFN and NT clauses for service providers. These clauses should guarantee European companies at least the same treatment and market access as US firms under a potential future US-Chile PTA (Dür, 2007, pp. 845–846; Manger, 2009, pp. 174–177). Third, Spanish banks lobbied for the lifting of the 20% ceiling on foreign content for Chilean pension plans. The issue was arguably the only demand from service providers for additional market access (Dür, 2007, pp. 845–846; Manger, 2009, pp. 174–177). In contrast to the negotiations with Mexico, manufacturers and exporters of goods seem to have hardly lobbied for a PTA with Chile due to its small market size and low tariffs.

8.3.2 The Commission mandate

The Commission was responsive and proactive in order to satisfy and to use these business demands to advance its policy and institutional agenda. To speed up the negotiating process, it submitted to the Council of Ministers a comprehensive draft mandate for the EU-Chile PTA negotiations in July 1998 – well before the entry into force of the 'Framework Agreement' (Dür, 2007, p. 847; Manger, 2009, p. 172). The Member States were slow to react and examined the draft mandate only during the weeks prior to the EU-Latin America Summit in June 1999. This Summit brought together the EU, its Member States, the Mercosur countries and Chile. The main purpose of the summit was to evaluate the prospects of a region-to-region PTA between the EU and the Latin American countries. The idea of such a region-to-region PTA reflected the fact that Chile had applied for accession to the Mercosur. European policymakers thus wanted to conduct the EU-Chile and

EU-Mercosur negotiations in parallel in order to fuse them in case Chile acceded to the Mercosur in time for the conclusion of the negotiations (Agence Europe, 1999h).

First discussions in the Council of Ministers on the Commission's draft mandate prior to the EU-Latin America Summit showed that the Member States did not disagree so much over the substance of the draft mandate but, once again, over the proposed timing. Spain, Portugal, Denmark, Sweden and Germany pushed for the swift adoption of both mandates for the EU-Chile and EU-Mercosur negotiations (Dür, 2007, p. 847). They intended to use the upcoming summit as a platform to launch the PTA negotiations. Other Member States did not share their enthusiasm for these PTA negotiations. In particular, France and Ireland acted as brakemen in EU-internal debates (Dür, 2007, p. 847). France argued that PTA negotiations with major agricultural exporters like Chile and the Merocsur countries could only start once the EU had completed the reform of the Common Agricultural Policies (Agence Europe, 1999h, 1999i, 1999j). With regard to Chile, French wine producers feared competition with cheap Chilean produce. France also warned that Chilean agricultural produce might drive produce from French overseas territories and ACP countries out of the market. Greece, Italy and Ireland shared these concerns. On the other hand, France also stressed that it was bad timing to launch bilateral trade negotiations only a few months before the Seattle ministerial meeting of the WTO and the planned opening of a new multilateral round. The United Kingdom and the Netherlands agreed with France on this point. Germany, which held the Council Presidency, proposed setting 2003 as the deadline for the conclusion of the PTA negotiations with Chile and Mercosur. This compromise should give the EU more time to observe developments at the multilateral level and advance the CAP reform, but also provide for a clear timeframe. France and the United Kingdom rejected the proposal. They suggested starting with non-tariff negotiations on issues like investment, services, intellectual property rights, competition rules and rules of origin in the near future and to delay negotiations on industrial and agricultural tariffs until the WTO talks had delivered results (Agence Europe, 1999h, 1999i, 1999j).

In early June 1999, the European Council finally took a decision on the matter (Agence Europe, 1999h). The heads of states instructed their trade ministers to provide the Commission with mandates to open both PTA negotiations at the occasion of the EU-Latin America Summit. Their decision was based on an elaborate substantive and procedural compromise between the promoters and opponents of the PTA negotiations. The Commission should initially negotiate with Chile on non-tariff barriers and issues like investment, services and capital movements. In a second phase – after summer 2001 – the Commission should then start negotiations on the reduction of tariffs. The sequencing should enable the Commission to take developments in agricultural negotiations in the EU-Mercosur and planned WTO talks into account. The procedural linkage was reportedly a concession to France to gain its support for the opening of the PTA negotiations (Agence Europe, 1999h). Second, the mandate instructed the Commission to reach for an ambitious liberalisation of investments and services (Agence Europe, 2001a; Interview, telephone,

14 November 2013). The explicit mention of investment and services reflected the fear of European service providers that the conclusion of a comprehensive NAFTA-like US-Chile PTA in the following years might translate into discrimination against them. Following a pre-emptive logic, European service providers thus demanded European policymakers to seek the conclusion of an equivalent agreement with Chile. The mandate nevertheless clarified in an unusual degree of detail that the relevant chapter and liberalisation commitments should build on a positive list (Agence Europe, 2001a; Interview, telephone, 14 November 2013). The mandate's emphasis on the positive list approach was arguably an anticipating concession and first omen of the looming clash between the Commission and France over the negative list approach three months later in September 1999. It needs mention here that no source suggests that the Member States ever seriously discussed special representation modalities for these issues. The Member States seem to have assumed from the outset that the Commission would, as customary, act as their single voice in PTA negotiations regardless of the EU-internal distribution of competences. The Council of Ministers ultimately endorsed the mandate in time for the EU-Latin America Summit, which formally opened the PTA negotiations between the EU, Chile and Mercosur.

8.3.3 The core negotiations on the EU-Chile PTA

The EU and Chile met for the first symbolic consultations in November 1999 (Agence Europe, 2000b; Mulligan, 2000). As usual in PTA negotiations, the Commission spoke on behalf of the Member States on all agenda items including investment, services and capital movements. DG Relex was in the lead of the overall negotiating process, but DG Trade handled technical negotiations. The Member States typically sent officials to observe the negotiations, take notes and support the Commission on the spot. The joint EU-Chile negotiating committee agreed to structure the negotiations in three working groups: 1) trade in goods, 2) services and investment and, finally, 3) regulatory issues like rules of origin, public procurement, intellectual property rights and so on. The joint EU-Chile negotiating committee and the working groups should meet five times per year for five days. European sources reported that they expected the negotiations to take around three to four years. Chilean representatives, however, expressed their hope of finishing the negotiations within two years, before the second EU-Latin America Summit in 2002 (Agence Europe, 2000b; Mulligan, 2000).

The first round of substantive negotiations between the EU and Chile took place in March 2000 in Santiago de Chile. The negotiators established the working groups and agreed on a preliminary timetable for the talks (Agence Europe, 1999k). The second and third rounds, in June and November 2000, focused on the exchange of technical information on the parties' respective trade policies and regulations (Agence Europe, 2000c). The fourth round of negotiations, in March 2001, brought considerable progress. Chile and the EU made the first attempt to draft parts of the future agreement, notably on rules of origins, standards, intellectual property rights, public procurement and alike (Agence Europe, 2001b, 2001c).

Several Commission negotiators recalled that the EU-Chile negotiations were an easy enterprise as the Chilean negotiators were highly trained, very eager and Chile had already unilaterally dismantled many critical trade barriers (Interview, Brussels, 24 July 2012b; Interview, telephone, 14 November 2013).

Thanks to the Chilean and Commission entrepreneurship, the EU-Chile negotiations, moreover, made a procedural leap forward in spring 2001. While the first rounds of negotiations between the EU and Chile had been fruitful, many observers felt that the procedural linkage of the EU-Chile talks with the EU-Mercosur and WTO negotiations considerably decelerated the talks (Agence Europe, 2001d; Manger, 2009, pp. 172–173). The Mercosur negotiations had started but hardly progressed. The WTO negotiations had not even been launched as planned, due to the disastrous failure of the WTO ministerial meeting in Seattle. The Chilean government came to the conclusion that it was necessary to set the EU-Chile negotiations on an independent negotiating track so as to prevent stalemate. In summer 2000, the Chilean minister of foreign affairs thus toured with the support of the Commission the Member States to convince his European partners to delink the EU-Chile negotiations from the EU-Mercosur and WTO negotiations. In October 2000, the Commission requested the Council of Ministers and the European Parliament to adjust its negotiating mandate accordingly (Agence Europe, 2001d; Manger, 2009, pp. 172–173). The Council of Ministers was, however, divided on the matter. The sequencing and linking of the EU-Chile PTA negotiations had been a concession of favourable Member States toward hesitant ones. France and other mostly Southern European Member States had specifically asked for the sequencing and linking of the EU-Chile PTA negotiations in exchange for their assent to the EU-Chile PTA to prevent a too far-reaching liberalisation of agricultural trade. After lengthy discussion, the Council and the European Parliament nonetheless bought into the Chilean and Commission's arguments and accepted the request in spring 2001 (Agence Europe, 2001d; Manger, 2009, pp. 172–173). They changed the mandate and set the EU-Chile PTA negotiations on an independent track. The willingness of the Council to revise the mandate reportedly was due to the Commission's pedagogical campaigning and attempts to explain the greater negotiating context. It moreover raised awareness in the Council that after the failure of the Seattle ministerial meeting the EU may have to develop a stronger bilateral strategy and profile as the prospects of further multilateral liberalisation were dim. The Commission's proactive attitude allowed the EU-Chile PTA negotiations to progress, which ultimately consolidated the EU's role in international investment policy (Manger, 2009, pp. 172–173; Interview, Brussels, 25 September 2013a; Interview, telephone, 14 November 2013).

Early 2001 brought another important change. France passed the rotating Council Presidency on to Sweden. While the French government under Lionel Jospin was critical of economic liberalism and the PTA negotiations, Sweden was a liberal trading nation in favour of the PTA negotiations. Sweden, moreover, typically sided with the Commission in EU-internal debates on trade policy. The incoming Swedish Council Presidency identified the advancement of the PTA negotiations with Chile as a priority of its term. The Swedish Presidency understood that the main obstacles to a swift conclusion of a comprehensive and ambitious PTA with Chile were not located outside the EU but in Member State capitals. Many national administrations mistrusted the Commission and Brussels, had an aversion to free trade and sought to protect their competences against European encroachment. Sweden – in close cooperation with the Commission – came to the conclusion that they had to step up efforts to convince the Member States of the benefits of an ambitious EU-Chile PTA (Interview, telephone, 26 January 2012b).

8.3.4 Commission entrepreneurship for comprehensive investment disciplines

Sweden and the Commission subsequently acted as policy entrepreneurs and devised a campaign to build and to maintain a broad consensus among the Member States for ambitious investment, services and capital movement provisions. The Commission and Sweden used their technical expertise and agenda-setting powers to frame Council discussions and to logically link the EU-Chile negotiations to the EU's ambitions for upcoming WTO negotiations. In more concrete terms, Commission officials and Swedish diplomats and Commission negotiators reportedly toured Member State capitals – and in particular Paris – in order to build confidence and to inform national administrations about the merits of a comprehensive PTA. Sweden and the Commission felt that this approach reflected the EU's best economic interests. What is more, the campaign at the same time also consolidated the Commission's role and the EU's de facto competences in international investment policy. This instance of joined policy entrepreneurship of the Commission and Council Presidency thus echoed functional and power considerations. It needs mention that European business reportedly did not propose or lobby for this initiative (Interview, telephone, 26 January 2012b).

The primary objective of the joint initiative of Sweden and the Commission was to prevent another clash on investment, service and capital movement provisions, as had been the case at the end of the EU-Mexico negotiations (Heydon and Woolcock, 2009, p. 112). Swedish diplomats and Commission negotiators sought to ensure continuous support for the Commission's negotiating mandate and results in these domains. They reassured Member State administrations that the positive list approach used in the EU-Chile talks allowed for greater control over the liberalisation of services and service-related investment than the negative list approach used in the EU-Mexico talks. They, moreover, added that – at the behest of the Member States – the EU was pushing for a new round of multilateral trade negotiations in the WTO (see Chapter 7). The official EU position stipulated that the new round should seek a further liberalisation of services trade and extend the WTO regime toward the so-called Singapore Issues – investment, public procurement, competition and trade facilitation. The Swedish diplomats and Commission negotiators explained in meetings with sceptical Member State governments that the EU could not credibly advocate a comprehensive new round, if the Member States vetoed the inclusion of comparable disciplines into the EU's PTAs. The very *raison d'être* of PTAs in the multilateral trade regime was to enable countries to go beyond WTO commitments and to reach for a broader (WTO+) and deeper (WTOx) liberalisation of their economic relations. This line of argument was reportedly quite effective with Member State governments and in particular with the French government. In the run-up to the PTA negotiations with Mexico, the Mercosur and Chile, France had constantly reiterated that its trade policy priority were the upcoming WTO negotiations. In consequence, France could hardly veto an ambitious service chapter in the PTA with Chile, if it intended to remain credible (Interview, telephone, 26 January 2012b).

Swedish diplomats and the Commission negotiators used the same argument in order to convince the Member States to finally include investment provisions for non-service sectors (Interview, telephone, 26 January 2012b). They reiterated that the EU was formally seeking negotiations on 'investment' per se – i.e. investment across all economic sectors – in the upcoming WTO round. So if the EU wanted to be seen as a credible actor in related WTO debates, the EU had to reach for similar provisions in its PTAs. Swedish diplomats and Commission negotiators proposed negotiating on a comprehensive positive list on 'establishment', which should codify investment liberalisation commitments for services and non-service sectors. From the point of view of regulators, as a Swedish diplomat elaborated, such an encompassing approach to investment made much more sense than the artificial distinction between service-related and non-service-related investments. Sceptical Member States – and notably France – found it again difficult to object to this logic. Only two years before, France had withdrawn from the MAI negotiations in the OECD by publically claiming that negotiations on investment should continue in the WTO as part of the Singapore Issues, because the WTO was a more suitable forum for such talks. This remained France's official position in the Council of Ministers in the following years. Hence, it would have undermined France's credibility to veto the inclusion of such provisions in the EU-Chile PTA (Interview, telephone, 26 January 2012b).

The efforts of the Swedish Council Presidency and Commission facilitated EU-internal debates on the PTA negotiations. Commission negotiators commented that the EU-Chile negotiations took place in an atmosphere of much greater trust between the Commission and the Member States than the previous EU-Mexico talks (Interview, Brussels, 24 July 2012b; Interview, telephone, 14 November 2013). At the fifth negotiating round between the EU and Chile in July 2001, the EU was thus able to present its first full offer to Chile. It proposed to do away with 100% of industrial tariffs and 93% of agricultural tariffs within ten years of the PTA coming into force. It also proposed that all commitments on non-tariff barriers – for instance establishment/investment and services – should take immediate effect (Agence Europe, 2001e). The consequent discussions between the EU and Chile showed that both parties agreed on most aspects of the offer. In consequence, Commission President Romano Prodi and Chilean President Ricardo Lagos announced in September 2001 that it might be possible to close the negotiations by the end of the year (Agence Europe, 2001f).

The optimism of Commissioner Prodi and President Lagos was premature. In October 2001, the sixth round of negotiations saw further in-depth discussions on tariffs, services and other non-tariff issues. The discussions shed light on three points of persisting disagreement among the parties. First, Spain demanded access to Chile's territorial waters for European fishery fleets, which Chile was unwilling to grant. The so-called *Swordfish Issue* became the most difficult issue of the entire negotiations. Second, France, Greece and other wine producing Member States demanded that Chile adjust to the European regime for the protection of geographical indicators. Third, the Commission demanded greater liberalisation commitments in financial services from Chile. While Chile did not categorically refuse to further open its financial sector for European companies, it insisted that it would first negotiate on this matter with the USA before taking on further commitments. The Commission dismissed the Chilean point of view and underlined that the EU would not adjust to US rules later on. The disagreements could not be resolved during the sixth round (Agence Europe, 2001a, 2002a; Manger, 2009, pp. 173–174). The EU and Chile therefore held another three negotiating rounds in January, March and April 2002, which finally closed all chapters and ultimately even resolved the aforementioned points of disagreement (Agence Europe, 2002b, 2002c, 2002d, 2002e, 2002f). The negotiations on the EU-Chile PTA drew to an end in time for the second EU-Latin America Summit in May 2002. The agreement was signed in November 2002 and entered into force in February 2003 (European Commission, 2014b).

The conclusion of the EU-Chile PTA marks a milestone in the emergence of the EU's international investment policy for several reasons. First, the EU-Chile PTA contains comprehensive commitments on market access for investors in services[12] and non-services[13] sectors like agriculture, mining and manufacturing. Investors generally benefit from MFN and/or NT under the PTA. The commitments are scheduled in the form of a GATS-like positive list. This list did not significantly enhance market access for European investors in Chile, but it codified and consolidated the existing degree of openness. It is therefore much easier for investors to use than the EU-Mexico PTA, which merely includes a standstill clause regarding service-related investment but no consolidated schedule. The inclusion of investment commitments in non-service sectors, moreover, marks the 'emancipation' and emergence of a proper European approach to the regulation of investments in PTAs, which is independent from the regulation of services trade. Second, the EU-Chile PTA also partly liberalises the movement of key personnel.[14] The establishment of investments not only requires the transfer of capital but also the ability of investors to manage and build their affiliates. The movement of key personnel is thus crucial to investment liberalisation. Third, the EU-Chile PTA includes a clause encouraging Chile and the Member States to conclude BITs.[15] The PTA thus seeks to establish an encompassing investment framework. Finally, the EU-Chile PTA provides for the liberalisation of capital movements – including FDI, payments and profits – under specific commitments as well as under the relevant OECD codes.[16]

8.3.5 Conclusion

The analysis of the negotiations on the EU-Chile PTA draws a nuanced picture. European business lobbied for the negotiations and favoured a comprehensive

PTA including investment provisions in order to pre-empt any future competitive disadvantages, which may arise from a US-Chile PTA. The Member States were generally receptive to these demands, but maintained reservations with regard to the breadth and the speed of negotiations. The European Commission aimed for an ambitious PTA with investment provisions. It joined forces with the Swedish Council Presidency to prevent another debacle and sovereigntist backlash against an ambitious PTA with investment provisions. The Commission and Sweden used their agenda-setting powers and expertise to build trust, to frame and to politically link the PTA negotiations to ongoing efforts of the EU to establish multilateral investment disciplines in the WTO. The joint efforts of the Commission and the Swedish Council Presidency were successful. They managed to maintain the Member States' commitment to an ambitious PTA and even convinced them to include investment commitments from services to non-services sectors. The observations primarily lend support to institutionalist and supranational thinking on cooperation, delegation and integration.

8.4 Beyond Chile – investment provisions in EU PTAs agreements

The negotiations on the EU-Mexico and EU-Chile PTAs were the first bilateral trade negotiations between the EU and third countries to cover comprehensive investment commitments. At the same time, the Member States negotiated on the Treaty of Nice (2000–2001) and the Constitutional Treaty (2002–2003). While the Nice Treaty extended the Union's exclusive competence under the CCP toward the regulations of services trade and service-related investments, the draft Constitution even proposed to generally bring FDI regulation under exclusive Union competence (see Chapter 9). Taken together, these events triggered reflections in the Council of Ministers about the EU's long-term strategy on international investment. The '113/133 Committee' reportedly established an expert group which examined, in cooperation with the Commission, the cast of investment chapters in future EU trade and investment agreements (Interview, Brussels, 24 July 2012a; Interview, telephone, 14 November 2013).

In 2006, the Commission presented its so-called Minimum Platform on Investment (MPoI) (European Commission, 2006). The MPoI codified and standardised in many regards the investment approach adopted in the EU-Chile PTA. It proposed a single chapter on establishment – i.e. investment for future EU trade and investment agreements. Investment liberalisation should proceed on the basis of a GATS-like positive list. Investors in liberalised sectors should benefit from MFN and NT at the pre- and post-establishment stage and have the right to send key personnel to their affiliates in host countries. The MPoI, moreover, proposed the inclusion of a non-lowering of standards clause into the establishment chapter. The clause would prevent countries from lowering their social, health, labour or environmental standards to the end of attracting additional inward investments. The MPoI laid out the first comprehensive EU approach to market access and post-establishment treatment under future EU trade and investment agreements.

It did not, however, contain any provisions on investment protection and dispute settlement as typically found in Member State BITs or NAFTA-like trade and investment agreements.

The MPoI was not in use for long. While the Constitutional Treaty was rejected in referenda in France and the Netherlands in 2005, the Member States signed the Treaty of Lisbon in December 2007. Article 207 TFEU finally provides the EU with the exclusive competences to regulate FDI. It arguably empowered the EU to conclude full-fledged trade and investment agreements covering market access, post-establishment treatment and investment protection provisions. The Council of Ministers consequently instructed the Commission to reach for comprehensive investment chapters – covering market access, post-establishment treatment and investment protection – in the PTA negotiations with Malaysia, Singapore, India, Canada and the USA.

8.5 Conclusion

This chapter examined the PTA negotiations between the EU and Mexico as well as the EU and Chile. It sought to answer two questions. *First, why was the EU allowed to negotiate on investment provisions with these countries? And second, why does the EU-Mexico PTA contain only limited investment provisions, whereas the EU-Chile PTA encompasses significant investment commitments?* The observations from this chapter draw an intriguing picture of cooperation, delegation and integration dynamics. European business, the Member States and the European Commission saw the need to negotiate ambitious PTAs inter alia with investment provisions with Mexico and Chile in order to mitigate adverse economic effects of competing PTA projects. The findings largely confirm existing research on the proliferation of PTAs in the world economy (Bhagwati, 2008; Dür, 2007; Grossmann and Helpman, 1995; Heydon and Woolcock, 2009; Manger, 2009).

The chapter however suggests that global competitive pressures and related business lobbying are insufficient to account for the inclusion of investment provisions into European PTAs. Commission entrepreneurship was decisive in adding investment provisions to the standard agenda of European PTAs. The comparative assessment of the EU-Mexico and EU-Chile negotiations underscores this reading. While at first supportive, the Member States suddenly vetoed in a last-minute revolt fairly ambitious investment provisions agreed with Mexico. The Member States reportedly sought to protect their competences from European encroachment. In the end, the European Commission could save only a fraction of investment-related provisions from deletion. To avoid another diplomatic debacle, the Commission was highly proactive in the following PTA negotiations with Chile. It engaged together with the Swedish Council Presidency in a campaign to build trust and to convince critical Member States of the value added of the an ambitious PTA with investment provisions. The Commission underlined that the EU could not – on behest of the Member States – push for investment negotiations in the WTO, but reject investment provisions as part of PTAs. The Commission stressed that PTAs were in essence a trade policy instrument to go beyond

WTO commitments. The Commission omitted that it had previously gone to great lengths to include investment into the WTO work agenda (see Chapter 7). The Member States accepted the reasoning and subsequently even accepted investment liberalisation commitments in non-service sectors in the EU-Chile PTA. The EU-Chile PTA became the first PTA with noteworthy investment provisions. It moreover decoupled investment from services provisions in European trade policy and triggered more systemic reflection on the EU's approach to international investment regulation as part of its trade policy.

The chapter thus points to a striking instance of policy entrepreneurship through agenda setting and forum linkage. As Chapter 7 showed, the Commission had invested considerable energy in putting investment onto the work agenda of the WTO as part of the Singapore Issues. It, moreover, persistently and ultimately successfully pushed for shifting multilateral investment negotiations back from the OECD into the WTO. In the EU-Chile negotiations, the Commission then referred to investment work and negotiations in the WTO to justify the inclusion of investment provisions into European PTAs. The Commission thereby linked different policy fora to build up functional systemic pressures to consolidate the EU's role in international investment policy. From a historical institutionalist perspective, the Commission promoted institutional drift. It shaped the policy environment to alter the effect of an institution and to bring about institutional change. To conclude, Member State cooperation and delegation of international investment policymaking in PTA negotiations confirm institutionalist supranational thinking rather than societal and liberal intergovernmental thinking.

Notes

1 The chapter disregards accession, association and partnership and cooperation agreements. Accession agreements typically contain very comprehensive investment provisions. Nevertheless, they cannot be considered as part of the EU's foreign economic policy strategy. They seek to fully integrate third countries into the legal and economic regime of the EU. Early association as well as Partnership and Cooperation Agreements – such as with the former Soviet Republics or Mediterranean countries concluded in the 1990s – are of economic and geopolitical nature alike. These agreements contain very shallow provisions indirectly touching on investment activities (e.g. liberalisation of current or capital accounts), which albeit cannot be considered as a manifestation of a proper EU international investment policy.
2 The Mercosur is a Common Market between Argentina, Brazil, Paraguay, Uruguay and Venezuela.
3 The EU includes into its PTAs and Association Agreements clauses, which stipulate that both parties are committed to the protection of Human Rights and democracy.
4 The so-called Agreement on Political and Economic Association and Cooperation.
5 The Interim Agreement was a de facto fast track authority. It should automatically enter into force after the conclusion of the global agreement and provided for the establishment of the joint EU-Mexico committee in charge of the PTA negotiations.
6 The Joint Declaration, finally, was a peculiar document. It essentially underlined that agenda items like investment, services, capital movements and intellectual property rights came under shared or national competences and thus were subject to specific negotiating and decision-making rules. Hence, the Joint Declaration should be considered as an expression of the Member States' preoccupation with competence questions.

194 *PTA negotiations*

7 See, for instance, the annexes of Directive 88/361/EEC, which provide an inconclusive albeit binding definition of the term.
8 For more information, see, for instance Hindelang (2009) and OECD (2002).
9 For text of PTA see European Commission (2001).
10 See articles 4, 5 and 6 of the services part of the PTA.
11 See article 35 of the services part of the PTA and Chapter IV, title III.
12 See Annexe VII of the EU-Chile PTA.
13 See Annexe X of the EU-Chile PTA.
14 See Annexe X of the EU-Chile PTA, pp. 1,212–1,220.
15 See article 21(b) of the EU-Chile PTA.
16 See articles 164 and 165 of the EU-Chile PTA.

References

Agence Europe, 2002a. EU/Chile: EU and Chile to intensify rate of negotiations on free trade agreement (26 January 2002).
Agence Europe, 2002b. EU/Chile: Negotiations over a free-trade agreement between the EU and Chile are on right path (2 February 2002).
Agence Europe, 2002c. EU/Chile: Last round of free trade negotiations (7 March 2002).
Agence Europe, 2002d. EU/Chile: Home straight before signing of association agreement (13 April 2002).
Agence Europe, 2002e. EU/Chile: EU and Chile expected to finish negotiations for free-trade agreement on Friday before (26 April 2002).
Agence Europe, 2002f. EU/Chile: EU and Chile conclude negotiations for association and free trade agreement (27 April 2002).
Agence Europe, 2001a. EU/Chile: 6th negotiating round over free-trade agreement clarifies stances on agriculture (5 October 2001).
Agence Europe, 2001b. EU/Chile: On Thursday both parties should come up with joint text, at end of 4th round of negotiations on free-trade agreement (15 March 2001).
Agence Europe, 2001c. EU/Chile: Parties welcome success of the 4th round of negotiation for free trade agreement and open (16 March 2001).
Agence Europe, 2001d. EU/Merocsur/Chile (9 February 2001).
Agence Europe, 2001e. EU/Chile: Liberalisierung innerhalb von zehn Jahren vorgeschlagen (13 July 2001).
Agence Europe, 2001f. EU/Chile: Chilea President announces that two sides intend technically concluding negotiations on (14 September 2001).
Agence Europe, 2000a. EU/Mexico (20 July 2000).
Agence Europe, 2000b. EU/Chile: Negotiation instruments and procedures toward association agreement are set in place (24 June 2000).
Agence Europe, 2000c. EU/Chile: Third negotiating session for association and free trade agreement begins Monday in Santiago (14 November 2000).
Agence Europe, 1999a. EU/Mexico (22 May 1999).
Agence Europe, 1999b. EU/Mexico (5 March 1999).
Agence Europe, 1999c. EU/Mexico: Free trade (24 July 1999).
Agence Europe, 1999d. EU/Mexico: Eight (and last?) round of negotiations over a free-trade agreement (16 October 1999).
Agence Europe, 1999e. EU/Mexico: Analysis of issues still on the table in trade negotiations (21 October 1999).
Agence Europe, 1999f. EU/Mexico (6 November 1999).

Agence Europe, 1999g. EU/Mexico: Negotiations on free trade agreement are prolonged (13 November 1999).
Agence Europe, 1999h. EU/Chile/Mercosur: EU seeks compromise to allow start of trade negotiations with Chile and the Mercosur (21 September 1999).
Agence Europe, 1999i. EU/Chile/Mercosur: Rahmenabkommen mit Chile tritt in Kraft (20 February 1999).
Agence Europe, 1999j. EU/Mercosur/Chile (4 June 1999).
Agence Europe, 1999k. EU/Chile/Mercosur: EU trade negotiations with Mercosur and Chile on 24 November at ministerial level (18 November 1999).
Agence Europe, 1998a. EU/Mexico: Trade liberalisation (28 April 1998).
Agence Europe, 1998b. EU/Mexico: First joint council meeting on Tuesday 14 July will kick off trade liberalisation negotiations (11 July 1998).
Agence Europe, 1998c. EU/Mexico: Trade liberalisation negotiations to open on 9 November in Mexico City (14 October 1998).
Agence Europe, 1998d. EU/Mexico: Trade negotiations to start on 9 November (7 November 1998).
Agence Europe, 1998e. EU/Mexico: Trade liberalization negotiations could begin in the second half this year (18 February 1998).
Agence Europe, 1997a. EU/Mexico: Member states elaborate global approach to relaunch negotiations of envisaged agreement (15 March 1997).
Agence Europe, 1997b. EU/Mexico: End of negotiations for an interim, global and political agreement (13 June 1997).
Agence Europe, 1997c. EU/Mexico: "Adjustments" to Human Rights clause raise difficulties (20 June 1997).
Agence Europe, 1997d. EU/Mexico: Compromise in sight (1 July 1997).
Agence Europe, 1997e. EU/Mexico: Trade liberalisation (9 December 1997).
Agence Europe, 1996a. EU15 disagree on nature and contents of Mexican agreement (14 February 1996).
Agence Europe, 1996b. Spain speaks up for free trade deal with Mexico (22 March 1996).
Agence Europe, 1996c. EU/Mexico (21 May 1996).
Agence Europe, 1996d. EU/Mexico (14 May 1996).
Agence Europe, 1996e. EU/Mexico (23 November 1996).
Agence Europe, 1995a. Commission recommends liberalisation of trade with Mexico (10 February 1995).
Agence Europe, 1995b. Council favours rapid start to talks with Mercosur (12 April 1995).
Agence Europe, 1995c. Commission outlines aims of agreement with Mexico (26 October 1995).
Baldwin, D., 2013. Power in international relations, in: *Handbook of international relations*. Sage Publications, London, pp. 271–297.
Bhagwati, J., 2008. *Termites in the trading system*. Oxford University Press, Oxford.
Ceyssens, J., 2005. Towards a common foreign investment policy? Foreign investment in the European Constitution. *Leg. Issues Econ. Integr.* 32, 259–291.
Cottier, T., Elsig, M., 2011. *Governing the World Trade Organization: Past, present and beyond Doha*. Cambridge University Press, Cambridge.
Dür, A., 2007. EU trade policy as protection for exporters: The agreements with Mexico and Chile. *J. Common Mark. Stud.* 45, 833–855.
European Commission, 2017. EU trade commissioner in Mexico: "Trade deal possible by year's end" [WWW Document]. URL http://trade.ec.europa.eu/doclib/press/index.cfm?id=1659 (accessed 5.9.17).

European Commission, 2014a. Countries and regions: Mexico [WWW Document]. URL http://ec.europa.eu/trade/policy/countries-and-regions/countries/mexico/ (accessed 5.23.14).
European Commission, 2014b. Countries and regions: Chile [WWW Document]. URL http://ec.europa.eu/trade/policy/countries-and-regions/countries/chile/ (accessed 8.8.14).
European Commission, 2006. Minimum platform on investment for EU FTAs: Provisions on establishment in template for a title on "Establishment, trade in services and e-commerce" (D (2006) 9219), Brussels.
European Commission, 2001. Decision No. 2/2001 of the EU-Mexico Joint Council of 27 February 2001. Brussels.
Financial Times, 1997. FT news digest: Talks planed on free trade (11 December 1997).
Grossmann, G., Helpman, E., 1995. The politics of free trade agreements. *Am. Econ. Rev.* 85, 667–690.
Harding, G., 1999. Obstacles remain to EU-Mexico trade deal (7 October 1999). *Eur. Voice.*
Heydon, K., Woolcock, S., 2009. *The rise of bilateralism: Comparing American, European and Asian approaches to preferential trade agreements*. United Nations University Press, Tokyo.
Hindelang, S., 2009. *The free movement of capital and foreign direct investment: The scope of protection in EU law*. Oxford University Press, Oxford.
Manger, M., 2009. *Investing in protection: The politics of preferential trade agreements between north and south*. Cambridge University Press, Cambridge.
Mulligan, M., 2000. World news: The Americas – Chile and EU in new trade talks (10 April 2000). *Financ. Times* 3.
Odell, J., 2000. *Negotiating the world economy*, Cornell studies in political economy. Cornell University Press, Ithaca, NY.
OECD, 2002. *Forty years' experience with the OECD codes of liberalisation of capital movements*. OECD, Paris.
Sanahuja, J.A., 2000. Trade, politics, and democratization: The 1997 global agreement between the European Union and Mexico. *J. Interam. Stud. World Aff.* 42, 35–62.
Tallberg, J., 2003. The agenda-shaping powers of the EU Council presidency. *J. Eur. Public Policy* 10, 1–19.
Woolcock, S., 2011. *European Union economic diplomacy: The role of the EU in external economic relations*, Global finance series. Ashgate, Burlington.
Zimmerman, H., 2007. Realist power Europe? The EU in the negotiations about China's and Russia's WTO accession. *J. Common Mark. Stud.* 45, 813–832.

9 The evolution of the EU's legal competences in international investment policy

The previous chapters examined the EU's involvement in multilateral and bilateral investment negotiations since the 1980s despite the Union's manifest lack of legal competences to regulate international investment flows. The present chapter complements the preceding analysis. It traces debates on the EU's legal competences in international investment policy as enshrined in European primary and secondary law since the 1950s. Special attention is afforded to how the EU's de facto competences and involvement in international investment negotiations shaped these debates. The chapter builds on the theoretical assumption laid out in the analytical framework that the evolution of the EU's de facto competences influences the evolution of the EU's legal competences. De facto and legal competences are considered as interdependent and consecutive stages of Member State cooperation. If the Member States informally cooperate to regulate an issue area, it may gradually alter the preferences of involved policymakers and create path dependencies promoting a formalisation of cooperation, delegation and integration (Kleine, 2013; Pierson, 1994; Stacey and Rittberger, 2003). The book and chapter thus break with the analytical methodological tradition in European studies to separately analyse and explain on the one hand informal cooperation and integration in daily policy-making and, on the other, formal cooperation and integration in IGCs.

The chapter finds that European business was passive or divided regarding an extension of the EU's legal competences in international investment policy. Business preferences and lobbying cannot account for the extension of the EU's legal competences. The Member States, moreover, continuously opposed an extension of the EU's legal competences in this domain. They sought to protect their competences against European encroachment. The chapter shows that the extension of the EU's legal competences to international investment regulation is predominantly the result of Commission entrepreneurship. In accordance with principal-agent research and historical institutionalist concepts of agency-driven institutional change, the Commission used its agenda-setting powers, had strategic recourse to the CJEU to claim competence and continuously underlined the evolving trade policymaking environment to emphasise vis-à-vis the Member States the need to extend the EU's legal competences to international investment policy. The Commission thereby promoted institutional 'conversion', 'layering' and 'drift' so as to extend its powers in foreign economic relations. After several decades, the

Commission's policy entrepreneurship finally succeeded during the Convention on the Future of Europe. The Convention differed from IGCs in terms of composition and working method. Open discussions among generalist politicians rather than secret bargaining among highly specialised technocrats were at the heart of the Convention. The Convention participants followed the Commission's functionalist plea that the EU's legal competences under the CCP had to be brought back in line with the agenda of modern PTAs and WTO negotiations to maintain the EU's ability to represent European interests in the global investment regime. The Commission, however, omitted in these debates that it had spared no efforts to put investment provisions onto the agenda of WTO negotiations and European PTAs and thereby promoted this problematique institutional drift. The chapter thus points to an intriguing instance of Commission entrepreneurship across multiple policy fora and over an extensive time period to consolidate and to formalise the EU's role and competences in international investment policymaking. The observations lend support to supranational and challenge liberal intergovernmental thinking on European Integration. The emergence of the EU's international investment policy is manifestly the result of Commission entrepreneurship and institutional dynamics rather than business or Member State preferences.

A brief note on the place of this chapter in the overarching structure of the book is appropriate. It has been suggested that the analysis of the EU's legal competences should be chronologically integrated with the analyses of the international investment negotiations. The analysis of the IGC on the Maastricht Treaty, for instance, should follow the examination of the Uruguay Round. This suggestion is convincing at first sight, but there are good reasons for the here chosen structure. First, many negotiations took place in parallel. A truly chronological account would be confusing for the reader. Second, the Convention on the Future of Europe, which ultimately initiated the extension of the CCP to FDI regulation, sits at the end of a long chain of international investment negotiations and EU-internal debates. The purpose of this chapter is to shed light on the way toward, and debates during, the Convention leading to the CCP reform. To analyse the Convention after the chapters on international investment negotiations constitutes the logical endpoint of the book.

9.1 First steps – the EU and international investment regulation from the 1950s to the 1980s

Veritable debates on the EU's role and legal competences in international investment policy did not start before the late 1980s. International investment was a marginal phenomenon and of limited economic importance before then (see Chapter 3). Neither European business nor policymakers took a strong interest in international investment policy in general or the EU's role and competences in particular. EU-internal policymaking debates, nonetheless, touched twice on this issue during the first three decades of European Integration. First, the preparatory debates on the Treaty of Rome briefly raised the question of the EU's role in the regulation of international investment flows. Second, the Commission proposed the creation of a European export policy in the 1970s, which would, inter alia, encompass the conclusion of investment protection agreements between the EU and third countries. The Member States, however, rejected the Commission's plans.

9.1.1 The Treaty of Rome

The Treaty of Rome did not provide the EU with legal competences in the regulation of international investment flows. The preparatory debates on the Treaty of Rome nevertheless touched on the issue. The publication of the Spaak Report in April 1956 marked the kick-off for in-depth discussions on the Treaty of Rome and the establishment of the EU. The Member States of the ECSC – Belgium, France, Germany, Luxemburg, the Netherlands and Italy – had commissioned an intergovernmental committee headed by the Belgian minister of foreign affairs, Paul-Henri Spaak, to evaluate and further develop the plan to create a Common Market. The report discussed the objectives, overarching rules and institutions of a Common Market (Bakker, 1996, pp. 30–33).

The report's section on the CCP did not touch on investment-related questions. Instead, it exclusively focused on the establishment of a customs union, a common external tariff and the abolishment of import and export quotas vis-à-vis third countries (Comité intergouvernemental créé par la conférence de Messine, 1956, p. 75). This focus reflected the then still limited working agenda of the GATT. Issues like international investment, trade in services or technical barriers to trade did not become the subject of GATT discussions before the 1970s and 1980s.

The report, nonetheless, touched upon the EU's potential role in the regulation of international investment flows in its section on the free movement of capital. The report stipulated that the Common Market should provide for the free movement of goods, services, labour and capital. The free movement of capital – a scarce production factor in post-war Europe – should promote its efficient allocation, stimulate economic growth and welfare gains (Comité intergouvernemental créé par la conférence de Messine, 1956, pp. 92–93). The report, however, cautioned that the liberalisation of capital movements – including FDI – would require several accompanying actions[1] and, notably, the creation of a common external capital regime. The absence of such a regime, the report warned, would create a regulatory gap. Capital could enter and exit the Common Market through Member States with liberal external capital regimes and then flow into Member States with more protectionist external capital regimes.

> *Le [. . .] obstacle, c'est la possibilité que les capitaux passent d'un pays vers un autre, non pour s'y investir mais pour échapper vers l'extérieur au bénéfice d'une inégalité dans la rigueur des contrôles. La liberté de la circulation des capitaux à l'intérieur du marché commun appelle donc dans les relations avec les pays tiers une certaine attitude commune qui [. . .] au stade finale, aboutirait à une égale liberté ou à un dégrée de contrôle équivalent.[2]*
> (Comité intergouvernemental créé par la conférence de Messine, 1956, pp. 93–94)

The report implicitly advised the states to empower the EU to regulate market access for foreign investors to maintain regulatory coherence across the Common Market. Since the EU's very inception, institutional dynamics in the form of spillovers thus exerted pressure to integrate the regulation of international investment activities.

The Spaak Report became the basis for negotiations on the Treaty of Rome, which were held between June 1956 and March 1957. The governments followed the recommendations of the Spaak Report in regard to trade policy. They provided the Union with the exclusive competence to regulate the Common Market's external trade relations in article 113 EEC. The wording of article 113 EEC clearly reflected the as yet limited understanding of trade policy of the 1950s and did not encompass the regulation of international investment flows. The governments followed only partly the recommendations of the Spaak Report in regard to capital movements due to sovereignty concerns. They did not provide the EU with competences to regulate capital movements between the Common Market and third countries. This diversion from the Spaak Report is not surprising. The Member States adopted a cautious approach to the liberalisation of capital movements within the Common Market. While articles 67–73 EEC in principle liberalised capital movements, article 69 EEC underlined that the free movement of capital was only a subordinate treaty freedom. The liberalisation of capital movements should only proceed to the extent necessary for the functioning of the Common Market for goods and services (Bakker, 1996, pp. 42–44; Ohler, 2002, pp. 1–3; Usher, 1992, pp. 35–37). What is more, the articles regarding the free movement of capital should not be directly enforceable but require the implementation of secondary legislation (Ohler, 2002, pp. 1–3). The Member States waited almost three decades before enacting any significant implementing legislation so as to advance the liberalisation of capital movements within the Common Market. The manifest hesitation of most Member State governments reflected their worries that a liberalisation of capital movements would undermine their Keynesian macroeconomic policies, taxation regimes and, lastly, sovereignty (Bakker, 1996, pp. 32–36). It was only with the demise of the Keynesian economic paradigm and the emergence of the neoliberal one in the 1980s that the Member States revised their positions on capital movements.

9.1.2 First debates on European BITs in the 1970s

Following the entry into force of the Treaty of Rome in 1958, the EU's legal competences in international investment policy did not resurface as a topic in EU-internal discussions for more than a decade. Only the debates on the creation of a European export policy and related Opinion 1/75 of the CJEU brought the topic up again. While previous EU-internal debates had only indirectly touched on the EU's competences in international investment regulation, these debates indeed focused on whether and how the EU could regulate the activities of international investors under the CCP. The debates constitute a first instance of Commission entrepreneurship to the end of consolidating the EU's legal competences in international investment regulation.

In late 1972 and 1975, the Commission published two draft regulations, which sought to establish a European export policy as an integral part of the CCP (Deutscher Bundestag, 1976; Johannsen, 2009, pp. 5–6; Seidl-Hohenveldern, 1977, pp. 54–59). One draft regulation foresaw the creation of a European investment guarantee agency. The agency should provide investment guarantees to European investment projects in third countries. The Commission explained in its proposal that joint investment projects of investors from different Member States had insufficient coverage through national schemes. The European scheme should be complementary. The investment guarantees should insure investors against non-commercial investment risks like war, riots, expropriation, payment restrictions and major exchange rate fluctuations. Access to common investment guarantees should be conditional on the existence or conclusion of investment protection agreements – i.e. BITs between the EU and the concerned third countries (Johannsen, 2009, pp. 5–6; Seidl-Hohenveldern, 1977, pp. 54–59). The Commission's proposal thus emulated the German approach to international investment policy. The German government had conceived of BITs in order to lower its financial exposure under state-backed investment guarantees (Interview, Berlin, 17 February 2012; Poulsen, 2010, pp. 555–557). The Commission's draft regulation referred to article 113 EEC as the competence basis for the creation of the EU investment guarantee agency and the conclusion of EU BITs covering post-establishment treatment, protection and compensation standards.

In July 1975, the Commission stepped up pressure on the Member States to accept its draft regulations and to acknowledge the EU's competence over export policy through the strategic recourse to legal review by the CJEU. It called on the CJEU to assess in Opinion 1/75 the EU's legal competences to enter into the so-called *Understanding on a Local Cost Standard* drafted in the OECD. This gentlemen's agreement sought to establish ground rules for export policies including investment guarantee schemes in order to prevent unfair international competition among OECD exporters and investors. The Commission argued that the EU should adhere and enforce the OECD standard on behalf of the Member States due to its exclusive competence over export policy under the CCP. The CJEU partly confirmed the EU's competence under article 113 EEC to adhere to the agreement and to harmonise Member States' export policies. Lawyers interpreted the CJEU's Opinion as an encouragement and wake-up call for the Commission to get active and to regulate in this domain as foreseen in the CCP provisions (Seidl-Hohenveldern, 1977, pp. 56–57).

The Member States did not receive the draft regulations and Opinion 1/75 well. They were unwilling to create a European export policy. The Council criticised the Commission's draft regulations and argued that the CCP provisions and Opinion 1/75 provided for the harmonisation of national export policies but did not call for the creation of a complementary EU policy. The German government stressed that national export policies provided sufficient coverage to all European investment and export projects. The German Bundestag warned that the creation of an EU investment guarantee scheme would bear incalculable financial risks for German taxpayers and was unacceptable. The French government sought to protect its competences and sovereignty. The EU was entitled to harmonise national policies, but did not hold the necessary competences to become a proper actor in this domain (Johannsen, 2009, pp. 5–6; Seidl-Hohenveldern, 1977, pp. 56–59).

9.2 The Treaty of Maastricht

The previous section highlighted two isolated instances of EU-internal discussions, which touched on the EU's legal competences and role in international investment policy. They imply that since the EU's earliest days Commission entrepreneurship played a pivotal role in promoting the EU's involvement in international investment policy. Focused in-depth discussions on the scope of the EU's legal competences to regulate international investments albeit only really started with the Uruguay Round (see Chapter 5) and the IGC on the Treaty of Maastricht in the late 1980s and early 1990s. The negotiations during the IGC on the Treaty of Maastricht touched directly and indirectly on the EU's legal competences in this domain. The Commission again acted as policy entrepreneur and pointed to the evolving trade agenda in the GATT (see Chapter 5) and invoked implied competences – or in its own words sought to 'clarify' the EU's existing legal competences – so as to consolidate the EU's role inter alia in international investment policy. In the absence of business support for such plans, the Member States blocked the Commission's attempt. The Treaty of Maastricht, nevertheless, provided the EU with implicit shared external competences to regulate market access for investment 'by accident'. The Member States created a common external capital regime for the emerging Single Market for capital, which necessarily affected the regulation of international investment flows.

9.2.1 Unsuccessful commission entrepreneurship to 'update' the CCP

The Member States convened for the IGC on the Treaty of Maastricht between December 1991 and February 1992. In March 1991, the Commission published a report on the functioning of the EU and advisable modifications to the European Treaties so as to prepare the IGC and facilitate negotiations. The Commission used its agenda-setting powers to highlight vis-à-vis the Member States the CCP as an area in urgent need of reform. The Commission proposed to rename the CCP the 'Common Policy of External Economic Relations'. It stressed that the new external economic relations policy would encompass the regulation of trade in goods, services, export policy, intellectual property rights, capital movements, investments, establishment and competition through trade agreements and autonomous measures. It underlined that the EU would be competent to regulate investment liberalisation as well as investment protection (Conference of the representatives of the governments of the Member States, 1991a).

The Commission, moreover, emphasised that the EU had always held implied legal competences in these areas. Advancing a teleological interpretation of the CCP provisions, it argued that the proposed modifications only sought to consolidate and to clarify the EU's implied competences. They did not substantially broaden the scope of the EU's legal competences in foreign economic relations (Conference of the representatives of the governments of the Member States, 1991a, pp. 28–29). The Commission argued that the main purpose of the EU's competences under the CCP should be the effective representation of the EU's Single Market regime in GATT negotiations. Hence, the scope of the CCP – as intermediary between the Single Market and the GATT regime – had to be congruent with the agenda of GATT negotiations (Eeckhout, 2011, p. 28).

Finally – and relatedly – the Commission pointed out that the EU already held de facto competences over these issues in the Uruguay Round (see Chapter 5). It was thus only a matter of formalising existing realities. The proposed modifications would finally end the long-lasting controversy with the Member States over the scope of the CCP and would ensure the effective *"representation of the union on the external scene and notably in dealings with international organizations"* (Conference of the representatives of the governments of the Member States, 1991a, p. 28).

European business showed fairly little interest in debates on the reform of the CCP. The archive of the Council of Ministers contains the formal submission of UNICE to the IGC (Conference of the representatives of the governments of the Member States, 1991b, p. 9). The UNICE position paper of 10 April 1991 did not exclusively focus on the reform of the CCP. It discussed the views of UNICE on all treaty chapters and advisable changes. The paper remained comparatively vague on the CCP, which implies that the CCP reform was not a priority for European business. The only substantive demand from UNICE to European policymakers was that trade policy measures should be subject to qualified majority voting in the Council of Ministers so as to ensure swift and effective decision-making (Conference of the representatives of the governments of the Member States, 1991b, p. 9). The paper thus implicitly called upon the Member States to bring the scope of the CCP in line with the agenda of the Uruguay Round. The absence of any explicit mention of investment regulation suggests that European business did not take a strong interest in this particular issue. It needs to be mentioned here though that it is difficult to reconstruct the detailed preferences of European business since more than two decades have passed. Business federations tend to have short institutional memories; their archives are limited and their employees typically change jobs every few years.

The Member States did not receive the Commission's recommendations during the IGC well. As reported in Chapter 5, during the debates on the Commission's negotiating mandate in September 1986 the Member States had collectively underlined that the Commission's role as their single voice in the Uruguay Round would not prejudge the distribution of legal competences on the *new trade issues*. The Member States obviously felt that most *new trade issues* came under national competence and that there was no functional need to delegate and extend the

EU's legal competences. From the Member States' point of view, the Commission was arguably trying to overthrow the EU-internal gentlemen's agreement not to raise competence questions during the Uruguay Round. Instead, the Commission exploited the EU's de facto competences in the Uruguay Round so as to extend the EU's legal competences under the CCP. The Council archive unfortunately does not cover in detail the intergovernmental debates on the Treaty of Maastricht. It does, nevertheless, contain several draft Treaties discussed during the IGC. The evolution of these draft Treaties allows for some inference regarding the positions of the Member States on the recommendations of the Commission. A first draft Treaty of 17 April 1991 maintained the new name of the CCP as 'Common Policy of External Economic Relations' (Conference of the representatives of the governments of the Member States, 1991c, p. 31). It stated, however, that the new policy should only cover the regulation of trade in goods and services. The Member States directly discarded the proposed reference to international investment regulation. Hence, the Member States must have immediately concurred that international investment regulation was and should remain under national competence. The following treaty drafts consecutively revoked all other proposed modifications to the CCP articles. The final text of the Treaty of Maastricht did not contain any changes to the CCP and hence the EU's competences in foreign economic relations (Conference of the representatives of the governments of the Member States, 1991d, p. 31, 1991e, p. 30, 1991f, p. 3159, 1991g; Eeckhout, 2011, pp. 26–27).

9.2.2 Competence 'by accident' – a common external capital regime for the single market

The Treaty of Maastricht did not reform the CCP. It, nevertheless, provided the EU with first legal competences relevant for the regulation of international investment flows under the chapter on capital movements. As mentioned earlier, the Treaty of Rome in theory liberalised capital movements within the Common Market. The liberalisation of capital movements, however, was not directly enforceable but required the implementation of secondary legislation. The Member States were unwilling to enact measures, which would substantially liberalise capital movements within the Common Market, during the first three decades of European Integration. Most Member States feared that a liberalisation of capital and current accounts would trigger capital flights and exchange rate fluctuations, which would undermine their Keynesian macroeconomic policies and ability to tax (Interview, Paris, 19 October 2011; Bakker, 1996, pp. 31–36; Ohler, 2002, pp. 1–3).

The Member States reconsidered their stance on the liberalisation of capital movements in the late 1970s and early 1980s. During the 1970s, the Member States had to deal with profound economic crises. Keynesian macroeconomic and monetary policies did not succeed in easing these crises, but instead produced stagflation. The failure of Keynesian policies fuelled the emergence of the neoliberal economic paradigm in Western countries. The neoliberal paradigm prescribed the reduction of state intervention and the deregulation and international opening of national economies in order to strengthen market mechanisms and the efficient use of production factors. In line with this new paradigm, several Member States unilaterally liberalised capital movements (Bakker, 1996, pp. 169–177). In 1982, the European Council, moreover, decided to advance and to finalise the Single Market for goods, services, and labour as well as capital by 1992 in order to inject a new impetus into the ailing European economy. Intergovernmental debates on the liberalisation of capital movements, and thus the creation of a Single Market for capital, continued during the mid-1980s (Bakker, 1996, pp. 161–162; European Commission, 1985, pp. 5–6; OECD, 2002, pp. 27–28). The Single European Act (SEA, 1987) and a new capital movements directive (1986) did not significantly advance the liberalisation of capital movements within the EU (Bakker, 1996, pp. 177–181). They, nonetheless, underlined the political will of European policymakers to create a Single Market for capital. In 1988, the Commission's long-standing insistence on a comprehensive liberalisation of capital movements finally paid off. The Council of Ministers came around and adopted the Commission's draft directive 88/361/EEC. The directive instantaneously liberalised capital movements, obliged the Member States to dismantle their capital control systems and finally created a veritable Single Market for capital (Bakker, 1996, pp. 210–212).

The creation of the Single Market for capital was perceived as a milestone of European Integration. European policymakers, nevertheless, soon realised that the job was not finished yet. Directive 88/361/EEC had dismantled all capital controls and barriers within the Single Market. But it had not established a common external capital regime. The directive had thus created the regulatory gap, which had already been problematised in the Spaak Report three decades earlier in 1956. Capital could circumvent the external capital regimes of rather protectionist Member States, like France, by flowing in and out of the Single Market through liberal Member States without capital controls, like the United Kingdom. The Council of Ministers soon started looking into this problem and possible remedies (Bakker, 1996, pp. 230–231). In the course of these debates, which started in late 1988 and continued until the end of the IGC on the Treaty of Maastricht, two camps formed.

The first camp wanted the creation of an external capital regime based on the 'erga omnes' principle. In other words, the unconditional liberalisation of capital movements within the Single Market should be extended toward third countries. The Commission and a majority of Member States – namely Belgium, Denmark, Germany, the Netherlands and Italy – supported this plan. Three considerations informed their position (Bakker, 1996, pp. 230–231). First, the freeing of capital movements to and from the Single Market was thought to enhance the functioning of market mechanisms and thus to promote welfare. Second, an open Single Market for capital should bolster the confidence of investors in the European Monetary Union and force the Member States to pursue sustainable budgetary policies. Third, several Member States had unilaterally liberalised their capital markets during the 1980s and were unwilling to partially close them again (Hindelang, 2009, pp. 24–30; Ohler, 2002, p. 39).

The second camp favoured a common external capital regime based on a differential and reciprocal liberalisation of capital movements between the Single

Market and third countries. The United Kingdom and France were the main supporters of this position. The United Kingdom held a strong offensive interest in this domain due to its important financial services sector. It wanted a liberalisation of capital movements vis-à-vis third countries on the basis of reciprocity. The British government worried that a liberalisation of capital movements based on the 'erga omnes' principle would deprive the EU of its bargaining power in international negotiations on market access. France, on the other hand, felt that only close partners should enjoy free access to the Single Market for capital (Bakker, 1996, pp. 193, 230).

In the end, the former camp prevailed during the IGC debates. Article 70 EC implemented the 'erga omnes' principle. It comprehensively liberalised all capital movements between the Single Market and third countries. Article 70 EC, moreover, stated that the EU – but not the individual Member States – could reimpose temporary capital restriction in the event of major economic and monetary turmoil in a Member State or in order to comply with international sanctions (Hindelang, 2009, pp. 37–38; Usher, 1992, pp. 42–43, 46–47). After the conclusion of the Maastricht Treaty, the CJEU and expert lawyers concluded that article 70 EC provided the Union with a shared, implicit, external competence to regulate market access regarding extra-EU FDI flows (Dimopoulos, 2011, p. 78). The Maastricht Treaty thereby created an essential building block for an EU international investment policy although neither the Member States nor the Commission had aimed for this. The EU acquired its first legal competence in international investment policy very much by accident.

9.3 The commission calls on the CJEU to recognise the EU's legal competences

During the IGC on the Maastricht Treaty, the Member States had immediately brushed off the Commission's attempt to 'clarify' the allegedly highly comprehensive scope of the CCP. But despite this first political defeat, the Commission remained determined to have the Member States recognise the EU's exclusive competence under the CCP to regulate all *new trade issues* of the Uruguay Round, including international investment. The Commission sought to invoke alleged implied competences, the evolving trade agenda and made strategic use of legal recourse in order to make the Member States accept the EU's alleged legal competences over international investment policymaking. From a historical institutionalist perspective, the Commission sought to promote 'conversion' (re-interpretation of existing competences) and 'layering' (adding of new subordinate rules to an institution). By 1995, the Commission and the Member States opposed each other in two legal proceedings before the CJEU, which in essence examined the scope of the CCP and inter alia the EU's legal competences in international investment policy. The Member States determinedly rejected the Commission's claim and harshly criticised the Commission's power-maximising behaviour. The pleadings of the Commission and the Member States provide important insights into the dynamics behind the emergence of the EU's international investment policy. This

The evolution of the EU's legal competences 207

section remains silent on business preferences, as European business rarely takes an interest in technical CJEU proceedings on competence delimitations.

9.3.1 Opinion 1/94 – the commission seeks to revisit its Maastricht defeat

Opinion 1/94 was, in essence, a continuation of the IGC debates on the scope of the CCP. After eight years of negotiations, the GATT parties had finally concluded the Uruguay Round in April 1994 (Eeckhout, 2011, p. 27; Koutrakos, 2006, p. 41). The outcome of these lengthy negotiations was the WTO Agreement, which encompassed in its annexe, inter alia, the GATS and the Agreement on Trade-Related Intellectual Property Rights (TRIPs). As could be expected, the Commission and the Member States disagreed over the question of whether the scope of the CCP was sufficiently broad to enable the EU to conclude the WTO Agreement and its annexes or whether it had to be concluded as a mixed agreement under participation of the individual Member States. In April 1994, the Commission decided to refer this legal question to the CJEU.

The Commission invoked in its submission to the CJEU alleged implied competences and pointed to the evolving trade policy environment in order to claim exclusive Union competence over the conclusion of the WTO Agreement and its annexes (European Court of Justice, 1994). Mixed ratification under participation of the Member States was, it argued, not a legal necessity. The Commission developed a twofold justification for its position. First, the CCP articles had to be interpreted in a teleological manner. In other words, the authors of the Treaties had conceived the CCP in 1956/57 in order to ensure the effective representation of the Union in trade negotiations and notably in GATT talks. Hence, the legal scope of the CCP had to evolve in line with the international trade and GATT agenda. The Commission had advanced the same argument during the IGC debates (Koutrakos, 2006, pp. 40–41). Second, the Commission added that the Union also held implied, exclusive, external competences regarding all issues covered in the WTO Agreement and its annexes under other treaty chapters (Eeckhout, 2011, pp. 87–89). It needs mention that although the Commission's submission did not explicitly dwell on the Union's legal competences in international investment policy, it contained the implicit claim that the Union held comprehensive competences in this domain. The WTO Agreement and its annexes covered investment liberalisation (GATS) and post-establishment treatment (TRIMs & TRIPs Agreements), which accordingly had to fall under exclusive Union competence (Johannsen, 2009, p. 7). The Commission's teleological interpretation of the CCP, moreover, implied that it was only a matter of time before all aspects of international investment policy would come under Union competence. As Chapter 5 reported, the USA had indeed embarked upon the Uruguay Round with the objective of creating a comprehensive multilateral investment framework. The USA failed to convince many critical countries of its plan during the Uruguay Round. But the idea of creating a comprehensive multilateral investment framework within the GATT/WTO was not off the table in 1994.

The Member States rejected the Commission's position and arguments (European Court of Justice, 1994). They demanded a mixed ratification of the WTO Agreement and its annexes. The submission of the Council of Ministers – i.e. the entirety of the Member States – and the individual submissions of the United Kingdom, France, Spain, Greece, the Netherlands, Germany, and Denmark underlined that the broad scope of the WTO Agreement and its annexes fell partly into the scope of the CCP, other EU policies and national policies and competences. They criticised in particular the Commission's overbearing claim that the Union held the exclusive competence under the CCP to conclude the GATS and TRIPs Agreements. The Member States assumed that these agreements, which inter alia affected international investment regulation, came predominantly under national competence (European Court of Justice, 1994). The Council, moreover, harshly rebuked the Commission for its alleged attempt to extend the Union's competences under the CCP through the backdoor after the failure to convince the Member States to acknowledge an extensive interpretation of the CCP during the IGC debates.

> *At the intergovernmental conference on Political Union, the Commission had proposed such an extension of Community competence. The concept of a common commercial policy was to be replaced by that of a common policy of external economic relations, comprising in particular 'economic and trade measures in respect of services, capital, intellectual property, investment, establishment and competition' with the possibility of extension of that ambit. This policy was to fall within the exclusive competence of the Community [. . .] The Community was to be exclusively represented by the Commission in its relations with non-member countries and international organizations and at international conferences [. . .] The Commission is seeking in its request for an Opinion to have implemented by means of judicial interpretation, the proposals which were rejected at the intergovernmental conference on Political Union.*
> (European Court of Justice, 1994, p. I–5306)

The CJEU delivered its opinion on this matter in November 1994. To the great surprise of most observers, the CJEU sided with the Member States (European Court of Justice, 1994). It found that the Union did not hold all necessary competences to conclude the WTO Agreement and its annexes either under the CCP or under other treaty chapters. Hence, the WTO Agreement and its annexes had to be concluded as mixed agreements.[3] Although Opinion 1/94, at first sight, was perceived as an objurgating of the Commission, observers soon interpreted the quite startling ruling as a fierce wake-up call to the Member States to finally take up their responsibility and to make political decisions regarding the modernisation of the CCP (Dimopoulos, 2011, pp. 85–86; Koutrakos, 2006, pp. 46–48; Meunier and Nicolaidis, 1999, pp. 491–493). Like the submissions of the Member States and the Commission, the CJEU ruling did not examine in detail the Union's competences in international investment policy. It, nevertheless, shed some light on the

EU's legal competences in this domain. First and foremost, Opinion 1/94 advanced a non-teleological, textual and thus narrow interpretation of the CCP. The CJEU thereby refuted the Commission's claim that the *new trade issues*, including international investment regulation, already came under the scope of the CCP. Second, the CJEU ruled that GATS mode III – i.e. establishment – did not come under the scope of the CCP (Eeckhout, 2011, p. 30; Johannsen, 2009, p. 7). It followed from this clarification that investment liberalisation in general was unlikely to fall under exclusive Union competence under the CCP. And finally, the CJEU did not challenge the EU's competence to conclude the TRIMs Agreement. The TRIMs Agreement regulated trade-related post-establishment treatment standards. The CJEU's silence on this issue implied that the EU was, at least partly, competent under the CCP in this domain of international investment policy. In conclusion, Opinion 1/94 was a telling instance of Commission entrepreneurship to extend the EU's legal competences to *new trade issues* including investment regulation, but the Member States and the CJEU determinedly rebuked the Commission for its activism.

9.3.2 *Opinion 2/92 – the commission claims competence over post-establishment treatment*

Opinion 1/94 had only indirectly touched on the EU's legal competences in international investment policy. Shortly after delivering Opinion 1/94, the CJEU rendered Opinion 2/92 in March 1995. Opinion 2/92 is of great interest to this study, because it essentially examined the EU's competence to regulate post-establishment treatment. Opinion 2/92 sought to identify the adequate competence basis for the EU's adhesion to the 'Third Revised Decision of the OECD on National Treatment' (hereinafter the 'Third Revised Decision'). The Third Revised Decision was a gentlemen's agreement among OECD countries, which stipulated that OECD countries should grant established investors from other OECD countries NT. The Commission and the Member States again disagreed over the competence basis for the EU's adhesion to the Third Revised Decision. This legal controversy translated into the more practical question of whether the EU alone or the EU and the Member States together should formally adhere to the Third Revised Decision. Belgium ultimately decided to refer this question to the CJEU in 1992 (Vedder and Folz, 1997, pp. 510–511).

The Commission advanced the view that the EU was exclusively competent to adhere to the Third Revised Decision. It presented several, highly interesting arguments to justify its position (European Court of Justice, 1995, pp. I-543–I-546). First, the Commission argued that the Third Revised Decision was, in essence, a trade policy measure coming under the scope of the CCP. It elaborated that international investment was a modern form of trade. International investment, on the one hand, substituted traditional trade through local business and production activities. On the other hand, international investment complemented traditional trade as it generated intra-firm trade. The NT obligation enshrined in the Third Revised Decision, the Commission argued, sought to increase investment activity and hence trade in goods and services. The Commission's line of argument implied that all aspects of international investment policy – market access, post-establishment treatment and protection – were in essence trade policy measures falling under the scope of the CCP. Second, the Commission advanced once again its well-known teleological interpretation of the CCP. The Commission explained that the main purpose of the CCP was to ensure the effective international representation of European interests and the Single Market at the international level. As international investment was a modern form of trade and becoming a standard agenda item of international trade negotiations, international investment regulation should come under the CCP. Finally, the Commission added that should the court disagree with the previous arguments, the EU nevertheless held an implied exclusive external competence to adhere to the Third Revised Decision under article 57 EC (establishment) and article 100 EC (approximation of legislation) (European Court of Justice, 1995, pp. I-543–I-546).

Several Member States refuted the Commission's position and justifications (European Court of Justice, 1995, pp. I-542–I-549). Their submissions to the CJEU draw an intriguing picture of Member State views on the EU's role and competence in international investment policy, which in many regards complement missing information on detailed Member State positions from the IGC on the Maastricht Treaty. First, the Belgian, Greek, Spanish, French and British rejected the claim that the EU was competent to adhere to the Third Revised Decision under the CCP. Some Member States elaborated that international investment was not a modern form of trade and could thus not be regulated under the CCP. Other Member States added that the Third Revised Decision would not affect trade flows and could thus not be considered to be a trade policy measure falling within the scope of the CCP. Second, Belgium, Greece, France, the Netherlands and the United Kingdom explained that article 57 EC (establishment) was the more pertinent competence basis for the EU to adhere to the Third Revised Decision. They, however, discarded the Commission's view that the EU held an implied, exclusive, external competence under this article. The Third Revised Decision, rather, came under shared competence (European Court of Justice, 1995, pp. I-542–I-549).

The CJEU developed a nuanced argument (European Court of Justice, 1995, pp. I-542–I-549). It ruled that the Member States and the EU were jointly competent to adhere to the Third Revised Decision for several reasons. First, the Third Revised Decision was a trade policy measure coming under the CCP and exclusive Union competence as regards its effects on extra-EU trade and investment activities between Member States and non-EU countries. Second, it was also a measure touching on Single Market rules as regards its effects on intra-EU trade and investment activities. The CJEU elaborated that the Third Revised Decision fell partly under the EU's internal competence over establishment – as the Commission argued – but that the EU's implied external competences were not exclusive. EU legislation had not fully penetrated and covered the policy domain. In accordance with the *ERTA Doctrine*, the EU could at best assert a shared external competence in this domain. Finally, the CJEU underlined that the Third Revised Decision was also a transport policy measure coming under shared external competence as regards its effects on the transport sector. Opinion 2/92 thus clarified that the EU was indeed competent to regulate post-establishment treatment of extra-EU FDI under the CCP. Even more importantly, the CJEU seemed to implicitly recognise the Commission's claim that international investment was a modern form of trade. Opinion 2/92 thus constitutes an interesting case of 'conversion' as it clarified that the CCP indeed extended to investment regulation. This implicit recognition did not, however, have consequences for policymaking. The Member States continued concluding hundreds of BITs despite the EU's partial exclusive competence regarding post-establishment treatment.

9.4 The Treaty of Amsterdam

The debates on the scope of the EU's legal competences in foreign economic relations and international investment policy did not end with Opinions 1/94 and 2/92. In early 1995, the Member States arrived at the conclusion that they needed to amend the Treaty of Maastricht. The so-called Treaty of Amsterdam should enhance the democratic legitimacy and effectiveness of European policymaking in light of the future Eastern Enlargement. The Council of Ministers asked the Commission, as customary, to submit a report on necessary reforms of the EU and its Treaties. The Commission used this occasion to problematise once again the EU's legal competences in foreign economic relations, in general, and in international investment policy, in particular (European Commission, 1995a, pp. 1–7).

The Commission's report of May 1995 analysed in considerable detail a reform of the CCP (European Commission, 1995a, pp. 57–58). It first lamented that the IGC on the Maastricht Treaty had missed the opportunity to modernise and to extend the legal scope of the CCP. The recent rulings of the CJEU had further narrowed the scope. The standard agenda of international trade negotiations largely exceeded the EU's legal competences. As the EU held, however, de facto competences over these issues, the legal situation considerably complicated the negotiating process and EU-internal decision-making. The Commission warned that these changes in the institutional environment increasingly limited the effectiveness of European policymaking and harmed European interests in the world economy. Hence, the Commission advised the Member States to extend the scope of the CCP so as to bring it in line with the standard agenda of international trade negotiations and its de facto competences. It stressed that the CCP should cover, in particular, the regulation of services trade, intellectual property rights and FDI. It observed that FDI had become increasingly important for the world economy and had a trade complementing and substituting effect. The Commission cautioned that the continuous conclusion of BITs between the Member States and third countries undermined the exercise of the EU's competences regarding the regulation of capital movements and the EU's trade policy interests. It explained that many third countries conditioned their market access commitments for trade in goods and services on the amount of received direct investment. Whereas other countries could easily adjust to the new importance of FDI in trade negotiations, the EU was paralysed (European Commission, 1995a, pp. 57–58).

The Commission explained its position regarding international investment regulation in even greater detail in a communication which it released only few weeks before the publication of the aforementioned report (European Commission, 1995b, pp. 1–14). The communication was entitled *A Level Playing Field for Direct Investment World-Wide*. It clearly sought to influence EU-internal debates on the Treaty of Amsterdam, as well as the MAI negotiations, which were just beginning (see Chapter 7). The Commission underlined in this document that neither the EU nor the Member States possessed the necessary legal competences to negotiate NAFTA-like, state-of-the-art IIAs covering investment liberalisation, post-establishment treatment and protection. European investors therefore increasingly suffered from competitive disadvantages vis-à-vis Japanese and US investors in a key domain of international economic competition. The Commission derived from this analysis that the EU and the Member States had to closely cooperate and to pool their competences in international investment policy. The EU should, moreover, start negotiating state-of-the-art bilateral investment agreements – i.e. BITs. In the long run, the EU and the Member States should jointly work toward the creation of a multilateral investment framework in the WTO or OECD (European Commission, 1995b, pp. 1–14).

The Member State positions regarding the Commission's proposal to reform and extend the CCP toward international investment policy are, unfortunately, less well documented. It is, nonetheless, possible to establish two important observations. First and foremost, the Member States showed only marginal interest in a reform of the CCP during the IGC debates in 1996 and early 1997. Only the IGC submissions of Germany, Italy and Sweden mention the general intention to discuss the CCP (European Parliament, 1996a, 1996b, 1996c). Other Member States did not enumerate the CCP as a priority for IGC debates. Second, drawing on the aforeexamined Opinions 1/94, 2/92 as well as Member State behaviour during the MAI negotiations (see Chapter 7), one may safely conclude that most Member States met the Commission's proposal to extend the scope of the CCP, inter alia, to investment regulation with considerable hesitation. On these occasions, the broad majority of Member States refuted demands to reform the CCP both in order to preserve their national competences and because they considered these issues to be unrelated to international trade (European Court of Justice, 1995, pp. I-542–I-549; Johannsen, 2009, p. 8).

The Irish Council Presidency, which chaired the IGC in the second semester of 1996, nonetheless tried to take the Commission's recommendations to reform the CCP into account. Its first discussion paper of 5 December 1996 proposed to the Member States the permanent empowerment of the Commission to negotiate on investment, services trade and intellectual property rights in the WTO. The Member States should remain competent to regulate these issues in domestic settings and to negotiate in other international fora like the OECD, IMF and World Bank (Conference of the representatives of the governments of the Member States, 1996, pp. 78–80). Despite this pragmatic approach, the Member States – and in particular France – remained determined to protect their competences against European encroachment. The proposal of the Presidency was quickly discarded in IGC debates. One may recall here that at the same time, the British, Dutch, French and German governments went as far as to reject coordination with the Commission during the MAI negotiations on issues like investment protection clauses, because they were determined to stop European encroachment onto their competences (Interview, Brussels, 18 January 2012; Johannsen, 2009, p. 8). The Treaty of Amsterdam, which entered into force in 1999, did not reform the CCP. A new paragraph of article 113 EC merely empowered the Council of Ministers to decide by unanimity to extend the scope of the CCP to the regulation of services trade and intellectual property rights. It did not provide for such a possibility regarding international investment regulation. The Council, however, never availed itself of this possibility so that the Treaty of Amsterdam did not have a noteworthy impact on the CCP or the EU's legal competences in international investment regulation (Koutrakos, 2006, pp. 59–60).

9.5 The Treaty of Nice

The Treaty of Amsterdam was a more than humble agreement. Most experts agreed that the Treaty failed to enhance the democratic legitimacy of the EU or to streamline EU policymaking in light of the upcoming Eastern Enlargement. So as to prevent a paralysis of the EU after the Eastern Enlargement, the Member States soon decided to hold yet another IGC. The IGC should reform and streamline the European Institutions and European policymaking. The IGC on the Treaty of Nice started in February 2000 and came to an end in February 2001. As during the previous IGCs, the Commission used agenda setting to push for a reform of the CCP and an extension of the EU's legal competences to international investment regulation.

In early 2000, the Commission again submitted to the Council of Ministers a report on advisable reforms of the EU and its Treaties. The Commission further adapted its rhetoric on a CCP reform to the overarching purpose of the IGC, namely to prepare the EU for the Eastern Enlargement. The Commission underlined that the CCP had to be extended toward the *new trade issues*, including international investment regulation, in order to ensure qualified majority voting on trade policy measures in the Council of Ministers. It expanded that as investment, services trade and intellectual property rights had become standard agenda items of trade negotiations the EU held de facto competences in these domains. But as the CCP did not cover these issue areas, the EU had to conclude modern trade agreements as so-called mixed agreements, which required unanimous endorsement in the Council of Ministers as well as national ratification. In other words, the CCP had devolved during the 1980s and 1990s from a policy domain coming under the 'community method' and qualified majority voting toward a policy domain governed by intergovernmental processes and unanimity voting. The Commission warned that the 'mixity' of modern trade agreements would considerably complicate negotiations and slow down their ratification in an EU-25. In light of this problematic instance of institutional drift, a reform and extension of the CCP to, inter alia, international investment regulation was inevitable in order to keep the EU governable (European Commission, 2000, pp. 25–27).

The Member States remained hesitant regarding the Commission's recommendations. Unfortunately, the archive of the Council of Ministers again does not contain detailed information about specific Member State positions during the IGC. A series of progress reports nevertheless demonstrates how the proposed extension of the CCP to international investment regulation was gradually scrapped during the negotiating process. A first progress report of 3 November 2000 contained two reform options for the CCP, which still foresaw the extension of the EU's legal competences to 'investment' regulation (Conference of the representatives of the governments of the Member States, 2000a, pp. 23–28). The reference to investment was consequently narrowed down to 'direct investment' and put into brackets in the following progress report of 23 November 2000 (Conference of the representatives of the governments of the Member States, 2000b, pp. 34–37). The reference then was entirely deleted in the progress report of 30 November 2000, which contained the final wording of the CCP provisions of the Nice Treaty (Conference of the representatives of the governments of the Member States, 2000c, pp. 39–42).

Despite the Member States persistent opposition to provide the EU with explicit legal competences in international investment policy, the Treaty of Nice, nevertheless, provided the EU with an exclusive legal competences under the CCP to regulate certain international investment flows. Article 133 EC[4] of the Treaty of Nice finally brought the regulation of trade in services and intellectual property rights under the scope of the CCP. Soon after the conclusion of the IGC on the Nice Treaty, lawyers started discussing whether the notion of trade in services in the revised treaty provisions was congruent with the notion of trade in services under GATS and therefore comprised the regulation of GATS mode III. GATS mode III is by and large congruent with service-related FDI. At first, lawyers denied this assumption. They argued that the Treaty contained distinct chapters on establishment and capital movements, which had to be considered as the paramount competence basis for any EU measures in this domain (Johannsen, 2009, p. 9). Later the *opinion juris* formed that the Member States had indeed intended to empower the EU to participate in GATS-like negotiations on services trade (Cremona, 2003, pp. 68–70; Koutrakos, 2006, pp. 61–62). The term 'trade in services' in article 133 EC thus had to be interpreted in light of the definition enshrined in the GATS encompassing mode III. From a historical institutionalist perspective, the Treaty of Nice gave rise to an intriguing instance of institutional layering. The CCP amendment altered the overall effect of the policy on international investment policy. It needs to be mentioned here that although the Nice Treaty brought the regulation of services trade and intellectual property rights under the scope of the CCP, relevant measures basically remained subject to unanimity voting. The Treaty contained numerous exceptions and carve-outs; notably for cultural, social, health and educational services.

9.6 The Treaty of Lisbon

The Treaty of Nice, much like the Treaty of Amsterdam, was considered a failure. Policymakers and lawyers agreed that it did not prepare the EU for the upcoming accession of 12 new Member States in 2004 and 2007. The signatures under the

Treaty of Nice had not yet dried when in December 2001, the European Council of Laeken decided to embark on another attempt to reform the EU and the Treaties. The heads of state and government judged that the classic intergovernmental method of treaty revisions had shown inefficient, ineffective and undemocratic. They decided to approach a further treaty revision through the so-called convention method, which had been conceived and successfully used for the elaboration of the Charter of Fundamental Rights of the European Union in 1999/2000 (Deloche-Gaudez, 2001; European Convention, 2003a).

9.6.1 The convention method

The 'convention method' considerably differed from the classic intergovernmental method of treaty revisions. Instead of technocrats and high-ranking diplomats engaging in intergovernmental bargaining and exchanges of concessions behind closed doors, democratically legitimised politicians and generalists argued and deliberated in public over necessary reforms of the EU for the good of European citizens. The overarching objective, procedural rules, professional background and self-perception of the involved policymakers of such a convention thus stood in stark contrast to classic IGCs (Deloche-Gaudez, 2001). As the following paragraphs will show, these procedural differences decisively promoted the extension of the EU's legal competences to FDI regulation.

The so-called Convention on the Future of Europe[5] met between 28 February 2002 and 20 July 2003 in order to elaborate the draft text for the Treaty establishing a Constitution for Europe (hereinafter the 'Constitutional Treaty'). The draft text was then sent to the Member States for final discussions and ratification. The Convention comprised 15 delegates from the Member State governments, 13 delegates from the governments of the candidate countries,[6] 30 delegates from the national parliaments, 26 delegates from the national parliaments of the candidate countries, 16 delegates of the European Parliament and 2 delegates from the Commission. The 102 delegates took decisions by consensus. The delegates of the candidate countries could fully participate in the debates, but could not block a consensus reached among the delegates of the current Member States. Most delegates were politicians – i.e. not specialised technocrats. The Committee of the Regions, and the European Social and Economic Committee as well as its national counterparts, were invited to participate in the Convention as observers. A Praesidium of 12 delegates – led by former French president Valéry Giscard d'Estaing – chaired the Convention. The 102 delegates met for two days per month in public plenary sessions and more often in 11 issue-specific working groups in order to discuss advisable treaty changes (European Convention, 2003a).

9.6.2 Commission entrepreneurship in the open and behind the scenes

At the beginning of the Convention, the main work was carried out in the working groups. The CCP came under the responsibility of working group VII on external action, whose delegates showed little interest in discussing a reform of the CCP. Most delegates were politicians and found trade and investment regulation dull and technical. They primarily focused on issues of 'high politics'. The ongoing Iraq War, moreover, deeply divided the European governments, citizens and the delegates of working group VII. Hence, the discussions in this working group mostly revolved around the Common Foreign and Security Policy and European Security and Defence Policy (European Convention, 2002a, p. 3; Interview, Brussels, 12 October 2011).

On 15 October 2002, the Commissioner for Trade, Pascal Lamy, addressed working group VII. He used the Commission's agenda setting powers to point to the need to bring the CCP in line with the international trade agenda. He made a determined plea to convince the delegates of the necessity to finally bring all *new trade issues* under qualified majority voting and the scope of the CCP. Pascal Lamy stressed, in his rather non-technical speech, that the CCP was a major success story of European Integration. The EU had become an effective and accepted representative of Europe's trade policy interests in the world. He nevertheless warned that the current scope of the CCP increasingly undermined the efficient and effective representation of European interests in the world economy. Bilateral and multilateral trade negotiations increasingly focused on the regulation of investment, services trade and intellectual property rights. While the EU spoke with a single voice on these issues – i.e. held de facto competences, such modern negotiations and agreements were subject to unanimity voting within the Council of Ministers. Decision-making by unanimity made it easy for third countries to divide and paralyse an enlarged EU with 25 Member States. Decision-making by unanimity might thus translate into the exclusion of such provisions from European trade agreements, which would ultimately harm European interests in the world economy. In light of this problematic institutional drift, Pascal Lamy urged the delegates to extend qualified majority voting to all modern trade policy issues. Lamy thus de jure demanded an extension of the scope of the CCP to investment regulation as well as a dismantling of the many carve-outs of article 133 EC applying to services trade and intellectual property rights. Lamy stressed that such a reform was necessary to preserve the EU's ability to speak with a single voice in international trade negotiations. He did not mention at this occasion that the Commission had previously fought hard to include these new trade issues into ongoing WTO and bilateral PTA negotiations. Finally, he called on the delegates to extend the powers of the European Parliament under the CCP and to increase the involvement of civil society in CCP policymaking. The last request of Lamy arguably sought to calm down NGOs and civil society, which had violently expressed its discontent with the world trading system during the Seattle and Genoa ministerial meetings of the WTO and G8 (European Convention, 2002b, pp. 5–7; Interview, Brussels, 12 October 2011). It has also been speculated that Lamy thereby tried to strike a deal with the European Parliament, which should support his push for an extension of Union competences.

Lamy's efforts to convince the delegates of working group VII of the need for a comprehensive reform of the CCP were moderately successful. The final report on 'external action' of working group VII of 16 December 2001 recommended that all measures relating to services trade and intellectual property rights should in future be subject to qualified majority voting in the Council of Ministers. There was also support for the proposal to extend the involvement and powers of the European Parliament under the CCP. The final report of working group VII, however, ignored Lamy's advice to extend the scope of the CCP to international investment regulation. The following plenary session approved the recommendations and sent them to the Praesidium. The Praesidium should then elaborate a first draft text of the Constitutional Treaty on the basis of the recommendations of the 11 working groups of the Convention (European Convention, 2002c, pp. 7–8).

The Praesidium of the Convention convened for a decisive meeting on 23 April 2003. The purpose of this meeting, which took place behind closed doors, was to examine the recommendations of working group VII and to transpose them into a revised chapter on 'external action' for the Constitutional Treaty. With regard to the CCP, the Praesidium decided to divert from the recommendations of working group VII on an important point. The Praesidium proposed in its draft CCP articles to extend qualified majority voting also to the regulation of FDI. The proposal also extended the scope of the EU's legal competences to FDI regulation. The Praesidium briefly explained its diversion from the recommendations of working group VII by reiterating the Commission's long-standing argument that investment flows supplemented trade in goods and underlay a significant share of commercial exchanges today (European Convention, 2003b, pp. 53–55; Johannsen, 2009, pp. 9–10; Krajewski, 2005, pp. 102–106).

How did the Praesidium arrive at this decision? It was reported that John Bruton, delegate of the Irish Parliament and Praesidium member, proposed extending qualified majority voting under the CCP to the regulation of FDI. He reportedly stressed that FDI disciplines had become a standard item in multilateral trade negotiations in the WTO (see Chapters 5 and 7) and bilateral PTA negotiations (see Chapter 8). It was necessary to extend qualified majority voting under the CCP to FDI regulation, as Bruton explained, in order to enable the Commission to effectively use its long-standing de facto competences and to represent the EU's interests in these fora. The president of the Convention, Valéry Giscard d'Estaing, and the delegate of the Commission and Praesidium member, Michel Barnier, enthusiastically supported the proposal. In the discussion which followed, Michel Barnier, moreover, stressed that the revised CCP articles should not only extend qualified majority voting to measures regarding FDI but also contain a firm basis for exclusive Union competence in this domain (Interview, Brussels, 12 October 2011; Ceyssens, 2005, p. 273).

The dedication of John Bruton to bringing FDI regulation under the scope of the CCP and exclusive Union competence is noteworthy. It is surprising that a member of the Irish Parliament and former Irish minister proposed these modifications, since Ireland is the only Member State which has never concluded a single international investment agreement. What is more, the Irish government later showed to be among the most determined opponents to the FDI reference in the revised CCP articles. It is furthermore remarkable that Bruton – like the Commission – pointed to the evolving international trade environment as justification and used to the expert concept of 'FDI' rather than the layman's term of 'international investment'. One may therefore wonder whether Bruton acted on his own behalf; or whether Commission officials had asked John Bruton as well as Valéry Giscard d'Estaing to push for this modification as supposedly neutral non-suspect actors. This reading of the outcome of the Praesidium meeting of 23 April 2003 would point to a decisive instance of Commission entrepreneurship through agenda setting.

9.6.3 Member State delegates fight the FDI amendment

Following the drafting exercise of the Praesidium, the delegates of the Convention reconvened for plenary sessions to discuss the Praesidium's draft text of the 'external action' chapter. The delegates were highly interested in the draft chapter on 'external action' and even in the therein-included revised CCP articles. They tabled some 1,000 amendments regarding the entire chapter on 'external action' and 100 amendments regarding the revised CCP articles. Thirty-one amendments concerned the proposed extension of qualified majority voting and the scope of the CCP to FDI regulation. Almost all amendments demanded the deletion of the FDI reference. The amendments document broad opposition to the FDI reference across Member States, political camps and political institutions.[7]

The delegates of the British, French, German, Irish and Spanish governments tabled ten amendments regarding the FDI reference. The British government argued that FDI regulation was not a matter of trade policy or customs union and should thus be deleted. The French government stressed that the chapter on the movement of capital already assigned to the EU a shared competence in the domain of FDI regulation. The German and Spanish governments merely commented that investment promotion and protection was, and should remain, a national competence. The Irish government expressed criticism that the purpose of the FDI reference remained unclear and should be deleted (European Convention, 2003c). A Convention participant interviewed for this book recalled that only the delegate of the German government supposedly understood the implications of the FDI reference for Member States' international investment policies and their BIT programmes. The opposition of France, the United Kingdom and Ireland mostly reflected their intention to protect their competences and sovereignty against European encroachment. The Spanish delegate reportedly supported France so as to gain political capital in consequent discussions on voting rights in the Council of Ministers (Interview, Brussels, 12 October 2011).

Delegates of the European Parliament tabled six amendments regarding the FDI reference. A collective amendment of several MEPs indicated that the FDI reference should be deleted because FDI regulation was not a matter of trade policy and the reference would trigger an immense and probably unintended increase in EU competence. Several other amendments tabled by MEPs merely demanded the deletion of the FDI reference without explanation (European Convention, 2003c).

Delegates of the national parliaments tabled eight amendments regarding the FDI reference. Most of these simply demanded the deletion of the FDI reference

The evolution of the EU's legal competences 219

without explanation. Few amendments highlighted that FDI regulation was either a shared competence under the Treaty chapter on capital movements or should remain a national competence (European Convention, 2003c).

The large number of amendments regarding the draft chapter on 'external action' overwhelmed the Praesidium, which declared that it was impossible to discuss all of them within the timeframe of the Convention. Valéry Giscard d'Estaing therefore called upon the delegates to prioritise their demands. Only the most important amendments should be examined in the plenary session (Krajewski, 2005, pp. 104–105; Interview, Brussels, 12 October 2011). Valéry Giscard d'Estaing's demand de facto saved the FDI reference from deletion. No delegate considered the FDI reference to be sufficiently important to prioritise it and to demand further discussions. Joschka Fischer, the delegate of the German government and minister of foreign affairs, reportedly decided, for instance, to ignore voices from the German Ministry of Economics in charge of international investment policy, which asked for the deletion of the FDI reference. Instead, he invested his political capital into his favourite project – the creation of the post of a European minister of foreign affairs (Interview, Brussels, 12 October 2011). The example illustrates how technocrats' lack of access to the Convention debates shifted the focus of debates away from low politics toward high politics. As no delegate had prioritised the FDI reference and asked for further discussion, the Praesidium interpreted it as tacit agreement to the revised CCP articles and included them in the final draft text. The draft text of the Constitutional Treaty was adopted and sent to the European Council for concluding intergovernmental negotiations and ratification on 18 July 2003 (Interview, Brussels, 12 October 2011).

9.6.4 *Business preferences – ambivalent and divided*

What role did European business play in these debates during the Convention? European business seemed generally little interested in the debates on a reform of the CCP. What is more, the preferences of European business were ambivalent and divided. Business lobbying can neither account for the Praesidium's decision to add the FDI reference to the CCP articles nor for Member State preferences mostly opposing this decision.

Only UNICE – today BusinessEurope – voiced its support for an extension of the CCP to FDI regulation. On 28 February 2002, UNICE released, in its capacity as formal observer to the Convention, a position paper enumerating its views on the Constitutional Treaty. UNICE advised extending qualified majority voting, and thereby the scope of the CCP, to FDI regulation.

In the context of the next Inter-Governmental Conference, UNICE strongly supports an extension of qualified majority voting to issues of major importance to business, such as international negotiations and agreements on services, intellectual property rights and foreign direct investment.

(UNICE, 2002, p. 6)

UNICE's firm statement in support of an extension of the scope of the CCP to FDI regulation is quite remarkable. Many national member federations seemed much less interested and partly even opposed the proposed extension of the CCP to FDI regulation. The Confederation of British Industries (CBI), for instance, published its own position paper, in which it stressed that the EU should indeed play a role in international investment policy. It elaborated, however, that the Member States should remain competent in the core domains of international investment policy like investment protection.

> *There is a good case for the extension of Community competence and [qualified majority voting] to cover negotiations on foreign direct investment. However, certain areas, such as bilateral investment treaties, decisions on inward and outward investment, export promotion and export financing would need to be ring-fenced.*
>
> (CBI, n.d., p. 4)

German business was reportedly also critical (Tietje, 2009). The German Federation of Industries (BDI) expounded its hesitation in detail in a position paper (BDI, 2010), which it released later on the occasion of the discussions on the Commission's draft for the so-called grandfathering regulation.[8] The BDI explained that German business worried that future IIAs negotiated by the EU might not attain the high level of investment protection of German BITs. German business also feared that the competence transfer might raise question marks over the continued validity of German BITs and thereby increase investment risks and costs. German business, moreover, lamented that trade and investment disciplines should not be included in the same agreements. Investment negotiations were about setting legal standards, whereas trade negotiations were about bargaining over market access concessions. The BDI manifestly worried that high investment protection and post-establishment treatment standards might be traded off for enhanced market access commitments. Finally, interviewed BDI officials added that German business also generally preferred keeping policymaking at the national level, because they perceived the EU's political landscape as opaque and difficult to navigate (Interview, Berlin, 16 February 2012; Interview, Brussels, 26 January 2012a; Interview, 17 February 2012, Berlin).

Other major business federations, like the Mouvement des Entreprises de France (Medef), the Italian Confindustria, the Spanish CEOE, the Polish Leviathan or the ESF, took little interest in the debates on the CCP and its extension to FDI regulation. The Medef, for instance, participated in the Convention in its role as social partner in collective wage bargaining. It almost exclusively focused on influencing debates on the Single Market and social policies and by and large ignored other policy areas. The Medef reportedly only took note of the debates on a reform of the CCP in regard to the proposed greater role of the European Parliament in this domain (Interview, Paris, 3 October 2013). Confindustria and the CEOE reportedly were sympathetic to a greater role for the EU in foreign economic relations, because Italy and Spain were gradually losing in influence on the international political economy. They did not, however, lobby for a strengthening of the EU in this domain at the national or European level and did not hold specific preferences regarding the extension of the CCP to FDI regulation (Interview, Brussels, 27 September 2013a; Interview, Brussels, 27 September 2013b). The Polish Leviathan also adopted a generally pro-European attitude during the Convention debates. Polish business sought to counterbalance the Eurosceptic attitude of the Polish government. The Leviathan did not, however, voice specific demands regarding the CCP. Many other policy areas were much more important to Polish business than international trade and investment regulation (Interview, email, 4 September 2013). Finally, the ESF did not seek to influence the Convention debates on the CCP despite the investment intensiveness of international services trade. The ESF had been created in the mid-1990s to the end of representing European service providers in EU-internal debates on WTO and PTA negotiations. Its institutional mandate did not allow lobbying on treaty revisions. The ESF was only indirectly involved in the Convention debates through its membership of UNICE (Interview, Brussels, 25 September 2013b).

How can one explain the fairly determined position of UNICE in favour of a CCP reform and extension to FDI regulation in light of the ambivalent and divided preferences of its member federations? UNICE adopts its positions by consensus after consultation with its member federations. The UNICE position should have at least partly reflected the hesitation of the BDI and CBI and lack of interest of many other federations regarding an extension of the CCP to FDI regulation. It was reported that the UNICE Secretariat drafted the UNICE position paper and circulated it among its member federations prior to the Convention. The member federations did not take offense to the proposed UNICE position on the CCP reform on this occasion and endorsed the section without much discussion. It was only later in the process of drafting the Constitutional Treaty that certain member federations came to the conclusion – after having been alerted by their respective governments – that they actually preferred keeping international investment policymaking at the national level. These federations consequently tried to revise the official UNICE position regarding the extension of the CCP to FDI regulation. The UNICE Secretariat and other member federations showed, however, unwilling to reopen discussions. The UNICE Secretariat understood that the shifting of international investment policymaking from the national to the European level would strengthen its position and influence vis-à-vis member federations. Other member federations realised that even though they had not proactively pushed for an extension of the CCP's scope to FDI regulation it was likely to benefit them (Interview, Brussels, 26 January 2012a).

9.6.4 *The intergovernmental conferences focus on 'high politics'*

At the end of the Convention in summer 2003, the Constitutional Treaty – and the extension of the CCP to FDI regulation – were not yet set in stone. The Member States still had to give their formal blessing to the draft text in an IGC, which in principle allowed for the deletion of disagreeable articles. The European Council formally received the draft text of the Constitutional Treaty on 18 July 2003. It took the following intergovernmental conference almost a year, until 18 June 2004, to reach final agreement on the Constitutional Treaty. The work of the IGC was so time consuming for two reasons. First and foremost, the Convention had not resolved the most delicate disagreements over issues of high politics like national voting rights, the definition of the qualified majority for Council votes and the role and powers of the EU president and minister of foreign affairs. Forging compromises on these issues proved to be a herculean task. Second, the Member States still disagreed over many technical provisions of the draft treaty. The Convention and its draft text, however, arguably possessed democratic legitimacy, which limited the room for manoeuvre for possible modifications and intergovernmental trade-offs (Interview, Brussels, 12 October 2011).

The revised CCP articles were of little interest during the IGC on the Constitutional Treaty. The high politics of founding a European federal state clearly downgraded the CCP to a secondary issue. The Member States focused on other more important issues and unwillingly accepted the FDI reference as part of a bigger package deal. The IGC, nevertheless, introduced two changes to the revised CCP articles. Both amendments clearly reflect the preoccupation of the Member States to safeguard their influence, and thus indirectly their sovereignty in international investment policy, against European encroachment. First, France insisted on preserving the Treaty of Nice's exception clause regarding cultural and educational services. Article 133(6) EC of the Nice Treaty indicated that measures touching upon trade in cultural and educational services had to be adopted by unanimity in the Council. Sweden and Finland consequently insisted on keeping the same clause for trade measures affecting health and social services. Second, Portugal and Ireland were still opposed to the FDI reference, while some new Member States reportedly now welcomed the extension of the CCP to FDI regulation. Portugal and Ireland were unwilling to invest a lot of political capital in attaining its deletion. Instead, they struck an alliance with the like-minded German and French governments. This group of Member States managed to add a clause stating that the Council must adopt international agreements by unanimity, where such agreements contain investment provisions for which unanimity is required for internal rules (Krajewski, 2005, pp. 104–106; Krenzler and Pitschas, 2005, pp. 801–802; Interview, Brussels, 12 October 2011). Both amendments ran counter to Lamy's plea to strengthen qualified majority voting to ensure the effective and efficient operation of the CCP in an enlarged EU.

The Constitutional Treaty was signed on 29 October 2004. The final wording of Articles III-314 and III-315 of the Constitutional Treaty on the CCP finally brought FDI regulation under the scope of the CCP and exclusive Union competence. It empowered the EU to pursue a full-fledged international investment policy. The joy among European policymakers over this 'milestone' in modern European history was albeit short-lived. In spring 2005, the French and Dutch public opted in referenda to reject the Constitutional Treaty. The negative outcomes of these votes in allegedly pro-European founding Member States made it politically impossible to further pursue the ratification of the Constitutional Treaty. After a reflection period, European policymakers came to the conclusion that the EU had, nevertheless, to be reformed in order to keep it governable after the Eastern Enlargement. They decided to hold another IGC on the so-called Reform Treaty, which is today known as the Treaty of Lisbon.

The intergovernmental conference on the Treaty of Lisbon was held between 23 July 2007 and 13 December 2007. The objective of the IGC was to preserve most technical revisions while cutting back on the symbolic elements of the Constitutional Treaty. In consequence, the IGC decided not to reopen discussions on the – in relative terms – uncontroversial and technical CCP provisions. It was, moreover, reported that the leadership of DG Trade admonished its officials not to draw the attention of the Member States or NGOs to the FDI reference of the revised CCP articles. The Commission hoped that the IGC would not 'rediscover' the reference and simply nod it through (Interview, Brussels, 12 October 2011). And indeed, in the end Articles 206 and 207 TFEU of the Lisbon Treaty simply copied former Articles III-314 and III-315 of the Constitutional Treaty. The Treaty of Lisbon entered into force on 1 December 2009 and finally provided the EU with a fairly comprehensive legal competence to pursue an EU international investment policy (Interview, Brussels, 12 October 2011).

In conclusion, Commission entrepreneurship ultimately succeeded during the Convention due to the procedural particularities of this forum. It used agenda setting to highlight the need to adjust the CCP to the altered policy environment in order to effectively represent European interests in the world economy ('drift'). The Convention proposed the extension of the scope of the CCP to FDI regulation. While the Member States opposed the reference, they were unwilling to invest political capital in this technical detail and focused on matters of high politics. Businesses was little involved or divided over the benefits of an EU international investment policy.

9.7 Beyond Lisbon – from the Grandfathering Regulation to Opinion 2/15

The Treaty of Lisbon extended the scope of exclusive Union competence under the CCP to the regulation of FDI. The exact interpretation and policy implications of this new FDI reference in article 207 TFEU, however, remained controversial. The Commission adopted an offensive strategy and advanced a maximalist interpretation of the new competence after 2009. The Member States unwillingly acknowledged that the EU was now by and large in charge of international investment policy. But they questioned whether the EU had really gained exclusive competence to negotiate IIAs or PTAs with IIA-like investment chapters.

The release of the Commission's draft 'Grandfathering Regulation' in 2010 marked the upbeat for this new stage of competence struggles (Lavranos, 2013; Reinisch, 2014, pp. 119–122). The 'Grandfathering Regulation' should increase legal certainty over the validity of existing Member State BITs with third countries. From a public international law perspective, Member States' BITs remained in force and valid. From an EU law perspective, however, Member States' BITs had become 'unconstitutional' to the extent the EU had gained exclusive competence over international investment regulation (Lavranos, 2013; Reinisch, 2014, pp. 119–122). If the EU held a comprehensive exclusive competence to conclude modern IIAs, only the EU – but not the Member States – could be party to BITs. The Commission implicitly endorsed this view and proposed Regulation 1219/2012 to create a transitional regime for Member State BITs. The draft regulation inter alia foresaw that the Commission should review all Member State BITs within five years in view of their compatibility with EU law and policy objectives (Lavranos, 2013). If the Commission found that a Member State BIT was incompatible with EU law and policy objectives, it could order the Member State to cancel this agreement.

Many Member States perceived the Commission's draft regulation as an affront. A prominent Dutch investment policy official commented that the regulation "*has the sole purpose of solidifying and expanding the powers of the European Commission*" (Lavranos, 2013, p. 3). Critical Member States denied the need for a 'Grandfathering Regulation'. They rejected the claim that the EU had gained the exclusive competence to conclude BITs and in consequence that these BITs were unconstitutional. From their point of view, the Commission's draft regulation was a heavy-handed attempt to assert political control over international investment policy. After tense debates between the Commission, the Council of Ministers and the European Parliament, a significantly modified regulation entered into power in late 2012. The final text of Regulation 1219/2012 does not provide for a review of Member State BITs and potential cancellation of agreements. It endorses a 'replacement' approach. It foresees that Member State BITs remain in force, as long as no replacement agreement between the EU and a third country has been concluded (Lavranos, 2013).

Regulation 1219/2012 did not resolve the dispute over the delimitation of the EU's new exclusive competence. The competence dispute continued simmering and regularly resurfaced during policy debates for instance on ongoing PTA and IIA negotiations with third countries. It became increasingly clear that at some point the CJEU would have to assess the exact scope of the EU's new competence under article 207 TFEU. In 2015 – at the occasion of the signing of the EU-Singapore PTA – the Commission decided to ask the CJEU in Opinion 2/15 to evaluate whether the EU held the exclusive competence to ratify the agreement and notably its investment provisions (European Court of Justice, 2017). The EU-Singapore PTA is among the EU's first highly comprehensive PTAs to enter ratification. Its content is comparable to the content of CETA, TTIP and alike. Opinion 2/15 is thus of systemic importance. It clarifies the negotiating and ratification modalities for modern PTAs.

On 16 May 2017 – in the midst of finalising this book manuscript – the CJEU released its opinion (European Court of Justice, 2017). The CJEU finds in its opinion that the EU-Singapore PTA generally comes under exclusive Union competence but identifies two investment-related exceptions. First, the EU-Singapore PTA does not only regulate FDI but also portfolio investments (see Chapter 3). The regulation of portfolio investments does not come under the CCP and exclusive Union competence. The regulation of extra-EU portfolio investment flows relates to capital movements and comes under shared competence. Second, the EU-Singapore PTA contains investment protection and ISDS provisions. The CJEU rules that investment protection standards are of trade policy nature and thus come under the CCP and exclusive Union competence. It cautions, however, that ISDS provisions come under shared competences. ISDS provisions – as a mechanism to enforce substantive investment protection standards – allow foreign investors to circumvent national legal systems and courts. The CJEU holds that the individual Member States need to consent to such clauses through joint ratification. The EU cannot commit to ISDS on behalf of the Member States.

Opinion 2/15 has important policy implications for the EU's international investment policy. First, it clarifies that the Member States have by and large lost the necessary competences to enter into BITs with third countries. The EU sits firmly in the 'driver's seat' of international investment policymaking. As far as FDI regulation is concerned, the EU is competent under the CCP to enter into agreements regulating market access, post-establishment treatment and protection standards. Second, the EU must, however, conclude modern IIAs and PTAs with ISDS commitments as mixed agreements. Taking into consideration the current political climate – and notably the considerable scepticism in several Member States regarding globalisation, free trade and ISDS – it seems unlikely that the EU will enter into comprehensive PTAs and IIAs in the near future. Opinion 2/15 thus is likely to create a 'joint decision trap' (Scharpf, 1999, 1988). Neither the EU nor individual Member States can pursue a veritable international investment policy. Opinion 2/15 thus represents a setback for the Commission's long-standing attempts to develop and to pursue an EU international investment policy. The CJEU's view that ISDS provisions must come under shared competence as they provide for the circumvention of Member State courts, moreover, implies that future treaty revisions are unlikely to bring IIAs and modern PTAs with ISDS commitments under the scope of exclusive Union competence.

9.8 Conclusion

The chapter traced debates about the EU's legal competences in international investment policy from the 1950s until the entry into force of the Treaty of Lisbon in 2009. Despite the considerable timespan covered in this analysis, a remarkably homogenous picture emerges. The observations confirm the assumptions formulated in the analytical framework and notably principal-agent research and historical institutionalist concepts of agency-driven incremental institutional change. While European business was little interested in the EU's legal competences, the Member States sought to protect their competences against European encroachment. The Commission, however, acted as a highly resourceful policy entrepreneur to promote its institutional objectives. The Commission used agenda setting, legal recourse at the CJEU and its growing de facto competences in PTA and WTO negotiations to push for a transfer of the relevant legal competences. In particular, the Commission's reference to PTA and WTO negotiations was ultimately decisive and convinced a key group of policymakers of the necessity to extend the EU's legal competences. As previous chapters showed, the Commission's central role in investment regulation in these negotiating fora however equally reflected to a large extent Commission activism and policy entrepreneurship. The chapter thereby draws the picture of encompassing multi-fora and long-term Commission entrepreneurship to promote institutional change in the form of an extension of the EU's legal competence to international investment regulation. From a theoretical perspective, the observations fit historical institutionalist assumptions on agency-driven institutional change though 'conversion', 'layering' and 'drift'. The Commission persistently advanced extensive re-interpretations of the Union's existing competences ('conversion'), promoted the adoption of new amendments to the CCP ('layering') and emphasised the need of a CCP reform due to the evolving policy context undermining the effectiveness of the policy ('drift'). The observations overall lend support to supranational and challenge liberal intergovernmental thinking on European Integration. The Member States exercised only imperfect control over integration dynamics in the analysed policy domain and failed to contain the Commission's activism.

Notes

1 The Spaak Report stresses that the creation of a Common Market for Capital would require 1) the harmonisation of capital taxation to prevent capital flight, 2) the harmonisation of monetary policies to prevent exchange rate fluctuations and 3) the creation of structural development funds in order to channel capital back into less competitive regions of the Common Market.
2 *"The problem is that capital may flow from one country to another not for investment purposes but to exit the Common Market by taking advantage of varying national external capital regimes. The free movement of capital within the Common Market thus requires at the final stage a common approach in relation to third countries which should end in a common level of openess or degree of control"* (author's translation).
3 For a detailed analysis see for instance Eeckhout, 2011, pp. 27–35; Koutrakos, 2006, pp. 40–48.
4 The Nice Treaty changed the numbering of Articles. The CCP provisions shifted from articles 110–116 EC to articles 131–134 TFEU.
5 For a first-hand report of a key delegate of the Convention – however in French – please see Lamassoure (2004).
6 This group encompassed the 12 new Member States, which joined the EU in 2004 and 2007 as well as Turkey.
7 For access to amendments, please see the website of the European Convention http://european-convention.europa.eu/.
8 See European Commission, 2010b.

References

Bakker, A., 1996. *The liberalization of capital movements in Europe: The monetary committee and financial integration, 1958–1994*, Financial and monetary policy studies. Kluwer Academic Publishing, Dordrecht.

BDI, 2010. Positionspapier: Internationale Investitionsfördervertträge: Position der Deutschen Industrie zum Übergang der Kompetenzen auf die Europäische Union.

CBI, n.d. Delivering a more competitive Europe: The CBI's view of the convention on the future of Europe.

Ceyssens, J., 2005. Towards a common foreign investment policy? Foreign investment in the European Constitution. *Leg. Issues Econ. Integr.* 32, 259–291.

Comité intergouvernemental créé par la conférence de Messine, 1956. Spaak Report.

Conference of the representatives of the governments of the Member States, 2000a. Progress report on the intergovernmental conference on institutional reform (CONFER 4790/00). Brussels.

Conference of the representatives of the governments of the Member States, 2000b. Revised summary: Intergovernmental conference on institutional reform (CONFER 4810/00). Brussels.

Conference of the representatives of the governments of the Member States, 2000c. Revised summary: Intergovernmental conference on institutional reform (CONFER 4815/00). Brussels.

Conference of the representatives of the governments of the Member States, 1996. The European Union today and tomorrow: Adapting the European Union for the benefit of its peoples and preparing it for the future: A general outline for a draft revision of the Treaties (CONF2500/96). Brussels.

Conference of the representatives of the governments of the Member States, 1991a. CONF-UP 1788/91.

Conference of the representatives of the governments of the Member States, 1991b. CONF-UP 1792/91.

Conference of the representatives of the governments of the Member States, 1991c. CONF-UP 1800/91.

Conference of the representatives of the governments of the Member States, 1991d. CONF-UP 1845/91.

Conference of the representatives of the governments of the Member States, 1991e. CONF-UP 1850/91.

Conference of the representatives of the governments of the Member States, 1991f. CONF-UP 1862/91.

Conference of the representatives of the governments of the Member States, 1991g. CONF-UP-UEM 2017/91.

Cremona, M., 2003. A policy of bits and pieces? The Common Commercial Policy after nice, in: Dashwood, A., Hillion, C., Spencer, J., Ward, A. (Eds.), *Cambridge yearbook of European legal studies (2001–2002)*. Oxford University Press, Oxford.

Deloche-Gaudez, F., 2001. The convention on a Charter of Fundamental Rights: A method for the future? *Notre Eur. Res. Policy Pap.* 15.

Deutscher Bundestag, 1976. Drucksache 7/4882 – Unterrichtung durch die Bundesregierung "Vorschlag einer Verordnung (EWG) des Rates zur Errichtung einer Europäischen Ausfuhrbank".

Dimopoulos, A., 2011. *EU foreign investment law*. Oxford University Press, Oxford.

Eeckhout, P., 2011. *EU external relations law*, 2nd ed., Oxford EU law library. Oxford University Press, Oxford.

European Commission, 2010b. Proposal for a regulation of the European Parliament and the Council establishing transitional arrangements for bilateral investment agreements between Member States and third countries (COM(2010) 344 final). Brussels.

European Commission, 2000. Adapting the institutions to make success of enlargement (COM(2000)34 final). Brussels.
European Commission, 1995a. Report on the operation of the Treaty on the European Union (SEC(95)731 final). Brussels.
European Commission, 1995b. A level playing field for direct investment world-wide (COM(95)42 final). Brussels.
European Commission, 1985. Completing the Internal Market (COM(85) 310). Brussels.
European Convention, 2003a. The European Convention [WWW Document]. URL http://european-convention.eu.int (accessed 8.10.13).
European Convention, 2003b. Draft articles on external action in the Constitutional Treaty (CONV 685/03). Brussels.
European Convention, 2003c. Proposed amendments to the text of the articles of the Treaty establishing a Constitution for Europe: Common Commercial Policy [WWW Document]. URL http://european-convention.eu.int/EN/amendments/amendments3dd9.html?content=866&lang=EN (accessed 8.10.13).
European Convention, 2002a. Discussion paper on external action (CONV 161/02). Brussels.
European Convention, 2002b. Intervention de M. Pascal Lamy, membre de la Commission Européenne, lors de la réunion du groupe de travail VII, le 15 octobre 2002 (working group VII – working document 10). Brussels.
European Convention, 2002c. Final report of working group VII on external action (CONV 459/02). Brussels.
European Court of Justice, 2017. Opinion 2/15 (ECLI/EU/C/2017/376). Luxemburg.
European Court of Justice, 1995. Opinion 2/92 (Competence of the Community or one of its institutions to participate in the Third Revised Decisions of the OECD on national treatment), in: European Court of Justice Reports. European Court of Justice, Luxemburg, pp. I-00521–I-00578.
European Court of Justice, 1994. Opinion 1/94 (Competence of the Community to conclude international agreements concerning services and the protection of intellectual property – Article 228(6) of the EC Treaty), in: European Court of Justice Reports. European Court of Justice, Luxemburg, pp. I-5267–I-5422.
European Parliament, 1996a. White paper on the 1996 intergovernmental conference volume II: Germany [WWW Document]. URL www.europarl.europa.eu/igc1996/pos-de_en.htm (accessed 10.1.12).
European Parliament, 1996b. White paper on the 1996 intergovernmental conference volume II: Italy [WWW Document]. URL www.europarl.europa.eu/igc1996/pos-it_en.htm (accessed 10.1.12).
European Parliament, 1996c. White paper on the 1996 intergovernmental conference volume II: Sweden [WWW Document]. URL www.europarl.europa.eu/igc1996/pos-sv_en.htm (accessed 10.1.12).
Hindelang, S., 2009. *The free movement of capital and foreign direct investment: The scope of protection in EU law*. Oxford University Press, Oxford.
Johannsen, E.L., 2009. Die Kompetenz der Europäischen Union für ausländische Direktinvestitionen nach dem Vertrag von Lissabon. Beitr. Zum Transnationalem Wirtsch.
Kleine, M., 2013. *Informal governance in the European Union: How governments make international organizations work*. Cornell University Press, Ithaca, NY.
Koutrakos, P., 2006. *EU international relations law: Modern studies in European law*. Hart, Oxford.

Krajewski, M., 2005. External trade law and the constitutional treaty: Towards a federal and more democratic common commercial policy? *Common Mark. Law Rev.* 42, 91–127.

Krenzler, G., Pitschas, C., 2005. Die Gemeinsame Handelspolitik nach dem Entwurf des Europäischen Verfassungsvertrags – ein Schritt in die richtige Richtung. *Recht Int. Wirtsch.* 51, 801–811.

Lamassoure, A., 2004. *Histoire secrète de la Convention Européenne*. Albin Michel, Paris.

Lavranos, N., 2013. In defence of member states' BITs gold standard: The regulation 1219/2012 establishing a transitional regime for existing extra-EU BITs: A member state's perspective. *Transnatl. Dispute Manag.* 10.

Meunier, S., Nicolaidis, K., 1999. Who speaks for Europe? The delegation of trade authority in the EU. *J. Common Mark. Stud.* 37, 477–507.

OECD, 2002. *Forty years' experience with the OECD codes of liberalisation of capital movements*. OECD, Paris.

Ohler, C., 2002. *Europäische Kapital- und Zahlungsverkehrsfreiheit: Kommentar zu den Artikeln 56 bis 60 EGV, der Geldwäscherichtlinie und Überweisungsrichtlinie*. Springer-Verlag, Berlin.

Pierson, P., 1994. *The path to European integration: A historical institutionalist perspective*. Harvard University and Russel Sage Foundation, Cambridge, MA.

Poulsen, L., 2010. The importance of BITs for foreign direct investment and political risk insurance: Revisiting the evidence, in: Sauvant, K. (Ed.), *Yearbook of international investment law and policy 2009/2010*. Oxford University Press, Oxford, pp. 539–574.

Reinisch, A., 2014. The EU on the investment path – Quo Vadis Europe? The future of EU BITs and other investment agreements. *St. Clara J. Int. Law* 12, 111–157.

Scharpf, F., 1999. *Regieren in Europa – Effektiv und demokratisch?* Campus, Frankfurt.

Scharpf, F., 1988. The joint decision trap: Lessons from German federalism and European integration. *Public Adm.* 66, 239–278.

Seidl-Hohenveldern, I., 1977. *Verischerung nichtkommerzieller Risiken und die Europäische Gemeinschaft, Kölner Studien zur Rechtsvereinheitlichung, Band 1*. Carl Heymanns Verlag KG, Köln.

Stacey, J., Rittberger, B., 2003. Dynamics of formal and informal institutional change in the EU. *J. Eur. Public Policy* 10, 858–883. doi:10.1080/1350176032000148342

Tietje, C., 2009. Gastberitrag – Europa springt ein (29 January 2009). Frankf. Allg. Ztg.

UNICE, 2002. Commission White Paper on European Governance: UNICE position. Brussels.

Usher, J., 1992. Capital movements and the treaty on European Union, in: *Yearbook of European law*. Oxford University Press, Oxford, pp. 35–57.

Vedder, C., Folz, H.-P., 1997. A survey of principal decisions of the European court of justice pertaining to international law in 1995. *Eur. J. Int. Law* 508–532.

10 Conclusion

This book set out to theoretically and empirical answer the following research question. *Why has the EU acquired de facto and legal competences to regulate international investment flows since the 1980s?* It has analysed the EU's involvement in international investment negotiations since the 1980s and EU-internal debates on the EU's legal competences in international investment policy since the 1950s. It has drawn a remarkably homogenous picture of European Integration. It has shown that the European Commission acted as a resourceful and persistent policy entrepreneur to extend the Union's *de facto* and legal competence under the CCP to the regulation of international investment despite Member State hesitation. European business, on the other hand, was largely absent from these debates. Business preferences and lobbying cannot account for the EU's growing *de facto* and legal competences in international investment policy. The empirical findings of the book challenge liberal intergovernmental thinking and lend strong support to supranational and notably institutionalist thinking on European Integration. The following sections provide a more detailed empirical summary and theoretical assessment (Table 10.1).

10.1 Empirical summary

The EU first became involved in international investment policymaking during the Uruguay Round of the GATT (1986–1994). The USA started pushing for the so-called Uruguay Round and negotiations on investment provisions in the early 1980s. After initial hesitation, the Commission became an outspoken proponent of the US proposal. It sought to convince and mobilise European business and the Member States to support the proposal. While a critical mass of Member States came to endorse the plan to hold a new comprehensive round, European business was little receptive to the Commission's campaigning. On the occasion of the opening of the Uruguay Round in Punta del Este in 1986, the Member States authorised the Commission to negotiate on investment-related provisions on their behalf. The Member States were convinced that speaking with a single voice in the GATT negotiations would increase their bargaining power and deliver a better deal for both the EU and the individual Member States. Nevertheless, the Member States put it on record that their decision to delegate negotiating on *new trade issues* such as investment-related provisions did

Conclusion 231

not prejudge the competence question. In the following negotiations on the Agreement on Trade-Related Investment Measures (TRIMs), the EU only played a marginal role. Neither the Member States, European business, nor the Commission expected the negotiations to deliver important results. Moreover, the Member States' use of TRIMs significantly diverged so that the EU could not forcefully push for specific provisions

Table 10.1 Summary of empirical observations

	Commission preferences	*European business preferences*	*Member state references*	*De facto and legal competences*
Uruguay Round (1986–1994)	*After initial hesitation, the Commission endorses the US proposal for a new comprehensive round and seeks to mobilise Member States and business inter alia for investment negotiations.*	*Minor interest on the part of European business in investment-related negotiations.*	*The Member States gradually endorse the US and Commission position that investment negotiations benefit the EU and authorise the Commission to represent them so as to maximise bargaining power.*	**The EU negotiates on post-establishment treatment and service-related investment liberalisation.**
ECT (1990–1998)	*The Commission is highly proactive and seeks to consolidate its role as the single voice in the ECT negotiations.*	*European utilities oppose the ECT project; upstream energy companies doubt its effectiveness; energy consumers are disengaged.*	*The Member States allow the Commission to negotiate to reach an optimal economic and geopolitical outcome.*	**The EU negotiates on investment liberalisation, post-establishment treatment, investment protection and ISDS provisions.**
MAI (1995–1998)	*The Commission shows lukewarm support and seeks to become the EU's single voice; as the Member States want to contain the Commission, the Commission starts pushing for multilateral investment talks to be shifted back to the WTO.*	*Limited business interest in the MAI negotiations.*	*The Member States welcome the MAI project but in the light of recent competence clashes in the Maastricht IGC and in Opinion 1/94 they seek to contain the Commission's role in negotiations and investment regulation.*	**The EU only negotiates on provisions coming under shared or exclusive Union competence such as capital movements; the Member States negotiate on all the other investment provisions.**

(*Continued*)

232 Conclusion

Table 10.1 (Continued)

	Commission preferences	European business preferences	Member state references	De facto and legal competences
Singapore Issues and Doha Round (1996–2003)	The Commission is the main sponsor of investment as a Singapore issue; it decisively pushes for these talks to be upgraded to negotiations in the Doha Round.	Limited business interest in Singapore Issues and investment negotiations in the Doha Round.	The Member States accept that a WTO-based multilateral investment framework is desirable and delegate the Commission to be their WTO spokesperson.	**The EU negotiates on post-establishment and generic protection standards; the Member States do not negotiate on their own behalf.**
PTA negotiations with Mexico, Chile and beyond (1996–2003)	The Commission pushes for ambitious PTA negotiations, including on investment; when the Member States veto such provisions in the Mexico negotiations, it engages in policy entrepreneurship to ensure support in the following PTA talks.	Business interest primarily in investment liberalisation commitments.	The Member States authorise the Commission to negotiate on investment but have second thoughts in talks with Mexico; the Commission points to the EU's demand for investment disciplines in the WTO to ensure support for such provisions in subsequent PTA talks.	**The EU negotiates on investment liberalisation and post-establishment treatment provisions.**
IGCs and CJEU proceedings (1956–2017)	The Commission persistently pushes for an extension of the Union's exclusive competence in international investment regulation.	Business shows limited interest and is divided over the question of integrating investment policy at EU level.	The Member States persistently oppose calls to extend Union competence in international investment regulation.	n/a

vis-à-vis third countries. The situation looked different in the investment-related negotiations on the GATS. The Commission and – to a lesser extent – the Member States were eager to negotiate an ambitious agreement on services trade. In the light of the ongoing construction of the Single Market, they considered the European economy to be internationally competitive and likely to gain from multilateral liberalisation efforts. European business remained remarkably disengaged even during the GATS negotiations.

Conclusion 233

In 1991 – with the Uruguay Round still underway – the Dutch government proposed negotiating the ECT. This was to establish a European Energy Community comprising the EU and the former socialist Eastern European and Eurasian countries. From the outset, the ECT was intended to contain ambitious investment provisions including investment protection and investor-state dispute settlement provisions (ISDS). The Member States welcomed the project and agreed to cooperate and speak through the Council Presidency and the Commission with a single voice for geopolitical and economic reasons. They saw the ECT as a unique project which would not set legal or political precedents. Confronted with a faltering Soviet Union, the Member States were determined to maximise their bargaining power and influence on Moscow. While the Council Presidency initially acted as lead negotiator and the Commission provided support, the Commission gradually took over the role of lead negotiator – including in negotiations on investment liberalisation, post-establishment treatment and protection provisions – due to its proactive attitude, expertise, administrative resources and pivotal role in the construction of the Single Market for energy. The Commission successfully framed the ECT negotiations as the external relations component of its domestic milestone project. Due to its political and functional link with the Single Market for energy, European utilities determinedly opposed the ECT project. They perceived it to be a Commission-led attempt to undo their downstream monopolies. Other parts of European business were barely interested in the ECT. In 1995, the EU ratified the ECT, including its investment provisions. Pending the ratification of new comprehensive PTAs, the ECT remains the only IIA-like agreement with ISDS provisions to which the EU is party.

In the early 1990s, the USA proposed negotiating the so-called MAI (1995–1998) within the OECD. Disappointed with investment-related talks in the ongoing Uruguay Round of the GATT, the USA sought to create a state-of-the-art investment framework among the industrialised economies in the OECD and thereby to increase pressure on developing countries to start cooperating on investment regulation. The Member States were receptive to the US proposal, while the Commission was hesitant. The EU/Commission would have to participate in the MAI talks due to fringe competences, but it became clear that the Member States intended to marginalise the Commission and to negotiate on their own behalf as per usual in the OECD. European business showed some support but was not whole-heartedly interested in the MAI project. The MAI was a government-led rather than business-driven initiative. Shortly after the launch of the MAI negotiations, cooperation between the Commission and the Member States turned remarkably arduous. The Commission had unsuccessfully tried to claim legal competence in international investment regulation in the intergovernmental conference on the Maastricht Treaty (1990–1991) and in Opinions 1/94 and 2/92 (1994), antagonising many Member States. Member State investment policy officials refused to cooperate and to delegate negotiation to the Commission on any items coming under Member State competence such as investment protection. Member State officials were determined to keep the Commission at bay and to prevent it from encroaching on their competences. In consequence, the Commission started pushing for multilateral investment negotiations to be shifted back to the WTO, where it conventionally acts as the single voice for the

Member States regardless of competence questions. In 1996, the Commission succeeded in reaffirming investment as a work item at the WTO as part of the so-called Singapore Issues. An investment working group was established at the WTO and it gained critical importance in late 1997 when the MAI negotiations ran into stalemate over substantive disagreements. The USTR – and reportedly the Commission – sought to promote the end of the MAI negotiations with a view to upgrading the WTO-based deliberations to proper negotiations. The sudden French withdrawal from the MAI negotiations became the ultimate trigger of the collapse. The consequent shift of multilateral investment negotiations to the WTO indeed consolidated the EU's role in international investment policy and the Commission acted as a proactive single voice in the short-lived investment talks in the Doha Round of the WTO. Its strategic promotion of a specific international policy forum thus turned out to be highly effective. Moreover, its role as the EU's single voice in investment negotiations in the Doha Round would later help to justify the inclusion of investment disciplines in bilateral trade negotiations and would inform the critical decision of the Praesidium of the Convention on the Future of Europe to propose the extension of the CCP to FDI regulation. With hindsight, the Commission's strategic international forum shopping was of key importance in the emergence of the EU's international investment policy.

In the late 1990s, the EU started signing PTAs. Its new interest in PTAs reflected an economic domino effect. EU PTAs would mitigate the adverse effects of third-country and, particularly, US PTAs. In 1996, the EU launched PTA negotiations with Mexico in reaction to the entry into force of the North American Free Trade Agreement. NAFTA caused European firms to lose market share in Mexico and at the same time increased the attractiveness of Mexico as an entry point to the US economy. The Commission, most Member State policymakers and European businesses were supportive of the plan to negotiate a PTA with NAFTA-parity. The Member States empowered the Commission to negotiate on the liberalisation of service-related investments, post-establishment treatment and capital movements. The Commission agreed with Mexico on an ambitious negative list for the liberalisation of service-related investments and a comprehensive capital movement clause. However, toward the end of the negotiations France and others suddenly started worrying about the implications of these provisions on their competences. They claimed that the Commission had overstepped its mandate and declared they would block the conclusion of the PTA unless the Commission dropped some controversial – mostly investment-related – commitments. The Commission had to bow down. In consequence, not the EU-Mexico PTA (1996–2000) but the EU-Chile PTA (1999–2002) became the first comprehensive agreement with a noteworthy investment chapter. The Commission, European business and the Member States jointly pushed for the EU-Chile PTA in order to pre-empt an envisaged US-Chile PTA. The Member States again initially agreed in the mandate to include service-related investment commitments – but on the basis of a positive list. Given the competence clash in the EU-Mexico negotiations, the Commission and the Swedish Council Presidency devised a strategy to ensure continued support for investment provisions in the EU-Chile talks. They started touring Member State capitals, and particularly Paris, to build trust. They argued that the EU could not credibly push for ambitious services and investment disciplines in the Doha Round of the WTO – as the Council had previously decided – if the EU's PTAs did not contain such commitments. The Member States agreed with the Commission's line of argument and the EU-Chile PTA became the first EU PTA to comprise a proper investment chapter with liberalisation and post-establishment treatment provisions. The EU-Chile PTA thus set a new standard: all the following European PTAs contain similar chapters. Moreover, it triggered in-depth thinking about the EU's general strategy toward investment regulation, which led to the EU's adoption of the so-called MPoI in 2006.

The final empirical chapter of the book shifted the analytical focus from the EU's involvement in international investment negotiations to EU-internal debates on the EU's legal competences. The purpose of this chapter was to clarify how the EU's evolving *de facto* competences in international investment negotiations with third countries affected the decision to extend the CCP to FDI regulation in the Lisbon Treaty. The chapter drew a remarkably homogenous picture of integration dynamics. From the 1970s, the Commission persistently pushed for the extension of the EU's legal competences in international investment policy. It used its agenda-setting powers, claimed implied competences, took strategic recourse to the CJEU and underlined in EU-internal debates the EU's growing involvement in this policy domain and the functional need for a firm EU competence due to the evolving global policy context. The EU's steadily growing role in international investment regulation served as the functionalist backdrop and legitimation for the Commission's policy entrepreneurship for an extension of the EU's legal competences. For many years, these attempts were of limited success. However, the Convention on the Future of Europe (2002–2003) opened a window of opportunity. While the Commission drew on similar strategies to its previous ones to win over the Member States (agenda setting; invoking *de facto* competences; pointing to the evolving agenda of international trade negotiations), it was the procedural particularities of the Convention which finally led to the competence transfer. Instead of specialised technocrats, generalist politicians had to draft a first revision of the CCP. These generalist politicians accepted the Commission's narrative of the EU's growing role in international investment negotiations and accordingly modified the CCP articles during the Convention. National technocrats still vehemently opposed the CCP extension but failed to convince their political leaderships to spend political capital on deletion of the 'FDI' reference from the CCP articles. The Treaty of Lisbon thus finally established the EU's comprehensive legal competence in the field of international investment regulation.

10.2 Theoretical assessment and contributions

What are the theoretical implications of this empirical assessment of the EU's growing role in international investment policy? First and foremost, the empirical findings suggest that it is illuminating to think of Commission entrepreneurship as a long-term two-stage process. In accordance with principal-agent research (Da Conceição, 2010; Damro, 2007; De Bièvre and Dür, 2004; Delreux and Kerremans, 2008; Dür, 2006; Frennhoff Larsén, 2007; Hawkins et al., 2006; Kerremans, 2004, 2004; Meunier, 2005; Meunier and Nicolaidis, 2006; Pollack, 2003; Woolcock, 2010; Young, 2002, 2011), the Commission used agenda setting, informational asymmetries, international forum shopping, the invoking of implied and fringe competences and recourse to the CJEU to consolidate its role and influence in international investment negotiations. It used its agency autonomy to promote its substantive and institutional policy agenda, which only partly aligned with Member State preferences. Many studies on European policymaking stop here. To limit 'noise' and allow for the development of parsimonious theoretical explanations of cooperation and delegation, many scholars analyse daily policymaking and formal integration dynamics in the EU separately (Börzel, 2013; Moravcsik, 1991, 1998; Moravcsik and Schimmelfennig, 2009; Rosamond, 2000). This has book opted for a comprehensive empirical analytical approach. In this way, it has shown that the Commission's ability to consolidate its role in international investment negotiations – even in the face of Member State hesitation – affected long-term formal integration. This ability amounted to agency-driven incremental institutional change in the form of institutional 'layering', 'conversion' and 'drift' (Mahoney and Thelen, 2010; Pierson, 2004; Stacey and Rittberger, 2003; Streeck and Thelen, 2005; Thelen, 2004). On the one hand, the Commission's invoking of fringe and implied competences and agenda-setting powers gave existing Union competence new meaning ('conversion'). For instance, the Commission successfully argued and invoked during the negotiations on the ECT its competences and central political role in energy policy to consolidate its standing in inter alia international investment negotiations. Moreover, it ensured its involvement in the MAI negotiations despite Member State reluctance by invoking the Union's shared competence over capital movements, which had some relevance in international investment regulation. The Commission thus brought to bear and reinterpreted existing Union competences to strengthen its role in international investment policy. On the other hand, the Commission promoted the creation of new 'minor' competences ('layering') to consolidate its role in international investment policy. Its recourse to the CJEU in Opinion 2/92, for instance, clarified that the regulation of post-establishment treatment of extra-EU FDI should be considered a trade policy measure. For the first time, it created an authoritative functional and legal link between trade policy and investment regulation. It was also the main driver behind the extension of the CCP to the regulation of services trade under the Treaty of Nice. While the Member States did not intend to create an investment-related competence, this new competence provided the EU with an exclusive competence to regulate GATS mode III – in other words service-related FDI – and thereby created a firm legal foothold for the EU in international investment policy. Finally, the Commission's agenda-setting powers, information asymmetries and skilful use of international forum shopping reshaped the policymaking context and thereby altered the effects of the CCP ('drift'). The Commission went to great lengths to keep investment on the negotiating agenda in the WTO and added it to the standard agenda of PTAs. The EU's trade policy thereby *de facto* – but not *de jure* – came to include the regulation of international investment activities in these policy fora. Due to the altered policymaking context, it became increasingly difficult for Member States to reject Commission calls to formalise the EU's role and to extend the CCP to international investment regulation. This institutional 'drift' occurred most forcefully during the Convention, where key decision-makers endorsed the Commission's narrative that the international trade policymaking context had evolved and required the formalisation of the EU's role in 'FDI' regulation. To conclude, the joint assessment of daily policymaking and formal integration decisions illustrated how the Commission used its agency autonomy in international investment negotiations to shape short-term policy outcomes and long-term institutional change.

The empirical findings, moreover, underpin the theoretical argument about the (non-)role of European business in international investment policymaking and its gradual integration. European business rarely held preferences or lobbied in international investment negotiations. The empirical chapters have largely confirmed that business took little interest in post-establishment treatment and protection provisions. The assessments of the Uruguay Round, the ECT and MAI negotiations suggested that European business was little aware of economic benefits arising from ambitious investment rules or doubted their effectiveness. The perceived costs of preference formation and lobbying arguably surmounted the perceived economic benefits of an 'ideal' policy. Only negotiations on investment liberalisation, for instance in PTA talks with Mexico and Chile, triggered noteworthy proactive business lobbying. The finding is in line with Vinerian economics and the theoretical argument made in Chapter 2. As investment liberalisation has a well understood and direct economic effect on business operations and profits – unlike post-establishment treatment and protection provisions – business took an interest and lobbied for specific outcomes in this sub-domain of international investment policy. The analysis of EU-internal debates about extending the CCP to international investment regulation drew a similar picture. European business was little aware of and/or divided over the creation of an EU international investment policy. It did not push for the integration of this policy domain or decisively shape Member State preferences in the domain. Instead, it seems that some Member State governments sought to mobilise their national business communities in favour of their institutional agendas. The empirical and theoretical findings of this book thus tie in with emerging literatures (Bickerton et al., 2015; Eckhardt, 2015; Woll, 2008; Woll and Artigas, 2007; Young, 2016) which point to a need to critically rethink business preferences and lobbying in European Integration and foreign economic policymaking.

To summarise, the study points to the need for additional theoretical research in three domains. First, it shows that informal cooperation and formal integration are interdependent. This finding is not surprising *per se*. Since the emergence of liberal intergovernmentalism in the 1990s, research on European Integration, however, tend to focus on formal integration. Scholars analyse IGCs to explain treaty revisions. To fully understand integration dynamics, it might be important though to broaden our analytical focus and to intensify efforts to conceptualise the causal relationships between informal and formal integration. As Bickerton et al. (2015) observe, the distinction between informal and formal integration becomes increasingly fluid. Since the 1990s, the Member States have integrated numerous policy domains. The Member States, however, rarely use the ordinary legislative procedure but rather design atypical and sector-specific cooperation procedures to govern these domains. An overly narrow research focus on formal integration as enshrined in the European Treaties may obscure more than improve our understanding of European Integration. Second, the study challenges in fundamental ways liberal intergovernmentalism. It shows that the integration may come about despite Member State opposition. Liberal intergovernmentalism stipulates, however, that integration is a state-serving and state-led process. This study moreover cautions that societal interest groups may often not hold preferences and lobby for or against integration, because integration does not necessarily affect policy substance and redistribute welfare in society. Welfare-maximising societal interest groups are, nonetheless, modelled in liberal intergovernmentalism as a key factor shaping Member State preferences and ultimately integration. Liberal intergovernmental scholars may thus need to take a fresh look at the role of societal interest groups in integration. Finally, the study highlights the need for additional research on the formation of business preferences in foreign economic policy. The bulk of theoretical research on foreign economic policy builds on Vinerian economics. Business preferences and lobbying are seen to reflect welfare effects of policies. Modern foreign economic policies are, nevertheless, of regulatory nature and have often complex, distant or minor effects on business operations and profits. The rise of regulatory foreign economic policy thus requires a new generation of theoretical enquiry into the factors shaping business preferences and lobbying. Preferences and lobbying of international law firms working on trade and investment disputes should receive special attention. International law firms – advising actual traders and investors – have emerged as key policy actors in current debates on modern foreign economic policies.

10.3 Outlook and policy challenges

The EU – as an actor in the global investment regime – faces a number of policy challenges. By and large, the Treaty of Lisbon (2009) provided it with the exclusive competence to pursue an international investment policy. On the other hand, the Member States have lost the competence to pursue international investment policies and to conclude IIAs. At first sight, it seems that the Commission may have reached its long-standing objective to centralise international investment policymaking at the EU level. It has been arguing for decades that this would streamline policymaking, ensure coherent policy outcomes and strengthen the voice of Europeans in the global investment regime. However, the opposite may be true. Opinion 2/15 clarified that the EU now has exclusive competence to regulate investment liberalisation, post-establishment treatment and protection. Nevertheless, the CJEU stressed that the EU and the Member States shared competences over the regulation of portfolio investments and ISDS (European Court of Justice,

2017). Opinion 2/15 implies that IIAs and PTAs with IIA-like investment chapters require mixed ratification. Using their national constitutional procedures, all Member States have to ratify agreements between the EU and third countries containing ISDS provisions and rules for portfolio investments. It seems unlikely in the current political climate that all Member States would ratify such agreements because ISDS has attracted considerable public criticism. The integration of international investment policy at the EU level may therefore have created a 'joint decision trap' (Scharpf, 1988). Neither the EU nor the Member States can act individually and pursue an IIA programme in the current situation.

The EU needs to define a policy strategy to deal with the emerging 'joint decision trap'. Several options come to mind. First, it could conclude IIAs and PTAs without the highly controversial ISDS provisions (and rules on portfolio investments) to avoid mixed ratification. For instance, instead of ISDS the EU could aim for state-to-state dispute settlement provisions as standard for the resolution of disputes regarding trade in goods and services. Second, it could conclude IIAs and PTAs without portfolio investment and ISDS provisions for EU ratification and conclude an ISDS and portfolio agreement subject to mixed ratification. In this way, through treaty architecture it could contain the costs of a potential non-ratification of mixed agreements to provisions coming under shared competence. In a similar vein, it could re-empower interested Member States to conclude agreements on ISDS and portfolio investments. The so-called Grandfathering Regulation (No. 1219/2012) foresees the possibility of the EU authorising Member States to negotiate new BITs with third countries under certain circumstances. Finally, the EU could maintain ISDS provisions in its IIAs and PTAs but include a so-called exhaustion of local remedies clause. This would require foreign investors to use all available legal remedies in a host country before turning to ISDS. The clause may – potentially – sidestep the need for mixed ratification. In Opinion 2/15, the CJEU argued that ISDS had to come under shared competence as it allowed foreign investors to sidestep national legal systems and courts. The EU could not enter into such commitments without explicit Member State endorsement. An 'exhaustion of local remedies' clause might eventually satisfy the court's line of argument but risks being politically untenable. To conclude, it remains to be seen how the EU will use its new competence in international investment policy in view of mixed ratification and public resistance.

A second policy challenge relates to the changing geography of global investment flows and the evolving offensive and defensive interests of the EU in the global investment regime (see Chapter 3). In the past, investment flows between the EU and developing countries were practically unidirectional. European companies invested in developing countries but very few companies from developing countries invested in Europe. Therefore, in practice the bulk of BITs between Member States and developing countries only bound the developing countries. Only European investors could *de facto* use these BITs and launch ISDS proceedings against developing countries. For many decades, the structural risk of the Member States facing an ISDS claim was negligible so Member State BITs traditionally put the emphasis on offensive rather than defensive concerns. Member State BITs are considered to be very business-friendly and afforded little attention to host states' right to regulate

(Alschner, 2013; Gaukrodger and Gordon, 2012; Reinisch, 2013). Moreover, certain procedural aspects of standard ISDS clauses arguably do not fully comply with European standards of the rule of law (Baetens, 2015; Basedow, 2014; Van Harten, 2007; Kuijper et al., 2014; Mestral and Lévesque, 2013; Poulsen et al., 2013). These critical properties of Member State BITs – which for many years were ignored in the European policy debate – emerge as a major concern as companies from developing and emerging economies become potent investors in Europe. Since the early 2000s, ever more investors from China, East Asia and the Gulf countries have been buying European firms. The number of foreign investors which may use BITs and ISDS against the Member States and the EU is surging. Europe's defensive interests under IIAs and ISDS are therefore growing and call for a reform of the European approach to IIAs and ISDS. The current heated debate on investment rules under TTIP and CETA by and large ties in with the same fundamental discussion on how to re-balance states' offensive and defensive interests in the global investment regime. In this context, the Commission proposed an overhaul of the language on post-establishment treatment and protection standards in European IIAs as well as the creation of a multilateral investment court system (European Commission, 2016). Both proposals aim at rebalancing the substantive and procedural rights and obligations of investors and states. In particular, the court proposal received mixed reactions from third countries such as the USA, so quick progress is unlikely on this front. In a similar vein, the growing defensive interests of Europe beg the question how to deal with the approximately 1,300 traditional BITs, which are still in force between the Member States and third countries. It remains to be seen how the EU will balance its interest in protecting European investors abroad and protecting itself and the Member States from costly arbitration awards.

References

Alschner, W., 2013. Americanization of the BIT universe: The influence of Friendship, Commerce and Navigation (FCN) treaties on modern investment treaty law. *Goettingen J. Int. Law* 5, 455–486.

Baetens, F., 2015. Transatlantic investment treaty protection: A response to Poulsen, Bonnitcha and Yackee, CEPS Special Report. CEPS, Brussels.

Basedow, R., 2014. Licht in den Schutz der Investoren. Frankfurter Allgemeine Zeitung 20.

Bickerton, C., Hodson, D., Puetter, U., 2015. The new intergovernmentalism: European integration in the post-maastricht era. *J. Common Mark. Stud.* 53, 703–722.

Börzel, T., 2013. Comparative regionalism: European integration and beyond, in: Carlsnaes, W., Risse, T., Simmons, B. (Eds.), *Handbook of international relations*. Sage, London, pp. 501–530.

Da Conceição, E., 2010. Who controls whom? Dynamics of power delegation and agency losses in EU trade politics. *JCMS: J. Common Mark. Stud.* 48, 1107–1126. doi:10.1111/j.1468–5965.2010.02086.x

Damro, C., 2007. EU delegation and agency in international trade negotiations: A cautionary comparison. *J. Common Mark. Stud.* 45, 883–903.

De Bièvre, D., Dür, A., 2004. Delegation and control in European and American trade policy. Manheimer Zentrum für Europäische Sozialforschung Arbeitspapiere 82.

Delreux, T., Kerremans, B., 2008. *How agents control principals*, IIEB Work. Pap. 28.

Conclusion 241

Dür, A., 2006. Assessing the EU's role in international trade negotiations. *Eur. Poli. Sci.* 5, 362–376.

Eckhardt, J., 2015. *Business lobbying and trade governance*. Palgrave Macmillan, Basingstoke.

European Commission, 2016. The multilateral investment court project [WWW Document].

European Court of Justice, 2017. Opinion 2/15 (ECLI/EU/C/2017/376). Luxemburg.

Frennhoff Larsén, M., 2007. Principal-agent analysis with one agent and two principals: European Union trade negotiations with South Africa. *Poli. Policy* 35, 440–463.

Gaukrodger, D., Gordon, K., 2012. Investor-state dispute settlement: A scoping paper for the investment policy community. OECD Work. Pap. on International Investment 2012/2013. OECD Publishing, Paris.

Hawkins, D., Nielson, D., Tierney, M., Lake, D. (Eds.), 2006. *Delegation and agency in international organizations*. Cambridge University Press, Cambridge.

Kerremans, B., 2004. What went wrong in Cancún? A principal-agent view of the EU's rationale towards the Doha Development Round. *Eur. Foreign Aff. Rev.* 9, 363–393.

Kuijper, P.J., Pernice, I., Hindelang, S., Schwar, M., Reuling, M., 2014. Investor-State Dispute Settlement (ISDS) provisions in the EU's international investment agreements. European Parliament, INTA Committee, Brussels.

Mahoney, J., Thelen, K. (Eds.), 2010. *Explaining institutional change: Ambiguity, agency, and power*, 1st ed. Cambridge University Press, Cambridge.

Mestral, A.L.C.D., Lévesque, C., 2013. *Improving international investment agreements*. Routledge, London.

Meunier, S., 2005. *Trading voices: The European Union in international commercial negotiations*. Princeton University Press, Princeton.

Meunier, S., Nicolaidis, K., 2006. The European Union as a conflicted trade power. *J. Eur. Public Policy* 13, 906–925.

Moravcsik, A., 1998. *The choice for Europe: Social purpose and state power from Messina to Maastricht*. Cornell University Press, Ithaca, NY.

Moravcsik, A., 1991. Negotiating the single European Act: National interests and conventional statecraft in the European Community. *Int. Organ.* 45, 19–56.

Moravcsik, A., Schimmelfennig, F., 2009. *European Integration Theory*. Liberal intergovernmentalism, in: Wiener, A., Diez, T. (Eds.),. Oxford University Press, Oxford, pp. 67–87.

Pierson, P., 2004. *Politics in time: History, institutions, and social analysis*. Princeton University Press, Princeton.

Pollack, M.A., 2003. *The engines of European integration: Delegation, agency, and agenda setting in the EU*. Oxford University Press, Oxford.

Poulsen, L., Bonnitcha, J., Yackee, J.W., 2013. *Costs and benefits of an EU-USA investment protection treaty*. Department of Business, Innovation and Skills, London.

Reinisch, A., 2013. The future shape of EU investment agreements. *ICSID Review* 28, 179–196. doi:10.1093/icsidreview/sit007

Rosamond, B., 2000. *Theories of European integration*. Palgrave Macmillan, Basingstoke.

Scharpf, F., 1988. The joint decision trap: Lessons from German federalism and European integration. *Public. Adm.* 66, 239–278.

Stacey, J., Rittberger, B., 2003. Dynamics of formal and informal institutional change in the EU. *J. Eur. Public Policy* 10, 858–883. doi:10.1080/1350176032000148342

Streeck, W., Thelen, K.A. (Eds.), 2005. *Beyond continuity: Institutional change in advanced political economies*. Oxford University Press, Oxford.

Thelen, K., 2004. *How institutions evolve: The political economy of skills in Germany, Britain, the United States, and Japan*. Cambridge University Press, Cambridge.

Van Harten, G., 2007. *Investment treaty arbitration and public law*. Oxford University Press, Oxford.

Woll, C., 2008. *Firm interests: How governments shape business lobbying on global trade, Cornell studies in political economy*. Cornell University Press, Ithaca, NY.

Woll, C., Artigas, A., 2007. When trade liberalization turns into regulatory reform: The impact on business-government relations in international trade politics. *Regul. Gov.* 1, 99–182.

Woolcock, S., 2010. Trade policy: A further shift towards Brussels, in: Wallace, H., Pollack, M., Young, A. (Eds.), *Policy-making in the European Union*. Oxford University Press, Oxford, pp. 382–399.

Young, A., 2016. Not your parents' trade politics: The transatlantic trade and investment partnership negotiations. *Rev. Int. Pol. Econ.* 23, 345–378.

Young, A., 2011. The rise (and fall?) of the EU's performance in the multilateral trading system. *J. Eur. Integ.* 33, 715–739.

Young, A., 2002. *Extending European cooperation: The European Union and the 'new' international trade agenda*. Manchester University Press, Manchester.

Index

actors, policymaking 82–87
agenda setting: by the European Commission 19–20; theoretical note on bilateral and multilateral negotiations' 171
Alliance for Liberals and Democrats in Europe (ALDE) 86
arbitration and enforcement, investment 57–60

bargaining power, increased European 37–38
Barnier, M. 217–218
Barshefsky, C. 158
bilateral investment treaties (BITs) 1, 54–56, 61, 224–225; agenda setting in 171; first debates on, in the 1970s 200–202; MAI negotiations and 149–150
BITs *see* bilateral investment treaties (BITs)
British Petroleum 131
Brittan, L. 143, 153, 159
Bruton, J. 217–218
BusinessEurope 220
business preferences: ECT negotiations and 131–132; European integration and 27–29; foreign economic policy, lobbying and 31–33; lobbying and 30–31; modelled on communitarisation of international investment policy 37–39; modelled on international investment policy 33–35, *35–36*; Treaty of Lisbon and 219–222

Calvo, C. 63
Calvo Doctrine 63–65
CCP *see* Common Commercial Policy (CCP)
Centre for Settlement of Investment Disputes (ICSID) 58

CJEU *see* Court of Justice of the European Union (CJEU)
Clinton, B. 153
Common Commercial Policy (CCP) 1–2, 207, 207–209; unsuccessful Commission entrepreneurship to update the 202–204
Common Market 199–200
communitarisation of international investment policy 37–39
Convention on the Future of Europe 1
conversion and layering 23–24, *26*
Council of Ministers 20–22, 81, 84–85; authorisation for signing agreements 82; Commission proposal ability 79; ECT and 117–118, 122–127; EU-Mexico PTA and 173–174; *European Energy Charter: Fresh Impetus from the European Community* and 124; GATT agenda and 94, 96; GNS talks and 108; international investment as legal concept and 47; Lubbers Plan and 117; MAI negotiations and 140–146, 155–156, 161; negotiating directives submitted to 81; political duopoly with European Commission 83; TPA and 133; Uruguay round and 96–98
Court of Justice of the European Union (CJEU) 2, 17–18, 21, 201, 225, 240; EC strategic recourse to 22; recognition of EU's legal competences 206–211
creative destruction *17*
Customary International Law (CIL) 57, 62–64

Dahl, R. A. *17*
Declaration of the Rights of Man and of the Citizens 62

244   *Index*

Delors, J. 120
dispute resolution mechanism, IIA 34–35, 57–60
Doha Round, WTO 2, 4, 9, 66, 164, 165, 171
dot.com crisis 69
Drago-Porter Convention 63
drift 24–25, *27*

economic nationalism 68–69
ECT *see* Energy Charter Treaty (ECT)
efficiency-seeking FDI 50
Energy Charter Treaty (ECT) 2, 66, 114–115, 134; EU in negotiations on 127–134; European business preferences 131–132; European Energy Charter 119–121; Lubbers Plan 115–119; Member State preferences 132–134; negotiating history of 115–127; supplementary protocol 126–127
ERTA Doctrine 21, 211
EU-Chile PTA 170–171, 183–191, 233–234; agenda setting and 171; Commission entrepreneurship for comprehensive investment disciplines in 188–190; Commission mandate 184–186; core negotiations on 186–188; pre-negotiations 183–184
EU-Mexico PTA 170–182, 233–234; agenda setting and 171; assessment of investment commitments in 181–182; clashing over competencies on investment regulation 179–181; Commission mandate for 173–176; core negotiations 176–179; investment disciplines in negotiations on 172–182
European Chemical Industries Federation (CEFIC) 102
European Commission: agenda setting 19–20; argument behind emergence of 3–5; entrepreneurship and ECT 129–131; entrepreneurship and historical institutionalism 5–6, 14–26, *26–27*; entrepreneurship and the EU-Chile PTA 188–190; entrepreneurship and the Treaty of Lisbon 216–218; entrepreneurship for WTO-based investment negotiations 142–145; *European Energy Charter: Fresh Impetus from the European Community* and 124; GATS negotiations 107–110; information asymmetries and 20–21; integration theory (*see* European integration theory); international forum shopping 21; international investment policy 1–3; invoking implied and fringe competences 21–22; mandate for EU-Chile PTA 184–186; mandate for EU-Mexico PTA 173–176; mandate for the MAI negotiations 145–147; non-mandate of Punta del Este 96–99; policymaking actors 82–87; policymaking procedures 79–82; political duopoly with the Council of Ministers 83; preferences on European integration 16–18; strategic recourse to the CJEU 22; supranationalism and 15–16; theoretical, empirical and policy contributions to literature on 5–7, *8*; unsuccessful entrepreneurship to update the CCP 202–204
European Court of Justice (ECJ) 47–48
European Energy Charter 119–121, 128–129
European Energy Charter: Fresh Impetus from the European Community, The 124
European Free Trade Agreements (FTAs) 2
European integration theory 13–14; commission entrepreneurship and historical institutionalism in 14–26, *26–27*; conversion and laying in 23–24, *26*; from daily policymaking to formal integration 23–25; formal integration through conversion and layering 23–24; formal integration through drift 24–25, *27*; limits of business-centred liberal intergovernmental explanations and 27–39; methodological strategy 39–40; supranationalism in 15–16; understanding Commission preferences on 15–16
European Parliament 85–86
European Treaties and Single Market programme 22
European Union: ECT negotiations 127–134; empirical summary of policymaking role of 231–236; GATs negotiations 107–110; and international investment agreements 76–79; legal competences 74–79, 197–226; MAI negotiations 147–149; and national security reviews of foreign investments 76; negotiation of IIAs 80–82; outlook and policy challenges for global investment regime and 239–241; policymaking actors 82–87; policymaking procedures 79–82; and political support for

investors 75; pre-negotiations for Uruguay and 93–96; Singapore issues negotiations and 161–165; theoretical assessment and contributions of role of 237–239; TRIMs negotiations 101–103; *see also* EU-Chile PTA; EU-Mexico PTA
EU-Singapore Free Trade Agreement (EUSFTA) 57
extraterritoriality issues in MAI 152–153

factor-based models 31
fair and equitable treatment (FEET) 57
FDI *see* foreign direct investment (FDI)
foreign direct investment (FDI) 1, 2, 34; amendment in the Treaty of Lisbon 218–219; benefits of level international playing field on 38–39; economic and political impact on states 51–53; as economic concept 48–51; efficiency seeking 50; historical perspective on 67–70; as legal concept 47–48; versus portfolio investments 76–77; recent increases in 66–67; stakeholders in EU's international investment policy and *35–36*; as statistical concept 46–47; strategic asset-seeking 50
foreign economic policy, societal theories of 6–7
formal integration 23–25; business preferences and lobbying in 30–31; *see also* European integration theory
full protection and security (FPS) 57
functionalism 15–16

GATS negotiations 104–110
GATT *see* General Agreement on Trade and Tariffs (GATT)
General Agreement on Trade and Tariffs (GATT) 2, 66, 90; GATS negotiations 104–110; pre-negotiations on new multilateral trade round 91–99; TRIMs negotiations 99–103
geography and sectors of international investment activity, historical perspective on 67–70
Giscard d'Estaing, V. 219
global financial crises and FDI 69
Global Value Chains (GVCs) 32
Gorbachev, M. 120

Hague Conference on International Peace 63
Heckscher-Ohlin theorem 31, 32

Helms-Burton Act 153
historical institutionalism 5–6, 14–26, *26–27*; basic principles of *18–19*; conceptual overlaps between principal-agent research and *26–27*; drift and 24–25; relationship between informal and formal integration and 23–25
Hull Doctrine 64–66

IIAs *see* international investment agreements (IIAs)
informal integration and liberal intergovernmental logic 29; *see also* European integration theory
information asymmetries 20–21
international investment: brief history of 62–70; defining 46–51; economic and political impact on states 51–53; as economic concept 48–51; emergence of modern regime for 62–67; historical perspective of geography and sectors of 67–70; as legal concept 47–48; regulation from the 1950s to the 1980s 198–202; as statistical concept 46–47
international investment agreements (IIAs) 4, 33, 53; defining investors and investments 56–57; dispute resolution mechanism 34–35, 57–60; the EU and 76–79; importance of 54–56; investment arbitration and enforcement 57–60; investment liberalisation 34; landscape, today's 60–61; market access 60; negotiating 80–82; post-establishment treatment and protection standards 7, 34, 57; states' rights to regulate 7
international investment policy 1–7; empirical summary 231–236; EU regulation of 1–3, 13–14; investment guarantees 53; modelling business preferences on 33–35, *35–36*; modelling business preferences on communitarisation of 37–39; national security review mechanisms 54; objectives and policy instruments 53–61; outlook and policy challenges 239–241; political support and technical assistance 54; theoretical assessment and contributions of EU role in 237–239; treatification of 64–65; under the Treaty of Lisbon 74–87
International Monetary Fund (IMF) 47; EU-Mexico PTA and 180

International Trade Committee (INTA) 81, 86
investment guarantees 53
investment liberalisation 34, 77
investor-to-state dispute settlement (ISDS) mechanisms 34–35, 55, 77–78, 240–241; investment arbitration and enforcement 57–60; MAI negotiations and 150
Iran-Libya Sanctions Act 153
ISDS *see* investor-to-state dispute settlement (ISDS) mechanisms

Jospin, L. 158, 180

Keynesian policies 69, 94, 204

Lamy, P. 216, 216–217
legal competences, EU 74–79, 197–226; calls on the CJEU to recognise 206–211; common external capital regime for single market and 204–206; EU and international investment regulation from the 1950s to the 1980s and 198–202; first debates on European BITs in the 1970s and 200–202; grandfathering regulation to opinion 2/15 223–225; Treaty of Amsterdam and 211–213; Treaty of Maastricht and 202–206; Treaty of Nice and 75, 213–215
Level Playing Field for Direct Investment World-Wide, A 143, 212
liberal intergovernmentalism 6, 27–39; in business preferences and European Integration 27–29; explaining business preferences and lobbying 30–31; foreign economic policy and 31–33; logic extended to informal integration 29; modelling business preferences on international investment policy 33–35, *35–36*
liberalisation, investment 34, 77
lobbying 30–31
LOTIS Committee 95
Lubbers, R. 115, 127
Lubbers Plan 115–119, 127–128

MAI *see* Multilateral Agreement on Investment (MAI)
Marxism 63
materialist models 32–33
Member States: bargaining power of 37–38; Commission proposal ability 79; delegates fight of the FDI amdemdment in Treaty of Lisbon 218–219; EC agenda setting and 19–20; economic and political impact of foreign direct investment on 51–53; ECT project and 132–134; European single market and 204–206; first debates on European BITs in the 1970s and 200–202; GATT agenda and 94, 96; information asymmetries 20–21; political support for investors 75; preferences on cooperation and European Integration 28; second-order negotiations by 28–29; Treaty of Amsterdam and 212–213; Treaty of Lisbon and (*see* Treaty of Lisbon*); Treaty of Nice and 75, 213–215; TRIMs negotiations and 101–103; US demand for new multilateral trade round and 95–96; see also* European Commission; European Union
Mercosur 184–185
Multilateral Agreement on Investment (MAI) 2, 139–140, 165–166, 232–233; collapse of negotiations 155–160; Commission mandate for 145–147; lead up to 140–147; lukewarm business support for 141–142; negotiations 147–160; non-governmental organisations and campaign against 154–155, 156–157; REIO clause 151–152, 159; substantive disagreements among negotiating parties 149–154; theoretical assessment of 160; US pressure for 140–141
multilateral negotiations, agenda setting in 171

NAFTA *see* North American Free Trade Agreement (NAFTA)
nationalism, economic 68–69
national security reviews of foreign investments 54, 76
negotiation of IIAs 80–82
neo-functionalism 15–16
New International Economic Order (NIEO) 64
non-governmental organisations and anti-MAI campaign 154–155, 156–157
non-state actors 86–87
North American Free Trade Agreement (NAFTA) 66, 67, 149; MAI and 142; *see also* EU-Mexico PTA

OECD *see* Organisation for Economic Co-operation and Development (OECD)
OLI framework, 50

Organisation for Economic
    Co-operation and Development
    (OECD) 47, 48, 66–67; EU-Mexico
    PTA and 180; MAI and 140–141,
    150–151

policy entrepreneurs *17*
policymaking actors, EU 82–87
policymaking procedures, EU 79–82
political support and technical
    assistance 54
portfolio investments versus FDI 76–77
post-establishment treatment and
    protection standards 7, 34, 57, 77; EU's
    legal competences and 209–211
preferential trade agreements
    (PTAs) 5, 29, 170–171, 233–234;
    EU-Chile 183–191; EU-Mexico
    172–182; investment provisions
    in other 191–192; theoretical note
    on agenda setting in bilateral and
    multilateral negotiations and 171
principal-agent models 5–6; conceptual
    overlaps between historical
    institutionalism and *26–27*
Prodi, R. 189–190
PTAs *see* preferential trade agreements
    (PTAs)

Regional Economic Integration
    Organisation (REIO) 49
REIO clause, MAI 151–152, 159
Ricardo-Viner theorem 32
Royal Dutch Shell 131

Schumpeter, J. A. *17*
sector-based models 31–32
Singapore issues negotiations 161–165
Single European Act 205
single market 204–206
socialism 63–64, 68–69
Spaak Report 200
stakeholder consultations 87
Stopler-Samuelson theory 31, 32
strategic asset-seeking FDI 50
supranationalism 15–16
Swordfish Issue 190

*Towards a Comprehensive European
    International Investment Policy* 1
TPC *see* Trade Policy Committee (TPC)
Trade Policy Committee (TPC) 81, 133
Trade-Related Intellectual Property Rights
    (TRIPs) 207

treatification of international investment
    regime 64–65
Treaty of Amsterdam 211–213
Treaty of Lisbon 1–3, 37, 47, 239;
    business preferences and 219–222;
    Commission entrepreneurship in
    the open and behind the scenes
    and 216–218; convention method
    215–216; EU's legal competences
    and 74–79; evaluation of 78–79;
    intergovernmental conferences focus
    on 'high politics' 222–223; Member
    State delegates' fight of the FDI
    amendment in 218–219; policymaking
    actors 82–87; policymaking procedures
    under 79–82
Treaty of Maastricht 198, 202–206;
    and CJEU recognition of EU's legal
    competences 206–211
Treaty of Nice 75, 75, 213–215, 222
Treaty of Rome 199–200
TRIMs negotiations 99–103
Tungendhat, Christopher 93

UNCTAD 34–35
*Understanding on a Local Cost
    Standard* 201
UNICE 220, 220–222
United Nations Commission on
    International Trade Law (UNCITRAL)
    58, 58–60
Uruguay Round, WTO 2, 4, *8,* 9,
    40, 66, 90–91, 110–111, 198,
    231–232; Commission's non-
    mandate of Punta del Este 96–99;
    EU in pre-negotiations 93–96;
    GATS negotiations 104–110;
    pre-negotiations on new multitrade
    round 91–93; TRIMs negotiations
    99–103; way toward Punta del Este
    and 91–99
US Council on International Business
    (USCIB) 141

World Trade Organisation (WTO)
    2, 66; *see also* Doha Round,
    WTO; Multilateral Agreement on
    Investment (MAI); Uruguay Round,
    WTO
WTO *see* World Trade Organisation
    (WTO)

*Yukos Universal Limited (Isle of Man) vs
    Russia* 114